# VISUAL QUICKPRO GUIDE

# PHP 5 ADVANCED

**Larry Ullman**

Peachpit Press

Visual QuickPro Guide
**PHP 5 Advanced**
Larry Ullman

**Peachpit Press**
1249 Eighth Street
Berkeley, CA 94710
510/524-2178
510/524-2221 (fax)

Find us on the Web at: www.peachpit.com
To report errors, please send a note to: errata@peachpit.com
Peachpit Press is a division of Pearson Education.
Copyright © 2007 by Larry Ullman

Editor: Rebecca Gulick
Copy Editor: Robert Campbell
Technical Reviewer: Jay Blanchard
Proofreader: Liz Welch
Production Coordinator: Becky Winter
Compositor: Kate Kaminski
Indexer: Karin Arrigoni
Cover Design: Peachpit Press

ISBN-13: 978-0-321-37601-5     ISBN-10: 0-321-37601-3

9 8 7 6 5 4 3 2 1

Printed and bound in the United States of America

## Dedication

To my good friend Michael K. and his family:
I cannot thank you all enough for your continuing friendship, generosity, and kindness
over these many years.

## My utmost thanks to...

Jessica, the love of my life, for just about everything.

Zoe and Sam, for making my world a better place.

The grandparents, who traveled far and often, pitching in with babysitting and housework so that I might write this book.

Everyone at Peachpit Press for their support, for their dedication to putting out quality books, and for everything else they do to make all this happen.

The most excellent editor, Rebecca Gulick, for so many reasons.

Bob Campbell, for his spot-on copy editing and attention to detail.

The production coordinator, Becky Winter, the compositor, Kate Kaminski, the proof-reader, Liz Welch, and the indexer, Karin Arrigoni, who turn my mess of files into an actual book.

Jay Blanchard, for his technical review.

The readers, the readers, the readers!

# CONTENTS AT A GLANCE

# TABLE OF CONTENTS

# INTRODUCTION

If you're looking at this book, then I probably don't need to tell you how great PHP is. Presumably, since you're perusing the pages of an advanced text on the topic, you are already using PHP for developing dynamic Web sites. Maybe you've been doing so for a couple of years, perhaps just a couple of months. You could have learned PHP on your own, in a class, or by reading one of the many excellent books on the subject. (I'm referring not just to my own, of course!) Whatever the case, with some experience under your belt, you probably don't want another "here's how to use PHP and isn't it swell" book. What you probably want to learn is how to use PHP more efficiently, more securely, faster, and all-around better than you already are. If so, you've found the right book.

In this humble author's (or not-so-humble author's) opinion, advanced PHP is about learning: how to do different things, how to improve upon the basic things, and about technologies that intersect with PHP. In short, you know how to make a dynamic Web site with PHP, but you'd like to know how to make a *better* Web site, with every possible meaning of "better." That's the approach I've taken in writing this book. I've not set out to blow your mind discussing esoteric idiosyncrasies the language has, rewriting the PHP, MySQL, or Apache source code, or making theoretically interesting but practically useless code. In short, I present to you several hundred pages of beyond-the-norm but still absolutely necessary (and often cool) tips and techniques.

# About This Book

Simply put, I've tried to make this book's content accessible and useful for every PHP programmer out there. As I suggest in the introductory paragraphs, I believe that "advanced" PHP is mostly a matter of extended topics. You already possess all the basic knowledge—you retrieve database query results in your sleep—but want to go further. This may mean learning object-oriented programming (OOP), using PEAR (PHP Extension and Application Repository), incorporating Ajax (Asynchronous JavaScript and XML) into a site, or improving upon aspects of your existing skill set.

My definition of advanced PHP programming covers three loosely grouped skills:

◆ Doing what you already do better, faster, and more securely

◆ Learning more sophisticated PHP techniques

◆ Doing standard things using PHP and other technologies (like PEAR, Ajax, or OOP)

This book can be divided into three sections, corresponding to those skills. The first five chapters cover advanced PHP knowledge in general: programming techniques, Web applications, databases, security, and e-commerce. They all cover information that the average PHP programmer may not be familiar with but should be able to comprehend, providing useful code in the process.

The next six chapters focus on extending your knowledge to areas of PHP with which you might not be as familiar. Half of this section goes over object-oriented programming in great detail, from the fundamentals to advanced topics to some real-world examples. The other three chapters are on different ways you might use PHP: to communicate with networked servers, to communicate with the host server, or from a command-line interface. The remaining three chapters each deal with a specific technology tied into PHP: PEAR, Ajax, and XML.

Two bonus chapters, "Image Generation" and "Creating PDFs", can be downloaded from Peachpit's Web site. Those two chapters, which are available for free, provide another 100 pages of content showing how PHP ties into related, and very useful, technologies. Visit www.peachpit.com/title/0321376013 to learn how to register this book and download the chapters.

Most examples used in this book are intended to be applicable in the real world, omitting the frivolous code you might see in other books, tutorials, and manuals. I focus as much on the philosophies involved as on the coding itself so that, in the end, you will come away with not just how to do this or that but also how to apply the overarching mentality to your own, individual projects.

Unlike with most of my other books, I do not expect that you'll necessarily read this book in sequential order, for the most part. Some chapters do assume that you've read others, like the object-oriented ones, which have a progression to them. Some later chapters also reference examples completed in earlier ones. If you read the later ones first, you'll just need to quickly hop over to the earlier ones to generate whatever database or scripts the later chapter requires.

Finally, I'll be using XHTML in my scripts instead of HTML. I'll also use some CSS, as warranted. I do not discuss either of these subjects in this book (and, to be frank, may not adhere to them perfectly). If you are not already familiar with the subjects, you should look at some online resources or good books (such as Elizabeth Castro's excellent Visual QuickStart Guides) for more information.

## What's new in this edition

The most important change in this edition of the book is that every bit of code has been updated, rewritten, or replaced to ensure 100 percent compatibility with PHP 5. Many of the examples have also been modified to take advantage of features added to the language.

What is also new is my approach. The first edition of this text was the second book I ever wrote. I've learned a lot since then, both in terms of PHP and in terms of what readers expect in a book. A lot of my valuable experience in this latter category comes from the constant interactions with other readers through email and my supporting forums (www.DMCInsights.com/phorum/). A fair amount of material is therefore based upon frequently asked questions I see.

## How this book compares to my others

Those readers who have come to this book from my *PHP for the World Wide Web: Visual QuickStart Guide* may find themselves in a bit over their heads. This book does assume comfort with standard PHP programming, in particular debugging your own scripts. I'm not suggesting you put this book down, but if you find it goes too fast for you, or assumes knowledge you don't currently possess, you may want to check out my *PHP and MySQL for Dynamic Web Sites: Visual QuickPro Guide* instead.

If you have read the *PHP and MySQL* book, or the first edition of this one, I'm hoping that you'll find this to be a wonderful addition to your library and skill set.

INTRODUCTION

# About PHP 5

Although version 5 of PHP has been out since July 2004 (when the first non-beta version was released), there are still a large number of servers running older versions of PHP, particularly outside of the United States. This book does assume you're using PHP 5, although some examples will work with older versions of the language.

The most important change in PHP 5, with respect to this book, is the completely different object model and syntax. Object-oriented programming in PHP 4 is a rather watered-down concept, really not worth using in comparison to PHP 5's OOP. The object-oriented chapters use PHP 5 syntax exclusively, and that code will not work on older versions of the language.

In addition, PHP 5 added support for the Improved MySQL extension, designed for use with MySQL 4.1 or later. With only one or two exceptions, I use these Improved MySQL functions instead of the older, "regular" MySQL functions. If your PHP installation (or MySQL installation) does not support these functions, you'll need to change the code accordingly.

INTRODUCTION

## What You'll Need

Just as this book assumes that you already possess the fundamental skills to program in PHP (and, more important, to debug it when things go awry), it also assumes that you already have everything you need to follow along with the material. For starters, this means a PHP-enabled server. At the time of this writing, the latest version of PHP was 5.2, and much of the book depends upon your using at least PHP 5.0.

Along with PHP, you'll often need a database application. I use MySQL for the examples, but you can use anything. And, for the scripts in some of the chapters to work—particularly the last five—your PHP installation will have to include support for the corresponding technology, and that technology's library may need to be installed, too. Fortunately PHP 5 comes with built-in support for many advanced features. If the scripts in a particular chapter require special extensions, that will be referenced in the chapter's introduction. This includes the few times where I make use of a PEAR or PECL class. Nowhere in this book will I discuss installation, though, as I expect you should already know or have accomplished that.

As with any issue, should you have questions or problems, you can always search the Web or post a message in my support forums for assistance.

Beyond PHP, you need the things you should already have: a text editor or IDE, an FTP application (if using a remote server), and a Web browser. All of the code in this book has been tested on both Windows XP and Mac OS X; you'll see screen shots in both operating systems.

# Support Web Site

I have developed a Web site to support this book, available at www.DMCinsights.com/phpvqp2/. This site:

◆ Has every script available for download

◆ Has the SQL commands available for download

◆ Has extra files, as necessary, available for download

◆ Lists errors that have been found in the book

◆ Has a support forum where you can get help or assist others

◆ Provides a way to contact me directly

When using this site, please make sure you've gone to the correct URL (the book's title and edition are plastered everywhere). Each book I've written has its own support area; if you go to the wrong one, the downloadable files won't match those in the book.

Two bonus chapters, "Image Generation" and "Creating PDFs," can be downloaded for free. Visit www.peachpit.com/title/0321376013 to learn how to register this book and access the chapters.

INTRODUCTION

# ADVANCED PHP TECHNIQUES

At the most basic level good programming is determined by whether or not an application or script works as intended. This is where the beginning programmer will leave things, and there is nothing wrong with that. However, the advanced programmer will work past that point, striving toward improved efficiency, reliability, security, and portability. This book teaches you how to develop the skills of an advanced PHP programmer.

One thing the advanced PHP programmer does better than the beginner is learning to take advantage of more obscure or harder-to-comprehend features of the language. For example, while you probably already know how to use arrays, you may not have mastered multidimensional arrays: creating them, sorting them, and so on. You have written your own functions by this point but may not understand how to use recursion and static variables. Issues like these will be discussed as well as other beyond-the-basics concepts, like the heredoc syntax and the `printf()`/`sprintf()` family of functions.

# Multidimensional Arrays

Because of their power and flexibility, arrays are widely used in all PHP programming. For advanced uses, the multidimensional array often solves problems where other variable types just won't do.

For the first of the two examples, I'll demonstrate how to sort a multidimensional array. It's a common question users have and isn't as hard as one might think. For the second example, I'll create a database-driven to-do list, which can have limitless dimensions (**Figure 1.1**).

**Figure 1.1** One use of multidimensional arrays will be to create a nested to-do list.

## Sorting multidimensional arrays

Sorting arrays is easy using PHP, thanks to the sort(), ksort(), and related functions. You can sort a one-dimensional array by key, by value, in reverse order, etc. But these functions will not work on multidimensional arrays (not as you'd probably like, at least).

Say you have an array defined like so:

```
$a = array (
array ('key1' => 940, 'key2' => 'blah'),
array ('key1' => 23, 'key2' => 'this'),
array ('key1' => 894, 'key2' => 'that')
);
```

This is a simple two-dimensional array (an array whose elements are also arrays) that you might need to sort using key1 (a numeric sort) or key2 (an alphabetical sort). To sort a multidimensional array, you define your own sort function and then tell PHP to use that function via the usort(), uasort(), or uksort() function. The function you define must take exactly two arguments and return a value indicating which should come first.

```
Array
(
    [0] => Array
        (
            [key1] => 23
            [key2] => this
        )

    [1] => Array
        (
            [key1] => 894
            [key2] => that
        )

    [2] => Array
        (
            [key1] => 940
            [key2] => blah
        )

)
```

**Figure 1.2** The multidimensional array sorted by numeric value (key1).

MULTIDIMENSIONAL ARRAYS

```
● ● ●        Mozilla Firefox        ◯

Iteration 1: 23 vs. 940

Iteration 2: 894 vs. 23

Iteration 3: 940 vs. 23

Iteration 4: 894 vs. 940

Array
(
    [0] => Array
        (
            [key1] => 23
            [key2] => this
        )

    [1] => Array
        (
            [key1] => 894
            [key2] => that
        )

    [2] => Array
        (
            [key1] => 940
            [key2] => blah
        )

)
```

**Figure 1.3** By printing out the values of $x['key1']$ and $y['key1']$, one can see how the user-defined sorting function is invoked.

```
● ● ●        Mozilla Firefox        ◯

Array
(
    [0] => Array
        (
            [key1] => 940
            [key2] => blah
        )

    [1] => Array
        (
            [key1] => 894
            [key2] => that
        )

    [2] => Array
        (
            [key1] => 23
            [key2] => this
        )

)
```

**Figure 1.4** An alphabetical sort on the example array using key2.

To sort the preceding array on the first key, the sorting function would like this:

```php
function mysort1 ($x, $y) {
    return ($x['key1'] > $y['key1']);
}
```

Then the PHP code would use this function by doing:

```php
usort ($a, 'mysort1');
```

**Figure 1.2** shows the same array at this point.

PHP will continue sending the inner arrays to this function so that they may be sorted. If you want to see this in detail, print the values being compared in the function (**Figure 1.3**).

The usort() function sorts by values and does not maintain the keys (for the outermost array). If you used uasort(), the keys would be maintained, and if you used uksort(), the sort would be based upon the keys.

To sort on the second key in the preceding example, you would want to compare two strings. That code would be (**Figure 1.4** shows the result):

```php
function mysort2 ($x, $y) {
    return strcasecmp($x['key2'],
→ $y['key2']);
}
usort ($a, 'mysort2');
```

Or you could just use strcmp(), to perform a case-sensitive sort.

To see this in action for yourself, let's run through an example.

**MULTIDIMENSIONAL ARRAYS**

## To sort a multidimensional array:

**1.** Create a new PHP script in your text editor or IDE, starting with the HTML code (**Script 1.1**).

```
<!DOCTYPE html PUBLIC "-//W3C//
→ DTD XHTML 1.0 Transitional//EN"
"http://www.w3.org/TR/xhtml1/DTD/
→ xhtml1-transitional.dtd">
<html xmlns="http://www.w3.org/1999/
→ xhtml" xml:lang="en" lang="en">
<head>
    <meta http-equiv="content-type"
→ content="text/html; charset=
→ iso-8859-1" />
    <title>Sorting Multidimensional
→ Arrays</title>
</head>
<body>
<?php # Script 1.1 - sort.php
```

**2.** Define a multidimensional array.

```
$students = array (
256 => array ('name' => 'Jon',
→ 'grade' => 98.5),
2 => array ('name' => 'Vance',
→ 'grade' => 85.1),
9 => array ('name' => 'Stephen',
→ 'grade' => 94.0),
364 => array ('name' => 'Steve',
→ 'grade' => 85.1),
68 => array ('name' => 'Rob',
→ 'grade' => 74.6)
);
```

The outer array, `$students`, has five elements, each of which is also an array. The inner arrays use the student's ID for the key (a made-up value) and store two pieces of data: the student's name and their grade.

*continues on page 6*

**Script 1.1** This script defines a two-dimensional array, which is then sorted based upon the inner array values.

```
1    <!DOCTYPE html PUBLIC "-//W3C//DTD XHTML 1.0 Transitional//EN"
2        "http://www.w3.org/TR/xhtml1/DTD/xhtml1-transitional.dtd">
3    <html xmlns="http://www.w3.org/1999/xhtml" xml:lang="en" lang="en">
4    <head>
5        <meta http-equiv="content-type" content="text/html; charset=iso-8859-1" />
6        <title>Sorting Multidimensional Arrays</title>
7    </head>
8    <body>
9    <?php # Script 1.1 - sort.php
10
11   /*  This page creates a multidimensional array
12    *  of names and grades.
13    *  The array is then sorted twice:
14    *  once by name and once by grade.
15    */
16
17   // Create the array:
18   // Array structure:
19   // studentID => array ('name' => 'Name', 'grade' => XX.X)
20   $students = array (
21   256 => array ('name' => 'Jon', 'grade' => 98.5),
22   2 => array ('name' => 'Vance', 'grade' => 85.1),
23   9 => array ('name' => 'Stephen', 'grade' => 94.0),
24   364 => array ('name' => 'Steve', 'grade' => 85.1),
25   68 => array ('name' => 'Rob', 'grade' => 74.6)
26   );
27
28   // Name sorting function:
29   function name_sort ($x, $y) {
30       return strcasecmp($x['name'], $y['name']);
31   }
32
33   // Grade sorting function:
34   // Sort in DESCENDING order!
35   function grade_sort ($x, $y) {
36       return ($x['grade'] < $y['grade']);
37   }
38
39   // Print the array as is:
40   echo '<h3>Array As Is</h3><pre>' . print_r($students, 1) . '</pre>';
41
42   // Sort by name:
43   uasort ($students, 'name_sort');
44
45   // Print the array now:
46   echo '<h3>Array Sorted By Name</h3><pre>' . print_r($students, 1) . '</pre>';
47
48   // Sort by grade:
49   uasort ($students, 'grade_sort');
50
51   // Print the array now:
52   echo '<h3>Array Sorted By Grade</h3><pre>' . print_r($students, 1) . '</pre>';
53
54   ?>
55   </body>
56   </html>
```

MULTIDIMENSIONAL ARRAYS

**5**

3. Define the name sorting function.

```
function name_sort ($x, $y) {
    return strcasecmp($x['name'],
→ $y['name']);
}
```

The strcasecmp() function returns a number—negative, 0, or positive—indicating how similar two strings are. If a negative value is returned, the first string comes before the second alphabetically; if a positive value is returned, the second string comes first. If 0 is returned, the strings are the same.

4. Define the grade sorting function.

```
function grade_sort ($x, $y) {
    return ($x['grade'] <
→ $y['grade']);
}
```

This example is like the demo in the introduction to these steps. One significant difference is that I want to perform a descending sort, so that the highest grades are listed first. This is easily accomplished: change the comparison operator from greater than to less than.

5. Print the array as it's initially defined.

```
echo '<h3>Array As Is</h3><pre>' .
→ print_r($students, 1) . '</pre>';
```

For improved legibility, I'll use the <pre> tags and print_r() to quickly reveal the arrays' structure and values.

6. Sort the array by name and print the results.

```
uasort ($students, 'name_sort');
echo '<h3>Array Sorted By
→ Name</h3><pre>' .
→ print_r($students, 1) . '</pre>';
```

Here the uasort() function is used so that the keys—the student IDs—are not lost. **Figure 1.5** shows the result if just usort() was used instead.

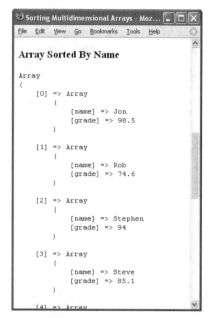

**Figure 1.5** Failure to use uasort() would cause the keys, which store meaningful values (see Script 1.1), to be lost.

**7.** Sort the array by grade and print the results.

```
uasort ($students, 'grade_sort');
echo '<h3>Array Sorted By
→ Grade</h3><pre>' .
→ print_r($students, 1) . '</pre>';
```

**8.** Complete the page.

```
?>
</body>
</html>
```

**9.** Save the file as sort.php, place it in your Web directory, and test in your Web browser (**Figures 1.6** and **1.7**).

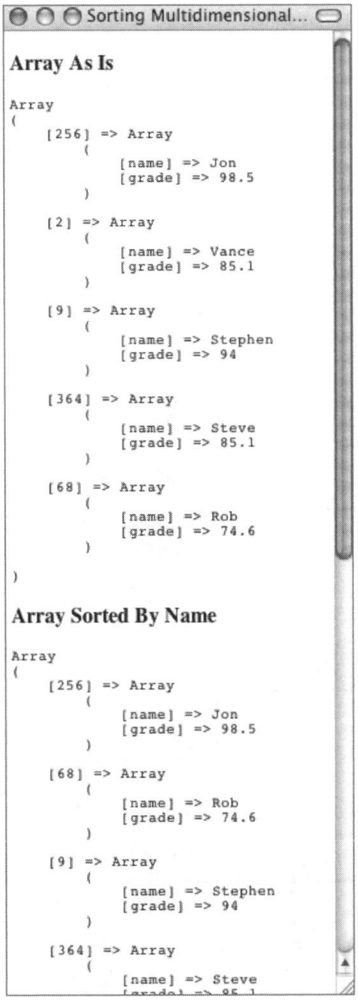

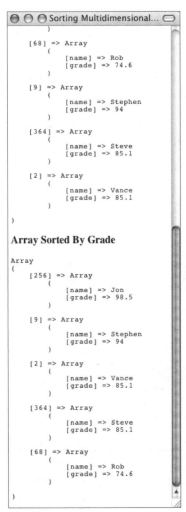

**Figure 1.6** The initial array and sorted by name.

**Figure 1.7** The array sorted by grade, in descending order (this is the same Web page as in Figure 1.6, but it couldn't all fit in one screenshot).

## Database-driven arrays

If you think about it, most database queries return a multidimensional array (**Figure 1.8**). If the query results are immediately sent to the Web browser one at a time, the multidimensional structure doesn't add any complication to your code. However, if you need to do something more elaborate with the results, you'll need a way to comprehend and manage the nested structure.

For this example, I want to create a database-driven, Web-based to-do list system. If the to-do list were one-dimensional, this wouldn't be that hard. But the list should be nestable, where each item can have multiple steps. The result will be a tree-like structure, where each branch can have its own offshoots (**Figure 1.9**).

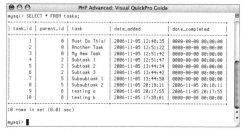

**Figure 1.8** Selecting multiple columns from multiple rows in a database results in a multidimensional array.

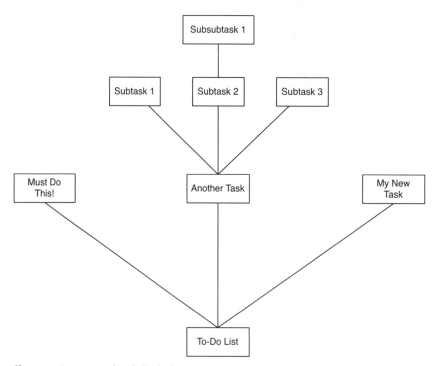

**Figure 1.9** How a nested to-do list looks as a tree.

**8**

**Figure 1.18** Adding a new task that's not linked to another task.

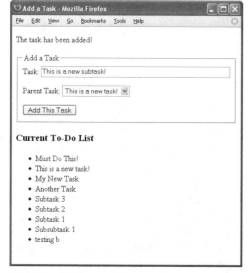

**Figure 1.19** Adding a task that's a subset of an existing task.

**13.** Sort the tasks by `parent_id`.

```
function parent_sort ($x, $y) {
    return ($x['parent_id'] >
→ $y['parent_id']);
}
usort ($tasks, 'parent_sort');
```

The `parent_id` value is what separates primary tasks from secondary ones, so working with this value in PHP is important. Using the information discussed earlier in the chapter, a user-defined function will sort the multidimensional array.

**14.** Display the full list of tasks.

```
echo '<h3>Current To-Do
→ List</h3><ul>';
foreach ($tasks as $task) {
    echo "<li>{$task['task']}
→ </li>\n";
}
echo '</ul>';
```

This loop will display each task in order of its `parent_id`. This is the first step toward making the list shown in Figure 1.1, although as you can see in Figure 1.16, the list isn't organized as it should be. This will be solved later in the chapter.

**15.** Complete the page.

```
?>
</body>
</html>
```

**16.** Save the file as `add_task.php`, place it in your Web directory, and test in your Web browser (**Figures 1.18** and **1.19**).

### ✔ Tip

■ If you wanted to implement this idea in a live site, one improvement you could make would be the ability to add multiple tasks at once. I'll provide further tips on fleshing out this example over the course of the chapter.

**MULTIDIMENSIONAL ARRAYS**

# Advanced Function Definitions

Being able to define and use your own functions is integral to any programming language. After even a modicum of PHP experience, you've no doubt created many. But there are three potential features of user-defined functions that arise in more advanced programming. These are:

◆ Recursive functions

◆ Static variables

◆ Accepting values by reference

While not often used, sometimes these concepts are indispensable. In discussing and demonstrating these first two concepts, I'll continue to build upon the tasks example just begun in the chapter.

## Recursive functions

Recursion is the act of a function calling itself.

```
function somefunction() {
    // Some code.
    somefunction();
    // Possible other code.
}
```

The end result is that your functions can act both as originally intended and as a loop. The one *huge* warning when using this technique is to make sure your function has an "out" clause. For example, the following code will run ad infinitum:

```
function add_one ($n) {
    $n++;
    add_one ($n);
}
add_one (1);
```

The lack of a condition that determines when to stop execution of the function creates a big programming no-no, the infinite loop. Compare that function to this one:

```
function count_to_100 ($n) {
    if ($n <= 100) {
        echo $n . '<br />';
        $n++;
        count_to_100 ($n);
    }
}
count_to_100 (1);
```

This function will continue to call itself until $n is greater than 100, at which point it will stop executing the function. (That's obviously a trivial use of this concept; a loop would do the same thing.)

Recursive functions are necessary when you have a process that may be followed to an unknown depth. For example, a script that searches through a directory may have to search through any number of subdirectories. Or an array might have an unknown number of dimensions....

With the tasks table created earlier in the chapter, retrieving and displaying all the tasks is not hard (see Figures 1.17 and 1.18). However, the method used in add_task.php (Script 1.2) does not properly nest the tasks like that in Figure 1.1. To accomplish that desired end, a multidimensional array and a recursive function are required.

## To use recursion:

**1.** Begin a new PHP script in your text editor or IDE, starting with the HTML (**Script 1.3**).

```
<!DOCTYPE html PUBLIC "-//W3C//
→ DTD XHTML 1.0 Transitional//EN"
"http://www.w3.org/TR/xhtml1/DTD/
→ xhtml1-transitional.dtd">
<html xmlns="http://www.w3.org/1999/
→ xhtml" xml:lang="en" lang="en">
```

```
<head>
    <meta http-equiv="content-type"
→ content="text/html; charset=
→ iso-8859-1" />
    <title>View Tasks</title>
</head>
<body>
<h3>Current To-Do List</h3>
<?php # Script 1.3 - view_tasks.php
```

*continues on page 21*

**Script 1.3** One recursive function and a potentially bottomless multidimensional array will properly display the nested list of tasks.

```
1   <!DOCTYPE html PUBLIC "-//W3C//DTD XHTML 1.0 Transitional//EN"
2          "http://www.w3.org/TR/xhtml1/DTD/xhtml1-transitional.dtd">
3   <html xmlns="http://www.w3.org/1999/xhtml" xml:lang="en" lang="en">
4   <head>
5       <meta http-equiv="content-type" content="text/html; charset=iso-8859-1" />
6       <title>View Tasks</title>
7   </head>
8   <body>
9   <h3>Current To-Do List</h3>
10  <?php # Script 1.3 - view_tasks.php
11
12  /*  This page shows all existing tasks.
13   *  A recursive function is used to show the
14   *  tasks as nested lists, as applicable.
15   */
16
17  // Function for displaying a list.
18  // Receives one argument: an array.
19  function make_list ($parent) {
20
21      // Need the main $tasks array:
22      global $tasks;
23
24      // Start an ordered list:
25      echo '<ol>';
26
27      // Loop through each subarray:
28      foreach ($parent as $task_id => $todo) {
29
```

*(script continues on next page)*

**Script 1.3** *continued*

```
     ⦿⦿⦿                          📄 Script
30            // Display the item:
31            echo "<li>$todo";
32
33            // Check for subtasks:
34            if (isset($tasks[$task_id])) {
35
36                // Call this function:
37                make_list($tasks[$task_id]);
38
39            }
40
41            // Complete the list item:
42            echo '</li>';
43
44        } // End of FOREACH loop.
45
46        // Close the ordered list:
47        echo '</ol>';
48
49    } // End of make_list() function.
50
51
52    // Connect to the database:
53    $dbc = @mysqli_connect ('localhost', 'username', 'password', 'test') OR die ('<p>Could not
       connect to the database!</p></body></html>');
54
55    // Retrieve all the uncompleted tasks:
56    $q = 'SELECT task_id, parent_id, task FROM tasks WHERE date_completed="0000-00-00 00:00:00"
       ORDER BY parent_id, date_added ASC';
57    $r = mysqli_query($dbc, $q);
58
59    // Initialize the storage array:
60    $tasks = array();
61
62    while (list($task_id, $parent_id, $task) = mysqli_fetch_array($r, MYSQLI_NUM)) {
63
64        // Add to the array:
65        $tasks[$parent_id][$task_id] =  $task;
66
67    }
68
69    // For debugging:
70    //echo '<pre>' . print_r($tasks,1) . '</pre>';
71
72    // Send the first array element
73    // to the make_list() function:
74    make_list($tasks[0]);
75
76    ?>
77    </body>
78    </html>
```

**2.** Begin defining a function.

```
function make_list ($parent) {
    global $tasks;
    echo '<ol>';
```

The purpose of the function will be to display an array of items in an ordered list:

```
<ol>
<li>Item 1</li>
<li>Item 2</li>
<li>Item 3</li>
</ol>
```

This function will take one argument, which will always be an array. Within the function, the $tasks array (the main array) needs to be available—you'll soon see why. Then the ordered list is begun.

**3.** Loop through the array, printing each item.

```
foreach ($parent as $task_id
→ => $todo) {
    echo "<li>$todo";
```

A foreach loop will go through the array, printing each item within <li> tags. Those are begun here.

*continues on next page*

**4.** Check if any subtasks exist.

```
if (isset($tasks[$task_id])) {
    make_list($tasks[$task_id]);
}
```

This is the most important part of the script. The tasks retrieved from the database will be tossed into a multidimensional array like that in **Figure 1.20**. For the main array, each key is a parent_id and the elements are arrays of tasks that fall under that parent_id. So after printing the initial <li> task, the function needs to check if this task has any subtasks; in other words: is there an array element in $tasks whose key is this task ID? If so, then this function should be called again, sending that other part of the array (the element whose key is this task_id and whose value is an array of subtasks) as the argument. That will result in the code:

```
<ol>
<li>Item 1</li>
<li>Item 2
    <ol>
    <li>Subitem 1</li>
    <li>Subitem 2</li>
    </ol>
</li>
<li>Item 3</li>
</ol>
```

**5.** Complete the foreach loop and the function.

```
        echo '</li>';
    } // End of FOREACH loop.
    echo '</ol>';
} // End of make_list() function.
```

**Figure 1.20** The PHP script takes the tasks from the database and creates this multidimensional array.

ADVANCED FUNCTION DEFINITIONS

**6.** Connect to the database.

```
$dbc = @mysqli_connect ('localhost',
→ 'username', 'password', 'test') OR
→ die ('<p>Could not connect to the
→ database!</p></body></html>');
```

With the recursive function defined, the rest of the script needs to retrieve all the tasks, organize them in an array, and then call the make_list() function.

**7.** Define and execute the query.

```
$q = 'SELECT task_id, parent_id, task
→ FROM tasks WHERE
date_completed="0000-00-00 00:00:00"
→ ORDER BY parent_id, date_added
→ ASC';

$r = mysqli_query($dbc, $q);
```

The query retrieves three pieces of information for each task: its ID, its parent_id, and the task itself. The conditional means that only noncompleted tasks are selected. The results are also ordered by the parent_id, so that every top-level task (with a parent_id of 0) is returned first. A secondary ordering by the date_added returns the tasks in the order they were added (an assumption being that's how they are prioritized).

**8.** Add each task to an array.

```
$tasks = array();
while (list($task_id, $parent_id,
→ $task) = mysqli_fetch_
→ array($r, MYSQLI_NUM)) {
    $tasks[$parent_id][$task_id]
→ = $task;
}
```

The $tasks array will store every task. Figure 1.20 shows the final structure. As described in Step 4, the array's outermost key is the parent_id value from the table. The value of this outermost array is an array of the tasks with that parent_id.

**9.** Add a debugging line, if desired.

```
//echo '<pre>' . print_r($tasks,1) .
→ '</pre>';
```

When dealing with multidimensional arrays, it's vitally important to know and understand the structure you're working with. When you uncomment this line (by removing the two slashes), the script will print the array like you see in Figure 1.20.

**10.** Call the make_list() function, sending it the array of top-level tasks.

```
make_list($tasks[0]);
```

Although the $tasks variable is a multidimensional array, the make_list() function needs to be called only once, sending it the first array element. This element's value is an array of tasks whose parent_id is 0. Within the function, for each of these tasks, a check will see if there are subtasks. So the function will end up accessing every task thanks to its recursive nature.

**11.** Complete the page.

```
?>
</body>
</html>
```

*continues on next page*

**12.** Save the file as `view_tasks.php`, place it in your Web directory, and test in your Web browser (**Figure 1.21**).

**13.** Add some more subtasks and retest in your Web browser (**Figure 1.22**).

### ✔ Tips

- The PHP manual suggests that you should avoid any recursive function that may call itself over 100 to 200 times. Doing so could crash the script or the Web server.

- This page does assume that some tasks were returned by the database. You may want to add a conditional checking that `$tasks` isn't empty prior to calling the `make_list()` function.

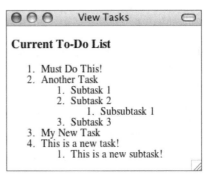

**Figure 1.21** The page of tasks, as a bunch of nested lists.

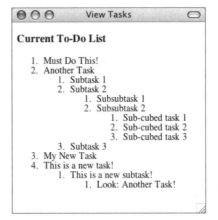

**Figure 1.22** There is no limit to the number of subtasks that this system supports.

## Using static variables

When working with recursion or, in fact, any script in which the same function may be called multiple times, you might want to consider using the `static` statement. `static` forces the function to remember the value of a variable from function call to function call, without using global variables. The example `count_to_100()` function (see the preceding section of this chapter) could be rewritten like so with the same result:

```php
function count_to_100 () {
    static $n = 1;
    if ($n <= 100) {
        echo $n . '<br />';
        $n++;
        count_to_100 ();
    }
}
count_to_100 ();
```

Of course, that's not a very useful implementation of the concept. The very astute reader may have wondered how I achieved the result in Figure 1.3. Showing the values being compared is not hard, but counting the iterations requires the use of `static`. Toward this end, `sort.php` will be modified.

### Completing This Example

This example was primarily written to demonstrate multidimensional arrays and recursive functions. Still, it's a nice example and worth implementing in a live site (the ability to nest tasks is great). If you wanted to do so, one feature you'd likely need is the ability to mark a task as completed. An example later in the chapter will do just that. Another alteration would be to change the `add_task.php` page so that the drop-down menu reflects the hierarchy as well.

Another likely addition would be the ability to add multiple tasks at once. And you may want to consider an edit task option. While you're at it, the view tasks page could have a link that passes a value in the URL indicating whether all tasks should be displayed or just uncompleted ones. These are just some ideas. Turn to the book's supporting forum (www.dmcinsights.com/phorum/) for assistance and more!

ADVANCED FUNCTION DEFINITIONS

## To use static variables:

1. Open sort.php (Script 1.1) in your text editor or IDE.

2. Modify the name_sort() function to read (**Script 1.4**):

```
function name_sort ($x, $y) {
    static $count = 1;
    echo "<p>Iteration $count:
→ {$x['name']} vs. {$y['name']}
→ </p>\n";
    $count++;
    return strcasecmp($x['name'],
→ $y['name']);
```

Three lines of code have been added to the function. The first is the declaration of a static variable called $count. It's initially set to 1, but that assignment only applies the first time this function is called (because it's a static variable). Then the iteration number is printed (how many times this function has been called), along with the values being compared. Finally, the $count variable is incremented.

*continues on page 28*

**Script 1.4** This modified version of the sorting script will reveal how many times each sorting function is invoked, thanks to a static variable.

```
1   <!DOCTYPE html PUBLIC "-//W3C//DTD XHTML 1.0 Transitional//EN"
2        "http://www.w3.org/TR/xhtml1/DTD/xhtml1-transitional.dtd">
3   <html xmlns="http://www.w3.org/1999/xhtml" xml:lang="en" lang="en">
4   <head>
5       <meta http-equiv="content-type" content="text/html; charset=iso-8859-1" />
6       <title>Sorting Multidimensional Arrays</title>
7   </head>
8   <body>
9   <?php # Script 1.4 - sort2.php
10
11  /*  This page creates a multidimensional array
12   *  of names and grades.
13   *  The array is then sorted twice:
14   *  once by name and once by grade.
15   *  A static variable has been added to both
16   *  functions to see how many times they are called.
17   */
18
19  // Create the array:
20  // Array structure:
21  // studentID => array ('name' => 'Name', 'grade' => XX.X)
22  $students = array (
23  256 => array ('name' => 'Jon', 'grade' => 98.5),
```

**Script 1.4** *continued*

```
24    2 => array ('name' => 'Vance', 'grade' => 85.1),
25    9 => array ('name' => 'Stephen', 'grade' => 94.0),
26    364 => array ('name' => 'Steve', 'grade' => 85.1),
27    68 => array ('name' => 'Rob', 'grade' => 74.6)
28    );
29
30    // Name sorting function:
31    function name_sort ($x, $y) {
32        static $count = 1;
33        echo "<p>Iteration $count: {$x['name']} vs. {$y['name']}</p>\n";
34        $count++;
35        return strcasecmp($x['name'], $y['name']);
36    }
37
38    // Grade sorting function:
39    // Sort in DESCENDING order!
40    function grade_sort ($x, $y) {
41        static $count = 1;
42        echo "<p>Iteration $count: {$x['grade']} vs. {$y['grade']}</p>\n";
43        $count++;
44        return ($x['grade'] < $y['grade']);
45    }
46
47    // Print the array as is:
48    echo '<h3>Array As Is</h3><pre>' . print_r($students, 1) . '</pre>';
49
50    // Sort by name:
51    uasort ($students, 'name_sort');
52
53    // Print the array now:
54    echo '<h3>Array Sorted By Name</h3><pre>' . print_r($students, 1) . '</pre>';
55
56    // Sort by grade:
57    uasort ($students, 'grade_sort');
58
59    // Print the array now:
60    echo '<h3>Array Sorted By Grade</h3><pre>' . print_r($students, 1) . '</pre>';
61
62    ?>
63    </body>
64    </html>
```

ADVANCED FUNCTION DEFINITIONS

**3.** Modify the `grade_sort()` function to read:

```
function grade_sort ($x, $y) {
    static $count = 1;
    echo "<p>Iteration $count:
{$x['grade']} vs.
{$y['grade']}</p>\n";
    $count++;
    return ($x['grade'] <
$y['grade']);
}
```

The same three lines of code that were added to `name_sort()` are added to `grade_sort()`, except the key being compared here is *grade*, not *name*.

**4.** Save the file as `sort2.php`, place it in your Web directory, and test in your Web browser (**Figures 1.23** and **1.24**).

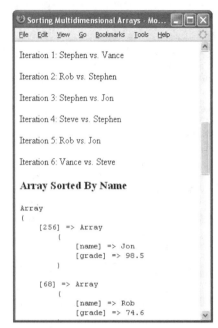

**Figure 1.23** Sorting the original five-element array by name requires six calls of the sorting function.

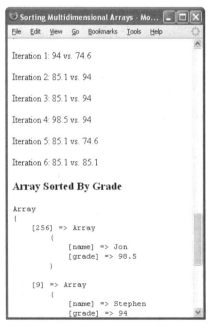

**Figure 1.24** Sorting the same array by grade also requires six iterations.

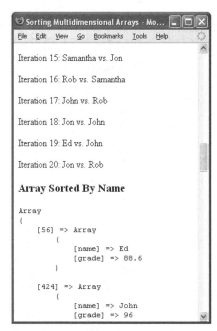

**Figure 1.25** After adding three more elements to the main array, the name sort now takes 20 iterations...

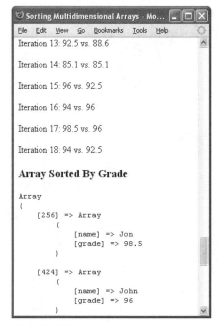

**Figure 1.26** ...but the grade sort can be done in 18.

**5.** Add more items to the $students array and rerun the script (**Figures 1.25** and **1.26**).

For the result in the figures, I changed the array definition to:

```
$students = array (
256 => array ('name' => 'Jon',
→ 'grade' => 98.5),
2 => array ('name' => 'Vance',
→ 'grade' => 85.1),
9 => array ('name' => 'Stephen',
→ 'grade' => 94.0),
364 => array ('name' => 'Steve',
→ 'grade' => 85.1),
68 => array ('name' => 'Rob', 'grade'
→ => 74.6),
56 => array ('name' => 'Ed', 'grade'
→ => 88.6),
365 => array ('name' => 'Samantha',
→ 'grade' => 92.5),
424 => array ('name' => 'John',
→ 'grade' => 96.0)
);
```

## References and Functions

As a default, functions receive arguments on a call-by-value basis. This means that a function receives the value of a variable, not the actual variable itself. The function can also be described as making a copy of the variable. This is fine, as long as that variable does not need to be altered within the function. To alter the value of a variable within a function, you need to either use the `global` statement or pass the variable by reference.

To pass a variable by reference instead of by value, precede the variable in the argument list with the ampersand (&).

```
function increment (&$var) {
    $var++;
}
$num = 2;
increment($num);
echo $num; // 3
```

Alternatively, the function definition can stay the same and how the function is called would change:

```
function increment ($var) {
    $var++;
}
$num = 2;
increment(&$num);
echo $num; // 3
```

You probably won't (or shouldn't) find yourself passing values by reference often, but like the other techniques in this chapter, it's often the perfect solution to an advanced problem.

# The Heredoc Syntax

Heredoc, in case you've never heard the term before, is an alternative way for encapsulating strings. It's used and seen much less often than the standard single or double quotes, but it fulfills the same role. Heredoc is like putting peanut butter on bananas: you either grow up doing it or you don't. The heredoc method works just like a double quote in that the values of variables will be printed, but you can define your own delimiter, which is particularly nice when printing oodles of HTML (with its own double-quotation marks). The only catch to heredoc is that its syntax is very particular!

The heredoc syntax starts with <<<, immediately followed by an identifier. The identifier is normally a word in all caps. It can only contain alphanumeric characters plus the underscore (no spaces), and it cannot begin with a number. There should be nothing on the same line after the initial identifier, not even a space! So usage of heredoc might begin like

```
echo <<<EOT
blah...
```

or

```
$string = <<<EOD
blah...
```

*continues on next page*

At the end of the string, use the same identifier without the <<<. The closing identifier has to be the very first item on the line (it cannot be indented at all) and can only be followed by a semicolon! Examples:

```
echo <<<EOT

Somevar $var

Thisvar $that

EOT;

$string = <<<EOD

string with $var \n

EOD;
```

Using EOD and EOT as delimiters is common (they're unlikely to show up in the string) but not required. The heredoc syntax is a nice option but—and I'm trying to drive this point home—it's very particular. Failure to get the syntax 100 percent correct—even an errant space—results in a parse error.

As an example of this, let's write a new version of the view_tasks.php page that allows for marking tasks as updated (**Figure 1.27**).

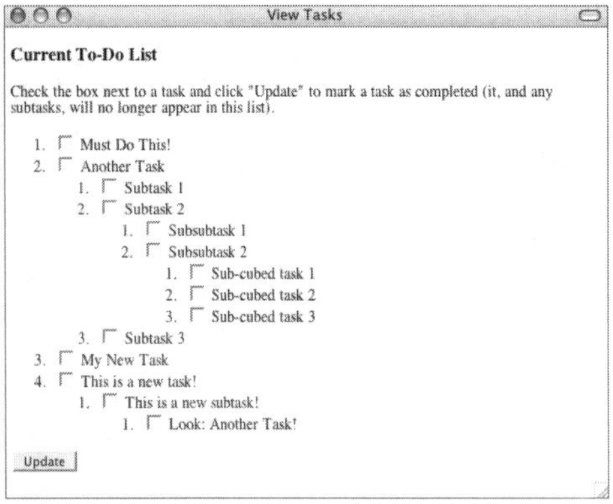

## To use the heredoc syntax:

1. Open view_tasks.php (Script 1.3) in your text editor or IDE.

2. Within the make_list() function, change the printing of the task to (**Script 1.5**):

```
echo <<<EOT

<li><input type="checkbox"
→ name="tasks[$task_id]" value="done"
→ /> $todo

EOT;
```

This is a good use of the heredoc syntax, as it's an alternative to:

```
echo "<li><input type=\"checkbox\"
→ name=\"tasks[$task_id]\"
→ value=\"done\" />$todo";
```

That syntax, in my opinion, has way too many double quotation marks to escape. The single quotation mark example isn't as bad but requires concatenation:

```
echo '<li><input type="checkbox"
→ name="tasks['. $task_id . ']"
→ value="done" /> ' . $todo;
```

With the heredoc code, be absolutely certain that nothing follows the opening identifier (EOT) except a return (a carriage return or newline) and that the closing identifier starts as the very first thing on its own line.

*continues on page 35*

**Figure 1.27** The page for viewing tasks will now have check boxes to mark tasks as complete.

**The Heredoc Syntax**

**Script 1.5** The original `view_tasks.php` page (Script 1.3) has been modified as a form so that tasks can be checked off. The heredoc syntax aids in the creation of some of the HTML.

```
1    <!DOCTYPE html PUBLIC "-//W3C//DTD XHTML 1.0 Transitional//EN"
2         "http://www.w3.org/TR/xhtml1/DTD/xhtml1-transitional.dtd">
3    <html xmlns="http://www.w3.org/1999/xhtml" xml:lang="en" lang="en">
4    <head>
5        <meta http-equiv="content-type" content="text/html; charset=iso-8859-1" />
6        <title>View Tasks</title>
7    </head>
8    <body>
9    <h3>Current To-Do List</h3>
10   <?php # Script 1.5 - view_tasks2.php
11
12   /*  This page shows all existing tasks.
13    *  A recursive function is used to show the
14    *  tasks as nested lists, as applicable.
15    *  Tasks can now be marked as completed.
16    */
17
18   // Function for displaying a list.
19   // Receives one argument: an array.
20   function make_list ($parent) {
21
22       // Need the main $tasks array:
23       global $tasks;
24
25       // Start an ordered list:
26       echo '<ol>';
27
28       // Loop through each subarray:
29       foreach ($parent as $task_id => $todo) {
30
31           // Display the item:
32           // Start with a checkbox!
33           echo <<<EOT
34   <li><input type="checkbox" name="tasks[$task_id]" value="done" /> $todo
35   EOT;
36
37           // Check for subtasks:
38           if (isset($tasks[$task_id])) {
39
40               // Call this function:
41               make_list($tasks[$task_id]);
42
43           }
44
45           // Complete the list item:
46           echo '</li>';
47
48       } // End of FOREACH loop.
49
50       // Close the ordered list:
51       echo '</ol>';
52
53   } // End of make_list() function.
54
55   // Connect to the database:
56   $dbc = @mysqli_connect ('localhost', 'username', 'password', 'test') OR die ('<p>Could not
     connect to the database!</p></body></html>');
57
```

*(script continues on next page)*

**Script 1.5** *continued*

```
58    // Check if the form has been submitted:
59    if (isset($_POST['submitted']) && isset($_POST['tasks']) && is_array($_POST['tasks'])) {
60
61        // Define the query:
62        $q = 'UPDATE tasks SET date_completed=NOW() WHERE task_id IN (';
63
64        // Add each task ID:
65        foreach ($_POST['tasks'] as $task_id => $v) {
66            $q .= $task_id . ', ';
67        }
68
69        // Complete the query and execute:
70        $q = substr($q, 0, -2) . ')';
71        $r = mysqli_query($dbc, $q);
72
73        // Report on the results:
74        if (mysqli_affected_rows($dbc) == count($_POST['tasks'])) {
75            echo '<p>The task(s) have been marked as completed!</p>';
76        } else {
77            echo '<p>Not all tasks could be marked as completed!</p>';
78        }
79
80    } // End of submission IF.
81
82    // Retrieve all the uncompleted tasks:
83    $q = 'SELECT task_id, parent_id, task FROM tasks WHERE date_completed="0000-00-00 00:00:00"
      ORDER BY parent_id, date_added ASC';
84    $r = mysqli_query($dbc, $q);
85
86    // Initialize the storage array:
87    $tasks = array();
88
89    while (list($task_id, $parent_id, $task) = mysqli_fetch_array($r, MYSQLI_NUM)) {
90
91        // Add to the array:
92        $tasks[$parent_id][$task_id] = $task;
93
94    }
95
96    // For debugging:
97    //echo '<pre>' . print_r($tasks,1) . '</pre>';
98
99    // Make a form:
100   echo '<p>Check the box next to a task and click "Update" to mark a task as completed (it, and any
      subtasks, will no longer appear in this list).</p>
101   <form action="view_tasks2.php" method="post">
102   ';
103
104   // Send the first array element
105   // to the make_list() function:
106   make_list($tasks[0]);
107
108   // Complete the form:
109   echo '<input name="submitted" type="hidden" value="true" />
110   <input name="submit" type="submit" value="Update" />
111   </form>
112   ';
113
114   ?>
115   </body>
116   </html>
```

**3.** After connecting to the database, begin a conditional that checks for the form submission.

```php
if (isset($_POST['submitted']) &&
→ isset($_POST['tasks']) &&
→ is_array($_POST['tasks'])) {
```

The database update (marking the tasks as complete) will only occur if the form has been submitted, `$_POST['tasks']` has a value, and it is an array. Even if only one check box is selected, `$_POST['tasks']` would still be an array.

**4.** Write the update query.

```php
$q = 'UPDATE tasks SET
→ date_completed=NOW() WHERE task_id
→ IN (';
foreach ($_POST['tasks'] as $task_id
→ => $v) {
    $q .= $task_id . ', ';
}
$q = substr($q, 0, -2) . ')';
$r = mysqli_query($dbc, $q);
```

The update query will be something like

```php
UPDATE tasks SET date_completed=NOW()
→ WHERE task_id IN (X, Y, Z)
```

This will set each applicable task's `date_completed` column to the current date and time, so that it will no longer show up in the view list (because that query checks for a 0 `date_completed` value).

**5.** Report on the results and complete the submission conditional.

```php
if (mysqli_affected_rows($dbc)
→ == count($_POST['tasks'])) {
        echo '<p>The task(s)
→ have been marked as
→ completed!</p>';
    } else {
        echo '<p>Not all tasks
→ could be marked as completed!</p>';
    }
} // End of submission IF.
```

**6.** Before calling the `make_list()` function, add the initial form tag.

```php
echo '<p>Check the box next to a task
→ and click "Update" to mark a task
→ as completed (it, and any subtasks,
→ will no longer appear in this
→ list).</p>
<form action="view_tasks2.php"
→ method="post">
';
```

Because of the way the `make_list()` function works, if a parent task is marked as completed, its subtasks will never be shown. A comment indicating such is added to the form.

*continues on next page*

**THE HEREDOC SYNTAX**

**35**

**7.** After calling the `make_list()` function, complete the form.

```
echo '<input name="submitted"
→ type="hidden" value="true" />
<input name="submit" type="submit"
→ value="Update" />
</form>
';
```

**8.** Save the file as `view_tasks2.php`, place it in your Web directory, and test in your Web browser (**Figures 1.28** and **1.29**).

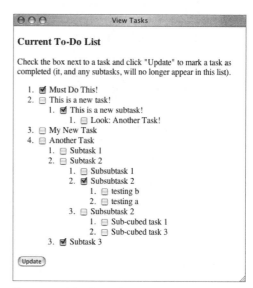

**Figure 1.28** Selecting tasks to be marked as completed.

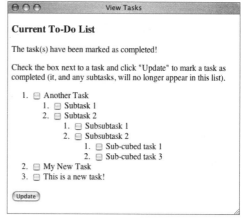

**Figure 1.29** The updated tasks list (some of the tasks had the exact same `date_added` value, hence the slight reshuffling of the order—see Figure 1.28).

# Using printf() and sprintf()

For most PHP programmers, the print()
and echo() functions are all they need for
printing text and variables. The advanced
PHP programmer might occasionally use the
more sophisticated printf() function. This
function prints text but also has the ability
to format the output. The PHP manual definition of this function is

```
printf(string format [, mixed
→ arguments]);
```

The *format* is a combination of literal text
and special formatting parameters, beginning with the percent sign (%). After that you
may have any combination of (in order):

◆ A sign specifier (+/-) to force a positive
number to show the plus sign.

◆ A padding specifier that indicates the
character used for right-padding (space is
the default, but you might want to use 0
for numbers).

◆ An alignment specifier (default is right-
justified, use - to force left-justification).

◆ A number indicating the minimum width
to be used.

◆ A precision specifier for how many decimal digits should be shown for floating-
point numbers (or how many characters
in a string).

◆ The type specifier; see **Table 1.2**.

*continues on next page*

**Table 1.2** These type specifiers are used to format
values used in the printf() and sprintf() functions.

| Type Specifiers | |
|---|---|
| CHARACTER | MEANING |
| b | binary integer |
| c | ASCII integer |
| d | standard integer |
| e | scientific notation |
| u | unsigned decimal integer |
| f | floating-point number |
| o | octal integer |
| s | string |
| x | hexadecimal integer |

This all may seem complicated, and well, it kind of is. You can start practicing by playing with a number (**Figure 1.30**):

```
printf('b: %b <br />c: %c <br /> d: %d
→ <br /> f: %f <br />', 80, 80, 80, 80);
```

That's four different representations of the same number. The first format will print 80 as a binary number, the second as 80's corresponding ASCII character (the capital letter *P*), the third as an integer, and the fourth as a floating-point number.

From there, take the two most common number types—*d* and *f*—and add some formatting (**Figure 1.31**):

```
printf('%0.2f <br />%+d <br />%0.2f <br
→ />', 8, 8, 1235.456);
```

First, the number 8 is printed as a floating-point number, with two digits after the decimal and padded with zeros. Next, the number 8 is printed as a signed integer. Finally, the number 1235.456 is printed as a floating-point number with two digits after the decimal (resulting in the rounding of the number).

Taking this idea further, mix in the string type (**Figure 1.32**):

```
printf('The cost of %d %s at $%0.2f each
→ is $%0.2f.', 4, 'brooms', 8.50,
→ (4*8.50));
```

The sprintf() function works exactly like printf(), but instead of printing the formatted string, it returns it. This function is great for generating database queries, without an ugly mixing of SQL and variables (and potentially function calls).

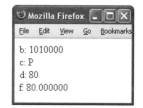

**Figure 1.30** The same number printed using four different type specifiers.

**Figure 1.31** Using printf() to format how numbers are printed.

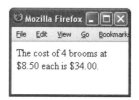

**Figure 1.32** Printing a mix of numbers and strings.

**USING PRINTF() AND SPRINTF()**

## To use sprintf():

1. Open `add_task.php` (Script 1.1) in your text editor or IDE.

2. Delete the call to the `mysqli_real_escape_string()` function (**Script 1.6**).

   I'll now call this function in the line that defines the query (Step 3).

*continues on page 41*

**Script 1.6** A minor modification to the `add_task.php` page (Script 1.1) shows a cleaner way to create a database query.

```
1    <!DOCTYPE html PUBLIC "-//W3C//DTD XHTML 1.0 Transitional//EN"
2           "http://www.w3.org/TR/xhtml1/DTD/xhtml1-transitional.dtd">
3    <html xmlns="http://www.w3.org/1999/xhtml" xml:lang="en" lang="en">
4    <head>
5        <meta http-equiv="content-type" content="text/html; charset=iso-8859-1" />
6        <title>Add a Task</title>
7    </head>
8    <body>
9    <?php # Script 1.6 - add_task2.php
10
11   /*  This page adds tasks to the tasks table.
12    *  The page both displays and handles the form.
13    *
14    */
15
16   // Connect to the database:
17   $dbc = @mysqli_connect ('localhost', 'username', 'password', 'test') OR die ('<p>Could not
     connect to the database!</p></body></html>');
18
19   // Check if the form has been submitted:
20   if (isset($_POST['submitted']) && !empty($_POST['task'])) {
21
22       // Sanctify the input...
23
24       // The parent_id must be an integer:
25       if (isset($_POST['parent_id'])) {
26           $parent_id = (int) $_POST['parent_id'];
27       } else {
28           $parent_id = 0;
29       }
30
```

*(script continues on next page)*

**Script 1.6** *continued*

```
000                              📄 Script
31      // Add the task to the database.
32      $q = sprintf("INSERT INTO tasks (parent_id, task) VALUES (%d, '%s')", $parent_id,
        mysqli_real_escape_string($dbc, $_POST['task']));
33      $r = mysqli_query($dbc, $q);
34
35      // Report on the results:
36      if (mysqli_affected_rows($dbc) == 1) {
37          echo '<p>The task has been added!</p>';
38      } else {
39          echo '<p>The task could not be added!</p>';
40      }
41
42  } // End of submission IF.
43
44  // Display the form:
45  echo '<form action="add_task2.php" method="post">
46  <fieldset>
47  <legend>Add a Task</legend>
48
49  <p>Task: <input name="task" type="text" size="60" maxlength="100" /></p>
50
51  <p>Parent Task: <select name="parent_id"><option value="0">None</option>
52  ';
53
54  // Retrieve all the uncompleted tasks:
55  $q = 'SELECT task_id, parent_id, task FROM tasks WHERE date_completed="0000-00-00 00:00:00"
        ORDER BY date_added ASC';
56  $r = mysqli_query($dbc, $q);
57  while (list($task_id, $parent_id, $task) = mysqli_fetch_array($r, MYSQLI_NUM)) {
58
59      // Add to the select menu:
60      echo "<option value=\"$task_id\">$task</option>\n";
61
62  }
63
64  echo '</select></p>
65
66  <input name="submitted" type="hidden" value="true" />
67  <input name="submit" type="submit" value="Add This Task" />
68
69  </form>
70  </fieldset>
71  ';
72
73  ?>
74  </body>
75  </html>
```

USING PRINTF() AND SPRINTF()

**3.** Change the line that defines the INSERT query to read:

```
$q = sprintf("INSERT INTO tasks
→ (parent_id, task) VALUES (%d,
→ '%s')", $parent_id,
→ mysqli_real_escape_string($dbc,
→ $_POST['task']));
```

By using the sprintf() function, the query can be created without interspersing SQL and variables. While doing so wasn't too ugly in the original script, in more complex queries the result can be hideous (lots of {$var['index']} and such), prone to errors, and hard to debug. This syntax separates the query from the data being used and is still able to incorporate a function call, all without using concatenation or other techniques.

**4.** Change the action attribute of the form to add_task2.php.

```
echo '<form action="add_task2.php"
→ method="post">
<fieldset>
<legend>Add a Task</legend>
<p>Task: <input name="task"
→ type="text" size="60"
→ maxlength="100" /></p>
<p>Parent Task: <select
→ name="parent_id"><option
value="0">None</option>
';
```

This file will be renamed, so the form needs to be adjusted, too.

*continues on next page*

USING PRINTF() AND SPRINTF()

**5.** If you want, remove all the lines required to view the list of tasks.

The `view_tasks.php` page (and its second version) both do this much better, so there's no need to still include that code here.

**6.** Save the file as `add_task2.php`, place it in your Web directory, and test in your Web browser (**Figures 1.33** and **1.34**).

## ✔ Tips

■ To use a literal percent sign in a string, escape it with another percent sign:

```
printf('The tax rate is %0.2f%%',
→ $tax);
```

■ The `vprintf()` function works exactly like `printf()` but only takes two arguments: the format and an array of values.

■ The `scanf()` and `fscanf()` functions also work exactly like `printf()` and `sprintf()` in terms of formatting parameters. The `scanf()` function is used for reading input; `fscanf()` is used to read data from a file.

**Figure 1.33** The page should still work exactly as it had before.

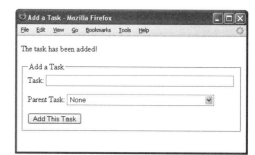

**Figure 1.34** Another thing to do!

# DEVELOPING
# WEB APPLICATIONS

The life of a PHP programmer normally begins with individual scripts, dedicated to a single purpose. From there one begins using more and more files, building up Web applications. Eventually you might get to developing sites on your own server and, if you're lucky, balanced over multiple servers. No matter how large your projects are, learning new and improved ways to develop Web applications is an important part of the life of the PHP programmer. As is being reminded to abide by the fundamentals.

In this chapter, the focus is on developing Web applications beyond the beginner or intermediate level. Assuming a mastery of standard Web application tools, like using sessions and templates, the topics here range from a reassertion of the fundamentals (which become more vital in larger projects) to changing the way you create pages. The chapter ends on two kinds of caching, both used to influence the client/server relationship.

# Documenting Code

Properly documenting one's code is so vitally important that I wish PHP would generate errors when it came across a lack of comments! Having taught PHP and interacted with readers for years, I am amazed at how often comments are omitted, occasionally under the guise of waiting until later. Proper documentation is something that should be incorporated into code for your own good, for your client's, for your co-workers' (if applicable), and for the programmer in the future who may have to alter or augment your work. Even—or especially—if that programmer is you.

Arguably, one cannot over-document one's work. Make notes about functions, variables, sections of code, and pages as a whole. And remember that documentation is something you should implement when you begin coding and continue to do as you work. Attempting to go in after the fact to make notes just isn't the same (and frequently won't happen at all). What seems obvious at the time of creation will be perplexing just three months later.

### Comments and White Space in Book Code

Because of the confines of the book format, the scripts developed in my books are never as well documented or organized as I would prefer (or as you should). But there's reasonably a limit as to how much valuable book space should be taken up with lines like

```
// Developed by: Larry E. Ullman.
```

Assuming that you are learning things from me and this book (that is the thinking, right?), then, when it comes to code documentation and layout, use what you see here as the base: the absolute minimum of what you should do. The amount of comments in my books may be sufficient but could be safely doubled.

## To document your code:

1. At the top of a script, thoroughly document all the meta-properties.

   "Meta-properties" refers to information about the file: who created it, when, why, as part of what site, etc. Also include information about yourself, even if you don't think anyone else will ever see the source code.

2. Document any contingencies.

   This is just a more specific type of documentation than that in Step 1. By "contingency," I mean what things must exist or happen for this script to do its job. Does it receive information from a form or a database? Does it rely upon PEAR or other external code? Does it use a template? Basically make a note of any other file that this script interacts with or includes. If the script assumes a minimum version of PHP, note that too.

3. Thoroughly describe every function.

   Functions should be commented like scripts: note their purpose, their contingencies, what values they take, what value(s) they return, etc.

4. Indicate the purpose of a variable if it would not be already completely obvious to the most basic programmer.

   Hopefully a variable's name is a good indicator of its purpose, but don't always assume such things are crystal clear.

5. Explain what sequences of code are going to do.

*continues on next page*

**DOCUMENTING CODE**

**6.** Indicate the purpose of a conditional.

Make sure it's clear why you're using the condition you're using and what the desired results are. If a conditional references a specific number or value, comment on why that number or value is being used.

**7.** Mark the closing brackets for complex functions and control structures (conditionals, loops, etc.).

You'll see this commonly in my scripts:

```
} // End of some_name() function.
```

**8.** Update your comments when you change your code!

This is a common and problematic mistake: you update your code but don't update the comment. Then, when you come back to review the code later, you read that the code does X but it actually does Y and you can't tell which is supposed to be correct.

## ✔ Tips

- The popular phpDocumentor (www.phpdoc.org, **Figure 2.1**) is used by PEAR to automatically generate package documentation. This tool, written in PHP and similar to the common JavaDoc (for Java programmers), creates comments within your scripts by actually reading the code itself. This shouldn't be used in lieu of your own comments, but it can add standardized documentation to a page.

- Somewhat outdated but still useful is the PHP Coding Standard. It's worth a read, even if you don't abide by all its suggestions. Unfortunately it tends to float around the Web a lot (its URL has changed several times over), so do a search to find it.

- You can also find many suggestions on comments, style, and structure by checking out coding standards for other languages.

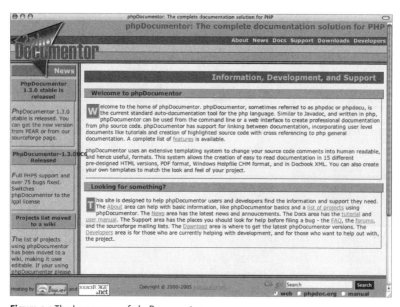

**Figure 2.1** The home page of phpDocumentor.

# Code Style and Structure

As the second topic to be discussed under the implied heading of "you know you should be doing these things but aren't for some reason," I want to take a couple pages to talk about code style and structure. The fundamentals of code structure refer to how you indent your code, skip blank lines, use braces and parentheses, and so forth. Proper syntax implies a certain amount of structure, but there are really two golden rules:

- Be consistent!

- Make your code easy to read.

I cannot stress enough that consistency is the most important consideration. Inconsistency will lead to unnecessary errors and extra hours of debugging.

Style is a much more subjective guideline, involving naming conventions (pages, variables, classes, and functions), where you define and how you organize functions, and so forth. Style is entirely a matter of user preference. Any recommendations anyone, including myself, has on the subject are merely suggestions. The only absolute must is that you be consistent!

## To structure and style your code:

◆ Always use curly braces, even if syntactically speaking you don't have to.

Many programmers will ignore this recommendation, but it's so much more foolproof to use curly braces all the time.

◆ Indent blocks of code (e.g., results of conditionals or function content) one tab stop or four spaces. (Formally, one should use spaces in lieu of tabs, but coders use the more convenient tab option regardless.)

How you indent your code goes directly toward how easy it is to read. Indentation should make clear the relationship between code and the control structures (loops, conditionals, etc.), functions, classes, and so on that the code is part of.

◆ Use blank lines to visually separate related sections of code.

◆ Put spaces between words, function arguments, operators, and so forth, as allowed (PHP is generally, but not universally, insensitive to white space).

◆ Place functions at the beginning of a document or in a separate file.

◆ Always use the formal PHP tags.

Because XML uses short tags (`<? ?>`) for its own purpose, you must use the formal PHP tags (`<?php ?>`) when using XML, as you'll see in Chapter 14, "XML and PHP." The recommendation is to use the formal tags regardless because that is the best way to ensure cross-server compatibility.

◆ It is suggested that `.php` always be used as the file extension for pages that are to be treated as PHP scripts. (Includes such as classes and configuration pages may use different extensions.)

Acceptable file extensions are determined by the Web server's configuration, but within the PHP community the movement is toward making `.php` the default.

## Site Structure

Much like your code structure and documentation, another overarching issue when developing larger Web applications is that of site structure: how the files are organized and stored on the server. Proper site structure is intended to improve security and administration of a site, as well as promote scalability, portability, and ease of modifications.

The key to site structure is to break up your code and applications into different pages and directories according to use, purpose, and function. Within the primary Web documents folder, which I'll call `html`, you would have one directory for images (most everyone does do this, at least), another for classes (if using object-oriented programming), another for functions, and so forth. Further, I would suggest that you use your own personalized folder names for security purposes. Anytime that a malicious user is blind to the names of folders and documents, the better. If you use the name *admin* for the administration section of a site, you're not doing yourself any favors, security-wise.

# Modularizing a Web Site

In my experience, the arc of a programmer's development starts with writing one-page applications that do just a single thing. These turn into two-page tools, and eventually into multipage sites, using templates, sessions, and/or cookies to tie them all together. For many programmers, though, the arc is actually a bell curve. After more and more experience, the seasoned PHP developer starts doing the same amount of work in fewer pages, like having the same script both display and handle a form. Or, conversely, the advanced PHP programmer may start making individual scripts that actually do less, by focusing each on a particular task. This is the premise behind modularizing a Web site.

For this example, I'll create a dummy Web site (i.e., it won't do much) that's broken into pieces. The new knowledge here will be how those features are separated, organized, and put back together. Instead of having individual pages (`contact.php`, `about.php`, `index.php`, etc.), the entire application will be run through one index page. That page will include the appropriate content module based upon values passed in the URL.

# Creating the configuration file

Every Web application I build begins with a configuration file. Configuration files serve several purposes, the four most important being:

◆ Defining constants

◆ Establishing site-wide settings

◆ Creating user functions

◆ Managing errors

Basically, any piece of information that every page in a site might need to access should be stored in a configuration file. (As a side note, if a function would not likely be used by the majority of site pages, I would put it in a separate file, thereby avoiding the extra overhead of defining it on pages where it won't be called.)

## To create the configuration file:

1. Begin a new PHP script in your text editor or IDE (**Script 2.1**).

   ```
   <?php # Script 2.1 - config.inc.php
   ```

   *continues on page 53*

**Script 2.1** The configuration file is the key back-end script. It defines site-wide constants and dictates how errors are handled.

```php
1    <?php # Script 2.1 - config.inc.php
2
3    /*
4     *  File name: config.inc.php
5     *  Created by: Larry E. Ullman of DMC Insights, Inc.
6     *  Contact: LarryUllman@DMCInsights.com, http://www.dmcinsights.com
7     *  Last modified: November 8, 2006
8     *
9     *  Configuration file does the following things:
10    *  - Has site settings in one location.
11    *  - Stores URLs and URIs as constants.
12    *  - Sets how errors will be handled.
13    */
14
15   # ****************** #
16   # ***** SETTINGS ***** #
17
18   // Errors are emailed here.
19   $contact_email = 'address@example.com';
20
21   // Determine whether we're working on a local server
22   // or on the real server:
23   if (stristr($_SERVER['HTTP_HOST'], 'local') || (substr($_SERVER['HTTP_HOST'], 0, 7) ==
     '192.168')) {
24       $local = TRUE;
25   } else {
26       $local = FALSE;
27   }
28
29   // Determine location of files and the URL of the site:
30   // Allow for development on different servers.
31   if ($local) {
32
33       // Always debug when running locally:
34       $debug = TRUE;
35
36       // Define the constants:
37       define ('BASE_URI', '/path/to/html/folder/');
38       define ('BASE_URL', 'http://localhost/directory/');
39       define ('DB', '/path/to/mysql.inc.php');
40
41   } else {
42
43       define ('BASE_URI', '/path/to/live/html/folder/');
44       define ('BASE_URL', 'http://www.example.com/');
45       define ('DB', '/path/to/live/mysql.inc.php');
46
47   }
48
49   /*
50    *  Most important setting...
51    *  The $debug variable is used to set error management.
52    *  To debug a specific page, add this to the index.php page:
53
54   if ($p == 'thismodule') $debug = TRUE;
55   require_once('./includes/config.inc.php');
56
```

*(script continues on next page)*

**Script 2.1** *continued*

```
57    *  To debug the entire site, do
58
59    $debug = TRUE;
60
61    *  before this next conditional.
62    */
63
64    // Assume debugging is off.
65    if (!isset($debug)) {
66        $debug = FALSE;
67    }
68
69    # ***** SETTINGS ***** #
70    # ******************** #
71
72
73    # *************************** #
74    # ***** ERROR MANAGEMENT ***** #
75
76    // Create the error handler.
77    function my_error_handler ($e_number, $e_message, $e_file, $e_line, $e_vars) {
78
79        global $debug, $contact_email;
80
81        // Build the error message.
82        $message = "An error occurred in script '$e_file' on line $e_line: \n<br />$e_message\n<br
          />";
83
84        // Add the date and time.
85        $message .= "Date/Time: " . date('n-j-Y H:i:s') . "\n<br />";
86
87        // Append $e_vars to the $message.
88        $message .= "<pre>" . print_r ($e_vars, 1) . "</pre>\n<br />";
89
90        if ($debug) { // Show the error.
91
92            echo '<p class="error">' . $message . '</p>';
93
94        } else {
95
96            // Log the error:
97            error_log ($message, 1, $contact_email); // Send email.
98
99            // Only print an error message if the error isn't a notice or strict.
100           if ( ($e_number != E_NOTICE) && ($e_number < 2048)) {
101               echo '<p class="error">A system error occurred. We apologize for the
                 inconvenience.</p>';
102           }
103
104       } // End of $debug IF.
105
106   } // End of my_error_handler() definition.
107
108   // Use my error handler:
109   set_error_handler ('my_error_handler');
110
111   # ***** ERROR MANAGEMENT ***** #
112   # *************************** #
113
114   ?>
```

2. Add some comments discussing the nature and purpose of this page.

```
/*
 *   File name: config.inc.php
 *   Created by: Larry E. Ullman of
→ DMC Insights, Inc.
 *   Contact:
→ LarryUllman@DMCInsights.com,
→ http://www.dmcinsights.com
 *   Last modified: November 8, 2006
 *
 *   Configuration file does the
→ following things:
 *     - Has site settings in one
→ location.
 *     - Stores URLs and URIs as
→ constants.
 *     - Sets how errors will be
→ handled.
 */
```

Because the configuration file is a common file, it ought to be the best-documented script in a site.

3. Set the email address to be used for errors.

```
$contact_email =
→ 'address@example.com';
```

For live sites, I prefer to be emailed when errors occur. So I declare a variable with the "to" email address. This may be my address while developing a site or a client's once the site goes live.

4. Determine if the script is running on the live server or a test server.

```
if (stristr($_SERVER['HTTP_HOST'],
→ 'local') ||
```

```
→ (substr($_SERVER['HTTP_HOST'],
→ 0, 7) == '192.168')) {
    $local = TRUE;
} else {
    $local = FALSE;
}
```

I almost always develop on a local server and then upload the completed site to the live server. The two environments will have server-specific settings, so the configuration file ought to confirm which is the current environment. To see if the site is running locally, I check two conditions against $_SERVER['HTTP_HOST']. If that variable contains the word *local* (as in http://localhost or http://power-book.local) or if the IP address begins with 192.168 (indicating a local network), then a $local variable is set as TRUE. Otherwise, it is FALSE.

5. Set the server-specific constants.

```
if ($local) {
    $debug = TRUE;
    define ('BASE_URI',
→ '/path/to/html/folder/');
    define ('BASE_URL',
→ 'http://localhost/directory/');
    define ('DB',
→ '/path/to/mysql.inc.php');
} else {
    define ('BASE_URI',
→ '/path/to/live/html/folder/');
    define ('BASE_URL',
→ 'http://www.example.com/');
    define ('DB',
→ '/path/to/live/mysql.inc.php');
}
```

*continues on next page*

*continues on next page*

MODULARIZING A WEB SITE

I always use these three constants in my Web applications. The BASE_URI is the absolute path to where the site's root folder is on the server (**Figure 2.2**). This constant makes it easy to use absolute URLs when any script includes a file. The BASE_URL constant is the hostname and directory (if applicable). On a test server, that might be just http://localhost/ch02/. Finally, the DB constant is the absolute path to the file that contains the database connectivity information. For security purposes, it's best to keep this stored outside of the Web directory.

Note that each constant is represented twice: once for a test server and once for the live server. If this is a test server ($local is TRUE), I also turn on debugging, which will mean more shortly.

**6.** Set the debugging level.

```
if (!isset($debug)) {
    $debug = FALSE;
}
```

I use a $debug variable to indicate how errors should be handled. If the site is being run locally, $debug will be TRUE. To debug a live site, a page would need to use the line

```
$debug = TRUE;
```

prior to including the configuration file. In all other cases, debugging is turned off.

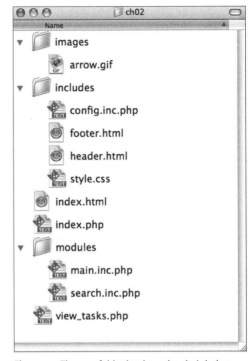

**Figure 2.2** The root folder is where the site's index page may be found. Within the root folder, other subfolders—such as images, includes, and modules—would be found.

**7.** Begin a function for handling errors.

```
function my_error_handler ($e_number,
→ $e_message, $e_file, $e_line,
→ $e_vars) {
    global $debug, $contact_email;
```

PHP allows you to define your own function for handling errors, rather than using the built-in behavior. For more information on this process or the syntax, see the PHP manual or my *PHP and MySQL for Dynamic Web Sites: Visual QuickStart Guide* book (Peachpit Press, 2005).

Two global variables will be used in this function.

**8.** Build up the error message.

```
$message = "An error occurred in
→ script '$e_file' on line $e_line:
→ \n<br />$e_message\n<br />";
$message .= "Date/Time: " . date('n-
→ j-Y H:i:s') . "\n<br />";
$message .= "<pre>" . print_r
→ ($e_vars, 1) . "</pre>\n<br />";
```

For debugging purposes, the error message should be as informative as possible. To start, it will include the name of the file where the error occurred and on what line. Then the date and time of the error are appended to the message. Finally, every existing variable is added. This can be a lot of data (**Figure 2.3**), but that's a good thing when you need to find and fix a problem.

*continues on next page*

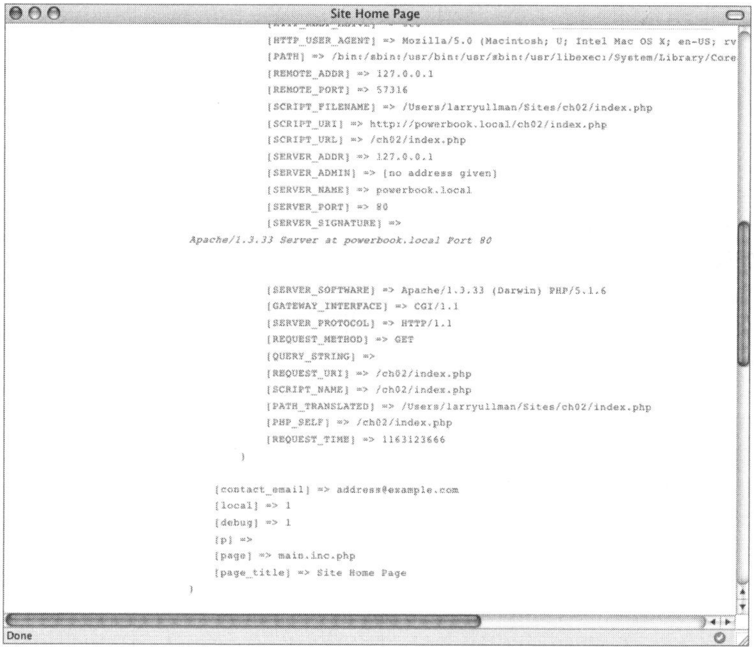

**Figure 2.3** This is just some of the data reported when an error occurs.

**9.** If debugging is turned on, print the error.

```
if ($debug) {
    echo '<p class="error">' .
→ $message . '</p>';
```

If debugging is turned on, then the full message will appear in the Web browser (**Figure 2.4**). This is great when developing a site but a huge security flaw on a live site. You can also edit this code to fit into your site's design.

**10.** If debugging is turned off, send the message in an email and print a default message.

```
} else {
    error_log ($message, 1,
→ $contact_email);
    if ( ($e_number != E_NOTICE) &&
→ ($e_number < 2048)) {
        echo '<p class=
→ "error">A system error occurred.
→ We apologize for the
→ inconvenience.</p>';
    }
} // End of $debug IF.
```

For a live site, the detailed error message should not be shown (unless debugging is temporarily enabled for that page) but should be emailed instead. The `error_log()` function will do this, if provided with the number 1 as its second argument. But the user probably needs to know that something didn't go right, so a generic message is displayed (**Figure 2.5**). If the error happens to be a notice or a strict error (having a value of 2048), no message should be printed, as the error is likely not interfering with the operation of the page.

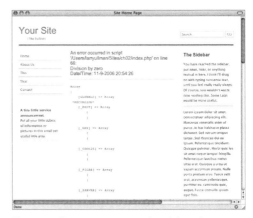

**Figure 2.4** How errors appear when debugging a page.

**Figure 2.5** On a live site, errors are handled more modestly (and securely).

**11.** Complete the function, tell PHP to use this error handler, and complete the page.

```
} // End of my_error_handler()
→ definition.
set_error_handler
→ ('my_error_handler');
?>
```

**12.** Save the file as `config.inc.php` and place it in your Web directory (in an `includes` subfolder).

Figure 2.2 shows the directory layout I'll use for this site.

## Creating the Database File

I have not, for this application, created a database configuration file, as the site does not involve any databases. If a database were required, I would write a `mysql.inc.php` (or `postgresql.inc.php` or `oracle.inc.php` or whatever) file that establishes the database connection. Such a file should also define any functions that involve the database application.

This file could also be stored in the `includes` directory but would preferably be stored outside of the Web directory. The `config.inc.php` file has a constant named `DB` that should be an absolute path to this file on the server.

Any page that needs a database connection could then include it by just using

```
require_once(DB);
```

Because `DB` represents an absolute path to that file, it wouldn't matter if the including script was in the main folder or a subdirectory.

# Creating the HTML template

Using an HTML template is a virtual certainty with any larger-scale application. You can use Smarty (http://smarty.php.net) or many other templating systems, but I prefer to use just two simple files: a header that contains everything in a page up until the page-specific content, and a footer that contains the rest of the page (**Figure 2.6**).

For this template, I'll use a design found on Open Source Web Design (www.oswd.org), an excellent Web design resource. This particular design (**Figure 2.7**) is by Anthony Yeung (www.smallpark.org) and is gratefully used with his kind permission.

### To create the template pages:

1. Design an HTML page in your text or WYSIWYG editor.

   To start creating a template for a Web site, design the layout like a standard HTML page, independent of any PHP code. For this example, as I already said, I'll be using the Leaves CSS design (Figure 2.7).

   Note: In order to save space, the CSS file for this example (which controls the layout) is not included in the book. You can download the file through the book's supporting Web site (www.DMCInsights.com/phpvqp2/, see the site's Extras page) or do without it (the template will still work; it just won't look as nice).

2. Copy everything from the first line of the layout's source to just before the page-specific content and paste it in a new document (**Script 2.2**). That is, start from

   ```
   <!DOCTYPE html PUBLIC "-//W3C//
   → DTD XHTML 1.0 Transitional//EN"
   → "http://www.w3.org/TR/xhtml1/DTD/
   → xhtml1-transitional.dtd">
   <html xmlns="http://www.w3.org/1999/
   → xhtml">
   <head>
   ```

   and continue through

   ```
           <div id="content">
       <!-- End of header. -->
   ```

   This first file will contain the initial HTML tags (from DOCTYPE through the head and into the beginning of the page body). It also has the code that makes the column of links on the left side of the browser window and the sidebar on the right (see Figure 2.7). I've omitted a good chunk of the HTML from this step. For the complete code, see Script 2.2 or just download the file from the book's Web site.

*continues on page 60*

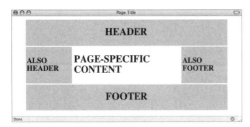

**Figure 2.6** A very crude representation of how to create a template for a site by wrapping two included files around the page-specific content area.

**Figure 2.7** The template this site will use for all its pages.

**Script 2.2** The header file begins the HTML template. It also includes the CSS file and uses a PHP variable for the browser window's title.

```
1    <?php # Script 2.2 - header.html
2
3    // This page begins the HTML header for the site.
4
5    // Check for a $page_title value:
6    if (!isset($page_title)) $page_title = 'Default Page Title';
7    ?>
8    <!DOCTYPE html PUBLIC "-//W3C//DTD XHTML 1.0 Transitional//EN"
     "http://www.w3.org/TR/xhtml1/DTD/xhtml1-transitional.dtd">
9    <html xmlns="http://www.w3.org/1999/xhtml">
10   <head>
11   <meta http-equiv="Content-Type" content="text/html; charset=ISO-8859-1" />
12   <title><?php echo $page_title; ?></title>
13   <link href="./includes/style.css" rel="stylesheet" type="text/css" />
14   </head>
15   <body>
16   <div id="container">
17       <div id="header">
18         <h1>Your Site</h1>
19         <p>i like bylines</p>
20           <form name="form1" id="form1" method="get" action="index.php">
21           <input type="text" name="terms" value="Search..." />
22           <input type="hidden" name="p" value="search" />
23           <input class="button" type="submit" name="Submit" value="GO" />
24         </form>
25       </div>
26
27       <div id="navigation">
28         <ul id="navlist">
29             <li><a href="index.php">Home</a></li>
30             <li><a href="index.php?p=about">About Us</a></li>
31             <li><a href="index.php?p=this">This</a></li>
32             <li><a href="index.php?p=that">That</a></li>
33             <li><a href="index.php?p=contact">Contact</a></li>
34   <li><p><strong>A tiny little service announcement.</strong><br/>Put all your little tidbits of
     information or pictures in this small yet useful little area. </p></li>
35           </ul>
36
37     </div>
38       <div id="sidebar">
39         <h2>The Sidebar</h2>
40         <p>You have reached the sidebar, put news, links, or anything textual in here. I think
     I'll drag on with typing nonsense text, until you feel really really sleepy. Of course, you
     wouldn't waste time reading this. Some Latin would be more useful.</p>
41         <p>Lorem ipsum dolor sit amet, consectetuer adipiscing elit. Maecenas venenatis enim ut
     purus. In hac habitasse platea dictumst. Sed rutrum tempus turpis. Sed rhoncus dui eu ipsum.
     Pellentesque tincidunt. Quisque pulvinar. Morbi quis leo sit amet neque tempor fringilla.
     Pellentesque faucibus metus vitae erat. Quisque a urna ut sapien accumsan ornare. Nulla porta
     pretium eros. Fusce velit erat, accumsan pellentesque, porttitor eu, commodo quis, augue. <a
     href="#">Fusce convallis ipsum eget felis</a>. </p>
42         <p>Aenean eros arcu, condimentum nec, dapibus ut, tincidunt sit amet, urna. Quisque
     viverra, eros sed imperdiet iaculis, est risus facilisis quam, id malesuada arcu nulla luctus
     urna. </p></div>
43
44       <div id="content">
45       <!-- End of header. -->
```

**3.** Change the page's title line to read:

```
<title><?php echo $page_title;
→ ?></title>
```

I'll want the page title (which appears at the top of the Web browser; *Page Title* in Figure 2.7) to be changeable on a page-by-page basis. To do so, I set this as a variable that will be printed out by PHP.

**4.** Before any HTML, create a PHP section that checks for a $page_title.

```
<?php # Script 2.2 - header.html

if (!isset($page_title)) $page_title
→ = 'Default Page Title';

?>
```

Just in case a PHP script includes the header file without having set a $page_title first, this PHP code declares a default page title (which you'll likely want to make more meaningful). If you don't do this and error reporting is turned on, the browser title could end up like **Figure 2.8**.

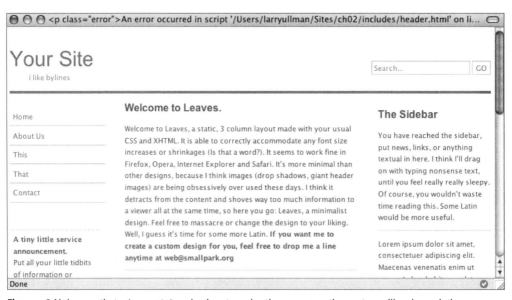

Your Site

i like bylines

Search...  GO

Home

About Us

This

That

Contact

A tiny little service announcement.
Put all your little tidbits of information or

**Welcome to Leaves.**

Welcome to Leaves, a static, 3 column layout made with your usual CSS and XHTML. It is able to correctly accommodate any font size increases or shrinkages (Is that a word?). It seems to work fine in Firefox, Opera, Internet Explorer and Safari. It's more minimal than other designs, because I think images (drop shadows, giant header images) are being obsessively over used these days. I think it detracts from the content and shoves way too much information to a viewer all at the same time, so here you go: Leaves, a minimalist design. Feel free to massacre or change the design to your liking. Well, I guess it's time for some more Latin. **If you want me to create a custom design for you, feel free to drop me a line anytime at web@smallpark.org**

**The Sidebar**

You have reached the sidebar, put news, links, or anything textual in here. I think I'll drag on with typing nonsense text, until you feel really really sleepy. Of course, you wouldn't waste time reading this. Some Latin would be more useful.

Lorem ipsum dolor sit amet, consectetuer adipiscing elit. Maecenas venenatis enim ut

**Figure 2.8** Make sure that a $page_title value is set, or else the error reporting system will end up printing a detailed error message there instead.

**Script 2.3** The footer file completes the HTML template.

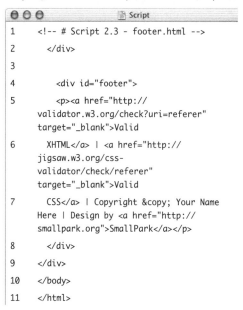

```
1    <!-- # Script 2.3 - footer.html -->
2        </div>
3
4          <div id="footer">
5          <p><a href="http://
      validator.w3.org/check?uri=referer"
      target="_blank">Valid
6      XHTML</a> | <a href="http://
      jigsaw.w3.org/css-
      validator/check/referer"
      target="_blank">Valid
7      CSS</a> | Copyright &copy; Your Name
      Here | Design by <a href="http://
      smallpark.org">SmallPark</a></p>
8        </div>
9      </div>
10     </body>
11     </html>
```

**5.** Save the file as `header.html`.

Included files can use just about any extension for the filename. Some programmers like to use `.inc` to indicate that a file is used as an include. In this case, you could also use `.inc.html`, which would indicate that it's both an include and an HTML file (to distinguish it from includes full of PHP code).

**6.** Copy everything in the original template from the end of the page-specific content to the end of the page and paste it in a new file (**Script 2.3**).

```
<!-- # Script 2.3 - footer.html -->
    </div>
    <div id="footer">
    <p><a
href="http://validator.w3.org/check?
→ uri=referer" target="_blank">Valid
  XHTML</a> | <a
href="http://jigsaw.w3.org/
→ css-validator/check/referer"
→ target="_blank">Valid
  CSS</a> | Copyright &copy; Your
→ Name Here | Design by <a
→ href="http://smallpark.org">Small
→ Park</a></p>
    </div>
</div>
</body>
</html>
```

The footer file contains the remaining formatting for the page body, including the page's footer, and then closes the HTML document.

**7.** Save the file as `footer.html`.

**8.** Place both files in the Web server's `includes` directory.

# Creating the index page

The index page is the main script in the modularized application. In fact, it's the only page that should ever be loaded in the Web browser. The index page has but a single purpose: to assemble all the proper pieces to make the complete Web page. Accomplishing this might involve:

◆ Including a configuration file

◆ Including a database connectivity file

◆ Incorporating an HTML template

◆ Determining and including the proper content module

With this in mind, it's really just a matter of thinking out all the code and making sure it's securely handled. I'll explain in more detail in the following steps.

## To create the main page:

1. Begin a new PHP script in your text editor or IDE (**Script 2.4**).

   `<?php # Script 2.4 - index.php`

2. Include the configuration file

   `require_once ('./includes/`
   `→ config.inc.php');`

   The configuration file defines many important things, so it should be included first.

*continues on page 64*

**Script 2.4** The index page is the script through which everything happens. It determines what module should be included, requires the configuration file, and pulls together the HTML template.

```
1    <?php # Script 2.4 - index.php
2
3    /*
4     *  This is the main page.
5     *  This page includes the configuration file,
6     *  the templates, and any content-specific modules.
7     */
8
9    // Require the configuration file before any PHP code:
10   require_once ('./includes/config.inc.php');
11
12   // Validate what page to show:
13   if (isset($_GET['p'])) {
14       $p = $_GET['p'];
15   } elseif (isset($_POST['p'])) { // Forms
16       $p = $_POST['p'];
17   } else {
18       $p = NULL;
19   }
20
21   // Determine what page to display:
22   switch ($p) {
23
```

*(script continues on next page)*

**Script 2.4** *continued*

```
    ⊖ ⊖ ⊖                                    📄 Script
24      case 'about':
25          $page = 'about.inc.php';
26          $page_title = 'About This Site';
27          break;
28
29      case 'this':
30          $page = 'this.inc.php';
31          $page_title = 'This is Another Page.';
32          break;
33
34      case 'that':
35          $page = 'that.inc.php';
36          $page_title = 'That is Also a Page.';
37          break;
38
39      case 'contact':
40          $page = 'contact.inc.php';
41          $page_title = 'Contact Us';
42          break;
43
44      case 'search':
45          $page = 'search.inc.php';
46          $page_title = 'Search Results';
47          break;
48
49      // Default is to include the main page.
50      default:
51          $page = 'main.inc.php';
52          $page_title = 'Site Home Page';
53          break;
54
55  } // End of main switch.
56
57  // Make sure the file exists:
58  if (!file_exists('./modules/' . $page)) {
59      $page = 'main.inc.php';
60      $page_title = 'Site Home Page';
61  }
62
63  // Include the header file:
64  include_once ('./includes/header.html');
65
66  // Include the content-specific module:
67  // $page is determined from the above switch.
68  include ('./modules/' . $page);
69
70  // Include the footer file to complete the template:
71  include_once ('./includes/footer.html');
72
73  ?>
```

**3.** Validate the page being shown.

```
if (isset($_GET['p'])) {
    $p = $_GET['p'];
} elseif (isset($_POST['p'])) {
    $p = $_POST['p'];
} else {
    $p = NULL;
}
```

The specific content being shown will be based upon a value sent to this page. When clicking links, the value will be sent in the URL. When most forms are submitted, the value will be sent in $_POST. If neither is the case, set $p to NULL.

**4.** Begin a switch conditional that determines the page title and file.

```
switch ($p) {
    case 'about':
        $page = 'about.inc.php';
        $page_title = 'About
→ This Site';
        break;
```

Each module has a name of *something*.inc.php, which is my way of indicating that it's both a PHP script but also an included file. Due to the way computers handle extensions, only the final extension really matters (i.e., if you were to run the file directly, it would be treated as a PHP script).

For each module, the page's title (which will appear in the browser window) is also set.

**5.** Complete the switch.

```
    case 'this':
        $page = 'this.inc.php';
        $page_title = 'This is
→ Another Page.';
        break;
    case 'that':
        $page = 'that.inc.php';
        $page_title = 'That is
→ Also a Page.';
        break;
    case 'contact':
        $page =
→ 'contact.inc.php';
        $page_title =
→ 'Contact Us';
        break;
    case 'search':
        $page =
→ 'search.inc.php';
        $page_title = 'Search
→ Results';
        break;
    default:
        $page = 'main.inc.php';
        $page_title = 'Site Home
→ Page';
        break;
} // End of main switch.
```

For each possible content module, another switch case is provided. For security purposes, the default case is critical. If $p does not have a value or does not have a valid value—one of the specific cases—then the main.inc.php file will be used. This is a necessary security step because some ill-intended person will see that your site has a URL like index.php?p=contact and will attempt to do something like index.php?p=*/path/to/something/useful*. In such a case, the page's main content will be included.

6. Confirm that the module file exists.

```
if (!file_exists('./modules/' .
→ $page)) {
    $page = 'main.inc.php';
    $page_title = 'Site Home Page';
}
```

This isn't absolutely necessary as long as the right module file exists for each case in the `switch`. However, including this code provides an extra layer of security.

7. Include the header file.

```
include_once
('./includes/header.html');
```

This is the start of the HTML template.

8. Include the module.

```
include ('./modules/' . $page);
```

This brings in all the specific content.

9. Include the footer file.

```
include_once
('./includes/footer.html');
```

This completes the HTML template.

10. Complete the page.

```
?>
```

11. Save the file as `index.php` and place it in your Web directory.

    You can't test it until you've created some of the content modules (at least `main.inc.php`).

### ✔ Tip

■ The `switch` conditional that validates proper `$p` values is an important security measure. Another is using a separate variable for the name of the included file (i.e., `$page`). The following code would be *highly* insecure:

```
include ($_GET['p']);
```

---

## My Security Anecdote

In the summer of 2006, I revamped my company's Web site (www.DMCInsights.com), using a modularized layout, to a small extent. Literally the first night the new version of the site went live, someone tried hacking the server by changing URLs like about.php?i=phpmysql2 into about.php?i=http://somesite.com/file.txt. The file.txt script on that other server contained PHP code that would reveal every file on my server. Had it run, my site's security would have been compromised.

The attempt did not work for two reasons. First, I was smart about validating my $_GET['i'] data, associating proper values to scripts. Second, I was careful about how files were included. Just as important, though, was the error reporting I had implemented. As the site was live, the user saw nothing informative when they tried to include an invalid file but I was notified via email of the attempt.

## Creating content modules

Now that all the legwork has been done and the configuration, template, and index files have been written, it's time to start creating the actual content modules. With this system, a content module is stunningly simple to implement. The content files do not need to include the configuration or the template files, as the main script already does that. And because all the content files are includes, they can contain literal HTML or PHP code.

There is one catch: the modules should not be loadable directly. If one were to directly access main.inc.php (or any other module) in their Web browser, they'd see the result without the HTML template (**Figure 2.9**), without the proper error management, and possibly without the database connectivity. So every module should have some code that redirects the user to the proper page, if accessed directly.

## To create the main module:

1. Begin a new PHP script in your text editor or IDE (**Script 2.5**).

   ```
   <?php # Script 2.5 - main.inc.php
   ```

   *continues on page 68*

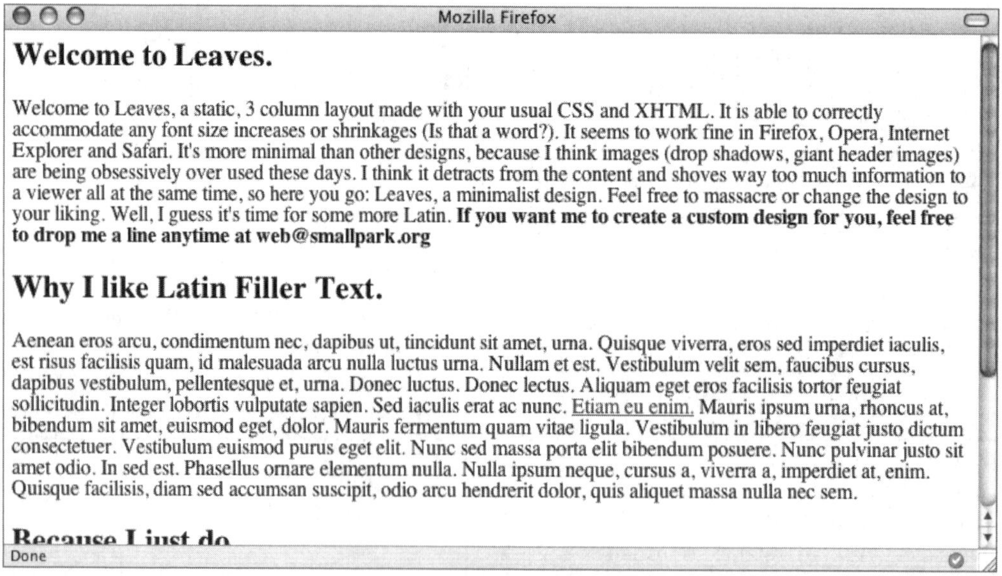

**Figure 2.9** Content modules shouldn't be accessed directly through a URL, since they would then lack the HTML template (among other things).

**Script 2.5** The first content module has the HTML for the main page. Some PHP code redirects the Web browser if this script was accessed directly.

```
1    <?php # Script 2.5 - main.inc.php
2
3    /*
4     *  This is the main content module.
5     *  This page is included by index.php.
6     */
7
8    // Redirect if this page was accessed directly:
9    if (!defined('BASE_URL')) {
10
11       // Need the BASE_URL, defined in the config file:
12       require_once ('../includes/config.inc.php');
13
14       // Redirect to the index page:
15       $url = BASE_URL . 'index.php';
16       header ("Location: $url");
17       exit;
18
19   } // End of defined() IF.
20   ?>
21
22       <h2>Welcome to Leaves.</h2>
23       <p>Welcome to Leaves, a static, 3 column layout made with your usual CSS and XHTML. It is
     able to correctly accommodate any font size increases or shrinkages (Is that a word?). It seems
     to work fine in Firefox, Opera, Internet Explorer and Safari. It's more minimal than other
     designs, because I think images (drop shadows, giant header images) are being obsessively over
     used these days. I think it detracts from the content and shoves way too much information to a
     viewer all at the same time, so here you go: Leaves, a minimalist design. Feel free to massacre
     or change the design to your liking. Well, I guess it's time for some more Latin. <strong>If you
     want me to create a custom design for you, feel free to drop me a line anytime at
     web@smallpark.org </strong></p>
24       <h2>Why I like Latin Filler Text. </h2>
25       <p>Aenean eros arcu, condimentum nec, dapibus ut, tincidunt sit amet, urna. Quisque
     viverra, eros sed imperdiet iaculis, est risus facilisis quam, id malesuada arcu nulla luctus
     urna. Nullam et est. Vestibulum velit sem, faucibus cursus, dapibus vestibulum, pellentesque et,
     urna. Donec luctus. Donec lectus. Aliquam eget eros facilisis tortor feugiat sollicitudin.
     Integer lobortis vulputate sapien. Sed iaculis erat ac nunc. <a href="#">Etiam eu enim.</a>
     Mauris ipsum urna, rhoncus at, bibendum sit amet, euismod eget, dolor. Mauris fermentum quam
     vitae ligula. Vestibulum in libero feugiat justo dictum consectetuer. Vestibulum euismod purus
     eget elit. Nunc sed massa porta elit bibendum posuere. Nunc pulvinar justo sit amet odio. In sed
     est. Phasellus ornare elementum nulla. Nulla ipsum neque, cursus a, viverra a, imperdiet at,
     enim. Quisque facilisis, diam sed accumsan suscipit, odio arcu hendrerit dolor, quis aliquet
     massa nulla nec sem. </p>
26       <h2>Because I just do. </h2>
27       <p><a href="#">Proin sagittis leo in diam</a>. Vestibulum vestibulum orci vel libero. Cras
     molestie pede quis odio. Phasellus tempus dolor eu risus. Aenean tellus tortor, dignissim sit
     amet, tempus eu, eleifend porttitor, ipsum. Fusce diam. Suspendisse potenti. Duis consequat
     scelerisque lacus. Proin et massa. Duis adipiscing, lectus a euismod consectetuer, pede libero
     ornare dui, et lacinia ipsum ipsum nec lectus. Suspendisse sed nunc quis odio aliquet feugiat.
     Pellentesque sapien. Phasellus sed lorem eu augue luctus commodo. Nullam interdum convallis nunc.
     Fusce varius. Ut egestas. Fusce interdum iaculis pede. Sed vehicula vestibulum odio. <a
     href="#">Donec id diam. </a></p>
```

MODULARIZING A WEB SITE

**2.** Check that this page has not been accessed directly.

```
if (!defined('BASE_URL')) {
```

There are any number of things you could check for, like whether $page or $p is set. But if register globals was enabled and the user went to main.inc.php?p=true, that check would fail. Instead, I'll see if a constant is defined. This constant is created in the configuration file, which should be included first thing in the index file, prior to including this page.

**3.** Redirect the user.

```
require_once ('../includes/
→ config.inc.php');
$url = BASE_URL . 'index.php';
header ("Location: $url");
exit;
```

The user should be redirected to the index page. Because an absolute URL redirection is desired (which is best), the configuration file must be included to get the BASE_URL value.

**4.** Complete the PHP section.

```
} // End of defined() IF.
?>
```

**5.** Add whatever content.

```
<h2>Welcome to Leaves.</h2>
    <p>Welcome to Leaves, a static,
→ 3 column layout made with your
→ usual CSS and XHTML. It is able to
→ correctly accommodate any font size
→ increases or shrinkages (Is that a
→ word?). It seems to work fine in
→ Firefox, Opera, Internet Explorer
→ and Safari. It's more minimal than
→ other designs, because I think
→ images (drop shadows, giant header
→ images) are being obsessively over
→ used these days. I think it
→ detracts from the content and
→ shoves way too much information to
→ a viewer all at the same time, so
→ here you go: Leaves, a minimalist
→ design. Feel free to massacre or
→ change the design to your liking.
→ Well, I guess it's time for some
→ more Latin. <strong>If you want me
→ to create a custom design for you,
→ feel free to drop me a line anytime
→ at web@smallpark.org </strong></p>
```

This can be any combination of HTML and PHP, just like any other PHP page. I'm omitting some of the content from this step, but you can find it in the downloadable version of the script.

**6.** Save the file as `main.inc.php`, place it in your Web directory (in the `modules` folder, Figure 2.2), and test by going to `index.php` in your Web browser (**Figure 2.10**).

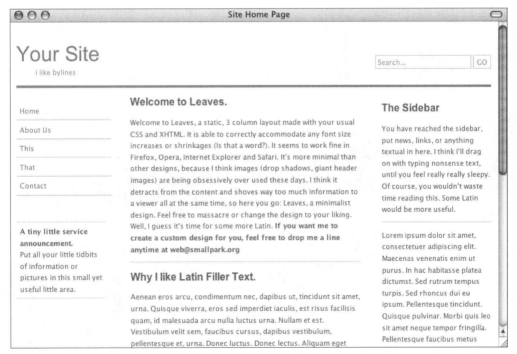

**Figure 2.10** The complete, modularized, template-driven site home page.

## Creating the search module

In the last example I created the main content module. It was surprisingly simple, so I want to run through another example to show some variety. As a demonstration of a PHP-driven module, I'll sketch out the search feature. Keep in mind that, having no real content and no database back end, it's impossible to implement a real search with this example. But that's not important anyway. The focus here is on how you would use PHP to handle forms within the modular structure. Once again, I think you'll be surprised by how uncomplicated it is.

## To create the search module:

1. Begin a new PHP script in your text editor or IDE (**Script 2.6**).

   ```
   <?php # Script 2.6 - search.inc.php
   ```

   *continues on page 72*

**Script 2.6** The search module pretends to return some results as a way of demonstrating how easy it is to handle forms, even in a modularized structure.

```php
1    <?php # Script 2.6 - search.inc.php
2
3    /*
4     *  This is the search content module.
5     *  This page is included by index.php.
6     *  This page expects to receive $_GET['terms'].
7     */
8
9    // Redirect if this page was accessed directly:
10   if (!defined('BASE_URL')) {
11
12       // Need the BASE_URL, defined in the config file:
13       require_once ('../includes/config.inc.php');
14
15       // Redirect to the index page:
16       $url = BASE_URL . 'index.php?p=search';
17
18       // Pass along search terms?
19       if (isset($_GET['terms'])) {
20           $url .= '&terms=' . urlencode($_GET['terms']);
21       }
22
23       header ("Location: $url");
24       exit;
25
26   } // End of defined() IF.
27
28   // Print a caption:
29   echo '<h2>Search Results</h2>';
30
31   // Display the search results if the form
32   // has been submitted.
33   if (isset($_GET['terms']) && ($_GET['terms'] != 'Search...') ) {
34
35       // Query the database.
36       // Fetch the results.
37       // Print the results:
38       for ($i = 1; $i <= 10; $i++) {
39           echo <<<EOT
40   <h4><a href="#">Search Result #$i</a></h4>
41   <p>This is some description. This is some description. This is some description. This is some
     description.</p>\n
42   EOT;
43       }
44
45   } else { // Tell them to use the search form.
46       echo '<p class="error">Please use the search form at the top of the window to search this
     site.</p>';
47   }
48   ?>
```

2. Redirect the browser if the page has been accessed directly.

```
if (!defined('BASE_URL')) {
    require_once ('../includes/
→ config.inc.php');
    $url = BASE_URL .
→ 'index.php?p=search';
    if (isset($_GET['terms'])) {
        $url .= '&terms=' .
→ urlencode($_GET['terms']);
    }
    header ("Location: $url");
    exit;
}
```

The bulk of the code here is like that in main.inc.php. There are two changes. First, the redirection URL is changed to BASE_URL plus index.php?p=search. This technique can be used for any module so that the user is redirected to the page they want—via index.php. Second, if, for some inexplicable reason, the user arrived on this page while submitting a form, then the search terms would be present in the URL. If so, those terms will be passed along as well. The end result will be that going directly to www.example. com/modules/search.inc.php?terms=blah still results in a valid search.

3. Print a caption.

```
echo '<h2>Search Results</h2>';
```

4. Check for a proper search term.

```
if (isset($_GET['terms']) &&
→ ($_GET['terms'] != 'Search...') ) {
```

The database search would only take place if a search term were passed along in the URL. The search box uses *Search...* as the default value, so that needs to be ruled out.

## Using Frameworks

Frameworks are libraries of established code meant to facilitate development. There are many well-conceived frameworks available for PHP, well over 40 at last count. Zend, the company behind the PHP engine, has recently entered the framework discussion with its own version (http://framework.zend.com).

Frameworks normally use a modular system, like the one implemented in this chapter, but on a much more elaborate scale. The arguments for using frameworks are the same as those for using OOP or PEAR: they allow you to quickly build applications with (hopefully) better features and security. The arguments against using frameworks are also comparable to OOP and PEAR: they require time and effort to learn, let alone master, and may be difficult to customize. It's also probable that framework-driven sites will run more slowly (due to extra processing required).

Personally, I'm not a framework person, as I like to get my hands dirty with code, but you may like them. For a good discussion and comparison of ten popular frameworks, see www.phpit.net/article/ten-different-php-frameworks/

**Figure 2.11** No search is performed without a term being submitted.

**Figure 2.12** Any search term will turn up these dummy results.

**5.** Print the search results.

```
for ($i = 1; $i <= 10; $i++) {
    echo <<<EOT
<h4><a href="#">Search Result
→ #$i</a></h4>
<p>This is some description. This is
→ some description. This is some
→ description. This is some
→ description.</p>\n
EOT;
}
```

Since there's no database to search, I'll just use a `for` loop to print ten search results. I'm using the heredoc syntax here, as described in Chapter 1, "Advanced PHP Techniques."

**6.** Complete the page.

```
} else {
    echo '<p class="error">Please
→ use the search form at the top of
→ the window to search this
→ site.</p>';
}
?>
```

This conditional applies if no valid search terms were entered (**Figure 2.11**).

**7.** Save the file as `search.inc.php`, place it in your Web directory (in the `modules` folder), and test by submitting the form (**Figure 2.12**).

MODULARIZING A WEB SITE

# Affecting the Browser Cache

Web browsers and proxy servers (something ISPs and other corporations create to improve network efficiency) habitually cache Web pages. Caching a page is a matter of storing its content (or part of its content, like an image or video) and then providing that stored version, rather than the version on the server, when a request is made.

For most end users, this is not a problem. In fact, they may not be aware that they are receiving an outdated version of a page or image. But if, while developing a site, you've struggled to get your Web browser (let's face it: the likely culprit is Internet Explorer) to recognize changes you know you've made in a page, then you've seen the dark side of caching. With your dynamic, PHP-driven sites, sometimes you want to make certain that end users are getting the most up-to-date version of your pages.

Caching—both in Web browsers and proxy servers—can be affected using PHP's `header()` function. There are four header types involved:

◆ Last-Modified

◆ Expires

◆ Pragma

◆ Cache-Control

The first three header types are part of the HTTP 1.0 standard. The *Last-Modified* header uses a UTC (Universal Time Coordinated) date-time value. If a caching system sees that the Last-Modified value is more recent than the date on the cached version of the page, it knows to use the new version from the server.

*Expires* is used as an indicator as to when a cached version of the page should no longer be used (in Greenwich Mean Time). Setting an Expires value in the past should always force the page from the server to be used:

```
header ("Expires: Mon, 26 Jul 1997
→ 05:00:00 GMT");
```

*Pragma* is just a declaration for how the page data should be handled. To avoid caching of a page, use:

```
header ("Pragma: no-cache");
```

The *Cache-Control* header was added in HTTP 1.1 and is a more finely tuned option. (You should still use the HTTP 1.0 headers as well.) There are numerous Cache-Control settings (**Table 2.1**).

Putting all this information together, to keep all systems from caching a page, you would use these headers:

```
header ("Last-Modified: Thu, 9 Nov 2006
→ 14:26:00 GMT"); // Right now!
header ("Expires: Mon, 26 Jul 1997
→ 05:00:00 GMT"); // Way back when!
header ("Pragma: no-cache");
header ("Cache-Control: no-cache");
```

While all too common, this is a heavy-handed approach. Certainly not every PHP script you use is uncacheable. Even the most active site could cache some of its scripts for a minute or more (and a very active site would get many requests within a minute; the cached version would save the server all those hits). As a more focused and proper use of these concepts, let's rewrite the `view_tasks.php` page (Script 1.3) from Chapter 1.

**Table 2.1**

## Cache-Control Directives

| Directive | Meaning |
| --- | --- |
| public | Can be cached anywhere |
| private | Only cacheable by browsers |
| no-cache | Cannot be cached anywhere |
| must-revalidate | Caches must check for newer versions |
| proxy-revalidate | Proxy caches must check for newer versions |
| max-age | A duration, in seconds, that the content is cacheable |
| s-maxage | Overrides the max-age value for shared caches |

## To affect caching:

1. Open view_tasks.php in your text editor or IDE (**Script 2.7**).

2. Before anything is sent to the Web browser, add the initial PHP tag (Script 2.7).

   `<?php # Script 2.7 - view_tasks.php`

   As you hopefully know, the header() function can only be called before anything is sent to the Web browser, including plain text, HTML, or even a blank space.

*continues on page 78*

**Script 2.7** This modified version of Chapter 1's view_tasks.php page (Script 1.3) uses the header() function to make caching recommendations.

```
1    <?php # Script 2.7 - view_tasks.php
2
3    // Connect to the database:
4    $dbc = @mysqli_connect ('localhost', 'username', 'password', 'test') OR die ('<p>Could not
     connect to the database!</p></body></html>');
5
6    // Get the latest dates as timestamps:
7    $q = 'SELECT UNIX_TIMESTAMP(MAX(date_added)), UNIX_TIMESTAMP(MAX(date_completed)) FROM tasks';
8    $r = mysqli_query($dbc, $q);
9    list($max_a, $max_c) = mysqli_fetch_array($r, MYSQLI_NUM);
10
11   // Determine the greater timestamp:
12   $max = ($max_a > $max_c) ? $max_a : $max_c;
13
14   // Create a cache interval in seconds:
15   $interval = 60 * 60 * 6; // 24 hours
16
17   // Send the header:
18   header ("Last-Modified: " . gmdate ('r', $max));
19   header ("Expires: " . gmdate ("r", ($max + $interval)));
20   header ("Cache-Control: max-age=$interval");
21   ?><!DOCTYPE html PUBLIC "-//W3C//DTD XHTML 1.0 Transitional//EN"
22         "http://www.w3.org/TR/xhtml1/DTD/xhtml1-transitional.dtd">
23   <html xmlns="http://www.w3.org/1999/xhtml" xml:lang="en" lang="en">
24   <head>
25       <meta http-equiv="content-type" content="text/html; charset=iso-8859-1" />
26       <title>View Tasks</title>
27   </head>
28   <body>
29   <h3>Current To-Do List</h3>
30   <?php
31
32   /*  This page shows all existing tasks.
33    *  A recursive function is used to show the
34    *  tasks as nested lists, as applicable.
35    */
36
37   // Function for displaying a list.
38   // Receives one argument: an array.
39   function make_list ($parent) {
40
```

*(script continues on next page)*

**Script 2.7** *continued*

```
                                                          📄 Script
41        // Need the main $tasks array:
42        global $tasks;
43
44        // Start an ordered list:
45        echo '<ol>';
46
47        // Loop through each subarray:
48        foreach ($parent as $task_id => $todo) {
49
50            // Display the item:
51            echo "<li>$todo";
52
53            // Check for subtasks:
54            if (isset($tasks[$task_id])) {
55
56                // Call this function:
57                make_list($tasks[$task_id]);
58
59            }
60
61            // Complete the list item:
62            echo '</li>';
63
64        } // End of FOREACH loop.
65
66        // Close the ordered list:
67        echo '</ol>';
68
69    } // End of make_list() function.
70
71    // Retrieve all the uncompleted tasks:
72    $q = 'SELECT task_id, parent_id, task FROM tasks WHERE date_completed="0000-00-00 00:00:00"
      ORDER BY parent_id, date_added ASC';
73    $r = mysqli_query($dbc, $q);
74
75    // Initialize the storage array:
76    $tasks = array();
77
78    while (list($task_id, $parent_id, $task) = mysqli_fetch_array($r, MYSQLI_NUM)) {
79
80        // Add to the array:
81        $tasks[$parent_id][$task_id] =  $task;
82
83    }
84
85    // For debugging:
86    //echo '<pre>' . print_r($tasks,1) . '</pre>';
87
88    // Send the first array element
89    // to the make_list() function:
90    make_list($tasks[0]);
91
92    ?>
93    </body>
94    </html>
```

**3.** Connect to the database.

```
$dbc = @mysqli_connect ('localhost',
→ 'username', 'password', 'test') OR
→ die ('<p>Could not connect to the
→ database!</p></body></html>');
```

To accurately determine when this page was last modified, the script will look at the database it uses. The `tasks` table contains two date/time columns—`date_added` and `date_completed`. Any time the page's content is updated, these two values are set to the current date and time (there is no delete option).

**4.** Get the latest date values from the table.

```
$q = 'SELECT UNIX_TIMESTAMP(MAX
→ (date_added)), UNIX_TIMESTAMP
→ (MAX(date_completed)) FROM tasks';
$r = mysqli_query($dbc, $q);
list($max_a, $max_c) =
mysqli_fetch_array($r, MYSQLI_NUM);
$max = ($max_a > $max_c) ? $max_a :
→ $max_c;
```

The query returns the largest `date_added` and `date_completed` values. Because they would be returned in a less usable format (**Figure 2.13**), the `UNIX_TIMESTAMP()` function is applied to make them both integers (**Figure 2.14**). Then, the ternary operator is used to assign the largest value (and therefore the most recent date) to the `$max` variable.

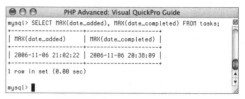

**Figure 2.13** How the timestamp fields would ordinarily be returned by the query.

**Figure 2.14** The query result used by this script.

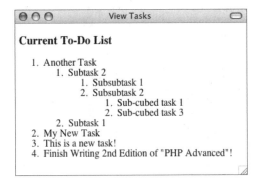

**Current To-Do List**

1. Another Task
    1. Subtask 2
        1. Subsubtask 1
        2. Subsubtask 2
            1. Sub-cubed task 1
            2. Sub-cubed task 3
    2. Subtask 1
2. My New Task
3. This is a new task!
4. Finish Writing 2nd Edition of "PHP Advanced"!

**Figure 2.15** The cache-controlled Web page.

**5.** Define a reasonable caching interval.

`$interval = 60 * 60 * 6;`

"Reasonable" depends upon your page, how many visitors you get (i.e., the server load), and how often it's updated. For this value, which is in seconds, I use six hours (60 seconds times 60 minutes time 6).

**6.** Send the Last-Modified header.

`header ("Last-Modified: " . gmdate`
`→ ('r', $max));`

This header sets the modification date of this script as the last time the database was updated. The "r" `gmdate()` (and `date()`) option will return the date formatted per the HTTP specifications.

**7.** Set the Expires header.

`header ("Expires: " . gmdate ("r",`
`→ ($max + $interval)));`

The expiration value is the current time plus the defined interval.

**8.** Set the Cache-Control header.

`header ("Cache-Control: max-age=`
`→ $interval");`

`?>`

This is just the HTTP 1.1 equivalent of the Expires header. Instead of giving a date value, `max-age` is set in seconds.

**9.** Delete the database connection that existed later on in the original script.

This has been moved to the top of the script in Step 3.

**10.** Save the file as `view_tasks.php`, place in your Web directory, and test in your Web browser (**Figure 2.15**).

*continues on next page*

**AFFECTING THE BROWSER CACHE**

### ✔ Tips

- Note that caching is, in theory, a very good thing, designed to minimize unnecessary server requests. If properly controlled, caches are great for both the server and the client.

- If you have cURL installed on your system, you can run this command to see a page's headers (**Figure 2.16**):

  ```
  curl --head http://www.example.com/
  → page.php
  ```

  Curl is discussed in Chapter 9, "Networking with PHP."

- If your applications make use of sessions, you can adjust session caching with the `session_cache_limit()` function. See the manual for more information.

- Page caching can also be affected using the `META` tags, placed within an HTML document's head. This may not work as reliably with some browsers as the `header()` method.

- Client/server performance can also be improved—for large scripts—using Zlib output compression or the function `ob_gzhandler()`. See the PHP manual for more on both.

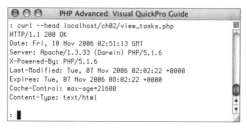

**Figure 2.16** Using cURL to view the headers returned by the `view_tasks.php` page.

## Server-Side Caching

There is an alternative type of caching you can use to affect the client/server relationship. When a PHP script is requested, the Web server asks the PHP module to read and process that code. Server-side caches store preprocessed versions of a script, so that they may be served without processing. Server-side caching can greatly improve your application's performance but normally requires more control over the server than the average user has (read: those using a shared hosting service).

If you want to look into and possibly implement server-side caching, there are many options. APC (Alternative PHP Cache) is very popular, so much so that it's now part of PECL (`http://pecl.php. net`). It's free, but installation can be tricky. Zend (`www.zend.com`) offers the free Zend Optimizer. It's fairly easy to install, but you must remember to upgrade it when you upgrade PHP (it's version-specific).

For options that do not require software installation on a server, there are the PEAR Cache and Cache_Lite packages. It's also possible to write your own caching system, although that's probably not the most efficient idea.

AFFECTING THE BROWSER CACHE

# ADVANCED DATABASE CONCEPTS

I had many goals in writing this second edition of my PHP Advanced book. The primary aim is to demonstrate what I consider to be "advanced" PHP programming: doing the things you already do but better, doing things tangentially related to PHP, and taking advantage of aspects of the language with which the average user may not be familiar. A second goal is to help solve some of the problems often put forth (to me or otherwise) in emails, forums, and newsgroups. This chapter addresses both goals equally.

For the first example, you'll see how to use a database to store session data. Doing so offers many advantages, improved security being at the forefront. Next, a thorough discussion on how to work with U.S. zip codes, demonstrated with a distance calculation script (i.e., how far various stores are from a given zip code). The third example introduces stored functions, a new addition to MySQL in version 5 (but present in other databases for some time). After that, a common question is addressed: how do you lay out query results horizontally?

Please note: for every example in this chapter I will be using MySQL as the database application. Most of these techniques are implementations of theories that are not database-specific. It shouldn't be difficult to translate them to whatever database application you're using. Second, I'll be exclusively using the Improved MySQL functions, available as of PHP 5 and MySQL 4.1. If you are using earlier versions of either, you'll need to modify the code to the earlier (the old standard) MySQL functions.

# Storing Sessions in a Database

By default PHP stores all session data in text files in the server. Normally these files are stored in a temporary folder (like /tmp on Unix and Mac OS X) with file-names matching the session IDs (e.g., *ei26b4i2nup742ucho9glmbh84*). PHP also supports the ability to store the same session data in a database.

The main reason I would recommend making this change is improved security. On shared hosting servers, every Web site is using the same temporary directory. This means that dozens upon dozens of applications are all reading and writing in the same place. It would be very easy to create a script that reads all the data from all the files in the sessions folder.

Second, moving the session data to a database would allow you to easily retrieve more information about your Web site's sessions in general. Queries could be run indicating the number of active sessions and session data can be backed up.

A third reason to store session data in a database is if you have a site running on multiple servers. When this is the case, the same user may be fed pages from different servers over the course of the same session. The session data stored in a file on one server would be unavailable to the pages on other servers. This isn't a situation that the majority of developers face, but if you do, there's really no other option but to go the database route.

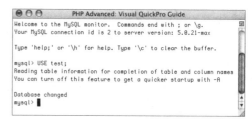

**Figure 3.1** I'll put the sessions table within the test database for this example.

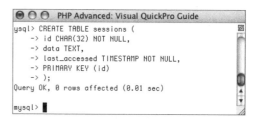

**Figure 3.2** This one table will handle all the session data.

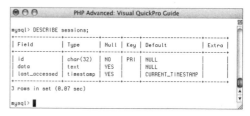

**Figure 3.3** Confirming the table's structure.

## ✔ Tip

■ Another fix for the security concern on a shared host is to change the session directory for your site. To do so, call the `session_save_path()` function prior to every `session_start()` call. You'll also need to make sure that the new directory exists, of course, and that it has the proper permissions.

## Creating the session table

The session data will be stored in a special table. This table can be part of an already existing database (like the rest of your application) or in its own. At a bare minimum, the table needs three columns (**Table 3.1**).

The session table can have more than those three columns, but it must have those three. Keep in mind, though, that many things you might be inclined to represent in another column—a user's ID, for example—would likely be stored in the session data.

### To create the sessions table:

1. Access your MySQL database using the `mysql` client.

   You can also use phpMyAdmin or whatever other interface you prefer.

2. Select the `test` database (**Figure 3.1**).

   `USE test;`

   Since this is just an example, I'll create the table within the `test` database.

3. Create the `sessions` table (**Figure 3.2**).

   `CREATE TABLE sessions (`
   `id CHAR(32) NOT NULL,`
   `data TEXT,`
   `last_accessed TIMESTAMP NOT NULL,`
   `PRIMARY KEY (id)`
   `);`

   The table contains the basic three fields. The `id` is the primary key. It will always contain a string 32 characters long and can never be `NULL`. The `data` column is a `TEXT` type and it can be `NULL` (when the session is first started, there is no data). The `last_accessed` column is a `TIME-STAMP`. It will therefore always be updated when the session is created (on `INSERT`) or modified (on `UPDATE`).

4. Confirm the `sessions` table structure (**Figure 3.3**).

   `DESCRIBE sessions;`

### ✔ Tips

- You don't have to use MySQL for this example; you could use PostgreSQL, Oracle, SQLite, or any other database.

- If your application stores a lot of data in sessions, you'd want to change the size of the session data column to `MEDIUMTEXT` or `LONGTEXT`.

**Table 3.1** A table with just three columns will suffice for storing session data in a database.

| Session Table Columns | |
|---|---|
| **COLUMN TYPE** | **STORES** |
| CHAR(32) | The session ID |
| TEXT | The session data |
| TIMESTAMP | The last time the session data was accessed |

## Defining the session functions

After creating the database table, storing session data in a database is a two-part process (from a PHP perspective):

1. Define the functions for interacting with the database.

2. Tell PHP to use these functions.

For this second step, the session_set_save_handler() function is called. This function should be called with six arguments, each a function name (**Table 3.2**).

I'll briefly discuss what each function should receive (as arguments) and do while creating them in the next script. I'll say up front that every function must return a Boolean value, except for the "read" function. That function must always return a string, even if that means an empty string.

For an understanding of when the different functions are called (from the perspective of what you'd do in the PHP code), see **Figure 3.4**.

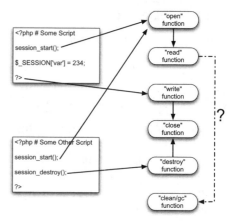

**Figure 3.4** Every time a session is started, the "open" and "read" functions are called. When the "read" function is called, garbage collection may take place (depending upon various factors). At the end of a script, the data is written, and then the "close" function is called, unless the session was destroyed, in which case the "write" function is not invoked.

**Table 3.2** The session_set_save_handler() function takes six arguments. Each should be the name of a function that is called when a particular event occurs.

| session_set_save_handler() Arguments | |
|---|---|
| ORDER | FUNCTION TO BE CALLED WHEN… |
| 1 | A session is started |
| 2 | A session is closed |
| 3 | Session data is read |
| 4 | Session data is written |
| 5 | Session data is destroyed |
| 6 | Old session data should be deleted (aka garbage collection performed) |

## To create new session handlers:

**1.** Begin a new PHP script in your text editor or IDE (**Script 3.1**).

```php
<?php # Script 3.1 -
→ db_sessions.inc.php
```

```php
$sdbc = NULL;
```

The **$sdbc** variable will store the database connection. I initialize it here and then make it global in each function.

*continues on page 88*

**Script 3.1** This script defines all the functionality required to store session data in a database. It can be included by any page that wants that feature.

```php
1   <?php # Script 3.1 - db_sessions.inc.php
2
3   /*
4    * This page creates the functional
5    * interface for storing session data
6    * in a database.
7    * This page also starts the session.
8    */
9
10  // Global variable used for the database
11  // connections in all session functions:
12  $sdbc = NULL;
13
14  // Define the open_session() function:
15  // This function takes no arguments.
16  // This function should open the database connection.
17  function open_session() {
18
19      global $sdbc;
20
21      // Connect to the database.
22      $sdbc = mysqli_connect ('localhost', 'username', 'password', 'test') OR die ('Cannot connect
    to the database.');
23
24      return true;
25
26  } // End of open_session() function.
27
```

*(script continues on next page)*

**Script 3.1** *continued*

```
   _____
   ○ ○ ○                          📄 Script
28    // Define the close_session() function:
29    // This function takes no arguments.
30    // This function closes the database connection.
31    function close_session() {
32
33        global $sdbc;
34
35        return mysqli_close($sdbc);
36
37    } // End of close_session() function.
38
39    // Define the read_session() function:
40    // This function takes one argument: the session ID.
41    // This function retrieves the session data.
42    function read_session($sid) {
43
44        global $sdbc;
45
46        // Query the database:
47        $q = sprintf('SELECT data FROM sessions WHERE id="%s"', mysqli_real_escape_string($sdbc,
      $sid));
48        $r = mysqli_query($sdbc, $q);
49
50        // Retrieve the results:
51        if (mysqli_num_rows($r) == 1) {
52
53            list($data) = mysqli_fetch_array($r, MYSQLI_NUM);
54
55            // Return the data:
56            return $data;
57
58        } else { // Return an empty string.
59            return '';
60        }
61
62    } // End of read_session() function.
63
64    // Define the write_session() function:
65    // This function takes two arguments:
66    // the session ID and the session data.
67    function write_session($sid, $data) {
68
69        global $sdbc;
70
71        // Store in the database:
72        $q = sprintf('REPLACE INTO sessions (id, data) VALUES ("%s", "%s")',
      mysqli_real_escape_string($sdbc, $sid), mysqli_real_escape_string($sdbc, $data));
73        $r = mysqli_query($sdbc, $q);
74
```

*(script continues on next page)*

**Script 3.1** *continued*

```
 75      return mysqli_affected_rows($sdbc);
 76
 77   } // End of write_session() function.
 78
 79   // Define the destroy_session() function:
 80   // This function takes one argument: the session ID.
 81   function destroy_session($sid) {
 82
 83      global $sdbc;
 84
 85      // Delete from the database:
 86      $q = sprintf('DELETE FROM sessions WHERE id="%s"', mysqli_real_escape_string($sdbc, $sid));
 87      $r = mysqli_query($sdbc, $q);
 88
 89      // Clear the $_SESSION array:
 90      $_SESSION = array();
 91
 92      return mysqli_affected_rows($sdbc);
 93
 94   } // End of destroy_session() function.
 95
 96   // Define the clean_session() function:
 97   // This function takes one argument: a value in seconds.
 98   function clean_session($expire) {
 99
100      global $sdbc;
101
102      // Delete old sessions:
103      $q = sprintf('DELETE FROM sessions WHERE DATE_ADD(last_accessed, INTERVAL %d SECOND) <
      NOW()', (int) $expire);
104      $r = mysqli_query($sdbc, $q);
105
106      return mysqli_affected_rows($sdbc);
107
108   } // End of clean_session() function.
109
110   # *************************** #
111   # ***** END OF FUNCTIONS ***** #
112   # *************************** #
113
114   // Declare the functions to use:
115   session_set_save_handler('open_session', 'close_session', 'read_session', 'write_session',
      'destroy_session', 'clean_session');
116
117   // Make whatever other changes to the session settings.
118
119   // Start the session:
120   session_start();
121
122   ?>
```

STORING SESSIONS IN A DATABASE

**2.** Define the function for opening a session.

```
function open_session() {
    global $sdbc;

    $sdbc = mysqli_connect
→ ('localhost', 'username',
→ 'password', 'test') OR die ('Cannot
→ connect to the database.');
    return true;
}
```

This function takes no arguments (which is to say that when PHP does whatever to open a session, it will call this function without sending any values to it). The intent of this function is to establish a database connection.

**3.** Define the function for closing a session.

```
function close_session() {
    global $sdbc;
    return mysqli_close($sdbc);
}
```

This function also takes no arguments. It will close the database connection, returning the success of that operation.

**4.** Define the function for reading the session data.

```
function read_session($sid) {
    global $sdbc;
    $q = sprintf('SELECT data FROM
→ sessions WHERE id="%s"',
→ mysqli_real_escape_string($sdbc,
→ $sid));
    $r = mysqli_query($sdbc, $q);
    if (mysqli_num_rows($r) == 1) {
        list($data) =
→ mysqli_fetch_array($r, MYSQLI_NUM);
        return $data;
    } else {
        return '';
    }
}
```

This function will receive one argument: the session ID (e.g., *ei26b4i2nup742ucho9glmbh84*). The function needs to retrieve the data for that session ID from the database and return it. If it can't do that, it should return an empty string instead. Although the session ID should be safe to use in a URL, one shouldn't make assumptions when it comes to security, so the mysqli_real_escape_string() function is used to make it safe (alternatively, you could use prepared statements).

If you're not familiar with the sprintf() function, which I use to compile the query, see Chapter 1, "Advanced PHP Techniques."

**5.** Define the function for writing data to the database.

```
function write_session($sid, $data) {
    global $sdbc;
    $q = sprintf('REPLACE INTO
→ sessions (id, data) VALUES ("%s",
→ "%s")',
mysqli_real_escape_string($sdbc,
→ $sid), mysqli_real_escape_
→ string($sdbc, $data));
        $r = mysqli_query($sdbc, $q);
        return mysqli_affected_
→ rows($sdbc);
}
```

This function receives two arguments: the session ID and the session data. The session data is a serialized version of the $_SESSION array (**Figure 3.5**). For the query, an INSERT must be run the first time the session record is created in the database and an UPDATE query every time thereafter. The lesser-known REPLACE query will achieve the same result. If a record exists whose primary key is the same as that given a value in this query (i.e., the session ID), an update will occur. Otherwise, a new record will be made.

**6.** Create the function for destroying the session data.

```
function destroy_session($sid) {
    global $sdbc;
    $q = sprintf('DELETE FROM
→ sessions WHERE id="%s"',
→ mysqli_real_escape_string($sdbc,
→ $sid));
    $r = mysqli_query($sdbc, $q);
    $_SESSION = array();
    return mysqli_affected_
→ rows($sdbc);
}
```

This function receives one argument, the session ID, when called. Normally this occurs when the `session_destroy()` function is invoked. This function then runs a `DELETE` query in the database and clears the `$_SESSION` array.

**7.** Define the garbage collection function.

```
function clean_session($expire) {
    global $sdbc;
    $q = sprintf('DELETE FROM
→ sessions WHERE DATE_ADD(last_
→ accessed, INTERVAL %d SECOND) <
→ NOW()', (int) $expire);
    $r = mysqli_query($sdbc, $q);
    return mysqli_affected_
→ rows($sdbc);
}
```

Garbage collection is something most PHP programmers do not think about. The premise is that PHP will automatically delete old sessions. There are two relevant settings in PHP: what is considered to be "old" and how likely it is that garbage collection is performed. For all session activity in a site, there is an $X$ percent chance that PHP will go into garbage collection mode (the exact percent is a PHP setting; the default value is 1%). If it does, then all "old" session data will be destroyed. So garbage collection is triggered by any session but attempts to clean up every session.

As for the garbage collection function, it will receive a time, in seconds, as to what is considered to be old. This can be used in a `DELETE` query to get rid of any session that hasn't been accessed in more than the set time.

**8.** Tell PHP to use the session handling functions.

```
session_set_save_handler('open_
→ session', 'close_session',
→ 'read_session', 'write_session',
→ 'destroy_session',
→ 'clean_session');
```

*continues on next page*

```
mysql> SELECT * FROM sessions\G
*************************** 1. row ***************************
           id: ei26b4i2nup742ucho9glmbh84
         data: blah|s:6:"umlaut";this|d:3615684.45000000018626451492309570312 5;that|s:4:"blue";
last_accessed: 2006-11-11 20:55:15
1 row in set (0.00 sec)

mysql>
```

**Figure 3.5** Session data is stored in the database (or in a file) as a serialized array. This serialized value says that indexed at blah is a string six characters long with a value of *umlaut*. Indexed at this is a decimal with a value of *3615684.4500* (and so on). Indexed at that is a string four characters long with a value of *blue*.

**9.** Start the session.

```
session_start();
```

Two important things to note here. First, the `session_set_save_handler()` function does not start a session. You still have to invoke `session_start()`. Second, you must use these two lines in this order. Calling `session_start()` prior to `session_set_save_handler()` will result in your handlers being ignored.

**10.** Complete the page.

```
?>
```

**11.** Save the file as `db_sessions.inc.php` and place it in your Web directory.

### ✔ Tips

■ The "write" session function is never called until all of the output has been sent to the Web browser. Then the "close" function is called. See Figure 3.4.

■ If `session.auto_start` is turned on in your PHP configuration (meaning that sessions are automatically started for each page), then you cannot use the `session_set_save_handler()` function.

## Using the new session handlers

Using the newly created session handlers is only a matter of invoking the function `session_set_save_handler()` function, as discussed in the preceding section of the chapter. Everything else you would do with sessions is unchanged, from storing data in them to accessing stored data to destroying a session.

To demonstrate this, the next script will create some session data if it doesn't exist, show all the session data, and even destroy the session data if a link back to this same page is clicked. As is often the case, there is one little tricky issue...

All of the session activity requires the database and, therefore, the database connection. The connection is opened when the session is started and closed when the session is closed. No problem there except that the "write" and "close" functions will be called after a script has finished running (see Figure 3.4). As you may already know, PHP does you the favor of automatically closing any database connections when a script stops running. For this next script, this means that after the script runs, the database connection is automatically closed, *and then* the session functions attempt to write the data to the database and close the connection. The result will be some confusing errors (and the—trust me on this—long "Where in the World Is My Database Connection?" search). To avoid this sequential problem, the `session_write_close()` function should be called before the script terminates. This function will invoke the "write" and "close" functions, while there's still a good database connection.

## To use the new session handlers:

1. Begin a new PHP script in your text editor or IDE (**Script 3.2**).

   ```
   <?php # Script 3.2 - sessions.php
   ```

**Script 3.2** This script includes the `db_sessions.inc.php` page (Script 3.1) so that session data is stored in a database. In order to have one page create a new session, access existing data, and close the session, a couple of conditionals are used in lieu of writing out multiple pages.

```
○○○                              Script
1    <?php # Script 3.2 - sessions.php
2
3    /*  This page does some silly things with sessions.
4     *  It includes the db_sessions.inc.php script
5     *  so that the session data will be stored in
6     *  a database.
7     */
8
9    // Include the sessions file:
10   // The file already starts the session.
11   require_once('db_sessions.inc.php');
12   ?><!DOCTYPE html PUBLIC "-//W3C//DTD XHTML 1.0 Transitional//EN"
13       "http://www.w3.org/TR/xhtml1/DTD/xhtml1-transitional.dtd">
14   <html xmlns="http://www.w3.org/1999/xhtml" xml:lang="en" lang="en">
15   <head>
16       <meta http-equiv="content-type" content="text/html; charset=iso-8859-1" />
17       <title>DB Session Test</title>
18   </head>
19   <body>
20   <?php
21
22   // Store some dummy data in the session,
23   // if no data is present.
24   if (empty($_SESSION)) {
25
26       $_SESSION['blah'] = 'umlaut';
27       $_SESSION['this'] = 3615684.45;
28       $_SESSION['that'] = 'blue';
29
30       // Print a message indicating what's going on:
31       echo '<p>Session data stored.</p>';
32
33   } else { // Print the already-stored data.
34       echo '<p>Session Data Exists:<pre>' . print_r($_SESSION, 1) . '</pre></p>';
35   }
36
37   // Log the user out, if applicable:
38   if (isset($_GET['logout'])) {
39
40       session_destroy();
41       echo '<p>Session destroyed.</p>';
42
43   } else { // Print the "Log Out" link:
44       echo '<a href="sessions.php?logout=true">Log Out</a>';
45   }
46
47   // Print out the session data:
48   echo '<p>Session Data:<pre>' . print_r($_SESSION, 1) . '</pre></p>';
49
50   ?>
51   </body>
52   </html>
53   <?php session_write_close(); ?>
```

2. Include the `db_sessions.inc.php` file.

```
require_once('db_sessions.inc.php');
?>
```

The `session_start()` function, which is in `db_sessions.inc.php`, must be called before anything is sent to the Web browser, so this file must be included prior to any HTML.

3. Create the initial HTML.

```
<!DOCTYPE html PUBLIC "-//W3C//DTD
→ XHTML 1.0 Transitional//EN"
→ "http://www.w3.org/TR/xhtml1/DTD/
→ xhtml1-transitional.dtd">
<html xmlns="http://www.w3.org/
→ 1999/xhtml" xml:lang="en"
→ lang="en">
<head>
    <meta http-equiv="content-type"
→ content="text/html; charset=iso-
→ 8859-1" />
    <title>DB Session Test</title>
</head>
<body>
```

4. Store some dummy data in a session if it is empty.

```
<?php
if (empty($_SESSION)) {
    $_SESSION['blah'] = 'umlaut';
    $_SESSION['this'] = 3615684.45;
    $_SESSION['that'] = 'blue';
    echo '<p>Session data
→ stored.</p>';
} else {
    echo '<p>Session Data
→ Exists:<pre>' . print_r
→ ($_SESSION, 1) . '</pre></p>';
}
```

Storing data in a database-managed session is no different than the regular method. This conditional is being used to replicate sessions on multiple pages. The first time the page is loaded, new data will be stored in the session. The second time the page is loaded, the existing data will be available. As a quick way to print the session data, the `print_r()` function will be used.

5. Create the logout functionality.

```
if (isset($_GET['logout'])) {
    session_destroy();
    echo '<p>Session
→ destroyed.</p>';
} else {
    echo '<a href="sessions.php?
→ logout=true">Log Out</a>';
}
```

Again, this conditional is used to fake a multipage site. When the page is accessed, a "Log Out" link is displayed. If the user clicks that link, `?logout=true` is passed in the URL, telling this same page to destroy the session.

6. Print the session data.

```
echo '<p>Session Data:<pre>' .
→ print_r($_SESSION, 1) .
→ '</pre></p>';
```

This is mostly a repeat of the code in Step 4. Unlike that line, this one will apply the first time the page is loaded. It will also be used to reveal the effect of destroying the session.

7. Complete the PHP and HTML.

```
?>
</body>
</html>
```

*continues on next page*

**STORING SESSIONS IN A DATABASE**

**8.** Call the `session_write_close()` function.

`<?php session_write_close(); ?>`

It really doesn't matter where in the script this function is called, as long as all the modifications to the session data are over. If you don't use this function, you might see results like those in **Figure 3.6**.

**Figure 3.6** Because PHP is nice enough to close open database connections after a script runs, the `write_session()` and `close_session()` functions—called after that point—would be without a database connection.

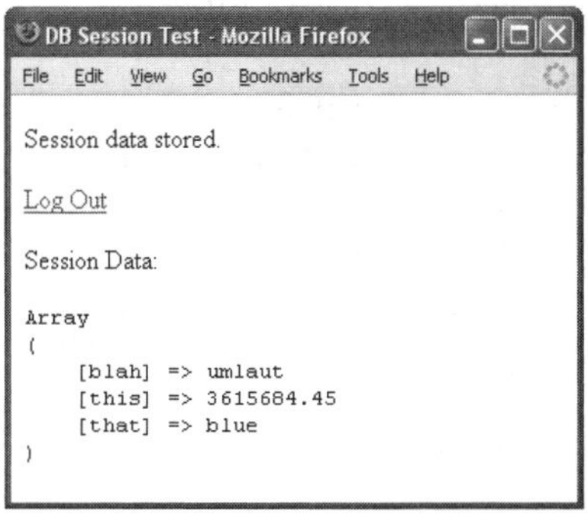

**Figure 3.7** The result the first time the page is loaded.

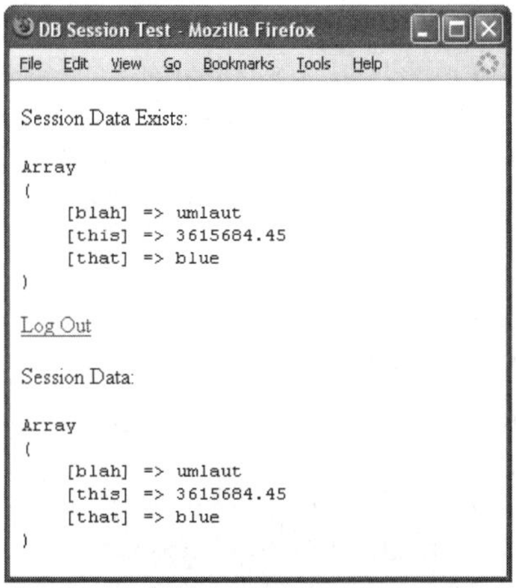

**Figure 3.8** Reloading the page allows it to access the already-stored session data.

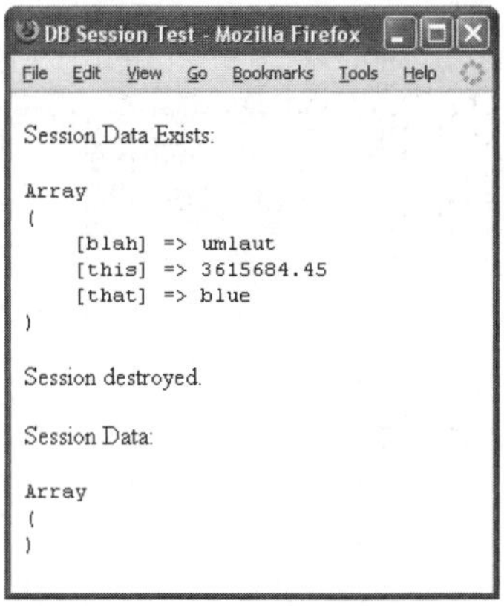

**Figure 3.9** Clicking the "Log Out" link ends up destroying the session.

**9.** Save the file as `sessions.php`, place it in your Web directory (in the same folder as `db_sessions.inc.php`), and test in your Web browser (**Figures 3.7**, **3.8**, and **3.9**).

### ✔ Tips

- The `session_write_close()` function is also necessary if your site uses frames. By calling it, you can close one page's access to a session so that the other page can load faster (because only one script can access the same session at a time).

- You should also call `session_write_close()` before redirecting the browser with a `header()` call. This only applies when using your own session handlers.

# Working with U.S. Zip Codes

One common need for Web sites is to be able to perform distance calculations between addresses. Although you can always go the full Mapquest or Google Maps route, simple distance estimates can be managed using just zip codes (in the United States, that is).

For every zip code, there is an associated longitude and latitude. Take two of these points on the earth, throw in some complicated math, and you have an approximate distance. In this section, I'll discuss how to obtain the necessary zip code data, create a "stores" table that will provide one of the two points, and then go over the formula used to calculate distances.

## Creating the zip code table

This whole example is predicated upon having a database with the latitude and longitude points for every zip code in the United States. You'll find three sources for this information:

◆ Commercial zip code databases

◆ Free zip code databases

◆ Free ZCTA databases

The first option will provide you with the most accurate, up-to-date information, but you'll have to pay for it (not a terrible amount, normally). The second option is free (free!) but harder to find and likely to be out of date. At the time of this writing, the Web site www.cfdynamics.com/zipbase/ provides this information, although there's no guarantee how long that will last. You can also search the Web for "free zip code database" to find alternatives.

As for the last option, ZCTA, the Zip Code Tabulation Areas, is a database created by the U.S. Census Bureau for its own purposes. This database ignores around 10,000 zip codes that are used by the U.S. Post Office or by specific corporations. It also groups some zip codes together and uses characters to represent others. For the vast majority of zip codes, this information will do just fine. Once source of a ZCTA database is http://zips.sourceforge.net, found by searching SourceForge.net for "zip code".

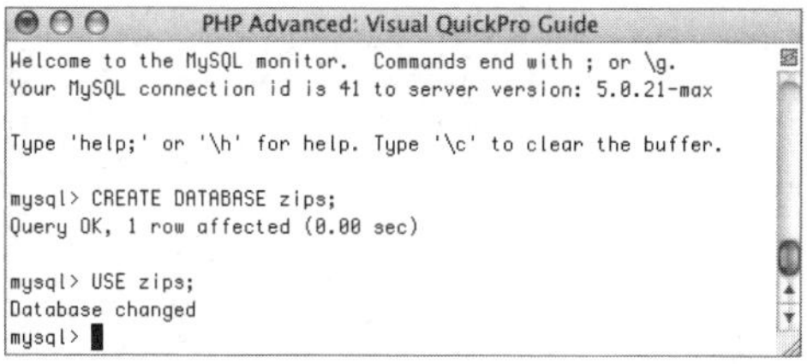

**Figure 3.10** Creating a new database to be used in this example.

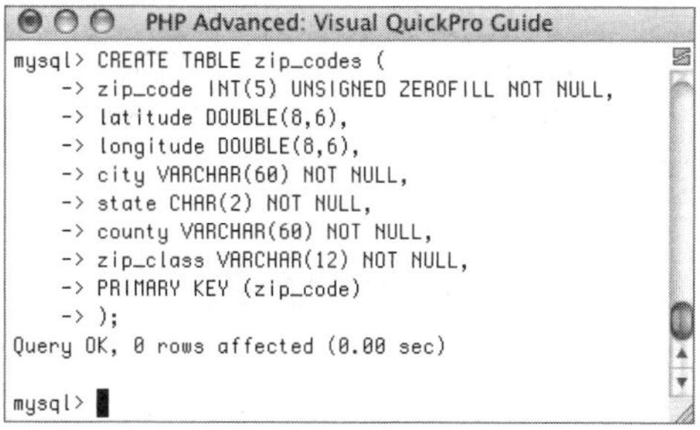

**Figure 3.11** The main table, whose structure is based upon the data to be inserted (Figure 3.12).

## To create the zip code database:

1. Find your data source.

   Which source (of the types and specific ones outlined) you use depends upon your situation. How important is accuracy? How much are you willing to spend? As a secondary consideration, what resources exist as you're reading this (search the Web and SourceForge)? I'll use the version from www.cfdynamics.com/zipbase/ for my example.

2. Create the database (**Figure 3.10**).

   ```
   CREATE DATABASE zips;
   ```

   I'm creating a database called zips, in MySQL, using the mysql command-line client. You could do most of the following using phpMyAdmin, the MySQL Administrator, or another tool.

3. Create a table that matches the data in the data file (**Figure 3.11**).

   ```
   CREATE TABLE zip_codes (
   zip_code INT(5) UNSIGNED ZEROFILL NOT
   → NULL,
   latitude DOUBLE(8,6),
   longitude DOUBLE(8,6),
   city VARCHAR(60) NOT NULL,
   state CHAR(2) NOT NULL,
   county VARCHAR(60) NOT NULL,
   zip_class VARCHAR(12) NOT NULL,
   PRIMARY KEY (zip_code)
   );
   ```

   *continues on next page*

**WORKING WITH U.S. ZIP CODES**

Some sources may already provide the necessary SQL commands to create the table and even insert the data, in which case you could skip Steps 3 and 4. If not, you should create a table whose structure matches the data to be inserted. **Figure 3.12** shows the file that I downloaded. The zip code column, which is the primary key, should be an unsigned, zero-filled integer five digits in length. The latitude and longitude columns should be some type of floating-point number. Because, in my case, some of the records have no values for the latitude and longitude, these two columns can't be defined as `NOT NULL`. My data contains four more columns: the city's name, a two-character state abbreviation, the county, and the "zip code class."

ZIP_CODES.txt

```
"00501","+40.922326","-072.637078","HOLTSVILLE","NY","SUFFOLK","UNIQUE"
"00544","+40.922326","-072.637078","HOLTSVILLE","NY","SUFFOLK","UNIQUE"
"00601","+18.165273","-066.722583","ADJUNTAS","PR","ADJUNTAS","STANDARD"
"00602","+18.393103","-067.180953","AGUADA","PR","AGUADA","STANDARD"
"00603","+18.455913","-067.145780","AGUADILLA","PR","AGUADILLA","STANDARD"
"00604","+18.493520","-067.135883","AGUADILLA","PR","AGUADILLA","STANDARD"
"00605","+18.465162","-067.141486","AGUADILLA","PR","AGUADILLA","STANDARD"
"00606","+18.172947","-066.944111","MARICAO","PR","MARICAO","STANDARD"
"00610","+18.288685","-067.139696","ANASCO","PR","ANASCO","STANDARD"
"00611","+18.279531","-066.802170","ANGELES","PR","UTUADO","PO BOX ONLY"
"00612","+18.450674","-066.698262","ARECIBO","PR","ARECIBO","STANDARD"
"00613","+18.458093","-066.732732","ARECIBO","PR","ARECIBO","STANDARD"
"00614","+18.429675","-066.674506","ARECIBO","PR","ARECIBO","STANDARD"
"00616","+18.444792","-066.640678","BAJADERO","PR","ARECIBO","STANDARD"
"00617","+18.447092","-066.544255","BARCELONETA","PR","BARCELONETA","STANDARD"
"00622","+17.998531","-067.187318","BOQUERON","PR","CABO ROJO","STANDARD"
"00623","+18.062201","-067.149541","CABO ROJO","PR","CABO ROJO","STANDARD"
"00624","+18.023535","-066.726156","PENUELAS","PR","PENUELAS","STANDARD"
"00627","+18.477891","-066.854770","CAMUY","PR","CAMUY","STANDARD"
"00631","+18.269187","-066.864993","CASTANER","PR","LARES","STANDARD"
"00636","+18.113284","-067.039706","ROSARIO","PR","SAN GERMAN","STANDARD"
"00637","+18.087322","-066.934911","SABANA GRANDE","PR","SABANA GRANDE","STANDARD"
"00638","+18.336160","-066.472087","CIALES","PR","CIALES","STANDARD"
"00641","+18.250027","-066.698957","UTUADO","PR","UTUADO","STANDARD"
"00646","+18.436060","-066.281954","DORADO","PR","DORADO","STANDARD"
"00647","+17.969594","-066.939754","ENSENADA","PR","GUANICA","STANDARD"
"00650","+18.360125","-066.562311","FLORIDA","PR","FLORIDA","STANDARD"
"00652","+18.457254","-066.603358","GARROCHALES","PR","ARECIBO","STANDARD"
"00653","+17.972468","-066.898661","GUANICA","PR","GUANICA","STANDARD"
"00656","+18.023280","-066.786909","GUAYANILLA","PR","GUAYANILLA","STANDARD"
```

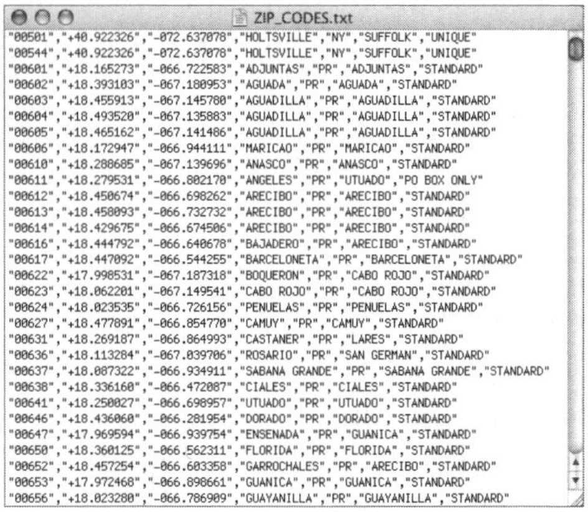

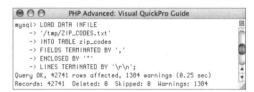

**Figure 3.12** The data file I'm working with.

PHP Advanced: Visual QuickPro Guide

```
mysql> LOAD DATA INFILE
    -> '/tmp/ZIP_CODES.txt'
    -> INTO TABLE zip_codes
    -> FIELDS TERMINATED BY ','
    -> ENCLOSED BY '"'
    -> LINES TERMINATED BY '\r\n';
Query OK, 42741 rows affected, 1384 warnings (0.25 sec)
Records: 42741  Deleted: 0  Skipped: 0  Warnings: 1384
```

**Figure 3.13** Importing the data into the table.

4. Import the data (**Figure 3.13**).

```
LOAD DATA INFILE
'/tmp/ZIP_CODES.txt'
INTO TABLE zip_codes
FIELDS TERMINATED BY ','
ENCLOSED BY '"'
LINES TERMINATED BY '\r\n';
```

It may take you a while to get this step working properly (you may also have more luck using phpMyAdmin for this). The `LOAD DATA INFILE` query takes the contents of a text file and inserts them into the given table. For this step to work, the number of columns in the table must match the number of values on each row in the text file. You might also need to change the `FIELDS TERMINATED BY`, `ENCLOSED BY`, and `LINES TERMINATED BY` values to match the text file you have. See the MySQL manual for more information on this syntax.

The name of the text file should match the absolute path to the file on your computer.

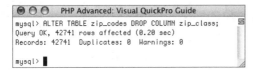

**Figure 3.14** Getting rid of unnecessary columns.

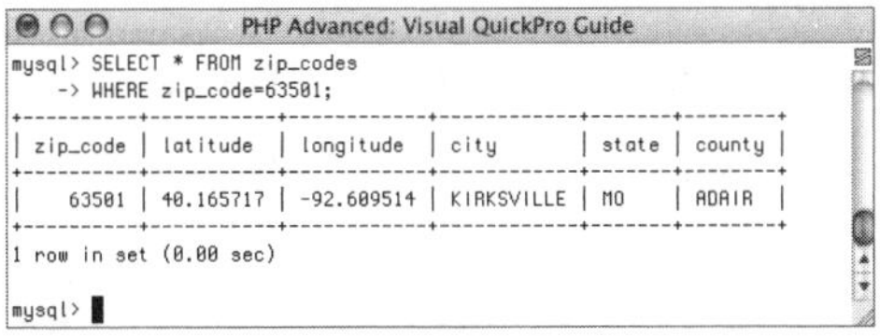

```
mysql> SELECT * FROM zip_codes
    -> WHERE zip_code=63501;
+----------+----------+-----------+------------+-------+--------+
| zip_code | latitude | longitude | city       | state | county |
+----------+----------+-----------+------------+-------+--------+
|    63501 | 40.165717| -92.609514| KIRKSVILLE | MO    | ADAIR  |
+----------+----------+-----------+------------+-------+--------+
1 row in set (0.00 sec)

mysql>
```

**Figure 3.15** The information for a single zip code.

5. Drop any columns you will not need (**Figure 3.14**).

   ```
   ALTER TABLE zip_codes DROP COLUMN
   → zip_class;
   ```

   The zip class data came with the downloaded file but isn't something I'll ever use.

6. Add indexes and update the data, if necessary.

   One additional step I took was to turn empty latitude and longitude values into formal NULL values. That query is:

   ```
   UPDATE zip_codes SET latitude=NULL,
   → longitude=NULL WHERE latitude='';
   ```

7. Check the information for your (or any) zip code (**Figure 3.15**).

   ```
   SELECT * FROM zip_codes
   WHERE zip_code=63501;
   ```

## Creating the stores table

After creating the zip code table, it's time to create the other required table. For this example, I'll want to be able to calculate the distance between a given zip code (like a user's home address) and a list of stores. Therefore, a `stores` table is necessary.

This table can contain whatever information you want. Likely, it would be something like **Table 3.3**.

Since the city and state are tied to the zip code, and that information is already in the `zip_codes` table, those columns can be removed. I'll also make the Address 2 column have a `NULL` option, as not all stores will use this field.

### To create the stores table:

1. Access the `zips` database using the `mysql` client or another interface.

2. Create the `stores` table (**Figure 3.16**).

   ```
   CREATE TABLE stores (
   store_id SMALLINT(5) UNSIGNED NOT
   → NULL AUTO_INCREMENT,
   name VARCHAR(60) NOT NULL,
   address1 VARCHAR(100) NOT NULL,
   address2 VARCHAR(100) default NULL,
   zip_code INT(5) UNSIGNED ZEROFILL NOT
   → NULL,
   phone VARCHAR(15) NOT NULL,
   PRIMARY KEY (store_id),
   KEY (zip_code)
   );
   ```

   The table models the data suggested in Table 3.3, except for the omission of the city and state (which are present in the `zip_codes` table). The `zip_code` column here should be defined exactly like that in the `zip_codes` table because the two fields will be used in a join (see the sidebar "Optimizing Joins," on page 102).

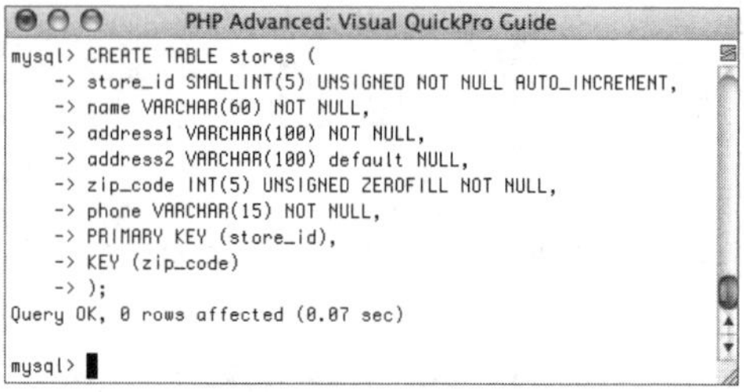

**Figure 3.16** Creating the second, and final, table.

**Table 3.3** An example record for a store.

| A Store's Information | |
| --- | --- |
| COLUMN | EXAMPLE |
| Name | Ray's Shop |
| Address 1 | 49 Main Street |
| Address 2 | Suite 230 |
| City | Arlington |
| State | Virginia |
| Zip Code | 22201 |
| Phone | (123) 456-7890 |

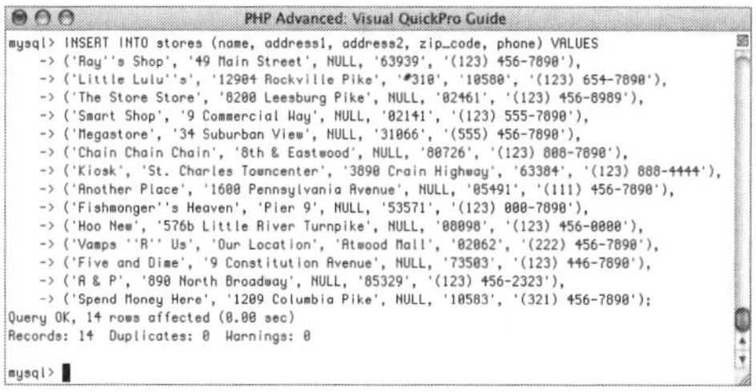

**Figure 3.17** Putting some sample records into the stores table.

3. Populate the stores table (**Figure 3.17**).

```
INSERT INTO stores (name, address1,
→ address2, zip_code, phone) VALUES
('Ray''s Shop', '49 Main Street',
→ NULL, '63939', '(123) 456-7890'),
('Little Lulu''s', '12904 Rockville
→ Pike', '#310', '10580', '(123) 654-
→ 7890'),
('The Store Store', '8200 Leesburg
→ Pike', NULL, '02461', '(123) 456-
→ 8989'),
('Smart Shop', '9 Commercial Way',
→ NULL, '02141', '(123) 555-7890'),
('Megastore', '34 Suburban View',
→ NULL, '31066', '(555) 456-7890'),
('Chain Chain Chain', '8th &
→ Eastwood', NULL, '80726', '(123)
→ 808-7890'),
('Kiosk', 'St. Charles Towncenter',
→ '3890 Crain Highway', '63384',
→ '(123) 888-4444'),
('Another Place', '1600 Pennsylvania
→ Avenue', NULL, '05491', '(111) 456-
→ 7890'),
('Fishmonger''s Heaven', 'Pier 9',
→ NULL, '53571', '(123) 000-7890'),
('Hoo New', '576b Little River
→ Turnpike', NULL, '08098', '(123)
→ 456-0000'),
('Vamps ''R'' Us', 'Our Location',
→ 'Atwood Mall', '02062', '(222) 456-
→ 7890'),
('Five and Dime', '9 Constitution
→ Avenue', NULL, '73503', '(123) 446-
→ 7890'),
('A & P', '890 North Broadway', NULL,
→ '85329', '(123) 456-2323'),
('Spend Money Here', '1209 Columbia
→ Pike', NULL, '10583', '(321) 456-
→ 7890');
```

*continues on next page*

You can enter whatever records you'd like. Or you can download this SQL from the book's corresponding Web site (www.DMCInsights.com/phpvqp2/).

4. Select the complete address for a couple of stores (**Figure 3.18**).

```
SELECT stores.*, zip_codes.city,
→ zip_codes.state
FROM stores LEFT JOIN zip_codes USING
→ (zip_code) LIMIT 2\G
```

To get a store's complete address, including the city and state, a join must be made across the two tables, using the `zip_code` column, which is common to both. If you're not familiar with it, using the \G closing character in the `mysql` client just returns the results in vertical groupings, not horizontal rows.

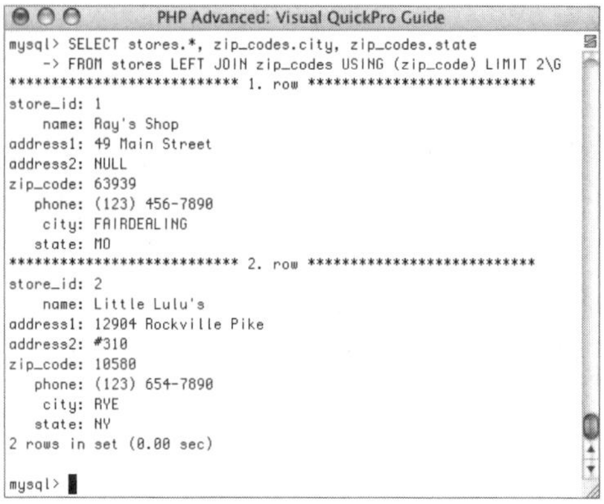

**Figure 3.18** By performing a join on the two tables, a store's complete address can be fetched.

## Optimizing Joins

The MySQL database does a lot of work to improve efficiency, often unbeknownst to the common user. This may involve changing the definition of a column or secretly altering how a query is run. But sometimes MySQL needs a little help.

Joins are expensive queries (in terms of database resources) because they require conditional matches to be made across two or more tables. In this example, a join will occur between the `zip_codes` and `stores` tables, using the `zip_code` column from both. To encourage MySQL to perform these joins faster, you should do two things.

First, an index should exist on both columns. Second, both columns should be defined in exactly the same way. If one column is a `TINYINT` and the other is an `INT`, MySQL will not use any indexes (which is bad).

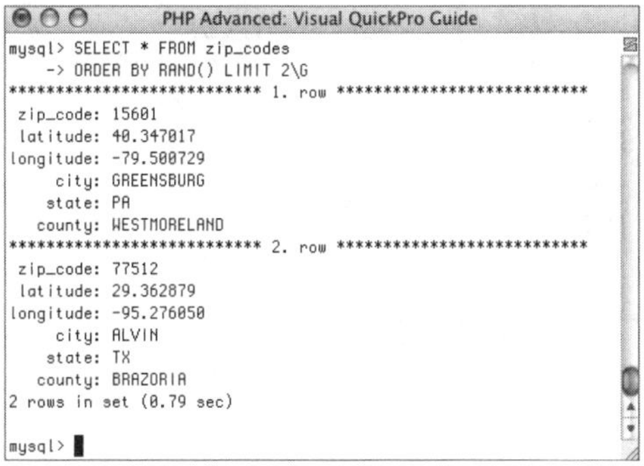

**Figure 3.19** To check the distance between two points, I select the information for two random zip codes.

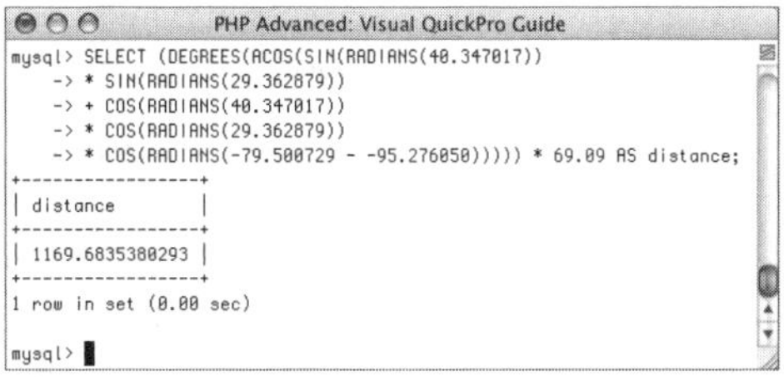

**Figure 3.20** The result of the distance calculation, using the latitudes and longitudes from Figure 3.19.

## Performing distance calculations

Now that two tables exist and are populated with data, it's time to perform the distance calculations. In PHP, the formula for doing so is:

```
$distance = sin(deg2rad($a_latitude))
* sin(deg2rad($b_latitude))
+ cos(deg2rad($a_latitude))
* cos(deg2rad($b_latitude))
* cos(deg2rad($a_longitude -
$b_longitude));
$distance = (rad2deg(acos($distance))) *
→ 69.09;
```

I could explain that formula in detail, except I don't really understand it (or, in truth, haven't tried to). All I know is that this works, and sometimes that's enough.

In MySQL, that same formula (requiring a couple of different functions) is:

```
SELECT (DEGREES(ACOS(SIN(RADIANS(lat_a))
* SIN(RADIANS(lat_b))
+ COS(RADIANS(lat_a))
* COS(RADIANS(lat_b))
* COS(RADIANS(long_a - long_b))))) *
→ 69.09
```

For example, taking the latitude and longitude for two random zip codes (**Figure 3.19**), this calculation returns a value of approximately 1,170 miles (**Figure 3.20**).

```
SELECT (DEGREES(ACOS
→ (SIN(RADIANS(40.347017))
* SIN(RADIANS(29.362879))
+ COS(RADIANS(40.347017))
* COS(RADIANS(29.362879))
* COS(RADIANS(-79.500729 - -
95.276050))))) * 69.09 AS distance;
```

To finally put all of this good knowledge into action, I'll create a PHP script that returns the three closest stores to a given zip code.

## To calculate distances in MySQL:

1. Begin a new PHP script in your text editor or IDE, starting with the HTML (**Script 3.3**).

```
<!DOCTYPE html PUBLIC "-//W3C//DTD
→ XHTML 1.0 Transitional//EN"
"http://www.w3.org/TR/xhtml1/DTD/
→ xhtml1-transitional.dtd">
<html xmlns="http://www.w3.org/
→ 1999/xhtml" xml:lang="en"
→ lang="en">
<head>
    <meta http-equiv="content-type"
→ content="text/html; charset=iso-
→ 8859-1" />
    <title>Distance
→ Calculator</title>
    <style type="text/css"
→ title="text/css" media="all">
.error {
    color: #F30;
}
h3 {
    color: #00F;
}
</style>
</head>
<body>
<?php # Script 3.3 - distance.php
```

I've thrown two CSS classes in here to be able to mark up the page a bit.

*continues on page 106*

**Script 3.3** This PHP script will return the three closest stores, using a zip code calculation, to a given zip code.

```
1    <!DOCTYPE html PUBLIC "-//W3C//DTD XHTML 1.0 Transitional//EN"
2         "http://www.w3.org/TR/xhtml1/DTD/xhtml1-transitional.dtd">
3    <html xmlns="http://www.w3.org/1999/xhtml" xml:lang="en" lang="en">
4    <head>
5        <meta http-equiv="content-type" content="text/html; charset=iso-8859-1" />
6        <title>Distance Calculator</title>
7        <style type="text/css" title="text/css" media="all">
8    .error {
9        color: #F30;
10   }
11   h3 {
12       color: #00F;
13   }
14   </style>
15   </head>
16   <body>
17   <?php # Script 3.3 - distance.php
18
19   /*  This page uses the zips database to
20    *  calculate the distance between a given
21    *  point and some stores.
22    *  The three closest stores are returned.
23    */
24
25   $zip = 64154; //User's zip code.
26
27   // Print a caption:
28   echo "<h2>Nearest stores to $zip:</h2>\n";
```

*(script continues on next page)*

**Script 3.3** *continued*

```
29
30    // Connect to the database:
31    $dbc = @mysqli_connect ('localhost', 'username', 'password', 'zips') OR die ('<p
      class="error">Cannot connect to the database.</body></html>');
32
33    // Get the origination latitude and longitude:
34    $q = "SELECT latitude, longitude FROM zip_codes WHERE zip_code='$zip' AND latitude IS NOT NULL";
35    $r = mysqli_query($dbc, $q);
36
37    // Retrieve the results:
38    if (mysqli_num_rows($r) == 1) {
39
40        list($lat, $long) = mysqli_fetch_array($r, MYSQLI_NUM);
41
42        // Big, main, complex, wordy query:
43        $q = "SELECT name, CONCAT_WS('<br />', address1, address2), city, state, stores.zip_code,
      phone, ROUND(DEGREES(ACOS(SIN(RADIANS($lat))
44    * SIN(RADIANS(latitude))
45    + COS(RADIANS($lat))
46    * COS(RADIANS(latitude))
47    * COS(RADIANS($long - longitude))))) * 69.09 AS distance FROM stores LEFT JOIN zip_codes USING
      (zip_code) ORDER BY distance ASC LIMIT 3";
48        $r = mysqli_query($dbc, $q);
49
50        if (mysqli_num_rows($r) > 0) {
51
52            // Display the stores:
53            while ($row = mysqli_fetch_array($r, MYSQLI_NUM)) {
54                echo "<h3>$row[0]</h3>
55    <p>$row[1]<br />" . ucfirst(strtolower($row[2])) . ", $row[3] $row[4]<br />
56    $row[5] <br />
57    (approximately $row[6] miles)</p>\n";
58
59            } // End of WHILE loop.
60
61        } else { // No stores returned.
62
63            echo '<p class="error">No stores matched the search.</p>';
64
65        }
66
67    } else { // Invalid zip code.
68
69        echo '<p class="error">An invalid zip code was entered.</p>';
70
71    }
72
73    // Close the connection:
74    mysqli_close($dbc);
75
76    ?>
77    </body>
78    </html>
```

**2.** Identify the point of origin.

```
$zip = 64154;

echo "<h2>Nearest stores to
→ $zip:</h2>\n";
```

This value could also be taken from a form (after validating it, of course).

**3.** Connect to the database.

```
$dbc = @mysqli_connect ('localhost',
→ 'username', 'password', 'zips') OR
→ die ('<p class="error">Cannot
→ connect to the database.</body>
→ </html>');
```

**4.** Define and execute the query.

```
$q = "SELECT latitude, longitude FROM
→ zip_codes WHERE zip_code='$zip' AND
→ latitude IS NOT NULL";

$r = mysqli_query($dbc, $q);
```

This first query—the script contains two—both validates the zip code (that it's an actual U.S. zip code) and retrieves that zip code's latitude and longitude. That information will be necessary for calculating distances between the given zip code and each store. Because the data I used lacks the latitude and longitude for some zip codes, I've added an `AND latitude IS NOT NULL` condition to the `WHERE` clause. This may not be necessary for all data sets.

**5.** Retrieve the results of the query.

```
if (mysqli_num_rows($r) == 1) {
    list($lat, $long) =
→ mysqli_fetch_array($r, MYSQLI_NUM);
```

If one row was returned, the zip code is valid and the returned data is assigned to these two variables.

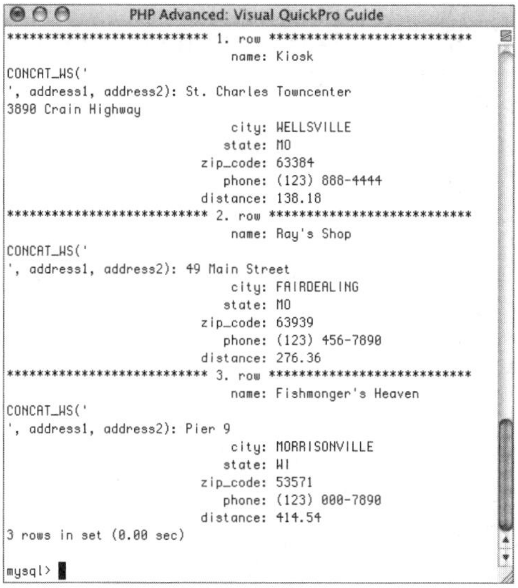

**Figure 3.21** The result of the main, rather unwieldy, query.

6. Perform the main query.

```
$q = "SELECT name, CONCAT_WS
→ ('<br />', address1, address2),
→ city, state, stores.zip_code,
→ phone, ROUND(DEGREES(ACOS(SIN
→ (RADIANS($lat))
* SIN(RADIANS(latitude))
+ COS(RADIANS($lat))
* COS(RADIANS(latitude))
* COS(RADIANS($long - longitude)))))
* 69.09 AS distance FROM stores LEFT
→ JOIN zip_codes USING (zip_code)
→ ORDER BY distance ASC LIMIT 3";
$r = mysqli_query($dbc, $q);
```

Getting to this main query is really the point of the whole script. As you can see in **Figure 3.21**, this query returns a store's name, full address, phone number, and distance from the given zip code. The two addresses lines are concatenated using CONCAT_WS(), which will place a <br /> between the lines if address2 has a value, but return just address1 otherwise. The store's city and state values come from the zip_codes table, and the zip_code could come from either. The phone number is also returned.

The big, complex calculation is also selected. For the "A" latitude and longitude, the values for the original zip code are used (already retrieved by the earlier query). For the "B" latitude and longitude, values from this query will be used. Only three stores are going to be returned, and they are ordered by the distance value, from smallest to largest. Whew!

*continues on next page*

WORKING WITH U.S. ZIP CODES

**7.** Print the results.

```
if (mysqli_num_rows($r) > 0) {
    while ($row = mysqli_fetch_
→ array($r, MYSQLI_NUM)) {
        echo "<h3>$row[0]</h3>
<p>$row[1]<br />" . ucfirst
→ (strtolower($row[2])) . ", $row[3]
→ $row[4]<br />
$row[5] <br />
(approximately $row[6] miles)</p>\n";
    }
} else {
    echo '<p class="error">No stores
→ matched the search.</p>';
}
```

The results are going to be printed with just a modicum of formatting. If no store was returned for some reason (which shouldn't happen), that message is displayed (**Figure 3.22**).

**8.** Complete the conditional begun in Step 5.

```
} else {
    echo '<p class="error">An
invalid zip code was entered.</p>';
}
```

This message applies if an invalid zip code is provided (**Figure 3.23**).

**Figure 3.22** Because no restriction is made as to how close a store should be, this message should never appear. Still, best not to make assumptions.

**Figure 3.23** The result should an invalid zip code (like 77777 here) be used.

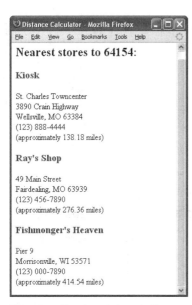

**Figure 3.24** The closest stores to the 64154 zip code.

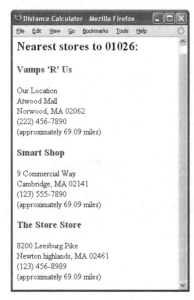

**Figure 3.25** The closest stores to the 01026 zip code.

**9.** Complete the page.

```
mysqli_close($dbc);
?>
</body>
</html>
```

**10.** Save the file as `distance.php`, place it in your Web directory, and test in your Web browser (**Figure 3.24**).

**11.** Change the zip code and test again (**Figure 3.25**).

To use a zip code that begins with a 0, put it in quotes:

```
$zip = '01026';
```

If you don't, PHP will think you're using another number form and translate it.

### ✔ Tips

■ Chapter 13, "Ajax," will use this example to demonstrate the magic of Ajax.

■ You could easily limit the stores returned to a certain area by adding `WHERE distance<=X` to the main query.

# Creating Stored Functions

Stored functions are half of a larger concept called *stored routines* (the other half are *stored procedures*). Present in many database applications but new to MySQL as of version 5, stored routines allow you to save a set sequence of code in the MySQL server, and then call that sequence as needed. Think of it like being able to write your own PHP functions but in SQL.

The topic of stored routines can be expansive, but I want to give you a little taste here. For more information, see the MySQL manual or my *MySQL: Visual QuickStart Guide* (Peachpit Press, 2006), where I dedicate many more pages to the subject. Before you follow this example, make sure that you have at least version 5 of MySQL (or are using a database application that supports them, like PostgreSQL).

The basic syntax for creating stored functions is:

```
CREATE FUNCTION name (arguments) RETURNS
→ type code
```

For the routine's name, you should not use an existing keyword, SQL term, or function name. As with most things you name in MySQL, you should stick to alphanumeric characters and the underscore.

The arguments section is used to pass values to the routine. The listed arguments are named and given types that correspond to the available data types in MySQL:

```
CREATE FUNCTION myfunc (myvar1 INT,
→ myvar2 CHAR) RETURNS type code
```

## Declaring Local Variables

Stored routines are like small programs, and they can even have their own variables. To do so, use the DECLARE statement:

```
DECLARE var_name var_type
```

The naming rules are pretty much the same as for everything else, but you absolutely want to make sure that your variables have unique identifiers. The types correspond to the MySQL data types:

```
DECLARE var1 INT
DECLARE var2 DECIMAL(5,2)
DECLARE var3 VARCHAR(20)
```

The only restrictions to declaring variables are:

◆ The declarations must take place within a BEGIN...END code block.

◆ The declarations must take place before any other statements (i.e., declarations must be immediately after the BEGIN).

Once you've declared a variable, you can assign it a value using SET:

```
SET name = value
```

Note, as well, that unlike variables in PHP, these stored routine variables do not begin with a dollar sign.

```
mysql> CREATE FUNCTION myfunc
    -> (myvar1 INT, myvar2 CHAR)
    -> RETURNS int
    -> BEGIN
    -> RETURN 2;
ERROR 1064 (42000): You have an error in your SQL syntax; check
the manual that corresponds to your MySQL server version for the
 right syntax to use near 'RETURN 2' at line 5
mysql> END
```

**Figure 3.26** You have to be careful when attempting to create stored routines within the `mysql` client.

The code section of this syntax is the most important. As your routines will normally contain multiple lines, you'll want to create a block by using `BEGIN` and `END`:

`CREATE FUNCTION` *name* (*arguments*) `RETURNS`
→ *type* `BEGIN`

    *statement1*;

    *statement2*;

`END`

Within the code block, each statement ends with a semicolon. This can cause a problem: when you go to add this stored function using the `mysql` client, it will think that the semicolon indicates the end of a command to be executed immediately (**Figure 3.26**). To prevent this, one solution is to change the delimiter (the semicolon) to something else. Another option is to use the MySQL Administrator, instructions for which you'll soon see.

Stored functions must contain a `RETURNS` clause, indicating the type of value returned by the function. Functions return scalar (single) values, like a number or a string. To do so, use

`RETURNS` *data*

within the function's code body. The type of the data returned must match the type indicated in the function's initial definition line. You cannot return a list of values from a stored function, but because stored functions return scalar values, they can be used in queries like any of the existing MySQL functions.

All of this information, along with the blip in the accompanying sidebar "Declaring Local Variables," is the five-minute guide to stored functions. In the next sequence of steps, I'll show you how to turn the complicated distance calculation formula (see Script 3.3) into a callable stored function.

CREATING STORED FUNCTIONS

## To create a stored function:

1. Download and install the MySQL Administrator.

   This free tool is part of MySQL's GUI Tools package, a wonderful suite of applications. Versions are available for most operating systems (Windows, Mac OS X, and Linux) and you can compile your own version if necessary.

2. Start the application.

   Windows users can use the Start menu shortcut. Mac users can double-click the application itself.

3. At the first prompt (**Figure 3.27**), enter the correct username, hostname, and password combination.

   To administer MySQL running on the same computer, you'll likely want to enter *localhost* as the host. You'll then want to use either *root* or another administrative account, and the correct password for that user. These values correspond to the users and permissions established within the MySQL server.

4. Click OK or Connect, depending upon your version of the application, to take you into the application.

   Assuming that you used a valid administrative username/hostname/password combination, this will connect to the MySQL server. **Figure 3.28** shows the result on Windows; **Figure 3.29** is the Mac OS X view.

**Figure 3.27** The MySQL Administrator connection prompt, where you enter the access information for the database server with which you will interact.

**Figure 3.28** MySQL Administrator on Windows, just after logging in.

**Figure 3.29** MySQL Administrator on Mac OS X.

**Figure 3.30** The view of the zips database.

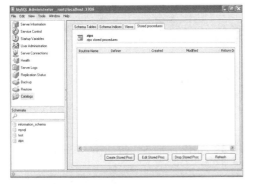

**Figure 3.31** The next step on Windows is to click Stored procedures.

**Figure 3.32** At this prompt, click Create FUNCTION.

**5.** Click Catalogs.

The Catalogs section is where you can look at and edit your databases.

**6.** Click on the zips database in the Schemata column (**Figure 3.30**).

Not sure why they don't just say *Databases* instead of *Schemata* (or Catalogs), but...

**7.** Find the stored function editor.

How the MySQL Administrator behaves on the different operating systems is stunningly varied. On Windows, you would:

**1.** Click Stored procedures (**Figure 3.31**).

**2.** Click Create Stored Proc.

**3.** Click Create FUNCTION at the next prompt (**Figure 3.32**).

*continues on next page*

CREATING STORED FUNCTIONS

On Mac OS X, you would:

**1.** Click Functions (**Figure 3.33**).

**2.** Click Create Function.

**8.** In the resulting window, enter (Figure 3.34):

```
CREATE FUNCTION zips.return_
→ distance (lat_a DOUBLE, long_
→ a DOUBLE,
lat_b DOUBLE, long_b DOUBLE)
→ RETURNS DOUBLE
BEGIN
    DECLARE distance DOUBLE;
    SET distance =
→ SIN(RADIANS(lat_a)) *
→ SIN(RADIANS(lat_b))
  + COS(RADIANS(lat_a))
  * COS(RADIANS(lat_b))
  * COS(RADIANS(long_a - long_b));
    RETURN((DEGREES(ACOS(distance)))
→ * 69.09);
END
```

This code wraps the complicated calculation within a stored function. The function is called *return_distance*. The *databasename.functionname* syntax associates the function with a specific database (here, `zips`). The function takes four arguments, all of type `DOUBLE`. It will return a `DOUBLE` value as well.

The first step in the function is to create a variable of type `DOUBLE`. Doing so will simplify the calculation to a degree (pardon the pun). The variable is assigned the value of most of the calculation. This variable is then run through a couple more functions and some arithmetic, then returned.

**9.** Click OK (Mac OS X) or Execute SQL (Windows).

**Figure 3.33** In the Catalogs pane on Mac OS X, click Functions.

**Figure 3.34** Using the SQL Editor (on Windows) to enter the stored function.

**Figure 3.35** The stored function is used to simplify the SQL query.

**10.** Test the function by running the following query in the mysql client (**Figure 3.35**):

```
SELECT return_distance(40.347017, -
→ 79.500729, 29.362879,
→ --95.276050);
```

This is the same query run in Figure 3.20, except now it calls the stored function.

**11.** If you want, modify distance.php (Script 3.3) to call the stored procedure. To do so, just change the main query to

```
SELECT name, CONCAT_WS('<br />',
→ address1, address2), city,
→ state, stores.zip_code, phone,
→ ROUND(return_distance($lat,
→ $long, latitude, longitude)) AS
→ distance FROM stores LEFT JOIN
→ zip_codes USING (zip_code) ORDER
→ BY distance ASC LIMIT 3
```

## ✔ Tips

■ All stored routines are associated with a specific database. This has the added benefit of not needing to select the database (USE *databasename*) when invoking them. This also means that you cannot have a stored routine select a database.

■ Because stored routines are linked with databases, if you drop the database, you'll also drop any associated stored routine.

**CREATING STORED FUNCTIONS**

**115**

# Displaying Results Horizontally

Another of the common questions I see involves displaying query results horizontally. It's quite easy to fetch the results and display them vertically (**Figure 3.36**), but creating an output like that in **Figure 3.37** does stymie some programmers. The code in Figure 3.37 uses an HTML table to create this output, with five records per row.

To achieve this effect using PHP, a counter is required that tracks how many records have been placed on a row. When zero records have been placed, the new row should be started. When the maximum number of records have been placed, the old row should be concluded. That's the premise, which I'll develop in this next script. For the data, I'll use the zip_codes table in the zips database (but you could use anything).

**Figure 3.36** A traditional vertical display of some records.

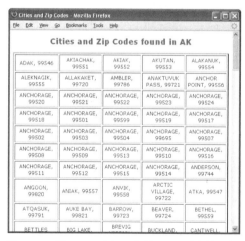

**Figure 3.37** The same data as in Figure 3.36, laid out in table form.

## To display results horizontally:

1. Begin a new PHP script in your text editor or IDE, starting with the HTML (**Script 3.4**).

```
<!DOCTYPE html PUBLIC "-//W3C//DTD
→ XHTML 1.0 Transitional//EN"
"http://www.w3.org/TR/xhtml1/DTD/
→ xhtml1-transitional.dtd">
<html xmlns="http://www.w3.org/1999/
→ xhtml" xml:lang="en" lang="en">
<head>
    <meta http-equiv="content-type"
→ content="text/html; charset=iso-
→ 8859-1" />
    <title>Cities and Zip
→ Codes</title>
    <style type="text/css"
→ title="text/css" media="all">
h2 {
    font-family: Verdana, Geneva,
→ Arial, Helvetica, sans-serif;
    font-size: 14pt;
    color : #960;
    text-align: center;
}
td {
    font-family: Verdana, Geneva,
→ Arial, Helvetica, sans-serif;
    font-size: 10pt;
    color : #333
}
.error {
    color: #F30;
}
</style>
</head>
<body>
<?php # Script 3.4 - display.php
```

To make the result a little nicer, I've defined formatting for the error CSS class and the <h2> and <td> tags.

*continues on page 120*

**Script 3.4** All of the cities and zip codes for a given state are retrieved by this PHP script. Instead of displaying them as a vertical list, they'll be displayed in a table with five cells per row.

```
                                          Script
1    <!DOCTYPE html PUBLIC "-//W3C//DTD XHTML 1.0 Transitional//EN"
2            "http://www.w3.org/TR/xhtml1/DTD/xhtml1-transitional.dtd">
3    <html xmlns="http://www.w3.org/1999/xhtml" xml:lang="en" lang="en">
4    <head>
5        <meta http-equiv="content-type" content="text/html; charset=iso-8859-1" />
6        <title>Cities and Zip Codes</title>
7        <style type="text/css" title="text/css" media="all">
8    h2 {
9        font-family: Verdana, Geneva, Arial, Helvetica, sans-serif;
10       font-size: 14pt;
11       color : #960;
12       text-align: center;
13   }
14   td {
15       font-family: Verdana, Geneva, Arial, Helvetica, sans-serif;
16       font-size: 10pt;
17       color : #333
18   }
```

*(script continues on next page)*

**Script 3.4** *continued*

```
     ○ ○ ○                                          Script
19   .error {
20       color: #F30;
21   }
22   </style>
23   </head>
24   <body>
25   <?php # Script 3.4 - display.php
26
27   /*  This page retrieves and displays all of the
28    *  cities and zip codes for a particular state.
29    *  The results will be shown in a table.
30    */
31
32   // Abbreviation of state to show:
33   $state = 'AK';
34
35   // Items to display per row:
36   $items = 5;
37
38   // Print a caption:
39   echo "<h2>Cities and Zip Codes found in $state</h2>\n";
40
41   // Connect to the database:
42   $dbc = @mysqli_connect ('localhost', 'username', 'password', 'zips') OR die ('<p
     class="error">Cannot connect to the database.</body></html>');
43
44   // Get the cities and zip codes, ordered by city:
45   $q = "SELECT city, zip_code FROM zip_codes WHERE state='$state' ORDER BY city";
46   $r = mysqli_query($dbc, $q);
47
48   // Retrieve the results:
49   if (mysqli_num_rows($r) > 0) {
50
51       // Start a table:
52       echo '<table border="2" width="90%" cellspacing="3" cellpadding="3" align="center">
53   ';
54
55       // Need a counter:
56       $i = 0;
57
58       // Retrieve each record:
59       while (list($city, $zip_code) = mysqli_fetch_array($r, MYSQLI_NUM)) {
60
61           // Do we need to start a new row?
62           if ($i == 0) {
```

*(script continues on next page)*

**Script 3.4** *continued*

```
63            echo "<tr>\n";
64        }
65
66        // Print the record:
67        echo "\t<td align=\"center\">$city, $zip_code</td>\n";
68
69        // Increment the counter:
70        $i++;
71
72            // Do we need to end the row?
73            if ($i == $items) {
74                echo "</tr>\n";
75                $i = 0; // Reset counter.
76            }
77
78        } // End of while loop.
79
80        if ($i > 0) { // Last row was incomplete.
81
82            // Print the necessary number of cells:
83            for (;$i < $items; $i++) {
84                echo "<td> </td>\n";
85            }
86
87            // Complete the row.
88            echo '</tr>';
89
90        } // End of ($i > 0) IF.
91
92        // Close the table:
93        echo '</table>';
94
95    } else { // Bad state abbreviation.
96
97        echo '<p class="error">An invalid state abbreviation was used.</p>';
98
99    } // End of main IF.
100
101    // Close the database connection:
102    mysqli_close($dbc);
103
104    ?>
105    </body>
106    </html>
```

**2.** Establish the necessary variables and print a caption.

```
$state = 'AK';
$items = 5;
echo "<h2>Cities and Zip Codes found
→ in $state</h2>\n";
```

**3.** Connect to and query the database.

```
$dbc = @mysqli_connect ('localhost',
→ 'username', 'password', 'zips') OR
→ die ('<p class="error">Cannot
→ connect to the database.</body>
→ </html>');
$q = "SELECT city, zip_code FROM
→ zip_codes WHERE state='$state'
→ ORDER BY city";
$r = mysqli_query($dbc, $q);
if (mysqli_num_rows($r) > 0) {
```

The query will return every city and zip code in the state in alphabetical order by city.

**4.** Begin a table and initialize a counter.

```
echo '<table border="2" width="90%"
→ cellspacing="3" cellpadding="3"
→ align="center">
';
$i = 0;
```

The $i counter will track how many items have already been placed on a row.

**5.** Retrieve each record.

```
while (list($city, $zip_code) =
→ mysqli_fetch_array($r,
→ MYSQLI_NUM)) {
```

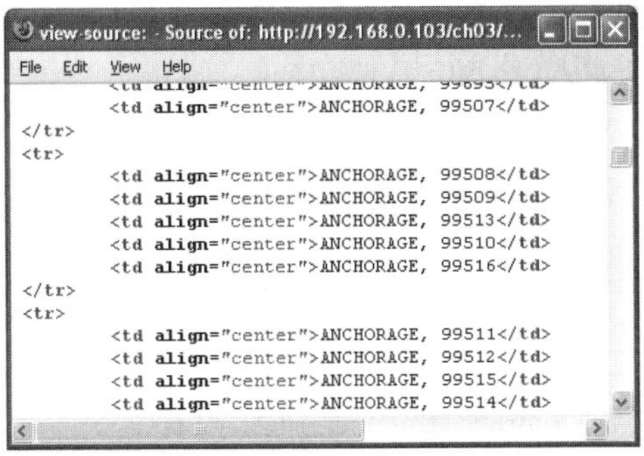

**Figure 3.38** The HTML source for part of the table.

**6.** Start a new row, if necessary.

```
if ($i == 0) {
        echo "<tr>\n";
}
```

Every time, within this while loop, the first item on a row is to be placed, a new row should be created by printing the <tr>. This applies the first time the loop is entered (because $i is initially 0) and after $i is reset (upon completing a row).

**7.** Print the record and increment the counter.

```
echo "\t<td align=\"center\">$city,
→ $zip_code</td>\n";

$i++;
```

To better format the HTML source of the page (**Figure 3.38**), each item appears on its own line and one tab in.

**8.** Complete the row, if necessary.

```
if ($i == $items) {
        echo "</tr>\n";
        $i = 0;
}
```

Once the counter equals the number of items to be placed on a row, it's time to end that row by printing </tr>. Then the counter needs to be reset so that the next time the loop is entered, a new row will be started.

**9.** Complete the while loop.

```
} // End of while loop.
```

**10.** Complete the last row, if necessary.

```
if ($i > 0) {
    for (;$i < $items; $i++) {
        echo
→ "<td> </td>\n";
    }
    echo '</tr>';
}
```

This is a step that's easy to miss. Unless the number of items displayed is easily divisible by the number to be displayed per row (i.e., there's no remainder of that division), the last row will be incomplete (**Figure 3.39**).

If `$i` has a value other than 0, some extra cells must be added (if it has a value of 0, then the last row was completed). A `for` loop can accomplish this task easily, starting with the current value of `$i` and stopping when `$i` equals `$items`. A little-known trick with the `for` loop is that each of the three parts is optional. Since no initial expression must be evaluated (like setting `$i` to some value), the loop begins with `(;`.

**11.** Close the table and complete the conditional started in Step 3.

```
    echo '</table>';
} else {
    echo '<p class="error">An
→ invalid state abbreviation was
→ used.</p>';
}
```

**12.** Complete the page.

```
mysqli_close($dbc);
?>
</body>
</html>
```

**13.** Save the file as `display.php`, place it in your Web directory, and test in your Web browser (Figure 3.37).

**14.** Change the value of `$items`, change the value of `$state`, and retest in your Web browser (**Figure 3.40**).

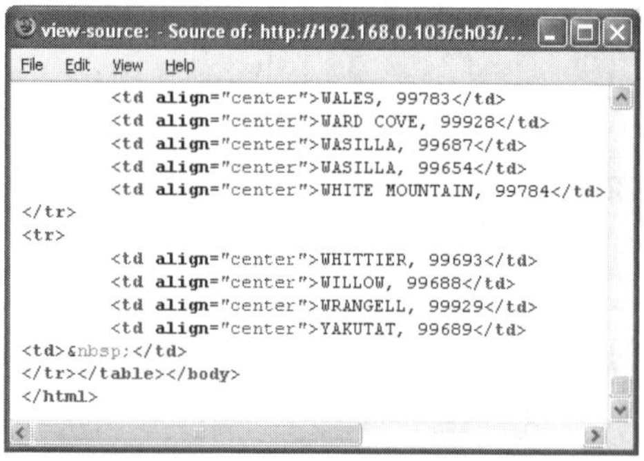


```
        <td align="center">WALES, 99783</td>
        <td align="center">WARD COVE, 99928</td>
        <td align="center">WASILLA, 99687</td>
        <td align="center">WASILLA, 99654</td>
        <td align="center">WHITE MOUNTAIN, 99784</td>
</tr>
<tr>
        <td align="center">WHITTIER, 99693</td>
        <td align="center">WILLOW, 99688</td>
        <td align="center">WRANGELL, 99929</td>
        <td align="center">YAKUTAT, 99689</td>
<td> </td>
</tr></table></body>
</html>
```

Figure 3.39 The last row had only four items in it, so one blank table cell had to be created.

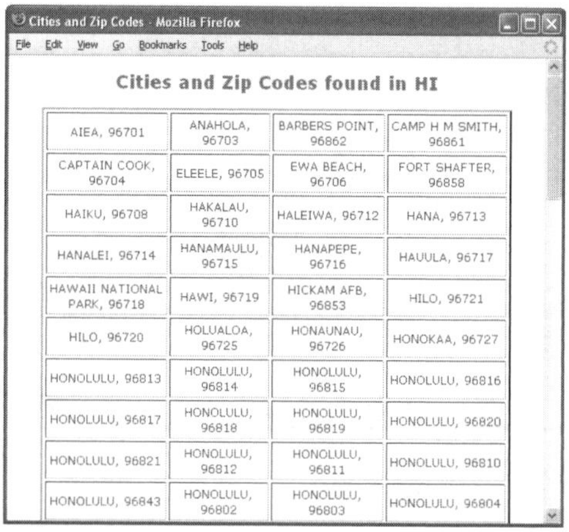


Figure 3.40 With two quick changes, the script now displays all the cities for another state (here, Hawaii), four per row.

# SECURITY
# TECHNIQUES

With more and more personal information being stored on the Web—credit card data, social security numbers, maiden names, favorite pets—today's PHP developer cannot afford to be ignorant when it comes to security. Sadly, most beginning programmers fail to understand the truth about security: there is no such thing as "secure" or "insecure." The wise programmer knows that the real question is *how secure* a site is. Once any piece of data is stored in a database, in a text file, or on a Post-it note in your office, its security is compromised. The focus in this chapter is therefore how to make your applications more secure.

This chapter will begin by rehashing the fundamentals of secure PHP programming. These are the basic things that I hope/assume you're already doing. After that a quick example shows ways to validate different kinds of data that might come from an HTML form. The third topic is the new-to-PHP 5 PECL library called Filter. Its usage isn't very programmer-friendly, but the way it wraps all of the customary data filtering and sanitizing methods into one interface makes it worth knowing. After that, two different uses of the PEAR Auth package show an alternative way to implement authorization in your Web applications. The chapter will conclude with coverage of the MCrypt library, demonstrating how to encrypt and decrypt data.

# Remembering the Basics

Before getting into demonstrations of more particular security techniques, I want to take a moment to go over the basics: those fundamental rules that every PHP programmer should abide by all of the time.

### To ensure a basic level of security:

1. Do not rely upon register_globals.

   The advent of register_globals once made PHP so easy to use, while also making it less secure (convenience often weakens security). The recommendation is to program as if register_globals is off. This is particularly important because register_globals will likely disappear in future versions of PHP.

2. Initialize variables prior to using them.

   If register_globals is still enabled—even if you aren't using them—a malicious user could use holes created by noninitialized variables to hack your system. For example:

   ```
   if (condition) {
       $auth = TRUE;
   }
   ```

   If $auth is not preset to FALSE prior to this code, then a user could easily make themselves authorized by passing $_GET['auth'], $_POST['auth'], or $_COOKIE['auth'] to this script.

3. Verify and purify all incoming data.

   How you verify and purify the data depends greatly upon the type of data. You'll see many different techniques in this chapter and the book.

## Avoiding Mail Abuses

A security concern exists in any Web application that uses the mail() function with form data. For starters, if someone enters their "to" email address as *someone@example.com,someone.else@example.com*, you'll now be sending two emails. If a malicious user enters 500 addresses (perhaps by creating their own form that submits to your same page), you're now sending out spam! You can avoid this by using regular expressions to guarantee that the submitted value contains just one address. Or you could search for a comma in the submitted email address, which wouldn't be allowed. But that won't solve the problem entirely.

Although the mail() function takes separate arguments for the "to" address, "from" address (or other additional headers), subject, and body, all four values are put together to create the actual message. By submitting specifically formatted text through any of these inputs, bad people can still use your form to send their spam. To guard against this, you should watch for newline (\n) and carriage returns (\r) within the submitted data. Either don't send emails with these values or replace them with spaces to invalidate the intended message format. You should probably also make sure that you (or someone involved with the site) receives a copy of every email sent so that close tabs can be kept on this area of the server.

**4.** Be careful if you use variables for included files.

If your code does something like

`require($page);`

then you should either make sure that `$page` does not come from an outside source (like `$_GET`) or, if it does, that you've made certain that it has an appropriate value. See the technique in Chapter 2, "Developing Web Applications."

**5.** Be extra, extra careful when using any function that runs commands on the server.

This includes `eval()`, `exec()`, `system()`, `passthru()`, `popen()`, and the backticks (` `` `). Because each of these runs commands on the server itself, they should never be used casually. And if you must use a variable as part of the command to execute, perform any and all security checks on that variable first. Also use the `escapeshellarg()` and `escapeshellcmd()` functions as an extra precaution.

**6.** Consider changing the default session directory or using a database to store session data.

An example as to how you would do this is discussed in Chapter 3, "Advanced Database Concepts."

**7.** Do not use browser-supplied filenames for storing uploaded files on the server.

When you move a file onto your server, rename it to something safe, preferably something not guessable.

**8.** Watch for HTML (and more important, JavaScript) in submitted data if it will be redisplayed in a Web page.

Use the `strip_tags()` or similar functions to clear HTML and potential JavaScript from submitted text.

**9.** Do not reveal PHP errors on live sites.

One of the most common ways to hack a site is to try to "break" it—do something unexpected to cause errors—in the hopes that the errors reveal important behind-the-scenes information.

**10.** Nullify the possibility of SQL injection attacks.

Use a language-specific database escaping function, like `mysqli_real_escape_data()`, to ensure that submitted values will not break your queries.

**11.** Program with error reporting on its highest level.

While not strictly a security issue, programming with error reporting on its highest level can often show potential holes in your code.

**12.** Never keep `phpinfo()` scripts on the server.

Although vital for developing and debugging PHP applications, `phpinfo()` scripts reveal too much information and are too easily found if left on a live site.

# Validating Form Data

Handling form data is still far and away the most common use of PHP (in this author's humble opinion, anyway). The security concern lies in the fact that the PHP page handling the form will do something with the information the user enters: store it in a database, pass it along to another page, or use it in an email. If the information the user enters is tainted, you could have a major problem on your hands. As a rule, do not trust the user! Mistakes can happen, either on purpose or by accident, that could reveal flaws in your code, cause the loss of data, or bring your entire system to a crashing halt.

Some good validation techniques are:

◆ Use the checkdate() function to confirm that a given date is valid.

◆ Typecast numbers.

◆ Use regular expressions to check email addresses, URLs, and other items *with definable patterns* (see the sidebar).

## When to Use Regular Expressions

I often see what I would call an overuse of regular expressions. You should understand that regular expressions require extra processing, so they shouldn't be used flippantly. Many types of data—comments and addresses being just two examples—really don't have a definable pattern. A regular expression that allows for any valid comment or address would allow for just about anything. So skip the server-intensive regular expressions in such cases.

As a guide, regular expressions *may be* the most exacting security measure, but they're almost definitely the least efficient and possibly the most problematic. I'm not suggesting you shouldn't use them—just make sure they're really the best option for the data being validated.

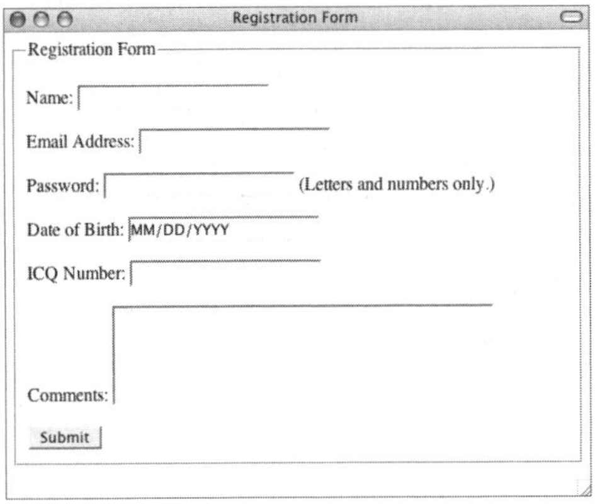

**Figure 4.1** When users first come to the registration page, this is the form they will see.

As with the basic security techniques already reviewed, the hope is that as a somewhat-experienced PHP programmer, you already know most of these things. To be certain, this next example will present a sample registration form (**Figure 4.1**), taking various types of information, which will then be precisely validated. In doing so, I'll make use of a couple of Character Type functions, added to PHP in version 4.3. Listed in **Table 4.1**, these functions test a given value against certain constraints for the current locale (established by the `setlocale()` function).

**Table 4.1** The Character Type functions provide validation specific to the given environment (i.e., the locale setting).

| Character Type Functions | |
| --- | --- |
| FUNCTION | CHECKS IF VALUE CONTAINS |
| ctype_alnum() | Letters and numbers |
| ctype_alpha() | Letters only |
| ctype_cntrl() | Control characters |
| ctype_digit() | Numbers |
| ctype_graph() | Printable characters, except spaces |
| ctype_lower() | Lowercase letters |
| ctype_print() | Printable characters |
| ctype_punct() | Punctuation |
| ctype_space() | White space characters |
| ctype_upper() | Uppercase characters |
| ctype_xdigit() | Hexadecimal numbers |

## To validate a form:

1. Begin a new PHP script in your text editor or IDE, starting with the HTML (**Script 4.1**).

   ```
   <!DOCTYPE html PUBLIC "-//W3C//DTD
   → XHTML 1.0 Transitional//EN"
   "http://www.w3.org/TR/xhtml1/DTD/
   → xhtml1-transitional.dtd">
   <html xmlns="http://www.w3.org/1999/
   → xhtml" xml:lang="en" lang="en">
   ```

   ```
   <head>
       <meta http-equiv="content-type"
   → content="text/html; charset=
   → iso-8859-1" />
       <title>Registration Form</title>
   </head>
   <body>
   <?php # Script 4.1 - register.php
   ```

   *continues on page 131*

**Script 4.1** This page both displays a registration form and processes it. The script validates the submitted data using various functions, and then reports any errors.

```
1    <!DOCTYPE html PUBLIC "-//W3C//DTD XHTML 1.0 Transitional//EN"
2            "http://www.w3.org/TR/xhtml1/DTD/xhtml1-transitional.dtd">
3    <html xmlns="http://www.w3.org/1999/xhtml" xml:lang="en" lang="en">
4    <head>
5        <meta http-equiv="content-type" content="text/html; charset=iso-8859-1" />
6        <title>Registration Form</title>
7    </head>
8    <body>
9    <?php # Script 4.1 - register.php
10
11   /*   This page creates a registration form
12    *   which is then validated using various functions.
13    */
14
15   if (isset($_POST['submitted'])) { // Handle the form.
16
17       // Store errors in an array:
18       $errors = array();
19
20       // Check for non-empty name:
21       if (!isset($_POST['name']) OR empty($_POST['name'])) {
22           $errors[] = 'name';
23       }
24
25       // Validate the email address using eregi():
26       if (!eregi('^[_a-z0-9-]+(\.[_a-z0-9-]+)*@[a-z0-9-]+(\.[a-z0-9-]+)*(\.[a-z]{2,4})$',
     $_POST['email'])) {
27           $errors[] = 'email address';
28       }
29
30       // Validate the password using ctype_alnum():
31       if (!ctype_alnum($_POST['pass'])) {
32           $errors[] = 'password';
33       }
```

*(script continues on next page)*

**Script 4.1** *continued*

```
34
35      // Validate the date of birth using check_date():
36      if (isset($_POST['dob']) AND
37      (strlen($_POST['dob']) >= 8) AND
38      (strlen($_POST['dob']) <= 10) ) {
39
40          // Break up the string:
41          $dob = explode('/', $_POST['dob']);
42
43          // Were three parts returned?
44          if (count($dob) == 3) {
45
46              // Is it a valid date?
47              if (!checkdate((int) $dob[0], (int) $dob[1], (int) $dob[2])) {
48                  $errors[] = 'date of birth';
49              }
50
51          } else { // Invalid format.
52              $errors[] = 'date of birth';
53          }
54
55      } else { // Empty or not the right length.
56          $errors[] = 'date of birth';
57      }
58
59      // Validate the ICQ number using ctype_digit():
60      if (!ctype_digit($_POST['icq'])) {
61          $errors[] = 'ICQ number';
62      }
63
64      // Check for non-empty comments:
65      if (!isset($_POST['comments']) OR empty($_POST['comments'])) {
66          $errors[] = 'comments';
67      }
68
69      if (empty($errors)) { // Success!
70
71          // Print a message and quit the script:
72          echo '<p>You have successfully registered (but not really).</p></body></html>';
73          exit();
74
75      } else { // Report the errors.
76
77          echo '<p>Problems exist with the following field(s):<ul>';
78
79          foreach ($errors as $error) {
80              echo "<li>$error</li>\n";
81          }
82
```

*(script continues on next page)*

**Script 4.1** *continued*

```
83          echo '</ul></p>';
84
85      }
86
87  } // End of $_POST['submitted'] IF.
88
89  // Show the form.
90  ?>
91  <form method="post">
92  <fieldset>
93  <legend>Registration Form</legend>
94  <p>Name: <input type="text" name="name" /></p>
95  <p>Email Address: <input type="text" name="email" /></p>
96  <p>Password: <input type="password" name="pass" /> (Letters and numbers only.)</p>
97  <p>Date of Birth: <input type="text" name="dob" value="MM/DD/YYYY" /></p>
98  <p>ICQ Number: <input type="text" name="icq" /></p>
99  <p>Comments: <textarea name="comments" rows="5" cols="40"></textarea></p>
100
101  <input type="hidden" name="submitted" value="true" />
102  <input type="submit" name="submit" value="Submit" />
103  </fieldset>
104  </form>
105
106  </body>
107  </html>
```

**2.** Create the section of the script that handles the submitted form.

```
if (isset($_POST['submitted'])) {
    $errors = array();
```

Your script should always handle the form before it could possibly redisplay it (on errors found). I like to use a hidden form input to check if a form was submitted. The hidden form input will always be passed to the page upon submission, unlike any other input (on Internet Explorer, if a user submits a button by pressing Enter, then the submit button won't be set).

One way I like to validate forms is to use an array that stores the errors as they occur. By checking if this array is empty, the script can tell if all validation tests have been passed. If the array isn't empty, its values can be used to print the error messages.

**3.** Check for a name.

```
if (!isset($_POST['name']) OR
→ empty($_POST['name'])) {
    $errors[] = 'name';
}
```

A person's name is one of those things that you can use regular expressions on, but it may not be worthwhile. A valid name can contain letters, spaces, periods, hyphens, and apostrophes. Under most circumstances, just checking for a nonempty name is sufficient.

**4.** Validate the submitted email address.

```
if (!eregi('^[_a-z0-9-]+(\.[_a-z0-
→ 9-]+)*@[a-z0-9-]+(\.[a-z0-9-]
→ +)*(\.[a-z]{2,4})$',
→ $_POST['email'])) {
    $errors[] = 'email address';
}
```

There are any number of patterns you can use to validate an email address, depending on how strict or liberal you want to be. This one is commonly seen. Certainly some invalid email addresses could slip through this expression, but it does add a sufficient level of security. Feel free to use a different pattern if you have one to your liking. Keep in mind that a user could enter a valid e-mail address that does not actually exist. Only some sort of activation process (sending the user an email containing a link back to the Web site) can confirm a real address.

**5.** Validate the submitted password.

```
if (!ctype_alnum($_POST['pass'])) {
    $errors[] = 'password';
}
```

The form indicates that the password must contain only letters and numbers. To validate such values, the function `ctype_alnum()` works perfectly.

In a real registration form, I would also recommend confirming the password with a second password input, then making sure both values match. I'm skipping that step here for brevity's sake.

*continues on next page*

**6.** Begin checking to see if the user entered a valid date of birth.

```
if (isset($_POST['dob']) AND
(strlen($_POST['dob']) >= 8) AND
(strlen($_POST['dob']) <= 10) ) {
    $dob = explode('/',
→ $_POST['dob']);
        if (count($dob) == 3) {
```

There is really no way of knowing if the information users enter is in fact their birthday, but PHP's built-in `checkdate()` function can confirm whether or not that date existed. Since the form takes the date of birth as a simple string in the format *MM/DD/YYYY*, the script must first confirm that something was entered. I also check if the string's length is at least eight characters long (e.g., 1/1/1900) but no more than ten characters long (e.g., 12/31/2000).

This string is then exploded on the slashes to theoretically retrieve the month, day, and year values. Next, a conditional checks that exactly three parts were created by the explosion.

**7.** Check if the date of birth is a valid date.

```
if (!checkdate((int) $dob[0], (int)
→ $dob[1], (int) $dob[2])) {
        $errors[] = 'date of birth';
}
```

The `checkdate()` function confirms that a date is valid. You might want to also check that a user didn't enter a date of birth that's in the future or the too-recent past. Each value is typecast as an integer as an extra precaution.

**8.** Complete the date of birth conditionals.

```
    } else {
            $errors[] = 'date of
→ birth';
        }
    } else {
        $errors[] = 'date of birth';
}
```

The first `else` applies if the submitted value cannot be exploded into three parts. The second `else` applies if the value isn't of the right length.

**9.** Validate the ICQ number.

```
if (!ctype_digit($_POST['icq'])) {
        $errors[] = 'ICQ number';
}
```

The ICQ number can only contain digits, so it makes sense to use the `ctype_digit()` function.

**10.** Check for some comments.

```
if (!isset($_POST['comments']) OR
→ empty($_POST['comments'])) {
        $errors[] = 'comments';
}
```

Comments really cannot be run through a regular expression pattern because any valid pattern would allow just about anything. Instead, a check for some value is made.

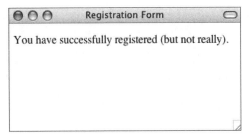

**Figure 4.2** If all of the data passed through the various checks, this message is displayed.

**Figure 4.3** A lot of mistakes were made in this registration attempt, each reported back to the user.

**11.** If there were no errors, report upon the success.

```
if (empty($errors)) {
    echo '<p>You have successfully
→ registered (but not
→ really).</p></body></html>';
    exit();
```

If no errors occurred, then `$errors` would still be empty. The script could then register the user (probably in a database). Here it just prints a message and terminates the script (so that the form isn't redisplayed) instead (**Figure 4.2**).

**12.** Report the errors.

```
} else {
    echo '<p>Problems exist with
→ the following field(s):<ul>';
    foreach ($errors as $error) {
        echo
→ "<li>$error</li>\n";
    }
    echo '</ul></p>';
}
```

If `$errors` isn't empty, it contains all of the fields that failed a validation test. These can be printed in a list (**Figure 4.3**).

**13.** Complete the main conditional and the PHP code.

```
} // End of $_POST['submitted'] IF.
?>
```

*continues on next page*

**14.** Create the HTML form.

```
<form method="post">
<fieldset>
<legend>Registration Form</legend>
<p>Name: <input type="text"
→ name="name" /></p>
<p>Email Address: <input type="text"
→ name="email" /></p>
<p>Password: <input type="password"
→ name="pass" /> (Letters and
→ numbers only.)</p>
<p>Date of Birth: <input type="text"
→ name="dob" value="MM/DD/YYYY" />
→ </p>
<p>ICQ Number: <input type="text"
→ name="icq" /></p>
<p>Comments: <textarea
→ name="comments" rows="5"
→ cols="40"></textarea></p>
<input type="hidden"
→ name="submitted" value="true" />
<input type="submit" name="submit"
→ value="Submit" />
</fieldset>
</form>
```

There's not much to say about the form except to point out that it does indicate the proper format for the password and date of birth fields. If you are validating data to a specification, it's important that the end user be made aware of the requirements as well, prior to submitting the form.

**15.** Complete the page.

```
</body>
</html>
```

**16.** Save the file as register.php, place it in your Web directory, and test in your Web browser.

## Using Captcha

Popular in many of today's forms is *captcha*, short for "completely automated public Turing test to tell computers and humans apart" (now *that's* an acronym!). A captcha test displays an image with a word or some letters written in it, normally in a nonlinear fashion. In order to successfully complete the form, the text from the image has to be typed into a box. This is something a human user could do but a bot could not.

If you do want to add this feature to your own sites, using the PEAR Text_CAPTCHA package would be the easiest route. Otherwise, you could generate the images yourself using the GD library. The word on the image should be stored in a session so that it can be compared against what the user typed.

The main caveat with captcha tests is that they do restrict the visually impaired from completing that form. You should be aware of this, and provide alternatives. Personally, I think that bots can be effectively stopped by just adding another input to your form, with an easy-to-answer question (like "What is 2 + 2?"). Humans can submit the answer, whereas bots could not.

### ✔ Tips

■ If possible, use the POST method in your forms. POST has a limitation in that the resulting page cannot be bookmarked, but it is far more secure and does not have the limit on transmittable data size that GET does. If a user is entering passwords, you really must use the POST method lest the password be visible.

■ Placing hidden values in HTML forms can be a great way to pass information from page to page without using cookies or sessions. But be careful what you hide in your HTML code, because those hidden values can be seen by viewing a page's source. This technique is a convenience, not a security measure.

■ Similarly, you should not be too obvious or reliant upon information PHP passes via the URL. For example, if a `homepage.php` page requires receipt of a user ID—and that is the only mandatory information for access to the account—someone else could easily break in (e.g., `www.example.com/userhome.php?user=2` could quickly be turned into `www.example.com/userhome.php?user=3`, granting access to someone else's information).

**VALIDATING FORM DATA**

135

# Using PECL Filter

New in PHP 5 and quite promising is the Filter library of PECL code. Being developed by PHP's creator and other major contributors, the future of Filter looks bright, even though it's still in beta form (at the time of this writing). The Filter package provides two types of security:

- Data validation by type
- Data sanitization

What Filter offers is a unified interface for performing common types of validation and sanitization. For example, I might commonly use code like this:

```
if (isset($_GET['id'])) {
    if (is_numeric($_GET['id'])) {
        $id = (int) $_GET['id'];
        if ($id > 0) {
            // Do whatever.
        }
    }
}
```

I could instead do this:

```
$id = filter_input(INPUT_GET, 'id',
→ FILTER_VALIDATE_INT, array('options'
→ =>array('min_range'=>1)));
if ($id) { …
```

That might look like jabberwocky, but once you get the hang of Filter, the amount of work you can do in just a line of code will be worth the learning curve.

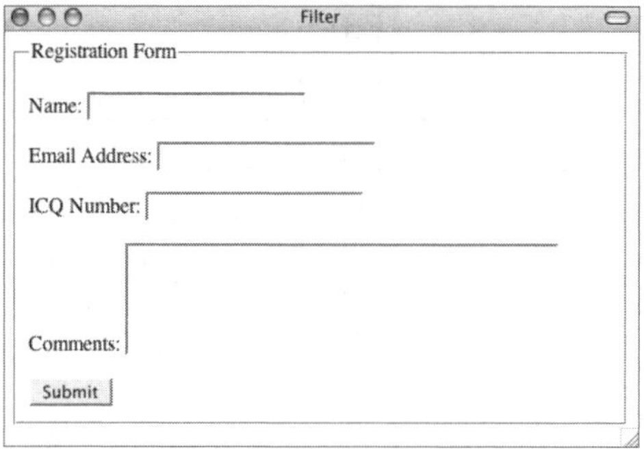

**Figure 4.4** This new registration form lacks the password and date of birth inputs.

To filter individual variables, there are two functions you'll use: `filter_input()` and `filter_var()`. The first one is for working with variables coming from an outside source, like forms, cookies, sessions, and the server. The second is for variables within your own code. I'll focus on `filter_input()` here. Its syntax is:

`$var = filter_input($variable_source,`
`→ $variable_name, $filter, $options);`

The sources, which the PHP manual calls "types," are: `INPUT_GET`, `INPUT_POST`, `INPUT_COOKIE`, `INPUT_SERVER`, `INPUT_ENV`, `INPUT_SESSION`, and `INPUT_REQUEST`. As you can probably guess, each of these corresponds to a global variable (`$_GET`, `$_POST`, etc.). For example, if a page receives data in the URL, you'd use `INPUT_GET` (not `$_GET`).

The second argument—the variable name—is the specific variable within the source that should be addressed. The `$filter` argument indicates the filter to apply, using the constants in **Table 4.2**. This argument is optional, as a default filter will be used if none is specified. Some filters also take options, like the `FILTER_VALIDATE_INT` in the preceding example (which can take a range).

The `filter_input()` function will return the filtered variable if the filtration or validation was successful, the Boolean `FALSE` if the filter didn't apply to the data, or the value `NULL` if the named variable didn't exist in the given input. Thus you have multiple levels of validation in just one step.

There's really a lot of information packed into just a few functions here, but I want to present a sample of how you would use the Filter library. To do so, I'll create a modified version of the registration form (**Figure 4.4**). Note that as of PHP 5.2, Filter is built into PHP. If you're using an earlier version, you may need to install it using the pecl installer (see the PHP manual for more).

**Table 4.2** These constants represent some of the filters that can be applied to data. For a complete list, see the PHP manual or invoke the `filter_list()` function.

| Filters by Name | |
| --- | --- |
| CONSTANT NAME | ACTION |
| FILTER_VALIDATE_INT | Confirms an integer, optionally in a range |
| FILTER_VALIDATE_FLOAT | Confirms a float |
| FILTER_ VALIDATE_REGEXP | Matches a PCRE pattern |
| FILTER_ VALIDATE_URL | Matches a URL |
| FILTER_ VALIDATE_EMAIL | Matches an email address |
| FILTER_SANITIZE_STRING | Strips tags |
| FILTER_SANITIZE_ENCODED | URL-encodes a string |

**USING PECL FILTER**

## To use PECL Filter:

1. Begin a new PHP script in your text editor or IDE, starting with the HTML (**Script 4.2**).

```
<!DOCTYPE html PUBLIC "-//W3C//DTD
→ XHTML 1.0 Transitional//EN"
"http://www.w3.org/TR/xhtml1/DTD/
→ xhtml1-transitional.dtd">
<html xmlns="http://www.w3.org/1999/
→ xhtml" xml:lang="en" lang="en">
<head>
    <meta http-equiv="content-type"
→ content="text/html; charset=iso-
→ 8859-1" />
```

```
<title>Filter</title>
    <style type="text/css"
→ title="text/css" media="all">
.error {
    color: #F30;
}
</style>
</head>
<body>
<?php # Script 4.2 - filter.php
```

The script has one CSS class for printing errors in a different color.

*continues on page 140*

**Script 4.2** With this minimalist registration form, the Filter library is used to perform data validation and sanitization.

```
1   <!DOCTYPE html PUBLIC "-//W3C//DTD XHTML 1.0 Transitional//EN"
2        "http://www.w3.org/TR/xhtml1/DTD/xhtml1-transitional.dtd">
3   <html xmlns="http://www.w3.org/1999/xhtml" xml:lang="en" lang="en">
4   <head>
5       <meta http-equiv="content-type" content="text/html; charset=iso-8859-1" />
6       <title>Filter</title>
7       <style type="text/css" title="text/css" media="all">
8   .error {
9       color: #F30;
10  }
11  </style>
12  </head>
13  <body>
14  <?php # Script 4.2 - filter.php
15
16  /*  This page uses the Filter functions
17   *  to validate form data.
18   *  This page will print out the filtered data.
19   */
20
21  if (isset($_POST['submitted'])) { // Handle the form.
22
23      // Sanitize the name:
24      $name = filter_input(INPUT_POST, 'name', FILTER_SANITIZE_STRING,
        FILTER_FLAG_NO_ENCODE_QUOTES);
25      if ($name) {
```

*(script continues on next page)*

**Script 4.2** *continued*

```
26        echo "<p>Name: $name<br />\$_POST['name']: {$_POST['name']}</p>\n";
27     } else {
28        echo '<p class="error">Please enter your name.</p>';
29     }
30
31     // Validate the email address using FILTER_VALIDATE_EMAIL:
32     $email = filter_input(INPUT_POST, 'email', FILTER_VALIDATE_EMAIL);
33     if ($email) {
34        echo "<p>Email Address: $email</p>\n";
35     } else {
36        echo '<p class="error">Please enter your email address.</p>';
37     }
38
39     // Validate the ICQ number using FILTER_VALIDATE_INT:
40     $icq = filter_input(INPUT_POST, 'icq', FILTER_VALIDATE_INT);
41     if ($icq) {
42        echo "<p>ICQ Number: $icq</p>\n";
43     } else {
44        echo '<p class="error">Please enter your ICQ number.</p>';
45     }
46
47     // Strip tags but don't encode quotes:
48     $comments = filter_input(INPUT_POST, 'comments', FILTER_SANITIZE_STRING);
49     if ($comments) {
50        echo "<p>Comments: $comments<br />\$_POST['comments']: {$_POST['comments']}</p>\n";
51     } else {
52        echo '<p class="error">Please enter your comments.</p>';
53     }
54
55  } // End of $_POST['submitted'] IF.
56
57  // Show the form.
58  ?>
59  <form method="post" action="filter.php">
60  <fieldset>
61  <legend>Registration Form</legend>
62  <p>Name: <input type="text" name="name" /></p>
63  <p>Email Address: <input type="text" name="email" /></p>
64  <p>ICQ Number: <input type="text" name="icq" /></p>
65  <p>Comments: <textarea name="comments" rows="5" cols="40"></textarea></p>
66
67  <input type="hidden" name="submitted" value="true" />
68  <input type="submit" name="submit" value="Submit" />
69  </fieldset>
70  </form>
71
72  </body>
73  </html>
```

**USING PECL FILTER**

**2.** Check for the form submission.

```
if (isset($_POST['submitted'])) {
```

**3.** Filter the name data.

```
$name = filter_input(INPUT_POST,
→ 'name', FILTER_SANITIZE_STRING,
→ FILTER_FLAG_NO_ENCODE_QUOTES);
```

For the name field, there's no type to validate against, but it can be filtered to remove any HTML tags. The FILTER_SANITIZE_STRING filter will accomplish that. The last argument, FILTER_FLAG_NO_ENCODE_QUOTES, says that any quotation marks in the name (e.g., O'Toole) shouldn't be turned into an HTML entity equivalent.

**4.** Print the name value or an error.

```
if ($name) {
        echo "<p>Name: $name<br
→ />\$_POST['name']:
→ {$_POST['name']}</p>\n";
} else {
        echo '<p class="error">Please
→ enter your name.</p>';
}
```

The conditional if ($name) will be true if the $_POST['name'] variable was set and passed the filter. In that case, I'll print the filtered version and the original version, just for comparison.

**5.** Validate the email address.

```
$email = filter_input(INPUT_POST,
→ 'email', FILTER_VALIDATE_EMAIL);
if ($email) {
        echo "<p>Email Address:
→ $email</p>\n";
} else {
        echo '<p class="error">Please
→ enter your email address.</p>';
}
```

The FILTER_VALIDATE_EMAIL filter is perfect here. If the submitted email address has a valid format, it will be returned. Otherwise, $email will equal either FALSE or NULL.

**6.** Validate the ICQ number.

```
$icq = filter_input(INPUT_POST,
→ 'icq', FILTER_VALIDATE_INT);
if ($icq) {
        echo "<p>ICQ Number:
→ $icq</p>\n";
} else {
        echo '<p class="error">Please
→ enter your ICQ number.</p>';
}
```

This is validated as an integer.

**7.** Filter the comments field.

```
$comments = filter_input(INPUT_POST,
→ 'comments', FILTER_SANITIZE_
→ STRING);
if ($comments) {
        echo "<p>Comments: $comments<br
→ />\$_POST['comments']:
{$_POST['comments']}</p>\n";
} else {
        echo '<p class="error">Please
→ enter your comments.</p>';
}
```

For the comments, any tags will be stripped (as with the name), but the quotation marks will also be encoded.

**8.** Complete the main conditional and the PHP code.

```
} // End of $_POST['submitted'] IF.
?>
```

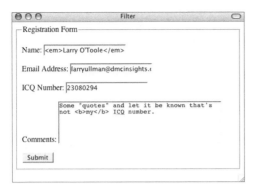

**Figure 4.5** These values will be submitted, then filtered, resulting in Figure 4.6.

**Figure 4.6** At the top of the form the filtered values are displayed.

**9.** Create the HTML form.

```
<form method="post"
→ action="filter.php">
<fieldset>
<legend>Registration Form</legend>
<p>Name: <input type="text"
→ name="name" /></p>
<p>Email Address: <input type="text"
→ name="email" /></p>
<p>ICQ Number: <input type="text"
→ name="icq" /></p>
<p>Comments: <textarea
→ name="comments" rows="5"
→ cols="40"></textarea></p>
<input type="hidden"
→ name="submitted" value="true" />
<input type="submit" name="submit"
→ value="Submit" />
</fieldset>
</form>
```

**10.** Complete the page.

```
</body>
</html>
```

**11.** Save the file as filter.php, place it in your Web directory, and test in your Web browser (**Figures 4.5** and **4.6**).

**12.** View the HTML source of the page to see how the name and comments fields were treated (**Figure 4.7**).

*continues on next page*

**Figure 4.7** The HTML source code shows how all tags are stripped from the name and comments fields, plus how quotation marks in the comments are encoded.

## ✔ Tips

- The `filter_has_var()` function checks to see if a variable with a given name exists within a greater array of variables. In this script, you could use this code to see if the form has been submitted:

```
if (filter_has_var(INPUT_POST,
→ 'submitted')) {
```

- To filter an array of variables, use `filter_input_array()`. In `filter.php`, you could just do this:

```
$filters = array(
'name' => FILTER_SANITIZE_STRING,
'email' => FILTER_VALIDATE_EMAIL,
'icq' => FILTER_VALIDATE_INT,
'comments' => array('filter' =>
→ FILTER_SANITIZE_STRING, 'flags' =>
→ FILTER_FLAG_NO_ENCODE_QUOTES)
);
$data = filter_input_array
→ (INPUT_POST, $filters);
```

From that point, you could just refer to `$data['name']`, etc.

- The `filter_var_array()` applies a filter, or an array of filters, to an array of data.

# Authentication with PEAR Auth

One of the more common elements in today's Web sites is an authentication system: users register with a site, they log in to gain access to some parts, and restricted pages allow or deny access accordingly. Such systems aren't hard to implement—I've done so in some of my other books—but here I'd like to look at what PEAR has to offer.

The PEAR Auth package provides a really easy, yet customizable authentication system. To show it off, I'll start with one very simple example. This will mostly demonstrate its basic usage. Then I'll show how to customize the authentication system to fit it into a larger application. For both examples, you'll need to install the PEAR Auth package. Because the authentication information is stored in a database, the PEAR DB package must also be installed. If you're not familiar with PEAR and its installation, see Chapter 12, "Using PEAR," or `http://pear.php.net`.

## ✔ Tip

- For these examples I will put both the authentication code and the restricted page data in the same file. In a larger Web site, you'll likely want to separate the authentication code into its own file, which is then included by any file that requires authentication.

## Simple authentication

This first, simple authentication example shows how easily you can implement authentication in a page. I'll run through the syntax and concepts first, and then create a script that executes it all.

To begin, require the Auth class:

```
require_once ('Auth.php');
```

Next, you'll need to define a function that creates a login form. This function will be called when an unauthorized user is trying to access a page. The form should use the POST method and have inputs called *username* and *password*.

Then, for database-driven authentication, which is the norm, you'll need to create a "DSN" within an options array. DSN stands for *data source name*. It's just a string of information that indicates the type of database application being used, the username, password, and hostname to connect as, and the database to select. That code might be:

```
$options = array('dsn' =>
→ 'mysql://username:password@localhost/
→ databasename');
```

Now that those two things have been defined—the function that makes the login form and the DSN—you can create an object of Auth type. Provide this object three arguments: the type of authentication back end to use (e.g., database or file), the options (that correspond to the authentication type), and the name of the login function:

```
$auth = new Auth('DB', $options,
→ 'login_form_function_name');
```

```
⊕ ○ ○     PHP Advanced: Visual QuickPro Guide
mysql> CREATE DATABASE auth;
Query OK, 1 row affected (0.00 sec)

mysql> USE auth;
Database changed
mysql> CREATE TABLE auth (
    -> username VARCHAR(50) NOT NULL,
    -> password VARCHAR(32) NOT NULL,
    -> PRIMARY KEY (username),
    -> KEY (password)
    -> )
    -> ;
Query OK, 0 rows affected (0.01 sec)

mysql> █
```

**Figure 4.8** Creating the database and table required by the simple authentication example.

The *DB* option tells Auth to use the PEAR DB package. If you wanted to use a file system instead, you would use *File* as the first argument and the name of the file as the second.

Now, start the authentication process:

`$auth->start();`

From there, you can check if a user is authenticated by calling the checkAuth() method:

```
if ($auth->checkAuth()) {
    // Do whatever.
```

And that's simple authentication in a nutshell! This next example will implement all this. It will also invoke the addUser() method to add a new authenticated user, which can then be used for logging in. One last note: this example will make use of a database called auth, which must be created prior to writing this script. It should have a table called auth, defined like so:

```
CREATE TABLE auth (
username VARCHAR(50) NOT NULL,
password VARCHAR(32) NOT NULL,
PRIMARY KEY (username),
KEY (password)
)
```

Be certain that you've created this database and table (**Figure 4.8**), and that you have created a MySQL user that has access to them, prior to going any further.

AUTHENTICATION WITH PEAR AUTH

## To perform simple authentication:

**1.** Begin a new PHP script in your text editor or IDE (**Script 4.3**).

```
<?php # Script 4.3 - login.php
```

Because Auth relies on sessions (it'll start the sessions for you), it's best to do as much as you can before sending any HTML to the Web browser. So I'll write most of the authentication code, and only then begin the HTML page.

*continues on page 148*

**Script 4.3** Using PEAR Auth and a MySQL table, this script enforces authentication.

```
1    <?php # Script 4.3 - login.php
2
3    /*  This page uses PEAR Auth to control access.
4     *  This assumes a database called "auth",
5     *  accessible to a MySQL user of "username@localhost"
6     *  with a password of "password".
7     *  Table definition:
8
9        CREATE TABLE auth (
10       username VARCHAR(50) default '' NOT NULL,
11       password VARCHAR(32) default '' NOT NULL,
12       PRIMARY KEY (username),
13       KEY (password)
14       )
15     *  MD5() is used to encrypt the passwords.
16     */
17
18   // Need the PEAR class:
19   require_once ('Auth.php');
20
21   // Function for showing a login form:
22   function show_login_form() {
23
24       echo '<form method="post" action="login.php">
25   <p>Username <input type="text" name="username" /></p>
26   <p>Password <input type="password" name="password" /></p>
```

*(script continues on next page)*

**Script 4.3** *continued*

```
     ┌─────────────────────────────────────────────────────────────────┐
     │ ○ ○ ○                         📄 Script                          │
     ├─────────────────────────────────────────────────────────────────┤
27   <input type="submit" value="Login" />
28   </form><br />
29   ';
30
31   } // End of show_login_form() function.
32
33   // Connect to the database:
34   $options = array('dsn' => 'mysql://username:password@localhost/auth');
35
36   // Create the Auth object:
37   $auth = new Auth('DB', $options, 'show_login_form');
38
39   // Add a new user:
40   $auth->addUser('me', 'mypass');
41
42   ?><!DOCTYPE html PUBLIC "-//W3C//DTD XHTML 1.0 Transitional//EN"
43           "http://www.w3.org/TR/xhtml1/DTD/xhtml1-transitional.dtd">
44   <html xmlns="http://www.w3.org/1999/xhtml" xml:lang="en" lang="en">
45   <head>
46       <meta http-equiv="content-type" content="text/html; charset=iso-8859-1" />
47       <title>Restricted Page</title>
48   </head>
49   <body>
50   <?php
51
52   // Start the authorization:
53   $auth->start();
54
55   // Confirm authorization:
56   if ($auth->checkAuth()) {
57
58       echo '<p>You are logged in and can read this. How cool is that?</p>';
59
60   } else { // Unauthorized.
61
62       echo '<p>You must be logged in to access this page.</p>';
63
64   }
65
66   ?>
67   </body>
68   </html>
```

AUTHENTICATION WITH PEAR AUTH

**2.** Include the Auth class.

```
require_once ('Auth.php');
```

If you haven't installed PEAR Auth yet, do so now. See the PEAR manual for instructions.

**3.** Define the function that creates the login form.

```
function show_login_form() {
echo '<form method="post"
→ action="login.php">
<p>Username <input type="text"
→ name="username" /></p>
<p>Password <input type="password"
→ name="password" /></p>
<input type="submit" value="Login" />
</form><br />
';
}
```

The only requirements are that this form has one input called *username* and another called *password*.

**4.** Create the options array.

```
$options = array('dsn' =>
→ 'mysql://username:password@
→ localhost/auth');
```

This code says that a connection should be made to a MySQL database called *auth*, using *username* as the username, *password* as the password, and *localhost* as the host.

**5.** Create the Auth object.

```
$auth = new Auth('DB', $options,
→ 'show_login_form');
```

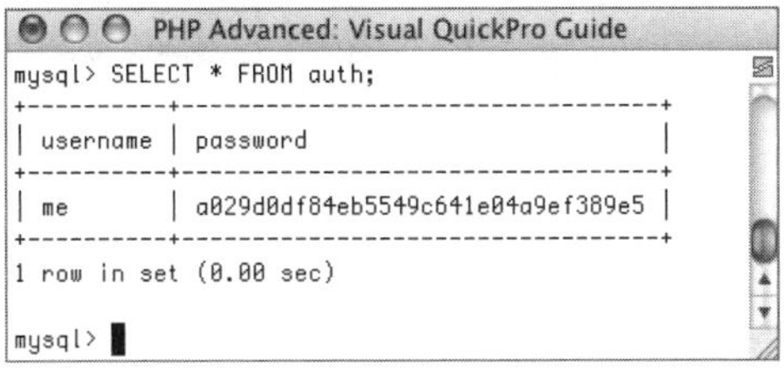

**Figure 4.9** One user has been added to the table. The password is encrypted using the MD5() function.

**6.** Add a new user and complete the PHP section.

```
$auth->addUser('me', 'mypass');
?>
```

The addUser() functions takes the username as its first argument and the password as the second. This record will be added to the database as soon as the script is first run (**Figure 4.9**). Because the username column in the table is defined as a primary key, MySQL will never allow a second user with the name of *me* to be added.

In a real application, you'd have a registration process that would just end up calling this function in the end.

**7.** Add the initial HTML code.

```
<!DOCTYPE html PUBLIC "-//W3C//DTD
→ XHTML 1.0 Transitional//EN"
"http://www.w3.org/TR/xhtml1/DTD/
→ xhtml1-transitional.dtd">
<html xmlns="http://www.w3.org/1999/
→ xhtml" xml:lang="en" lang="en">
<head>
    <meta http-equiv="content-type"
→ content="text/html; charset=iso-
→ 8859-1" />
    <title>Restricted Page</title>
</head>
<body>
```

**8.** Start the authentication.

```
<?php
$auth->start();
```

*continues on next page*

**AUTHENTICATION WITH PEAR AUTH**

**9.** Display different messages based upon the authentication status.

```
if ($auth->checkAuth()) {
    echo '<p>You are logged in and
→ can read this. How cool is
→ that?</p>';
} else {
    echo '<p>You must be logged in
→ to access this page.</p>';
}
```

When a user first comes to this page, and `$auth->checkAuth()` is false, they'll see the login form plus this second message (**Figure 4.10**). After logging in with a valid username/password combination, they'll see this first message (**Figure 4.11**).

**10.** Complete the page.

```
?>
</body>
</html>
```

**11.** Save the file as `login.php`, place it in your Web directory, and test in your Web browser.

Use *me* as the username and *mypass* as the password.

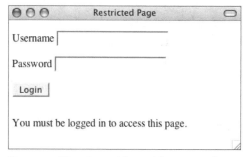

**Figure 4.10** When first arriving at this page, or after an unsuccessful login attempt, a user sees this.

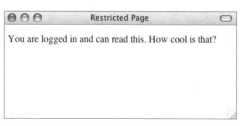

**Figure 4.11** The result after successfully logging in.

## Implementing Optional Authentication

If some of your Web site's pages do not require authentication but could still acknowledge logged-in users, that's an option with Auth, too. To make authentication optional, add a fourth parameter when creating the Auth object:

```
$auth = new Auth('DB', $options,
→ 'show_login_form', true);
```

To limit aspects of a page to authenticated users, invoke the `getAuth()` method:

```
if ($auth->getAuth()) {
    // Restricted access content.
}
```

# Custom authentication

The preceding example does a fine job of showing how easy it is to use PEAR Auth, but it doesn't demonstrate how you would actually use it in a more full-fledged application. By this I mean a site that has a table with more than two columns and needs to store, and retrieve, other information as well.

The first change you'll need to make is to the options array used when creating the Auth object. Different storage types ("containers" in Auth parlance) have different options. **Table 4.3** lists some of the other options you can use with DB.

For example, the DB container will use a combination of the *usernamecol* and *passwordcol* (encrypted using *cryptType*) to authenticate the user against the submitted values. The preceding example used the defaults, but you can change this information easily. Just as important, you can specify what other database columns should be retrieved. These will then be available in the session data and can be retrieved in your script through the getAuthData() function:

```
echo $auth->getAuthData('column_name');
```

Three other functions you can use to customize the authentication are setExpire(), setIdle(), and setSessionName(). The first takes a value, in seconds, when the session should be set to expire. The second takes a value, in seconds, when a user should be considered idle (because it's been too long since their last activity). The third function changes the name of the session (which is *PHPSESSID*, by default).

For this next example, a new table will be used, still in the auth database. To create it, use this SQL command (**Figure 4.12**):

```
CREATE TABLE users (
user_id INT UNSIGNED NOT NULL
→ AUTO_INCREMENT,
email VARCHAR(60) NOT NULL,
pass CHAR(40) NOT NULL,
first_name VARCHAR (20) NOT NULL,
last_name VARCHAR(40) NOT NULL,
PRIMARY KEY (user_id),
UNIQUE (email),
KEY (email, pass)
)
```

This table represents how you might already have some sort of user table, with its own columns, that you'd want to use with Auth.

**Table 4.3** These are some of the parameters you can set when creating a new Auth object that uses DB.

| DB Container Options | |
| --- | --- |
| OPTION | INDICATES |
| dsn | The Data Source Name |
| table | The database table to use |
| usernamecol | The name of the username column |
| passwordcol | The name of the password column |
| db_fields | What other table fields should be selected |
| cryptType | The function used to encrypt the password |

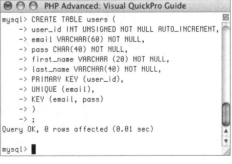

**Figure 4.12** Creating the table used by the custom authentication system.

## To use custom authentication:

1. Begin a new PHP script in your text editor or IDE, starting with the HTML (**Script 4.4**).

```
<?php # Script 4.4 - custom_auth.php

require_once ('Auth.php');
```

*continues on page 154*

**Script 4.4** In this script, Auth uses a different table, different column names, and a different encryption function for the password. It selects every column from the table, making all the previously stored data available to the page.

```
1    <?php # Script 4.4 - custom_auth.php
2
3    /*  This page uses PEAR Auth to control access.
4     *  This assumes a database called "auth",
5     *  accessible to a MySQL user of "username@localhost"
6     *  with a password of "password".
7     *  Table definition:
8
9        CREATE TABLE users (
10       user_id INT UNSIGNED NOT NULL AUTO_INCREMENT,
11       email VARCHAR(60) NOT NULL,
12       pass CHAR(40) NOT NULL,
13       first_name VARCHAR (20) NOT NULL,
14       last_name VARCHAR(40) NOT NULL,
15       PRIMARY KEY (user_id),
16       UNIQUE (email),
17       KEY (email, pass)
18       )
19
20     *  SHA1() is used to encrypt the passwords.
21     */
22
23    // Need the PEAR class:
24    require_once ('Auth.php');
25
26    // Function for showing a login form:
27    function show_login_form() {
28
29        echo '<form method="post" action="custom_auth.php">
30    <p>Email <input type="text" name="username" /></p>
31    <p>Password <input type="password" name="password" /></p>
32    <input type="submit" value="Login" />
33    </form><br />
34    ';
35
```

*(script continues on next page)*

**Script 4.4** *continued*

```
 36    } // End of show_login_form() function.
 37
 38    // All options:
 39    // Use specific username and password columns.
 40    // Use SHA1() to encrypt the passwords.
 41    // Retrieve all fields.
 42    $options = array(
 43    'dsn' => 'mysql://username:password@localhost/auth',
 44    'table' => 'users',
 45    'usernamecol' => 'email',
 46    'passwordcol' => 'pass',
 47    'cryptType' => 'sha1',
 48    'db_fields' => '*'
 49    );
 50
 51    // Create the Auth object:
 52    $auth = new Auth('DB', $options, 'show_login_form');
 53
 54    // Add a new user:
 55    $auth->addUser('me@example.com', 'mypass', array('first_name' => 'Larry', 'last_name' =>
       'Ullman'));
 56
 57    ?><!DOCTYPE html PUBLIC "-//W3C//DTD XHTML 1.0 Transitional//EN"
 58        "http://www.w3.org/TR/xhtml1/DTD/xhtml1-transitional.dtd">
 59    <html xmlns="http://www.w3.org/1999/xhtml" xml:lang="en" lang="en">
 60    <head>
 61        <meta http-equiv="content-type" content="text/html; charset=iso-8859-1" />
 62        <title>Restricted Page</title>
 63    </head>
 64    <body>
 65    <?php
 66
 67    // Start the authorization:
 68    $auth->start();
 69
 70    // Confirm authorization:
 71    if ($auth->checkAuth()) {
 72
 73        // Print the user's name:
 74        echo "<p>You, {$auth->getAuthData('first_name')} {$auth->getAuthData('last_name')}, are
       logged in and can read this. How cool is that?</p>";
 75
 76    } else { // Unauthorized.
 77
 78        echo '<p>You must be logged in to access this page.</p>';
 79
 80    }
 81
 82    ?>
 83    </body>
 84    </html>
```

AUTHENTICATION WITH PEAR AUTH

**2.** Define the show_login_form() function.

```
function show_login_form() {
        echo '<form method="post"
→ action="custom_auth.php">
<p>Email <input type="text"
→ name="username" /></p>
<p>Password <input type="password"
→ name="password" /></p>
<input type="submit" value="Login" />
</form><br />
';
}
```

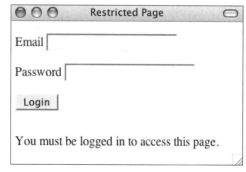

**Figure 4.13** The customized login form.

The function is mostly the same as it was before, except this time the action points to this script, custom_auth.php. The form also labels the one input as *Email* (**Figure 4.13**), even though it's named *username* (as required).

**3.** Establish the authorization options and create the object.

```
$options = array(
'dsn' => 'mysql://username:password@
→ localhost/auth',
'table' => 'users',
'usernamecol' => 'email',
'passwordcol' => 'pass',
'cryptType' => 'sha1',
'db_fields' => '*'
);
$auth = new Auth('DB', $options,
→ 'show_login_form');
```

The DSN is the same as it was before. Next, the *table*, *usernamecol*, and *passwordcol* values are all specified. These match the table already created (Figure 4.12). The *cryptType* value says that the passwords should be encoded using *SHA1()*, instead of the default MD5(). The final element in the $options array says that every column from the table should be retrieved. In this particular script, this will allow the page to refer to the logged-in user by name.

## Creating a Logout Feature

To add a logout to your authentication system, place this code on a logout page:

```
$auth = new Auth('DB', $options,
→ 'show_login_form');
$auth->start();
if ($auth->checkAuth()) {
    $auth->logout();
    $auth->start();
}
```

Just as when using sessions, you need to start the authentication in order to destroy it. You should then confirm that the user is authenticated, using checkAuth(), prior to logging out. Then call the logout() method to de-authenticate the user. Calling the start() method again will redisplay the login form.

**4.** Add a new user and complete the initial PHP section (**Figure 4.14**).

```
$auth->addUser('me@example.com',
→ 'mypass', array('first_name' =>
→ 'Larry', 'last_name' => 'Ullman'));
?>
```

Because the table has more than just the two columns, the extra columns and values have to be provided, as an array, as the third argument to the addUser() method. This call of the function is the equivalent of running this query:

```
INSERT INTO users (email, pass,
→ first_name, last_name) VALUES
→ ('me@example.com', SHA1('mypass'),
→ 'Larry', 'Ullman')
```

**5.** Create the initial HTML code.

```
<!DOCTYPE html PUBLIC "-//W3C//DTD
→ XHTML 1.0 Transitional//EN"
"http://www.w3.org/TR/xhtml1/DTD/
→ xhtml1-transitional.dtd">
<html xmlns="http://www.w3.org/1999/
→ xhtml" xml:lang="en" lang="en">
<head>
    <meta http-equiv="content-type"
→ content="text/html; charset=iso-
→ 8859-1" />
    <title>Restricted Page</title>
</head>
<body>
```

*continues on next page*

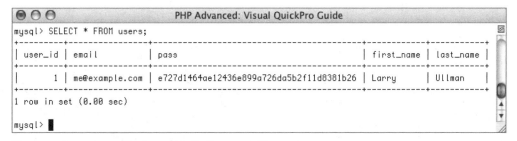

**Figure 4.14** A sample user has been added to the users table.

**AUTHENTICATION WITH PEAR AUTH**

**6.** Start the authorization.

```php
<?php
$auth->start();
```

**7.** Print the authorization status.

```php
if ($auth->checkAuth()) {
    echo "<p>You, {$auth->get
→ AuthData('first_name')}
→ {$auth->getAuthData('last_name')},
→ are logged in and can read this.
→ How cool is that?</p>";
} else {
    echo '<p>You must be logged in
→ to access this page.</p>';
}
```

The result if the user isn't logged in looks like Figure 4.13. When the user does log in, they are greeted by name (**Figure 4.15**). The getAuthData() function can access the values selected from the table and stored in the authentication session.

**8.** Complete the page.

```php
?>
</body>
</html>
```

**9.** Save the file as custom_auth.php, place it in your Web directory, and test in your Web browser.

### ✔ Tips

- You can add, on the fly, other data to the authentication session using setAuthData():

  ```php
  setAuthData($name, $value);
  ```

- You can also improve authentication security via the setAdvancedSecurity() method. It uses both cookies and JavaScript to lessen the possibility of someone hacking an authenticated session.

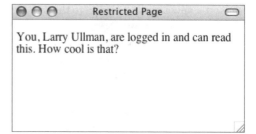

**Figure 4.15** After successfully logging in, the user is greeted by name. The name was pulled from the table and stored in the session.

## Using Auth_HTTP

One of the potential problems with Auth is that it relies upon sessions, which can introduce some security concerns. A more secure option is to use HTTP authentication via Auth_HTTP. HTTP authentication uses a pop-up window, separate from the HTML page, that takes a username and password.

The benefits of HTTP authentication are these:

- The entered username and password are remembered without needing to send cookies or establish sessions.

- The clean interface will not interfere with your page design.

The downsides are:

- Inability to create a logout feature

- Inability to establish user groups or specify access levels

- Inability to set an expiration time

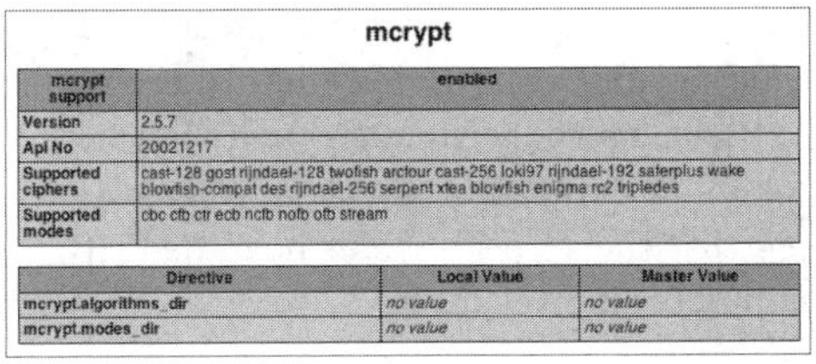
mcrypt

| mcrypt support | enabled |
|---|---|
| Version | 2.5.7 |
| Api No | 20021217 |
| Supported ciphers | cast-128 gost rijndael-128 twofish arcfour cast-256 loki97 rijndael-192 saferplus wake blowfish-compat des rijndael-256 serpent xtea blowfish enigma rc2 tripledes |
| Supported modes | cbc cfb ctr ecb ncfb nofb ofb stream |

| Directive | Local Value | Master Value |
|---|---|---|
| mcrypt.algorithms_dir | no value | no value |
| mcrypt.modes_dir | no value | no value |

**Figure 4.16** Run a `phpinfo()` script to confirm your server's support for MCrypt.

# Using MCrypt

Frequently Web applications will encrypt and decrypt data stored in a database, using the database-supplied functions. This is appropriate, as you want the database to do the bulk of the work whenever possible. But what if you want to encrypt and decrypt data that's not being stored in a database? In that situation, MCrypt is the best solution. To use MCrypt with PHP, you'll need to install the MCrypt library (libmcrypt, available from `http://mcrypt.sourceforge.net`) and configure PHP to support it (**Figure 4.16**).

For this example, I'll show you how to encrypt data stored in a cookie, making it that much more secure. Because the encryption process creates binary data, the `base64_encode()` function will be applied to the encrypted data prior to storing it in a cookie. Therefore, the `base64_decode()` function needs to be used prior to decoding the data. Other than that little tidbit, the focus in the next two scripts is entirely on MCrypt.

Do keep in mind that in the next several pages I'll be introducing and teaching concepts to which people have dedicated entire careers. The information covered here will be secure, useful, and valid, but it's just the tip of the proverbial iceberg.

# Encrypting data

With MCrypt libraries 2.4.x and higher, you start by identifying which algorithm and mode to use by invoking the `mcrypt_module_open()` function:

```
$m = mcrypt_module_open (algorithm,
→ algorithm_directory, mode,
→ mode_directory);
```

MCrypt comes with dozens of different algorithms, or *ciphers*, each of which encrypts data differently. If you are interested in how each works, see the MCrypt home page or search the Web. In my examples, I'll be using the Rijndael algorithm, also known as the Advanced Encryption Standard (AES). It's a very popular and secure encryption algorithm, even up to United States government standards. I'll be using it with 256-bit keys, for extra security.

As for the mode, there are four main modes: ECB (electronic codebook), CBC (cipher block chaining), CFB (cipher feedback), and OFB (output feedback). CBC will suit most of your needs, especially when encrypting blocks of text as in this example. So to indicate that you want to use Rijndael 256 in CBC mode, you would code:

```
$m = mcrypt_module_open('rijndael-
→ 256', '', 'cbc', '');
```

The second and fourth arguments fed to the `mcrypt_module_open()` function are for explicitly stating where PHP can find the algorithm and mode files. These are not required unless PHP is unable to find a cipher and you know for certain it is installed.

Once the module is open, you create an IV (initialization vector). This may be required, optional, or unnecessary depending upon the mode being used. I'll use it with CBC, to increase the security. Here's how the PHP manual recommends an IV be created:

```
$iv = mcrypt_create_iv
→ (mcrypt_enc_get_iv_size ($m),
→ MCRYPT_DEV_RANDOM);
```

By using the `mcrypt_enc_get_iv_size()` function, a properly sized IV will be created for the cipher being used. Note that on Windows, you should use `MCRYPT_RAND` instead of `MCRYPT_DEV_RANDOM`, and call the `srand()` function before this line to ensure the random generation.

The final step before you are ready to encrypt data is to create the buffers that MCrypt needs to perform encryption:

```
mcrypt_generic_init ($m, $key, $iv);
```

The second argument is a key, which should be a hard-to-guess string. The key must be of a particular length, corresponding to the cipher you use. The Rijndael cipher I'm using takes a 256-bit key. Divide 256 by 8 (because there are 8 bits in a byte and each character in the key string takes one byte) and you'll see that the key needs to be exactly 32 characters long. To accomplish that, and to randomize the key even more, I'll run it through `MD5()`, which always returns a 32-character string:

```
$key = MD5('some string');
```

Once you have gone through these steps, you are ready to encrypt data:

```
$encrypted_data = mcrypt_generic ($m,
→ $data);
```

Finally, after you have finished encrypting everything, you should close all the buffers and modules:

```
mcrypt_generic_denit ($m);

mcrypt_module_close($m);
```

For this example, I'm going to create a cookie whose value is encrypted. The cookie data will be decrypted in the next example. The key and data to be encrypted will be hardcoded into this script, but I'll mention alternatives in the following steps. Also, because the same key and IV are needed to decrypt the data, the IV will also be sent in a cookie. Surprisingly, doing so doesn't hurt the security of the application.

## To encrypt data:

1. Begin a new PHP script in your text editor or IDE (**Script 4.5**).

   ```
   <?php # Script 4.5 -
   → set_mcrypt_cookie.php
   ```

   Because the script will send two cookies, most of the PHP code will come before any HTML.

2. Define the key and the data.

   ```
   $key = md5('77 public drop-shadow
   → Java');
   $data = 'rosebud';
   ```

   For the key, some random words and numbers are run through the MD5() function, creating a 32-character-long string. Ideally, the key should be stored in a safe place, such as a configuration file located outside of the Web document root. Or it could be retrieved from a database.

   The data being encrypted is the word *rosebud*, although in real applications this data might come from the database or another source (and be something more worth protecting).

3. Open the cipher.

   ```
   $m = mcrypt_module_open('rijndael-
   → 256', '', 'cbc', '');
   ```

   This is the same code outlined in the text before these steps.

*continues on page 162*

**Script 4.5** This script uses MCrypt to encrypt some data to be stored in a cookie.

```php
1    <?php # Script 4.5 - set_mcrypt_cookie.php
2
3    /*  This page uses the MCrypt library
4     *  to encrypt some data.
5     *  The data will then be stored in a cookie,
6     *  as will the encryption IV.
7     */
8
9    // Create the key:
10   $key = md5('77 public drop-shadow Java');
11
12   // Data to be encrypted:
13   $data = 'rosebud';
14
15   // Open the cipher:
16   // Using Rijndael 256 in CBC mode.
17   $m = mcrypt_module_open('rijndael-256', '', 'cbc', '');
18
19   // Create the IV:
20   // Use MCRYPT_RAND on Windows instead of MCRYPT_DEV_RANDOM.
21   $iv = mcrypt_create_iv(mcrypt_enc_get_iv_size($m), MCRYPT_DEV_RANDOM);
22
23   // Initialize the encryption:
24   mcrypt_generic_init($m, $key, $iv);
25
26   // Encrypt the data:
27   $data = mcrypt_generic($m, $data);
28
29   // Close the encryption handler:
30   mcrypt_generic_deinit($m);
31
32   // Close the cipher:
33   mcrypt_module_close($m);
34
35   // Set the cookies:
36   setcookie('thing1', base64_encode($data));
37   setcookie('thing2', base64_encode($iv));
38   ?><!DOCTYPE html PUBLIC "-//W3C//DTD XHTML 1.0 Transitional//EN"
39        "http://www.w3.org/TR/xhtml1/DTD/xhtml1-transitional.dtd">
40   <html xmlns="http://www.w3.org/1999/xhtml" xml:lang="en" lang="en">
41   <head>
42       <meta http-equiv="content-type" content="text/html; charset=iso-8859-1" />
43       <title>A More Secure Cookie</title>
44   </head>
45   <body>
46   <p>The cookie has been sent. Its value is '<?php echo base64_encode($data); ?>'.</p>
47   </body>
48   </html>
```

**4.** Create the IV.

```
$iv = mcrypt_create_iv
→ (mcrypt_enc_get_iv_size($m),
→ MCRYPT_DEV_RANDOM);
```

Again, this is the same code outlined earlier. Remember that if you are running this script on Windows, you'll need to change this line to:

```
srand();
```

```
$iv = mcrypt_create_iv
→ (mcrypt_enc_get_iv_size($m),
→ MCRYPT_RAND);
```

**5.** Initialize the encryption.

```
mcrypt_generic_init($m, $key, $iv);
```

**6.** Encrypt the data.

```
$data = mcrypt_generic($m, $data);
```

If you were to print the value of $data now, you'd see something like **Figure 4.17**.

**7.** Perform the necessary cleanup.

```
mcrypt_generic_deinit($m);
mcrypt_module_close($m);
```

**8.** Send the two cookies.

```
setcookie('thing1',
→ base64_encode($data));
setcookie('thing2',
→ base64_encode($iv));
```

For the cookie names, I'm using meaningless values. You certainly wouldn't want to use, say, *IV*, as a cookie name! For the cookie data itself, you have to run it through `base64_encode()` to make it safe to store in a cookie. This applies to both the encrypted data and the IV (which is also in binary format).

If the data were going to be stored in a binary file or in a database (in a BLOB column), you wouldn't need to use `base64_encode()`.

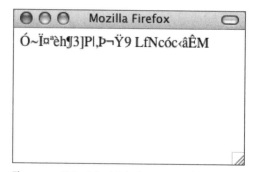

**Figure 4.17** This gibberish is the encrypted data in binary form.

**Figure 4.18** The result of running the page.

**Figure 4.19** The first cookie stores the actual data.

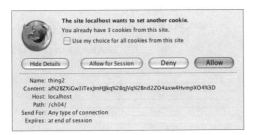

**Figure 4.20** The second cookie stores the base64_encode() version of the IV.

9. Add the HTML head.

```
?><!DOCTYPE html PUBLIC "-//W3C//DTD
→ XHTML 1.0 Transitional//EN"
"http://www.w3.org/TR/xhtml1/DTD/
→ xhtml1-transitional.dtd">
<html xmlns="http://www.w3.org/1999/
→ xhtml" xml:lang="en" lang="en">
<head>
    <meta http-equiv="content-type"
→ content="text/html; charset=iso-
→ 8859-1" />
    <title>A More Secure
→ Cookie</title>
</head>
<body>
```

10. Print a message, including the encoded, encrypted version of the data.

```
<p>The cookie has been sent. Its
→ value is '<?php echo
→ base64_encode($data); ?>'.</p>
```

I'm doing this mostly so that the page shows something (**Figure 4.18**), but also so that you can see the value stored in the cookie.

11. Complete the page.

```
</body>
</html>
```

12. Save the file as set_mcrypt_cookie.php, place it in your Web directory, and test in your Web browser.

If you set your browser to show cookies being sent, you'll see the values when you run the page (**Figures 4.19** and **4.20**).

## ✔ Tips

■ If you want to determine the length of the key on the fly, use the mcrypt_end_get_key_size() function:

```
$ks = mcrypt_end_get_key_size($m);
```

■ There's an argument to be made that you *shouldn't* apply the MD5() function to the key because it actually decreases the security of the key. I've used it here regardless, but it's the kind of issue that legitimate cryptographers think about.

## Decrypting data

When it's time to decrypt encrypted data, most of the process is the same as it is for encryption. To start:

```
$m = mcrypt_module_open('rijndael-
→ 256', '', 'cbc', '');
mcrypt_generic_init($m, $key, $iv);
```

At this point, instead of using mcrypt_generic(), you'll use mdecrypt_generic():

```
$data = mdecrypt_generic($m,
→ $encrypted_data);
```

Note, and this is very important, that to successfully decrypt the data, you'll need the *exact same key and IV* used to encrypt it.

Once decryption has taken place, you can close up your resources:

```
mcrypt_generic_deinit($m);
mcrypt_module_close($m);
```

Finally, you'll likely want to apply the rtrim() function to the decrypted data, as the encryption process may add white space as padding to the end of the data.

## To decrypt data:

1. Begin a new PHP script in your text editor or IDE, starting with the HTML (**Script 4.6**).

```
<!DOCTYPE html PUBLIC "-//W3C//DTD
→ XHTML 1.0 Transitional//EN"
"http://www.w3.org/TR/xhtml1/DTD/
→ xhtml1-transitional.dtd">
<html xmlns="http://www.w3.org/1999/
→ xhtml" xml:lang="en" lang="en">
<head>
    <meta http-equiv="content-type"
→ content="text/html; charset=iso-
→ 8859-1" />
    <title>A More Secure
→ Cookie</title>
</head>
<body>
<?php # Script 4.6 -
→ read_mcrypt_cookie.php
```

*continues on page 166*

**Script 4.6** This script reads in a cookie with encrypted data (plus a second cookie that stores an important piece for decryption); then it decrypts and prints the data.

```
Script
1    <!DOCTYPE html PUBLIC "-//W3C//DTD XHTML 1.0 Transitional//EN"
2          "http://www.w3.org/TR/xhtml1/DTD/xhtml1-transitional.dtd">
3    <html xmlns="http://www.w3.org/1999/xhtml" xml:lang="en" lang="en">
4    <head>
5        <meta http-equiv="content-type" content="text/html; charset=iso-8859-1" />
6        <title>A More Secure Cookie</title>
7    </head>
8    <body>
9    <?php # Script 4.6 - read_mcrypt_cookie.php
10
11   /*  This page uses the MCrypt library
12    *  to decrypt data stored in a cookie.
13    */
14
15   // Make sure the cookies exist:
16   if (isset($_COOKIE['thing1']) && isset($_COOKIE['thing2'])) {
17
18       // Create the key:
19       $key = md5('77 public drop-shadow Java');
20
21       // Open the cipher:
22       // Using Rijndael 256 in CBC mode.
23       $m = mcrypt_module_open('rijndael-256', '', 'cbc', '');
24
25       // Decode the IV:
26       $iv = base64_decode($_COOKIE['thing2']);
27
28       // Initialize the encryption:
29       mcrypt_generic_init($m, $key, $iv);
30
31       // Decrypt the data:
32       $data = mdecrypt_generic($m, base64_decode($_COOKIE['thing1']));
33
34       // Close the encryption handler:
35       mcrypt_generic_deinit($m);
36
37       // Close the cipher:
38       mcrypt_module_close($m);
39
40       // Print the data.
41       echo '<p>The cookie has been received. Its value is "' . trim($data) . '".</p>';
42
43   } else { // No cookies!
44       echo '<p>There\'s nothing to see here.</p>';
45   }
46   ?>
47   </body>
48   </html>
```

2. Check that the cookies exist.

```
if (isset($_COOKIE['thing1']) &&
→ isset($_COOKIE['thing2'])) {
```

There's no point in trying to decrypt the data if the page can't read the two cookies.

3. Create the key.

```
$key = md5('77 public drop-shadow
→ Java');
```

Not to belabor the point, but again, this must be the exact same key used to encrypt the data. This is another reason why you might want to store the key outside of these scripts.

4. Open the cipher.

```
$m = mcrypt_module_open('rijndael-
→ 256', '', 'cbc', '');
```

This should also match the encryption code (you have to use the same cipher and mode for both encryption and decryption).

5. Decode the IV.

```
$iv = base64_decode
→ ($_COOKIE['thing2']);
```

The IV isn't being generated here; it's being retrieved from the cookie (because it has to be the same IV as was used to encrypt the data). The base64_decode() function will return the IV to its binary form.

6. Initialize the decryption.

```
mcrypt_generic_init($m, $key, $iv);
```

7. Decrypt the data.

```
$data = mdecrypt_generic($m,
→ base64_decode($_COOKIE['thing1']));
```

The mdecrypt_generic() function will decrypt the data. The data is coming from the cookie and must be decoded first.

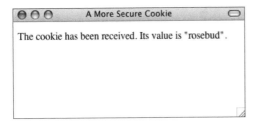

**Figure 4.21** The cookie data has been successfully decrypted.

**8.** Wrap up the MCrypt code.

```
mcrypt_generic_deinit($m);
mcrypt_module_close($m);
```

**9.** Print the data.

```
echo '<p>The cookie has been
→ received. Its value is "' .
→ trim($data) . '".</p>';
```

**10.** Complete the page.

```
} else {
    echo '<p>There\'s nothing to
→ see here.</p>';
}
?>
</body>
</html>
```

The `else` clause applies if the two cookies were not accessible to the script.

**11.** Save the file as `read_mcrypt_cookie.php`, place it in your Web directory, and test in your Web browser (**Figure 4.21**).

## ✔ Tip

■ If you rerun the first script, you'll see that the encrypted version of the data is actually different each time, even though the data itself is always the same. This is because the IV will be different each time. Still, the decryption will always work, as the IV is stored in a cookie.

# E-COMMERCE TECHNIQUES

In this chapter, a Web site explicitly for selling products will be developed. The information you learn will help you to understand the mechanics of an online store while giving you some viable code. The example will focus on the PHP coding itself, along with the database requirements, and it will lead you to the point of implementing a payment system. (Due to the vast number of online payment systems, attempting to demonstrate any one would be of limited use.)

This e-store will sell the ubiquitous *widget*. Unlike many similar examples, these will be some fancy widgets, organized under various categories and available in different sizes and colors. The specifics of these products are irrelevant; all I'm really trying to do is establish real-world factors for what might be sold online. You could also sell shirts in small, medium, and large that come in different colors or music available on compact disc, cassette tape, LP, or 8-track (admittedly not much of a market). Rarely will you get the chance to develop a site that sells only a handful of items, each in a singular format, so the example focuses on representational diversity.

# E-commerce Concepts

Even the most basic e-commerce site requires multiple features. For example, an administrator should be able to:

◆ Add new products

◆ Edit existing products

◆ Update product availability

◆ View orders

◆ Fulfill orders

Customers should be able to:

◆ Register and log in

◆ Possibly purchase without registration

◆ Browse for products

◆ Search for products

◆ Add products to a shopping cart

◆ Check out to complete an order

◆ View an order's status

To fully implement an e-commerce site with all of these features, addressing every possible security concern, would require a book in its own right. Instead, I'm going to focus on the most critical components. Features not implemented are those that are well documented elsewhere (like in my other books) or easy enough to add on your own. I will, throughout the chapter, make suggestions as to other things you could do. Additional information and code relating to this chapter is available on the companion Web site (www.DMCinsights.com/phpvqp2/), and you can also ask questions via the supporting forum (www.DMCinsights.com/phorum/).

# Creating the Database

The foundation for the store will be a database containing all the tables required for recording the customers, products, and orders. Under the premise of selling widgets that are categorized and can come in any color or size, I've come up with eight tables: five for the products, two for the orders, and another for the customer data.

This last table is roughed out in **Table 5.1**. This is a straightforward template for containing all of the customer information. I'm making the zip code and phone numbers text rather than number formats to allow for parentheses and dashes. This table also assumes only United States clients, but you can easily modify it for international addresses. One important note is that the database will not store the customer's credit card information. This means a slight inconvenience to the user (in having to reenter a credit card for each order), but it also significantly decreases the security risks involved.

In the database I suggest using two tables for the orders. The first (**Table 5.2**) records the *metadata* for the order: an order ID, the customer ID, the total amount, the credit card number used, and the order date. This table could also have fields indicating a shipping amount, the type of shipping selected, what coupons were applied and for how much, and so on. Now you might be thinking: didn't I just say I wasn't going to store the credit card information? Yes, I did. All that the credit_card_number field in this table plans on storing is the last four digits of the credit card used by the customer for that order. By recording this information, customers can review their orders and see they used card number *************1234, which will mean something to them but nothing to a potential thief.

*continues on next page*

**Table 5.1** The customers table keeps a list of every customer the site has. One update to the database would be to make the information in this table more international in scope by allowing for non-American addresses.

| Table customers | |
|---|---|
| COLUMN | DATA TYPE |
| customer_id | INT UNSIGNED |
| email | VARCHAR(40) |
| pass | CHAR(40) |
| first_name | VARCHAR(20) |
| last_name | VARCHAR(30) |
| address1 | VARCHAR(60) |
| address2 | VARCHAR(60) |
| city | VARCHAR(30) |
| state | CHAR(2) |
| zip | VARCHAR(10) |
| phone | VARCHAR(15) |

**Table 5.2** The orders table records the customer (via the customer's ID), the total amount of the order, the last four digits of the credit card used, and the date and time the order was placed.

| Table orders | |
|---|---|
| COLUMN | DATA TYPE |
| order_id | INT UNSIGNED |
| customer_id | INT UNSIGNED |
| total | DECIMAL(10,2) |
| credit_card_number | INT(4) |
| order_date | TIMESTAMP |

The second orders table stores the specific items in an order (**Table 5.3**). Each product purchased will be represented as one record in this table (so if a person ordered five different things, there would be five rows for that order). This table stores the product ID (called sw_id; you'll see why soon), the quantity purchased, and the price paid apiece. Each item also has its own shipping date, in case an order is shipping incrementally.

As I said, there are five tables just to represent the products. Of the five product tables, there are two "product attributes" tables: colors (**Table 5.4**) and sizes (**Table 5.5**). Both are required by a normalized design, as multiple products will be in the same color or same size. Plus, these tables would make it easy to search or sort by color and size. A third table allows the widgets to be categorized (**Table 5.6**). This makes browsing easier for the customer.

With the last two tables, a successful e-commerce database requires that each unique product sold has a unique ID (or SKU, in retail terms). Red, medium T-shirts are different than black, medium T-shirts, which are different than black, large T-shirts. Each variation of a unique thing gets its own ID! Getting to that point is the only way for an e-commerce system to work. If a family of products had the same identifier, regardless of size, color, and so on, there would be no way to track inventory or fulfill the order.

Toward that end, there will be a general widgets (or products) table that contains the generic information for an item: its name, its default price, a description, and the category under which it falls (**Table 5.7**). Second, there is a specific widgets table. It acts as the glue between general widgets,

**Table 5.3** The order_contents table has the details of an order; the actual products purchased, in what quantity, and at what price.

| Table order_contents | |
| --- | --- |
| COLUMN | DATA TYPE |
| oc_id | INT UNSIGNED |
| order_id | INT UNSIGNED |
| sw_id | INT UNSIGNED |
| quantity | TINYINT UNSIGNED |
| price | DECIMAL(6,2) |
| ship_date | DATETIME |

**Table 5.4** The colors table only has two columns.

| Table colors | |
| --- | --- |
| COLUMN | DATA TYPE |
| color_id | TINYINTINT UNSIGNED |
| color | VARCHAR(10) |

**Table 5.5** The sizes table also only has two columns.

| Table sizes | |
| --- | --- |
| COLUMN | DATA TYPE |
| size_id | TINYINTINT UNSIGNED |
| size | VARCHAR(10) |

**Table 5.6** The categories table stores a category name, its ID, and a text description.

| Table categories | |
| --- | --- |
| COLUMN | DATA TYPE |
| category_id | TINYINTINT UNSIGNED |
| category | VARCHAR(30) |
| description | TEXT |

the colors, and the sizes (**Table 5.8**). In this table, a widget of one general kind in a certain color and a certain size is represented as a row, with a unique ID. The same general widget in the same color but a different size is another record with a different ID, and so on. This table ensures that each unique product sold has its own ID. This table also has a field stating whether or not the product is currently in stock. That column could be used to reflect on-hand inventory instead.

A note on prices, which are reflected upward of three times for each product: This might seem like a violation of normalization (redundancy being a very bad thing), but it's really not. The general_widgets table stores the default price: what a product is assumed to sell for. The specific_widgets table provides for the ability to override a price. You might do this to put an item on sale, charge more for a different size or color, or close out an item. Finally, the order_contents table has the price actually paid for an item. It's very important that this field exist, as the price an item sells for might change, making that value different than what customers in the past paid for it.

Once you have all of the tables sketched out on paper, you can create them in your database. I'll be using MySQL, so if you use another RDMS (relational database management system), change the SQL and instructions as needed.

Also, to start things off, I'll populate all of the products tables here, rather than creating an administrative interface for that purpose. The PHP scripts required to do that would be easy enough for you to create. If you don't want to type all this text yourself, you can download the SQL commands from the book's corresponding Web site.

**Table 5.7** The general_widgets table stores general information about product lines. It also has a foreign key–primary key relationship with the categories table.

| Table general_widgets | |
|---|---|
| COLUMN | DATA TYPE |
| gw_id | MEDIUMINT UNSIGNED |
| category_id | TINYINT UNSIGNED |
| name | VARCHAR(30) |
| default_price | DECIMAL(6,2) |
| description | TEXT |

**Table 5.8** The specific_widgets table combines the general widgets, the colors, and the sizes, to define a distinct, sellable product.

| Table specific_widgets | |
|---|---|
| COLUMN | DATA TYPE |
| sw_id | INT UNSIGNED |
| gw_id | MEDIUMINT UNSIGNED |
| color_id | TINYINT UNSIGNED |
| size_id | TINYINT UNSIGNED |
| price | DECIMAL(6,2), |
| in_stock | CHAR(1) |

## To create the database:

1. Connect to your server via a command-line interface and connect to MySQL.

   If you'd rather, or are forced to, use phpMyAdmin or whatever other tool instead, that's fine.

2. Create the database.

   CREATE DATABASE ecommerce;

3. Choose the database (**Figure 5.1**).

   USE ecommerce;

4. Create the customers table (**Figure 5.2**).

   CREATE TABLE customers (

   customer_id INT UNSIGNED NOT NULL

   → AUTO_INCREMENT,

   email VARCHAR(40) NOT NULL,

   pass CHAR(40) NOT NULL,

   first_name VARCHAR(20) NOT NULL,

   last_name VARCHAR(30) NOT NULL,

   address1 VARCHAR(60) NOT NULL,

   address2 VARCHAR(60),

   city VARCHAR(30) NOT NULL,

   state CHAR(2) NOT NULL,

   zip_code VARCHAR(10) NOT NULL,

   phone VARCHAR(15),

   PRIMARY KEY (customer_id),

   UNIQUE (email),

   KEY email_pass (email, pass)

   ) ENGINE=MyISAM;

   The customer_id will be the primary key (automatically incremented), but email will also be unique and indexed. Although you won't directly use this table within the confines of this chapter, it's a viable part of any e-commerce site and it would be remiss of me not to include it. The assumption is that customers would register and then be able to log in using a combination of their email address and their password (encrypted using SHA1() or a similar function).

**Figure 5.1** Creating and selecting the database used in this chapter's example.

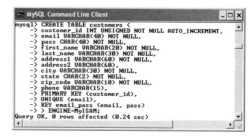

**Figure 5.2** Creating the customers table.

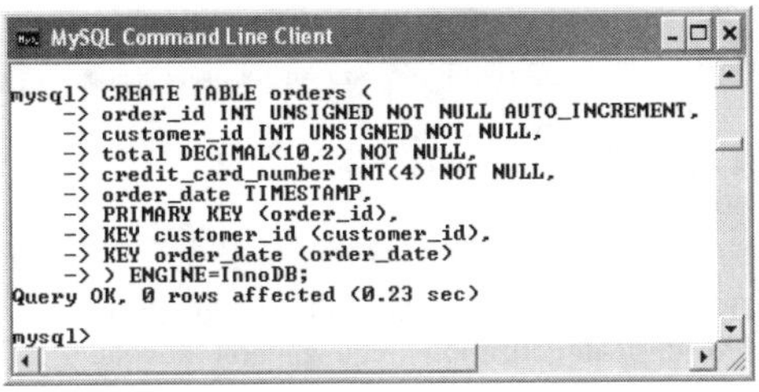

**Figure 5.3** Creating the orders table, which stores the metadata about the orders and uses a transaction-safe table type.

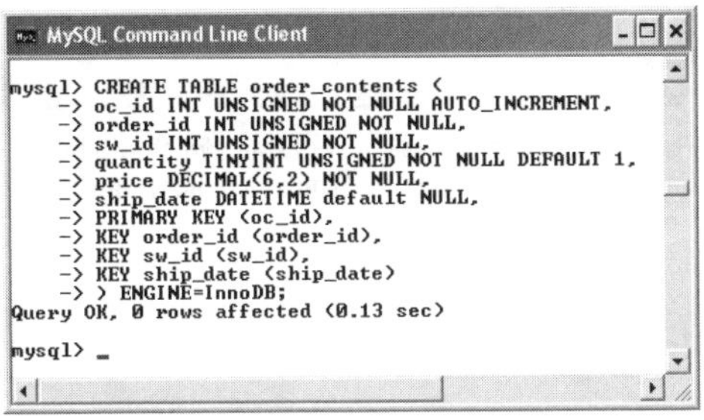

**Figure 5.4** Creating the order_contents table, which lists the details for every order.

**5.** Create the orders table (**Figure 5.3**).

```
CREATE TABLE orders (
order_id INT(10) UNSIGNED NOT NULL
→ AUTO_INCREMENT,
customer_id INT(5) UNSIGNED NOT NULL,
total DECIMAL(10,2) NOT NULL,
order_date TIMESTAMP,
PRIMARY KEY (order_id),
KEY customer_id (customer_id),
KEY order_date (order_date)
) ENGINE=InnoDB;
```

All of the orders fields are required, and three indexes have been created. Notice that a foreign key column here, like customer_id, is of the same exact type as its corresponding primary key (customer_id in the customers table). The order_date field will store the date and time an order was entered. Being defined as a TIMESTAMP, it will automatically be given the current value when a record is inserted.

Finally, because I'll want to use transactions with the orders and order_contents tables, both will use the InnoDB storage engine.

**6.** Create the order_contents table (**Figure 5.4**).

```
CREATE TABLE order_contents (
oc_id INT UNSIGNED NOT NULL
→ AUTO_INCREMENT,
order_id INT UNSIGNED NOT NULL,
sw_id INT UNSIGNED NOT NULL,
quantity TINYINT UNSIGNED NOT NULL
→ DEFAULT 1,
price DECIMAL(6,2) NOT NULL,
ship_date DATETIME default NULL,
PRIMARY KEY (oc_id),
KEY order_id (order_id),
KEY sw_id (sw_id),
KEY ship_date (ship_date)
) ENGINE=InnoDB;
```

*continues on next page*

**CREATING THE DATABASE**

In order to have a normalized database structure, I've separated out each order into its general information—the customer, the order date, and the total amount—and its specific information—the actual items ordered and in what quantity. This table has foreign keys to the orders and specific_widgets tables. The quantity has a default value of 1. The ship_date is defined as a DATETIME, so that it can have a NULL value, meaning that the item has not yet shipped. Again, this table must use the InnoDB storage engine in order to be part of a transaction.

7. Create the categories table (**Figure 5.5**).

CREATE TABLE categories (

category_id TINYINT UNSIGNED NOT NULL
→ AUTO_INCREMENT,

category VARCHAR(30) NOT NULL,

description TEXT,

PRIMARY KEY (category_id)

) ENGINE=MyISAM;

The categories table is just an added layer so that general widgets can be classified. In other e-commerce stores, the categories might be: shirts, sweaters, pants, etc., or music, movies, books, etc.

8. Create the colors table (**Figure 5.6**).

CREATE TABLE colors (

color_id TINYINT UNSIGNED NOT NULL
→ AUTO_INCREMENT,

color VARCHAR(10) NOT NULL,

PRIMARY KEY (color_id)

) ENGINE=MyISAM;

A very simple little table, this has just two columns, one of which is a primary key. Creating this table is implied by normalization, as you wouldn't want to use color names in the specific widgets table over and over again.

**Figure 5.5** Creating the categories table, which provides categorization for the general widgets.

**Figure 5.6** Creating the colors table, which will be tied to general widgets to define specific widgets.

**Figure 5.7** Creating the sizes table, which, along with colors, will define specific widgets.

**Figure 5.8** Creating the general_widgets table, which stores information about generic products.

9. Create the sizes table (**Figure 5.7**).

   CREATE TABLE sizes (

   size_id TINYINT UNSIGNED NOT NULL
   → AUTO_INCREMENT,

   size VARCHAR(10) NOT NULL,

   PRIMARY KEY (size_id)

   ) ENGINE=MyISAM;

10. Create the general_widgets table
    (**Figure 5.8**).

    CREATE TABLE general_widgets (

    gw_id MEDIUMINT UNSIGNED NOT NULL
    → AUTO_INCREMENT,

    category_id TINYINT UNSIGNED NOT
    → NULL,

    name VARCHAR(30) NOT NULL,

    default_price DECIMAL(6,2) NOT NULL,

    description TEXT,

    PRIMARY KEY (gw_id),

    UNIQUE (name),

    KEY (category_id)

    ) ENGINE=MyISAM;

    The general_widgets table is the second most important of the product tables. It links to the categories table and records a widget's name, default price, and description.

    *continues on next page*

**CREATING THE DATABASE**

**11.** Create the specific_widgets table (**Figure 5.9**).

```
CREATE TABLE specific_widgets (

sw_id INT UNSIGNED NOT NULL
→ AUTO_INCREMENT,

gw_id MEDIUMINT UNSIGNED NOT NULL,

color_id TINYINT UNSIGNED NOT NULL,

size_id TINYINT UNSIGNED NOT NULL,

price DECIMAL(6,2),

in_stock CHAR(1),

PRIMARY KEY (sw_id),

UNIQUE combo (gw_id, color_id,
→ size_id),

KEY (gw_id),

KEY (color_id),

KEY (size_id)

) ENGINE=MyISAM;
```

This final product table is an intermediary between general widgets, colors, and sizes. A widget's price can be overridden here and availability indicated.

**12.** Populate the categories table (**Figure 5.10**).

```
INSERT INTO categories (category)
→ VALUES

('Widgets That Wiggle'),

('Widgets That Bounce'),

('Widgets That Sit There'),

('Non-widget Widgets'),

('Fuzzy Widgets'),

('Razor-sharp Widgets');
```

As each widget falls under a category, the categories should be entered into the database first.

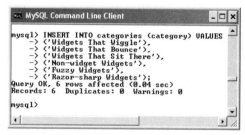

**Figure 5.9** Creating the final table, specific_widgets, whose IDs will be used as the product SKUs.

**Figure 5.10** Adding some records to the categories table, which will then be used when adding records to the general_widgets table.

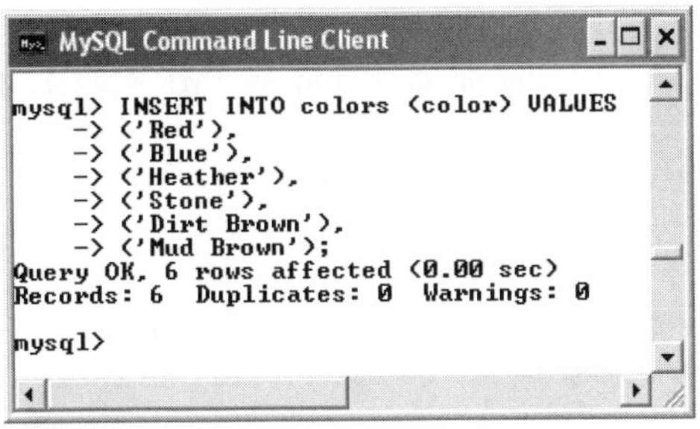

**Figure 5.11** Adding some sample colors to the colors table.

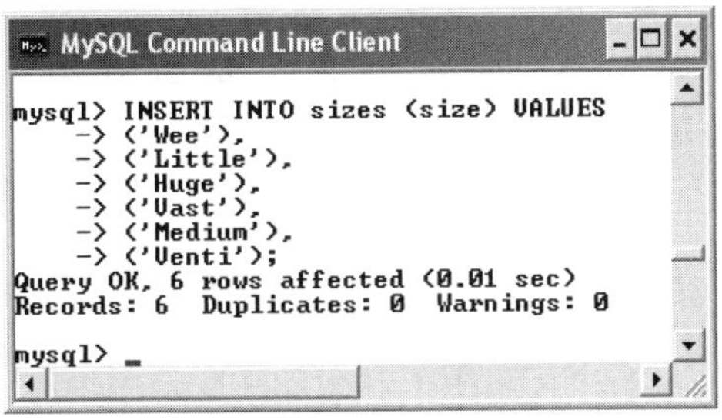

**Figure 5.12** Adding some widget sizes.

**13.** Populate the colors table (**Figure 5.11**).

```
INSERT INTO colors (color) VALUES
('Red'),
('Blue'),
('Heather'),
('Stone'),
('Dirt Brown'),
('Mud Brown');
```

**14.** Populate the sizes table (**Figure 5.12**).

```
INSERT INTO sizes (size) VALUES
('Wee'),
('Little'),
('Huge'),
('Vast'),
('Medium'),
('Venti');
```

*continues on next page*

CREATING THE DATABASE

**15.** Populate the `general_widgets` table.

```
INSERT INTO general_widgets
→ (category_id, name, default_price,
→ description) VALUES
(1, 'Wiggle Widget 1', 234.45, 'This
→ is the description of this widget.
→ This is the description of this
→ widget. This is the description of
→ this widget. This is the
→ description of this widget. '),
(1, 'Wiggle Widget 2', 200.99, 'This
→ is the description of this widget.
→ This is the description of this
→ widget. This is the description of
→ this widget. This is the
→ description of this widget. '),
(1, 'Wiggle Widget 3', 164.00, 'This
→ is the description of this widget.
→ This is the description of this
→ widget. This is the description of
→ this widget. This is the
→ description of this widget. '),
(2, 'Bouncy Widget 1', 1.16, 'This is
→ the description of this widget.
→ This is the description of this
→ widget. This is the description of
→ this widget. This is the
→ description of this widget. '),
(2, 'Bouncy Widget 2', 32.20, 'This
→ is the description of this widget.
→ This is the description of this
→ widget. This is the description of
→ this widget. This is the
→ description of this widget. '),
(3, 'Useless Widget', 985.00, 'This
→ is the description of this widget.
→ This is the description of this
→ widget. This is the description of
→ this widget. This is the
→ description of this widget. '),
(6, 'Barbed-wire Widget', 141.66,
→ 'This is the description of this
→ widget. This is the description of
→ this widget. This is the
→ description of this widget. This is
→ the description of this widget. '),
(6, 'Rusty Nails Widget', 45.25,
→ 'This is the description of this
→ widget. This is the description of
→ this widget. This is the
→ description of this widget. This is
→ the description of this widget. '),
(6, 'Broken Glass Widget', 8.00,
→ 'This is the description of this
→ widget. This is the description of
→ this widget. This is the
→ description of this widget. This is
→ the description of this widget. ');
```

The general widgets should be placed in categories; given names and default values; and optionally, they should have a description. So that you see in the e-commerce site where the description shows up, I'm putting in some text (the same text) for each widget.

**16.** Populate the `specific_widgets` table (**Figure 5.13**).

```
INSERT INTO specific_widgets (gw_id,
→ color_id, size_id, price,
→ in_stock) VALUES
(1, 1, 2, NULL, 'Y'),
(1, 1, 3, NULL, 'Y'),
(1, 1, 4, NULL, 'Y'),
(1, 3, 1, NULL, 'Y'),
(1, 3, 2, NULL, 'Y'),
(1, 4, 1, NULL, 'Y'),
(1, 4, 2, NULL, 'N'),
(1, 4, 3, NULL, 'N'),
(1, 4, 6, NULL, 'Y'),
(2, 1, 1, NULL, 'Y'),
(2, 1, 2, NULL, 'Y'),
(2, 1, 6, NULL, 'N'),
(2, 4, 4, NULL, 'Y'),
(2, 4, 5, NULL, 'Y'),
(2, 6, 1, NULL, 'N'),
(2, 6, 2, NULL, 'Y'),
(2, 6, 3, NULL, 'Y'),
(2, 6, 6, NULL, 'Y'),
(3, 1, 1, 123.45, 'N'),
(3, 1, 2, NULL, 'Y'),
(3, 1, 6, 846.45, 'Y'),
(3, 1, 4, NULL, 'Y'),
(3, 4, 4, NULL, 'Y'),
(3, 4, 5, 147.00, 'Y'),
(3, 6, 1, 196.50, 'Y'),
(3, 6, 2, 202.54, 'Y'),
(3, 6, 3, NULL, 'N'),
(3, 6, 6, NULL, 'Y'),
(4, 2, 5, NULL, 'Y'),
(4, 2, 6, NULL, 'Y'),
(4, 3, 2, NULL, 'N'),
(4, 3, 3, NULL, 'Y'),
(4, 3, 6, NULL, 'Y'),
(4, 5, 4, NULL, 'Y'),
(4, 5, 6, NULL, 'N'),
(4, 6, 2, NULL, 'Y'),
(4, 6, 3, NULL, 'Y');
```

This ends up being the most important query, as it populates the `specific_widgets` table with the actual products to be purchased: particular combinations of general widgets, colors, and sizes. To mix it up, I use a varying combination of general widgets, colors, sizes, availability, and overridden prices.

*continues on next page*

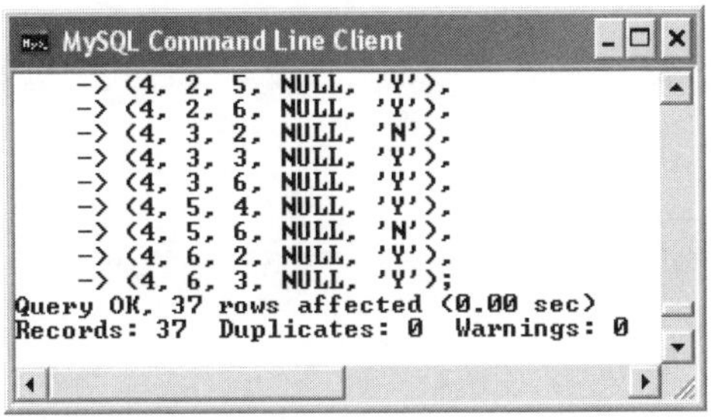

**Figure 5.13** The specific products are entered into the database.

## ✔ Tips

- The InnoDB storage engine will disappear in future versions of MySQL, being replaced with a different transaction-safe table type.

- Selling books, music, and videos is relatively straightforward, as these industries provide item-specific SKUs for the vendor (e.g., each book has its own ISBN number and the hardcover edition has a different ISBN than the paperback).

- If you wanted to store multiple addresses for users—home, billing, friends, etc.—create a separate addresses table. In this table store all of that information, including the address type, and link those records back to the customers table using the customer ID as a primary-foreign key.

# Creating the Configuration File

Every multipage Web application requires a configuration file, and certainly this is no exception. To make things easy—and because reusing code is just a smart thing to do—most of this configuration file will mimic the one developed in Chapter 2, "Developing Web Applications." For more information on most of this code, see that chapter. Also, because every page in the e-commerce site requires a database connection (and to save time and book space), I'll throw the database connectivity code into this file as well.

As with nearly every example in the book, I'll be using the Improved MySQL functions, available as of PHP 5 and MySQL 4.1. If you're using an earlier version of either, or a different database application entirely, you'll need to change the code accordingly.

## To create the configuration file:

1. Begin a new PHP script in your text editor or IDE (**Script 5.1**).

   ```
   <?php # Script 5.1 - config.inc.php
   ```

2. Set the email address to be used for errors.

   ```
   $contact_email =
   → 'address@example.com';
   ```

*continues on page 187*

**Script 5.1** The config.inc.php file is essentially the same as that written in Chapter 2, although it now also connects to the database.

```
  1   <?php # Script 5.1 - config.inc.php
  2
  3   /*
  4    *  Configuration file does the following things:
  5    *  - Has site settings in one location.
  6    *  - Stores URLs and URIs as constants.
  7    *  - Sets how errors will be handled.
  8    *  - Establishes a connection to the database.
  9    */
 10
 11
 12   # ******************* #
 13   # ***** SETTINGS ***** #
 14
 15   // Errors are emailed here.
 16   $contact_email = 'address@example.com';
 17
 18   // Determine whether we're working on a local server
 19   // or on the real server:
 20   if (stristr($_SERVER['HTTP_HOST'], 'local') || (substr($_SERVER['HTTP_HOST'], 0, 7) ==
      '192.168')) {
 21       $local = TRUE;
 22   } else {
 23       $local = FALSE;
 24   }
 25
 26   // Determine location of files and the URL of the site:
 27   // Allow for development on different servers.
 28   if ($local) {
 29
 30       // Always debug when running locally:
 31       $debug = TRUE;
 32
 33       // Define the constants:
 34       define ('BASE_URI', '/path/to/html/folder/');
 35       define ('BASE_URL', 'http://localhost/directory/');
 36
 37   } else {
 38
 39       define ('BASE_URI', '/path/to/live/html/folder/');
```

*(script continues on next page)*

**Script 5.1** *continued*

```
 40       define ('BASE_URL', 'http://www.example.com/');
 41
 42   }
 43
 44   /*
 45    *  Most important setting...
 46    *  The $debug variable is used to set error management.
 47    *  To debug a specific page, do this:
 48
 49   $debug = TRUE;
 50   require_once('./includes/config.inc.php');
 51
 52    *  on that page.
 53    *
 54    *  To debug the entire site, do
 55
 56   $debug = TRUE;
 57
 58    *  before this next conditional.
 59    */
 60
 61   // Assume debugging is off.
 62   if (!isset($debug)) {
 63       $debug = FALSE;
 64   }
 65
 66   # ***** SETTINGS ***** #
 67   # ******************** #
 68
 69
 70   # ************************** #
 71   # ***** ERROR MANAGEMENT ***** #
 72
 73   // Create the error handler.
 74   function my_error_handler ($e_number, $e_message, $e_file, $e_line, $e_vars) {
 75
 76       global $debug, $contact_email;
 77
 78       // Build the error message.
 79       $message = "An error occurred in script '$e_file' on line $e_line: \n<br />$e_message\n<br
      />";
 80
 81       // Add the date and time.
 82       $message .= "Date/Time: " . date('n-j-Y H:i:s') . "\n<br />";
 83
 84       // Append $e_vars to the $message.
 85       $message .= "<pre>" . print_r ($e_vars, 1) . "</pre>\n<br />";
 86
 87       if ($debug) { // Show the error.
 88
```

*(script continues on next page)*

**Script 5.1** *continued*

```
89           echo '<p class="error">' . $message . '</p>';
90
91      } else {
92
93           // Log the error:
94           error_log ($message, 1, $contact_email); // Send email.
95
96           // Only print an error message if the error isn't a notice or strict.
97           if ( ($e_number != E_NOTICE) && ($e_number < 2048)) {
98                echo '<p class="error">A system error occurred. We apologize for the
     inconvenience.</p>';
99           }
100
101     } // End of $debug IF.
102
103  } // End of my_error_handler() definition.
104
105  // Use my error handler:
106  set_error_handler ('my_error_handler');
107
108  # ***** ERROR MANAGEMENT ***** #
109  # ************************** #
110
111
112  # ************************** #
113  # ***** DATABASE STUFF ***** #
114
115  // Connect to the database:
116  $dbc = @mysqli_connect ('localhost', 'username', 'password', 'ecommerce') OR
     trigger_error("Could not connect to the database!\n<br />MySQL Error: " .
     mysqli_connect_error());
117
118  // Create a function for escaping the data.
119  function escape_data ($data) {
120
121     // Need the connection:
122     global $dbc;
123
124     // Address Magic Quotes.
125     if (ini_get('magic_quotes_gpc')) {
126          $data = stripslashes($data);
127     }
128
129     // Trim and escape:
130     return mysqli_real_escape_string($dbc, trim($data));
131
132  } // End of escape_data() function.
133
134  # ***** DATABASE STUFF ***** #
135  # ************************** #
136
137  ?>
```

**3.** Determine if the script is running on the live server or a test server.

```
if (stristr($_SERVER['HTTP_HOST'],
→ 'local') || (substr($_SERVER
→ ['HTTP_HOST'], 0, 7) == '192.168'))
→ {
    $local = TRUE;
} else {
    $local = FALSE;
}
```

**4.** Set the server-specific constants.

```
if ($local) {
    $debug = TRUE;
    define ('BASE_URI',
→ '/path/to/html/folder/');
    define ('BASE_URL',
→ 'http://localhost/directory/');
} else {
    define ('BASE_URI',
→ '/path/to/live/html/folder/');
    define ('BASE_URL',
→ 'http://www.example.com/');
}
```

Unlike in the script in Chapter 2, I am not defining a path to the database file here, as that code will appear later in this script. If you want to keep the database information separate, then define a DB constant here, with the full path to that file.

If necessary, you could also define server-specific database access constants here. You might do this if you use one set of username/password/hostname for your local server and another for the live server.

**5.** Set the debugging mode.

```
if (!isset($debug)) {
    $debug = FALSE;
}
```

*continues on next page*

CREATING THE CONFIGURATION FILE

**6.** Define the function for handling errors.

```
function my_error_handler ($e_number,
→ $e_message, $e_file, $e_line,
→ $e_vars) {
    global $debug, $contact_email;
    $message = "An error occurred in
→ script '$e_file' on line $e_line:
→ \n<br />$e_message\n<br />";
    $message .= "Date/Time: " .
→ date('n-j-Y H:i:s') . "\n<br />";
    $message .= "<pre>" . print_r
→ ($e_vars, 1) . "</pre>\n<br />";
    if ($debug) {
        echo '<p class="error">'
→ . $message . '</p>';
    } else {
        error_log ($message, 1,
→ $contact_email); // Send email.
        if ( ($e_number !=
→ E_NOTICE) && ($e_number < 2048)) {
            echo '<p
class="error">A system error
→ occurred. We apologize for the
→ inconvenience.</p>';
        }
    }
}
```

**Figure 5.14** Detailed error messages aid in debugging problems.

**Figure 5.15** Generic error messages are used on live sites so as not to give away anything important.

If debugging is turned on, a full, detailed message will appear in the Web browser (**Figure 5.14**). For a live site, the detailed error message should not be shown (unless debugging is temporarily enabled for that page) but should be emailed instead. The error_log() function will do this, if provided with the number 1 as its second argument. But the user probably needs to know that something didn't go right, so a generic message is displayed (**Figure 5.15**). If the error happens to be a notice or a strict error (having a value of 2048), no message should be printed, as the error is likely not interfering with the operation of the page.

**7.** Tell PHP to use this error handler.

```
set_error_handler
→ ('my_error_handler');
```

**8.** Establish a database connection.

```
$dbc = @mysqli_connect ('localhost',
→ 'username', 'password',
→ 'ecommerce') OR
→ trigger_error("Could not connect to
→ the database!\n<br />MySQL Error: "
→ . mysqli_connect_error());
```

If a database connection cannot be made, the `trigger_error()` function will invoke `my_error_handler()`, managing the error as appropriate for a live or local site. The error message will begin with *Could not connect to the database!*, followed by the MySQL connection error.

**9.** Define a function for escaping query data.

```
function escape_data ($data) {
    global $dbc;
    if (ini_get
→ ('magic_quotes_gpc')) {
        $data =
→ stripslashes($data);
    }
    return mysqli_real_escape_
→ string($dbc, trim($data));
}
```

This bit of code is one of my favorite creations, if I do say so myself. It takes a piece of data, strips any slashes if Magic Quotes is enabled (if the function didn't do this, the data would be over-escaped), and then trims and escapes the data using the secure `mysqli_real_escape_string()` function. Any data run through this function should be safe to use in a query.

**10.** Complete the page.

```
?>
```

**11.** Save the file as `config.inc.php` and place it in your Web directory (in an `includes` subfolder).

CREATING THE CONFIGURATION FILE

# Making the Template

This e-commerce application will also use a template, of course, just like the example in Chapter 2. For this template, I'll use another design found on Open Source Web Design (www.oswd.org). This particular design (**Figure 5.16**) is by Tjobbe Andrews (www.sitecreative.net) and is gratefully used with his kind permission.

I've modified it slightly (**Figure 5.17**) to show the store's name. The right-side column lists the categories of widgets for browsing purposes and also has areas that could be used to promote other products, reflect the contents of the shopping cart, or contain a search form. I haven't modified the top navigation, but you might want to make a spot there for quickly accessing the cart (such as a tab to cart.php).

In Chapter 2 I go through the steps involved in turning a sample page into a template. Here I'll just create the templates outright. In order to save space, the CSS file for this example (which controls the layout) is not included in the book. You can download the file through the book's supporting Web site (www.DMCInsights.com/phpvqp2/, see the Extras page).

**Figure 5.16** Tjobbe Andrews' original design.

**Figure 5.17** The slightly modified version of the design that will be used in this chapter.

## To create the template pages:

**1.** Begin a new PHP page in your text editor or IDE (**Script 5.2**).

```
<?php # Script 5.2 - header.html
```

**2.** Start the session and check for a $page_title variable.

```
session_start();

if (!isset($page_title)) $page_title
→ = 'WoW::World of Widgets!';
?>
```

The shopping cart relies upon sessions, so every page must have session access. As for the $page_title variable, that's used to set the browser window's title on a page-by-page basis. If one is not defined prior to including this file, a default title is used.

**Script 5.2** The header.html document contains the beginnings of an HTML page and starts the session.

```
1    <?php # Script 5.2 - header.html
2
3    /*
4     *    This page begins the HTML header for the site.
5     *    The header also creates the right-hand column.
6     *    This page calls session_start().
7     */
8
9    // Need sessions!
10   session_start();
11
12   // Check for a $page_title value:
13   if (!isset($page_title)) $page_title = 'WoW::World of Widgets!';
14   ?><!DOCTYPE html
15   PUBLIC "-//W3C//DTD XHTML 1.0 Strict//EN"
16   "http://www.w3.org/TR/xhtml1/DTD/xhtml1-strict.dtd">
17   <html xmlns="http://www.w3.org/1999/xhtml" xml:lang="en" lang="en">
18   <head>
19       <title><?php echo $page_title; ?></title>
20       <meta http-equiv="Content-Type" content="text/html; charset=iso-8859-1" />
21       <link href="./includes/style.css" rel="stylesheet" type="text/css" />
22   </head>
```

*(script continues on next page)*

MAKING THE TEMPLATE

**Script 5.2** *continued*

```
23    <body>
24    <div class="all">
25
26        <div class="box">
27            <div class="menu"><a href="#">home</a><a href="#">about</a><a href="#">products</a><a
      href="#">contact</a></div>
28            <div class="header"><img alt="" style="float:right; " src="./images/www.jpg" width="225"
      height="95" />
29            <h1>[<span class="style1">WoW</span>] World of Widgets</h1>
30            <div class="clearfix"></div>
31        </div>
32
33        <div class="newsbar">
34            <h1>Browse Widget Categories</h1>
35            <div class="p2"><ul>
36    <?php
37    // Get all the categories and
38    // link them to category.php.
39
40    // Define and execute the query:
41    $q = 'SELECT category_id, category FROM categories ORDER BY category';
42    $r = mysqli_query($dbc, $q);
43
44    // Fetch the results:
45    while (list($fcid, $fcat) = mysqli_fetch_array($r, MYSQLI_NUM)) {
46
47        // Print as a list item.
48        echo "<li><a href=\"category.php?cid=$fcid\">$fcat</a></li>\n";
49
50    } // End of while loop.
51
52            ?></ul></div>
53
54        <h1>Cart Contents?</h1>
55        <div class="p2">You could use this area to show something regarding the cart.</div>
56
57        <h1>Specials?</h1>
58        <div class="p2">
59            <p>Maybe place specials or new items or related items here.</p>
60        </div>
61
62    </div>
63
64        <div class="content">
```

MAKING THE TEMPLATE

**3.** Create the HTML head.

```
<!DOCTYPE html
PUBLIC "-//W3C//DTD XHTML 1.0
→ Strict//EN"
"http://www.w3.org/TR/xhtml1/DTD/
→ xhtml1-strict.dtd">
<html
xmlns="http://www.w3.org/1999/xhtml"
→ xml:lang="en" lang="en">
<head>
    <title><?php echo $page_title;
→ ?></title>
    <meta http-equiv="Content-Type"
→ content="text/html; charset=iso-
→ 8859-1" />
    <link href="./includes/
→ style.css" rel="stylesheet"
→ type="text/css" />
</head>
```

The $page_title variable is printed between the <title></title> tags.

**4.** Begin the body of the page.

```
<body>
<div class="all">
    <div class="box">
        <div class="menu"><a
→ href="#">home</a><a
→ href="#">about</a><a
→ href="#">products</a><a
→ href="#">contact</a></div>
        <div class="header"><img
→ alt="" style="float:right; "
→ src="./images/www.jpg" width="225"
→ height="95" />
        <h1>[<span
→ class="style1">WoW</span>] World of
→ Widgets</h1>
        <div
→ class="clearfix"></div>
        </div>
        <div class="newsbar">
        <h1>Browse Widget
→ Categories</h1>
        <div class="p2"><ul>
```

The body starts by printing the header and then goes into the right-side column. The first item in that column should be a list of widget categories, based upon the categories table in the database.

*continues on next page*

**5.** Print each category as a link.

```php
<?php
$q = 'SELECT category_id, category
→ FROM categories ORDER BY category';
$r = mysqli_query($dbc, $q);
while (list($fcid, $fcat) = mysqli_
→ fetch_array($r, MYSQLI_NUM)) {
    echo "<li><a href=\"category.
→ php?cid=$fcid\">$fcat</a></li>\n";
}
?>
```

The query fetches the category ID and category name from the `categories` table, in alphabetical order (**Figure 5.18**). Each is then printed as a link to `category.php`, with the category ID appended to the URL (**Figure 5.19**).

**6.** Complete the header.

```html
</ul></div>
            <h1>Cart Contents?</h1>
            <div class="p2">You
→ could use this area to show
→ something regarding the cart.</div>
            <h1>Specials?</h1>
            <div class="p2">
                <p>Maybe place
→ specials or new items or related
→ items here.</p>
            </div>
        </div>
        <div class="content">
```

**7.** Save the file as `header.html`.

The file should be placed in an `includes` folder within your Web directory. You'll also want to place `style.css` (downloadable from the book's corresponding Web site) in that same place.

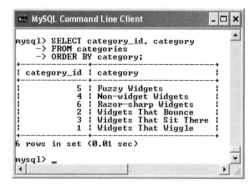

**Figure 5.18** The results of running the same query directly in the `mysql` client.

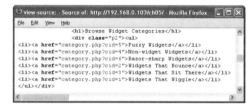

**Figure 5.19** The HTML source code shows how each category is linked to the `category.php` page.

MAKING THE TEMPLATE

**8.** Begin a new document in your text editor or IDE (**Script 5.3**).

```php
<?php # Script 5.3 - footer.html
if (isset($dbc)) {
    mysqli_close($dbc);
    unset($dbc);
}
?>
```

The footer file will forcibly close the database connection, if it's still open. Referring to the $dbc variable checks that status.

*continues on next page*

**Script 5.3** The footer.html file completes the HTML begun in header.html. It also closes an open database connection.

```
         Script
1    <?php # Script 5.3 - footer.html
2
3    // Close the database connection.
4    if (isset($dbc)) {
5        mysqli_close($dbc);
6        unset($dbc);
7    }
8    ?>
9            </div>
10           <div class="clearfix"></div>
11           <div class="footer">&copy; 2005, design by <a href="http://www.now-
     design.co.uk/">NOW:design</a> |
12               Template from <a href="http://www.oswd.org/">oswd.org</a></div>
13           </div>
14   </div>
15
16   </body>
17   </html>
```

MAKING THE TEMPLATE

**9.** Complete the HTML page.

```
            </div>
            <div class=
→ "clearfix"></div>
            <div
class="footer">&copy; 2005, design
→ by <a href="http://www.now-
→ design.co.uk/">NOW:design</a> |
            Template from <a
→ href="http://www.oswd.org/">oswd.
→ org</a></div>
        </div>
</div>
</body>
</html>
```

**10.** Save the file as footer.html, placing it your Web directory's includes folder (along with header.html, config.inc.php, and style.css).

## ✔ Tips

- Any variable you define in an included file that is only used in that file (like the category ID and name in the header) should be given a unique name. If you don't do that, you'll likely run into odd, hard-to-debug errors. For example, if I used $cid and $cat instead of $fcid and $fcat in header.html, I'd have conflicts with the $cid and $cat variables used in the category.php page (developed later in the chapter).

- One of the right-hand sections could be used for new products. To retrieve, say, the three latest products, you could just fetch those from the specific_widgets table with the highest sw_id values (since it's an automatically incrementing number).

# Creating the Index Page

The site's home page won't really do much, but it needs to exist regardless. It will show how all of the other pages are assembled, though. Let's whip that out quickly.

## To create the index page:

1. Begin a new PHP script in your text editor or IDE (**Script 5.4**).

   `<?php # Script 5.4 - index.php`

*continues on next page*

**Script 5.4** This script acts as the public home page.

```
1    <?php # Script 5.4 - index.php
2
3    /*
4     *  This is the main page.
5     *  This page doesn't do much.
6     */
7
8    // Require the configuration file before any PHP code:
9    require_once ('./includes/config.inc.php');
10
11   // Include the header file:
12   include_once ('./includes/header.html');
13
14   // Page-specific content goes here:
15   echo '<h1>[WoW] World of Widgets</h1>
16   <p>Put introductory information here. Marketing. Whatever. Put introductory information here.
        Marketing. Whatever. Put introductory information here. Marketing. Whatever. Put introductory
        information here. Marketing. Whatever. </p>
17   <p>Put introductory information here. Marketing. Whatever. Put introductory information here.
        Marketing. Whatever. Put introductory information here. Marketing. Whatever. Put introductory
        information here. Marketing. Whatever. </p>
18
19   <h1>[WoW] World of Widgets</h1>
20   <p>Put introductory information here. Marketing. Whatever. Put introductory information here.
        Marketing. Whatever. Put introductory information here. Marketing. Whatever. Put introductory
        information here. Marketing. Whatever. </p>
21   <p>Put introductory information here. Marketing. Whatever. Put introductory information here.
        Marketing. Whatever. Put introductory information here. Marketing. Whatever. Put introductory
        information here. Marketing. Whatever. </p>';
22
23   // Include the footer file to complete the template:
24   include_once ('./includes/footer.html');
25
26   ?>
```

**2.** Include the configuration file.

```
require_once ('./includes/
→ config.inc.php');
```

This file ought to be included first thing on every page, as it controls how the site handles errors and defines many settings.

**3.** Include the HTML header file.

```
include_once ('./includes/
→ header.html');
```

Because I haven't defined a $page_title variable prior to this inclusion, the default title will be used.

**4.** Add the page-specific content.

```
echo '<h1>[WoW] World of Widgets</h1>
<p>Put introductory information here.
→ Marketing. Whatever. Put
→ introductory information here.
→ Marketing. Whatever. Put
→ introductory information here.
→ Marketing. Whatever. Put
→ introductory information here.
→ Marketing. Whatever. </p>

<p>Put introductory information here.
→ Marketing. Whatever. Put
→ introductory information here.
→ Marketing. Whatever. Put
→ introductory information here.
→ Marketing. Whatever. Put
→ introductory information here.
→ Marketing. Whatever. </p>
```

```
<h1>[WoW] World of Widgets</h1>
<p>Put introductory information
→ here. Marketing. Whatever. Put
→ introductory information here.
→ Marketing. Whatever. Put
→ introductory information here.
→ Marketing. Whatever. Put
→ introductory information here.
→ Marketing. Whatever. </p>

<p>Put introductory information here.
→ Marketing. Whatever. Put
→ introductory information here.
→ Marketing. Whatever. Put
→ introductory information here.
→ Marketing. Whatever. Put
→ introductory information here.
→ Marketing. Whatever. </p>';
```

This page's content is pure drivel, but it could be made useful on a real site.

**5.** Include the footer file that completes the HTML.

```
include_once ('./includes/
→ footer.html');
```

**6.** Complete the page.

```
?>
```

**7.** Save the file as index.php, place it in your Web directory, and test in your Web browser (see Figure 5.17 for the result).

**Figure 5.20** The category page shows information about general widgets.

# Browsing by Category

Now that the database has been implemented and all of the base PHP files written, it's time to begin adding functionality to the site. With the example as I'm developing it, all of the products will be accessed by browsing. This starts with a widget category page, which is found by clicking a link in the right-hand column.

The category page should put the category's name in the browser window's title as well as on the page itself. After that, the page should contain a description of the category, if it exists, and every widget that falls under this category (**Figure 5.20**). These widgets would be linked to the widget-specific pages.

## To create the category page:

1. Begin a new PHP script in your text editor or IDE (**Script 5.5**).

   ```php
   <?php # Script 5.5 - category.php
   require_once ('./includes/
   → config.inc.php');
   ```

   *continues on page 202*

**Script 5.5** The category page is the first step in the browsing process (for the customer). It lists all the general widgets found in that category.

```
                                          Script
1    <?php # Script 5.5 - category.php
2
3    /*
4     *  This page represents a specific category.
5     *  This page shows all the widgets classified
6     *  under that category.
7     *  The page expects to receive a $_GET['cid'] value.
8     */
9
10   // Require the configuration file before any PHP code:
11   require_once ('./includes/config.inc.php');
12
13   // Check for a category ID in the URL:
14   $category = NULL;
15   if (isset($_GET['cid'])) {
16
17       // Typecast it to an integer:
18       $cid = (int) $_GET['cid'];
19       // An invalid $_GET['cid'] value would
20       // be typecast to 0.
21
22       // $cid must have a valid value.
23       if ($cid > 0) {
24
25           // Get the information from the database
26           // for this category:
27           $q = "SELECT category, description FROM categories WHERE category_id=$cid";
28           $r = mysqli_query($dbc, $q);
29
30           // Fetch the information:
31           if (mysqli_num_rows($r) == 1) {
32               list ($category, $description) = mysqli_fetch_array($r, MYSQLI_NUM);
33           } // End of mysqli_num_rows() IF.
34
```

*(script continues on next page)*

**Script 5.5** *continued*

```
35      } // End of ($cid > 0) IF.
36
37  } // End of isset($_GET['cid']) IF.
38
39  // Use the category as the page title:
40  if ($category) {
41      $page_title = $category;
42  }
43
44  // Include the header file:
45  include_once ('./includes/header.html');
46
47  if ($category) { // Show the products.
48
49      echo "<h1>$category</h1>\n";
50
51      // Print the category description, if it's not empty.
52      if (!empty($description)) {
53          echo "<p>$description</p>\n";
54      }
55
56      // Get the widgets in this category:
57      $q = "SELECT gw_id, name, default_price, description FROM general_widgets WHERE
category_id=$cid";
58      $r = mysqli_query($dbc, $q);
59
60      if (mysqli_num_rows($r) > 1) {
61
62          // Print each:
63          while (list($gw_id, $wname, $wprice, $wdescription) = mysqli_fetch_array($r, MYSQLI_NUM))
{
64
65              // Link to the product.php page:
66              echo "<h2><a href=\"product.php?gw_id=$gw_id\">$wname</a></h2><p>$wdescription<br
/>\$$wprice</p>\n";
67
68          } // End of while loop.
69
70      } else { // No widgets here!
71          echo '<p class="error">There are no widgets in this category.</p>';
72      }
73
74  } else { // Invalid $_GET['cid']!
75      echo '<p class="error">This page has been accessed in error.</p>';
76  }
77
78  // Include the footer file to complete the template:
79  include_once ('./includes/footer.html');
80
81  ?>
```

**2.** Begin validating the category ID.

```
$category = NULL;
if (isset($_GET['cid'])) {
    $cid = (int) $_GET['cid'];
    if ($cid > 0) {
```

First, a flag variable is created, called $category. The script will refer to this later on to tell if a valid category ID was received. Next, a check confirms that some $_GET['cid'] value was received, which is then typecast to an integer. This forces $cid to be an integer. Even if someone changed the URL to category.php?cid=/path/to/file, $cid would now equal 0. The next check confirms that the integer has a positive value.

**3.** Retrieve the category information.

```
$q = "SELECT category, description
→ FROM categories WHERE
→ category_id=$cid";
$r = mysqli_query($dbc, $q);
if (mysqli_num_rows($r) == 1) {
    list ($category, $description) =
→ mysqli_fetch_array($r, MYSQLI_NUM);
}
```

**4.** Complete the validation conditionals.

```
    } // End of ($cid > 0) IF.
} // End of isset($_GET['cid']) IF.
```

**5.** Make the category name be the page title and include the header file.

```
if ($category) {
    $page_title = $category;
}
include_once ('./includes/
→ header.html');
```

If the query in Step 3 did return a row, then that value (e.g., *Fuzzy Widgets*) should be used in the browser window.

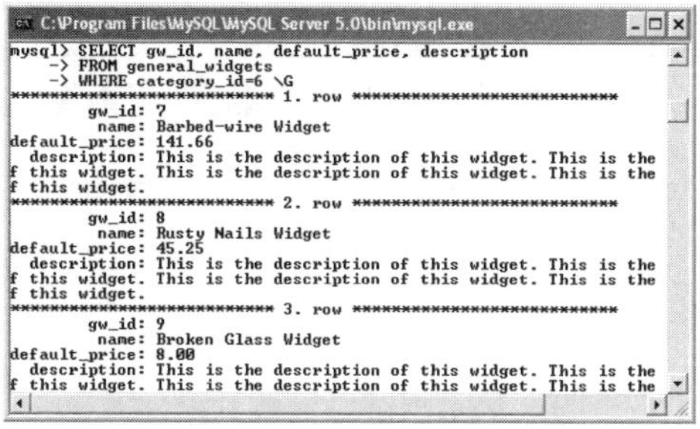

**Figure 5.21** The main query and its results for one of the category pages.

**Figure 5.22** The HTML source reveals how each general widget is linked to the product page, passing along the general widget ID in the URL.

**6.** If a valid category ID was used, print the category name and description.

```
if ($category) {
    echo "<h1>$category</h1>\n";
    if (!empty($description)) {
        echo "<p>$description
→ </p>\n";
    }
```

The description field in the database is optional (it can be NULL), so a conditional here checks for a value prior to printing it.

**7.** Retrieve all the widgets that are in this category.

```
$q = "SELECT gw_id, name,
→ default_price, description FROM
→ general_widgets WHERE
→ category_id=$cid";
$r = mysqli_query($dbc, $q);
if (mysqli_num_rows($r) > 1) {
```

This query retrieves all the general widget information for widgets associated with this category (**Figure 5.21**).

**8.** Print each widget, linking it to the products page.

```
while (list($gw_id, $wname, $wprice,
→ $wdescription) = mysqli_fetch_
→ array($r, MYSQLI_NUM)) {
    echo "<h2><a href=\"product.php?
→ gwid=$gw_id\">$wname</a></h2><p>$w
→ description<br />\$$wprice</p>\n";
}
```

It's not the most attractive layout, but I'll just print each widget in a vertical list. You could use the technique shown in Chapter 3, "Advanced Database Concepts," to lay the widgets out in horizontal rows. As you can see from the HTML source code of the page (**Figure 5.22**), each widget's name is linked to product.php, passing along the widget's ID (from the database), in the URL. The widget's description and default price are then under each name.

**9.** Complete the conditionals begun in Steps 7 and 6.

```
    } else {
            echo '<p
→ class="error">There are no widgets
→ in this category.</p>';
    }
} else {
    echo '<p class="error">This
→ page has been accessed in
→ error.</p>';
}
```

The first else clause applies if there are no widgets in this category. A message stating such will be printed in the browser (**Figure 5.23**). The second else applies if an invalid category ID is passed to this page (**Figure 5.24**).

**10.** Complete the page.

```
include_once ('./includes/
→ footer.html');
?>
```

**11.** Save the file as category.php, place it in your Web directory, and test in your Web browser by using the links in the right-hand column (**Figure 5.25**).

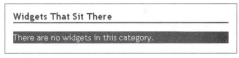

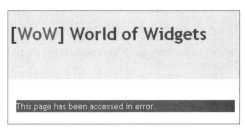

**Widgets That Sit There**

There are no widgets in this category.

**Figure 5.23** If a category has no products (general widgets) in it, the customer will see this message.

**[WoW] World of Widgets**

This page has been accessed in error.

**Figure 5.24** If a malicious user hacks the category ID value in the URL (or if something just goes wrong), this will be the result.

**Figure 5.25** Another category of widgets.

**Figure 5.26** The specific products page.

# Showing a Product

By clicking an individual product in the category page, customers will be taken to the product-specific page. This page should show all the general details about a widget—name and description, plus all of the specific versions of the widget available (**Figure 5.26**). Here is where all the widget colors and sizes get pulled out of the database and revealed.

The other feature of this page is a method that enables the customer to add an item to their shopping cart. This could be handled in any number of ways; I'll create a link that passes the specific product ID to `cart.php`. For the most part, this script will behave, and be written, like `category.php`.

## To make the product page:

1. Begin a new PHP script in your text editor or IDE (**Script 5.6**).

   ```php
   <?php # Script 5.6 - product.php
   require_once ('./includes/
   → config.inc.php');
   ```

   *continues on page 208*

**Script 5.6** The product page shows all the specific versions of a widget available for purchase.

```php
1    <?php # Script 5.6 - product.php
2
3    /*
4     *  This is the product page.
5     *  This page shows all the specific
6     *  products available for a given $_GET['gw_id'].
7     *  Links allow customers to add items to their cart.
8     */
9
10   // Require the configuration file before any PHP code:
11   require_once ('./includes/config.inc.php');
12
13   // Check for a general product ID in the URL.
14   $name = NULL;
15   if (isset($_GET['gw_id'])) {
16
17       // Typecast it to an integer:
18       $gw_id = (int) $_GET['gw_id'];
19
20       // $gw_id must have a valid value.
21       if ($gw_id > 0) {
22
23           // Get the information from the database
24           // for this product:
25           $q = "SELECT name, default_price, description FROM general_widgets WHERE gw_id=$gw_id";
26           $r = mysqli_query($dbc, $q);
27
28           if (mysqli_num_rows($r) == 1) {
29               list ($name, $price, $description) = mysqli_fetch_array($r, MYSQLI_NUM);
30           } // End of mysqli_num_rows() IF.
31
32       } // End of ($gw_id > 0) IF.
33
34   } // End of isset($_GET['gw_id']) IF.
35
36   // Use the name as the page title:
37   if ($name) {
38       $page_title = $name;
39   }
```

*(script continues on next page)*

**Script 5.6** *continued*

```
40
41    // Include the header file:
42    include_once ('./includes/header.html');
43
44    if ($name) { // Show the specific products.
45
46        echo "<h1>$name</h1>\n";
47
48        // Print the product description, if it's not empty.
49        if (!empty($description)) {
50            echo "<p>$description</p>\n";
51        }
52
53        // Get the specific widgets for this product.
54        $q = "SELECT sw_id, color, size, price, in_stock FROM specific_widgets LEFT JOIN colors using
      (color_id) LEFT JOIN sizes USING (size_id) WHERE gw_id=$gw_id ORDER BY size, color";
55        $r = mysqli_query($dbc, $q);
56
57        if (mysqli_num_rows($r) > 1) {
58
59            // Print each:
60            echo '<h3>Available Sizes and Colors</h3>';
61
62            while ($row = mysqli_fetch_array($r, MYSQLI_ASSOC)) {
63
64                // Determine the price:
65                $price = (empty($row['price'])) ? $price : $row['price'];
66
67                // Print most of the information:
68                echo "<p>Size: {$row['size']}<br />Color: {$row['color']}<br /> Price: \$$price<br
      />In Stock?: {$row['in_stock']}";
69
70                // Print cart link:
71                if ($row['in_stock'] == 'Y') {
72                    echo "<br /> <a href=\"cart.php?sw_id={$row['sw_id']}&do=add\">Add to Cart</a>";
73                }
74
75                echo '</p>';
76
77            } // End of WHILE loop.
78
79        } else { // No specific widgets here!
80            echo '<p class="error">There are none of these widgets available for purchase at this
      time.</p>';
81        }
82
83    } else { // Invalid $_GET['gw_id']!
84        echo '<p class="error">This page has been accessed in error.</p>';
85    }
86
87    // Include the footer file to complete the template:
88    include_once ('./includes/footer.html');
89
90    ?>
```

**2.** Begin validating the general widget ID.

```
$name = NULL;

if (isset($_GET['gwid'])) {

    $gwid = (int) $_GET['gwid'];

    if ($gwid > 0) {
```

First, a flag variable is created, called $name. The script will refer to this later on to tell if a valid general widget ID was received. Next, a check confirms that some $_GET['gwid'] value was received, which is then typecast to an integer. This forces $gwid to be an integer. The next check confirms that the integer has a positive value. All of this is exactly like the code in category.php.

**3.** Retrieve the general widget information and complete the validation conditionals.

```
        $q = "SELECT name,
→ default_price, description FROM
→ general_widgets WHERE gw_id=$gwid";
        $r = mysqli_query($dbc,
→ $q);
        if (mysqli_num_rows($r)
→ == 1) {
            list ($name,
→ $price, $description) =
→ mysqli_fetch_array($r, MYSQLI_NUM);
        }
    } // End of ($gwid > 0) IF.
} // End of isset($_GET['gwid']) IF.
```

This first query retrieves the general widget's name, description, and default price. This last value may or may not be overridden by a specific product's price.

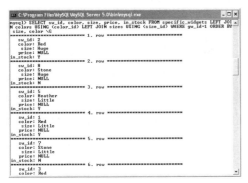

**Figure 5.27** The products page must retrieve all the particular information for the variety of specific widgets available. It does so using this query.

**4.** Make the widget name be the page title and include the header file.

```
if ($name) {
        $page_title = $name;
}
include_once ('./includes/
→ header.html');
```

If the query in Step 3 did return a row, then that value (e.g., *Bouncy Widget 1*) should be used in the browser window.

**5.** If a valid general widget ID was used, print the widget name and description.

```
if ($name) {
        echo "<h1>$category</h1>\n";
        if (!empty($description)) {
                echo "<p>$description
→ </p>\n";
        }
```

The description field in the database is optional (it can be NULL), so a check makes sure it has a value before attempting to print it.

**6.** Retrieve all the specific widgets that are of this general widget type.

```
$q = "SELECT sw_id, color, size,
→ price, in_stock FROM
→ specific_widgets LEFT JOIN colors
→ USING (color_id) LEFT JOIN sizes
→ USING (size_id) WHERE gw_id=$gwid
→ ORDER BY size, color";
$r = mysqli_query($dbc, $q);
if (mysqli_num_rows($r) > 1) {
        echo '<h3>Available Sizes and
→ Colors</h3>';
```

This query needs to get the specific widget ID, color, size, price, and stock status for every widget of the general widget type. This requires a join across three tables (**Figure 5.27**). If at least one item was returned, a caption is printed.

*continues on next page*

**7.** Begin printing each specific widget.

```
while ($row = mysqli_fetch_array($r,
→ MYSQLI_ASSOC)) {
    $price = (empty($row['price']))
→ ? $price : $row['price'];
    echo "<p>Size: {$row['size']}<br
→ />Color: {$row['color']}<br />
→ Price: \$$price<br />In Stock?:
→ {$row['in_stock']}";
```

As with the category page, this isn't the most attractive layout, just a vertical list. For each item, the price to use has to be determined. This is the default price (associated with the general widget) unless the specific widget has a new price.

The size, color, price, and availability are then printed.

**8.** Print a link to the shopping cart. Then complete the item and the `while` loop.

```
    if ($row['in_stock'] == 'Y') {
        echo "<br /> <a
→ href=\"cart.php?sw_id={$row['sw_
→ id']}&do=add\">Add to Cart</a>";
    }
    echo '</p>';
} // End of WHILE loop.
```

If the product is in stock, it should be purchasable. Customers can purchase an item just by clicking the link (this is a common method in most e-commerce sites). The link passes the specific widget ID to `cart.php` (**Figure 5.28**). Each link also passes another variable called *do*, with a value of *add*. This will provide an easy way, on the cart page, to know what should be done (the cart page will allow for both adding new items and updating quantities).

**Figure 5.28** The HTML source page shows how each available item is linked to the shopping cart, passing along the specific item ID in the URL.

**Bouncy Widget 2**

This is the description of this widget. This is the description of this widget. This is the description of this widget. This is the description of this widget.

There are none of these widgets available for purchase at this time.

**Figure 5.29** General widgets may not have any specific widgets available, resulting in this message.

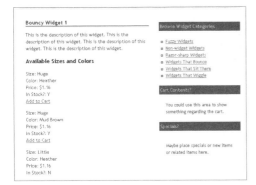

**Figure 5.30** Viewing another product.

9. Complete the conditionals begun in Steps 6 and 5.

```
    } else {
            echo '<p class=
→ "error">There are none of these
→ widgets available for purchase at
→ this time.</p>';
    }
} else {
    echo '<p class="error">This
→ page has been accessed in
→ error.</p>';
}
```

The first `else` clause applies if there are no specific widgets in this category (**Figure 5.29**). A message stating such will be printed in the browser. The second `else` applies if an invalid general widget ID is passed to this page.

10. Complete the page.

```
include_once ('./includes/
→ footer.html');
?>
```

11. Save the file as `product.php`, place it in your Web directory, and test in your Web browser by using the links in `category.php` (**Figure 5.30**).

# Implementing a Shopping Cart

The most important aspect of the e-commerce site is the shopping cart itself. A shopping cart should:

◆ Allow the customer to add items to the cart

◆ Allow for different quantities of each item

◆ Allow the customer to alter the quantities of an item

◆ Allow the customer to remove an item

◆ *Not allow the customer to hack an item's price*

All of the other functionality of an e-commerce site—from displaying products to processing the order—is separate from the cart. I'm going to write a shopping cart page that does all of this as well as display the cart's contents (**Figure 5.31**). There are a number of ways you can handle the cart contents, normally storing them in either a database or a session. I prefer the latter method, although this does mean you could potentially have session problems.

This page would be invoked under two situations: after the user clicks an "Add to Cart" link and after the user updates the cart's contents. The main `if-else` conditional checks for these two situations. Every time the cart is accessed, even directly without clicking "Add to Cart" or updating the form, the page will show the current cart's contents.

**Figure 5.31** The shopping cart page shows the cart's current contents as an updatable form.

## To make a shopping cart page:

1. Create a new PHP document in your text editor or IDE (**Script 5.7**).

```
<?php # Script 5.7 - cart.php
require_once ('./includes/
→ config.inc.php');
```

*continues on page 217*

**Script 5.7** The shopping cart script is the heart of the e-commerce application. It uses a simple multidimensional session array to store the specific item IDs and the quantities purchased. The script also shows the cart as an editable form (the quantities only), which is submitted back to this same page.

```
1    <?php # Script 5.7 - cart.php
2
3    /*
4     *  This is the shopping cart page.
5     *  This page has two modes:
6     *  - add a product to the cart
7     *  - update the cart
8     *  The page shows the cart as a form for updating quantities.
9     */
10
11   // Require the configuration file before any PHP code:
12   require_once ('./includes/config.inc.php');
13
14   // Include the header file:
15   $page_title = 'Shopping Cart';
16   include_once ('./includes/header.html');
17
18   echo '<h1>View Your Shopping Cart</h1>';
19
20   // This page will either add to or update the
21   // shopping cart, based upon the value of $_REQUEST['do']:
22   if (isset($_REQUEST['do']) && ($_REQUEST['do'] == 'add') ) { // Add new item.
23
24       if (isset($_GET['sw_id'])) { // Check for a product ID.
25
26           // Typecast to an integer:
27           $sw_id = (int) $_GET['sw_id'];
28
29           // If it's a positive integer,
30           // get the item information:
31           if ($sw_id > 0) {
32
33               // Define and execute the query:
34               $q = "SELECT name, color, size FROM general_widgets LEFT JOIN specific_widgets USING
     (gw_id) LEFT JOIN colors USING (color_id) LEFT JOIN sizes USING (size_id) WHERE sw_id=$sw_id";
35               $r = mysqli_query($dbc, $q);
```

*(script continues on next page)*

**Script 5.7** *continued*

```
36
37              if (mysqli_num_rows($r) == 1) {
38
39                  // Get the information:
40                  list ($name, $color, $size) = mysqli_fetch_array($r, MYSQLI_NUM);
41
42                  // If the cart already contains
43                  // one of these widgets, increment the quantity:
44                  if (isset($_SESSION['cart'][$sw_id])) {
45
46                      $_SESSION['cart'][$sw_id]++;
47
48                      // Display a message:
49                      echo "<p>Another copy of '$name' in color $color, size $size has been added to
        your shopping cart.</p>\n";
50
51                  } else { // New to the cart.
52
53                      // Add to the cart.
54                      $_SESSION['cart'][$sw_id] = 1;
55
56                      // Display a message:
57                      echo "<p>The widget '$name' in color $color, size $size has been added to your
        shopping cart.</p>\n";
58
59                  }
60
61              } // End of mysqli_num_rows() IF.
62
63          } // End of ($sw_id > 0) IF.
64
65      } // End of isset($_GET['sw_id']) IF.
66
67 } elseif (isset($_REQUEST['do']) && ($_REQUEST['do'] == 'update')) {
68
69      // Change any quantities...
70      // $k is the product ID.
71      // $v is the new quantity.
72      foreach ($_POST['qty'] as $k => $v) {
73
74          // Must be integers!
75          $pid = (int) $k;
76          $qty = (int) $v;
77
78          if ($qty == 0) { // Delete item.
79              unset ($_SESSION['cart'][$pid]);
80          } elseif ($qty > 0) { // Change quantity.
81              $_SESSION['cart'][$pid] = $qty;
82          }
83
```

*(script continues on next page)*

Script 5.7 *continued*

```
84       } // End of FOREACH.
85
86       // Print a message.
87       echo '<p>Your shopping cart has been updated.</p>';
88
89  } // End of $_REQUEST IF-ELSE.
90
91  // Show the shopping cart if it's not empty:
92  if (isset($_SESSION['cart']) && !empty($_SESSION['cart'])) {
93
94       // Retrieve all of the information for the products in the cart:
95       $q = "SELECT sw_id, name, color, size, default_price, price FROM general_widgets LEFT JOIN
    specific_widgets USING (gw_id) LEFT JOIN colors USING (color_id) LEFT JOIN sizes USING (size_id)
    WHERE sw_id IN (";
96
97       // Add each product ID.
98       foreach ($_SESSION['cart'] as $sw_id => $v) {
99           $q .= (int) $sw_id . ',';
100      }
101      $q = substr ($q, 0, -1) . ') ORDER BY name, size, color';
102      $r = mysqli_query ($dbc, $q);
103
104      if (mysqli_num_rows($r) > 0) {
105
106          // Create a table and a form:
107          echo '<table border="0" width="90%" cellspacing="2" cellpadding="2" align="center">
108          <tr>
109              <td align="left" width="20%"><b>Widget</b></td>
110              <td align="left" width="15%"><b>Size</b></td>
111              <td align="left" width="15%"><b>Color</b></td>
112              <td align="right" width="15%"><b>Price</b></td>
113              <td align="center" width="10%"><b>Qty</b></td>
114              <td align="right" width="15%"><b>Total Price</b></td>
115          </tr>
116  <form action="cart.php" method="post">
117  <input type="hidden" name="do" value="update" />
118      ';
119
120          // Print each item:
121          $total = 0; // Total cost of the order.
122          while ($row = mysqli_fetch_array ($r, MYSQLI_ASSOC)) {
123
124              // Determine the price:
125              $price = (empty($row['price'])) ? $row['default_price'] : $row['price'];
126
127              // Calculate the total and sub-totals:
128              $subtotal = $_SESSION['cart'][$row['sw_id']] * $price;
129              $total += $subtotal;
130              $subtotal = number_format($subtotal, 2);
```

*(script continues on next page)*

**Script 5.7** *continued*

```
131
132              // Print the row:
133              echo <<<EOT
134   <tr>
135      <td align="left">{$row['name']}</td>
136      <td align="left">{$row['size']}</td>
137      <td align="left">{$row['color']}</td>
138      <td align="right">\$$price</td>
139      <td align="center"><input type="text" size="3" name="qty[{$row['sw_id']}]"
      value="{$_SESSION['cart'][$row['sw_id']]}" /></td>
140              <td align="right">\$$subtotal</td>
141          </tr>\n
142   EOT;
143
144          } // End of the WHILE loop.
145
146          // Print the footer, close the table, and the form:
147          echo '   <tr>
148              <td colspan="5" align="right"><b>Total:<b></td>
149              <td align="right">$' . number_format ($total, 2) . '</td>
150          </tr>
151          <tr>
152              <td colspan="6" align="center">Set an item\'s quantity to 0 to remove it from your
      cart.</td>
153          </tr>
154          </table><div align="center"><button type="submit" name="submit" value="update">Update
      Cart</button>        
155              <a href="checkout.php"><button type="button" name="checkout"
      value="Checkout">Checkout</button></a></div>
156      </form>';
157
158      } // End of mysqli_num_rows() IF.
159
160   } else {
161      echo '<p>Your cart is currently empty.</p>';
162   }
163
164   // Include the footer file to complete the template:
165   include_once ('./includes/footer.html');
166
167   ?>
```

2. Include the header file.

```
$page_title = 'Shopping Cart';
include_once ('./includes/
→ header.html');
echo '<h1>View Your Shopping
→ Cart</h1>';
```

3. Check for a $_REQUEST['do'] variable.

```
if (isset($_REQUEST['do']) &&
→ ($_REQUEST['do'] == 'add') ) {
```

When an item is added to the cart by clicking the link on the products page, $_GET['do'] will have a value of *add*.

4. Validate the specific widget ID.

```
if (isset($_GET['sw_id'])) {
     $sw_id = (int) $_GET['sw_id'];
     if ($sw_id > 0) {
```

Just to be safe, you should make sure that the specific widget ID is a positive integer.

5. Retrieve the product information from the database.

```
$q = "SELECT name, color, size FROM
→ general_widgets LEFT JOIN
→ specific_widgets USING (gw_id) LEFT
→ JOIN colors USING (color_id) LEFT
→ JOIN sizes USING (size_id) WHERE
→ sw_id=$sw_id";
$r = mysqli_query($dbc, $q);
if (mysqli_num_rows($r) == 1) {
     list ($name, $color, $size) =
mysqli_fetch_array($r, MYSQLI_NUM);
```

In order to both confirm that a valid product ID was received, and to be able to display on this page the name and details of the product just added, this query is necessary. It performs a join across four tables in order to get the general widget name as well as the specific widget's color and size.

*continues on next page*

**6.** Update the cart.

```
if (isset($_SESSION['cart']
→ [$sw_id])) {
    $_SESSION['cart'][$sw_id]++;
    echo "<p>Another copy of '$name'
→ in color $color, size $size has
→ been added to your shopping
→ cart.</p>\n";
} else {
    $_SESSION['cart'][$sw_id] = 1;
    echo "<p>The widget '$name' in
→ color $color, size $size has been
→ added to your shopping
→ cart.</p>\n";
}
```

The `$_SESSION['cart']` array uses the specific product IDs for the keys and the quantities ordered for the values. If the item is already represented in the shopping cart, the assumption is that the customer wants to add another. In that case, `$_SESSION['cart'][$sw_id]` is incremented. Otherwise, a new array element is added to the cart, with a value of 1. Messages indicating what just happened are then printed (**Figures 5.32** and **5.33**).

**7.** Complete the conditionals started in Steps 4 and 5, and then check to see if `$_REQUEST['do']` equals *update*.

```
            } // End of
→ mysqli_num_rows() IF.
        } // End of ($sw_id > 0)
IF.
    } // End of
→ isset($_GET['sw_id']) IF.
} elseif (isset($_REQUEST['do']) &&
→ ($_REQUEST['do'] == 'update')) {
```

`$_REQUEST['do']` will have a value of *update* when the user updates their cart by submitting the form. At this point the shopping cart should attempt to update every quantity.

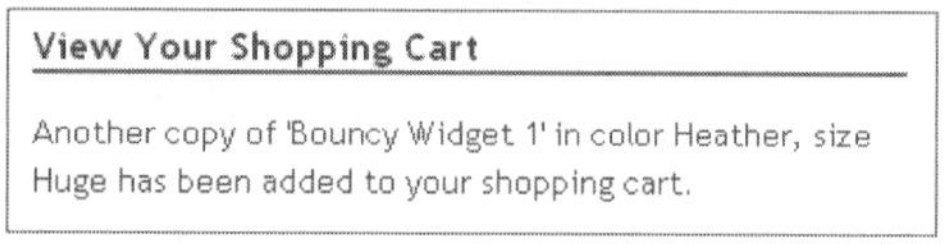

IMPLEMENTING A SHOPPING CART

View Your Shopping Cart

Another copy of 'Bouncy Widget 1' in color Heather, size Huge has been added to your shopping cart.

**Figure 5.32** This is the message a customer will see if they click the same "Add to Cart" link for a product already in the cart.

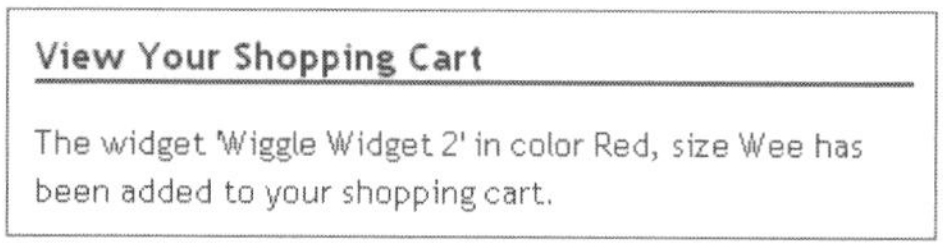

View Your Shopping Cart

The widget 'Wiggle Widget 2' in color Red, size Wee has been added to your shopping cart.

**Figure 5.33** Adding a new product to the shopping cart.

8. Update the cart quantities.

```
foreach ($_POST['qty'] as $k => $v)
{
    $pid = (int) $k;
    $qty = (int) $v;
    if ($qty == 0) {
        unset
→ ($_SESSION['cart'][$pid]);
    } elseif ($qty > 0) {
        $_SESSION['cart'][$pid]
→ = $qty;
    }
}
```

This is pretty simple. Both the key, which is the product ID, and the value, which is the quantity, are first typecast to integers. If the quantity equals 0, then the item is removed from the cart. This will also apply if a noninteger is entered as the quantity. Otherwise, as long as the quantity is positive, the cart is updated.

9. Print a message and complete the $_REQUEST if-else.

```
    echo '<p>Your shopping cart has
→ been updated.</p>';
} // End of $_REQUEST IF-ELSE.
```

10. Show the cart contents, if it's not empty.

```
if (isset($_SESSION['cart'])) &&
→ !empty($_SESSION['cart'])) {
```

If the customer goes directly to the cart page, then $_SESSION['cart'] will not be set. If the user deletes everything from their cart, then $_SESSION['cart'] will be empty.

*continues on next page*

11. Create the query for retrieving the cart content details.

```
$q = "SELECT sw_id, name, color,
→ size, default_price, price FROM
→ general_widgets LEFT JOIN
→ specific_widgets USING (gw_id)
→ LEFT JOIN colors USING (color_id)
→ LEFT JOIN sizes USING (size_id)
→ WHERE sw_id IN (";

foreach ($_SESSION['cart'] as $sw_id
→ => $v) {

    $q .= (int) $sw_id . ',';

}

$q = substr ($q, 0, -1) . ') ORDER
→ BY name, size, color';

$r = mysqli_query ($dbc, $q);
```

The query needs to perform a join across four tables in order to retrieve each item's name, color, size, and price. An **IN** clause will append each specific widget ID to the query. **Figure 5.34** shows the query and its result.

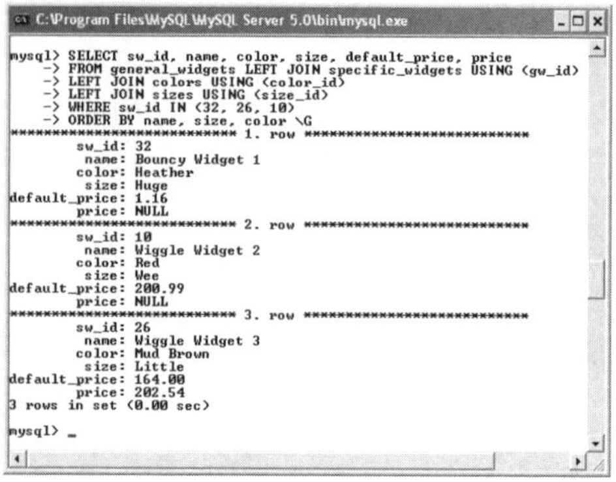

12. Begin creating the table and form.

```
if (mysqli_num_rows($r) > 0) {
    echo '<table border="0"
→ width="90%" cellspacing="2"
→ cellpadding="2" align="center">
    <tr>
        <td align="left"
→ width="20%"><b>Widget</b></td>
        <td align="left"
→ width="15%"><b>Size</b></td>
        <td align="left"
→ width="15%"><b>Color</b></td>
        <td align="right"
→ width="15%"><b>Price</b></td>
        <td align="center"
→ width="10%"><b>Qty</b></td>
        <td align="right"
→ width="15%"><b>Total
Price</b></td>
```

**Figure 5.34** The query used by the shopping cart to retrieve each item's details.

```
        </tr>
<form action="cart.php"
→ method="post">
<input type="hidden" name="do"
→ value="update" />
';
```

The table generated by this cart will list the products ordered, as well as how many and at what price. It will be created as an HTML form allowing the customer to alter the quantities, even deleting an item altogether. The recipient of the form will be the cart.php script, this same page. A hidden input named *do* with a value of *update* will indicate to this page that a cart update is in order once the form has been submitted (see Step 7).

**13.** Initialize a total variable and begin retrieving each item.

```
$total = 0;
while ($row = mysqli_fetch_array
→ ($r, MYSQLI_ASSOC)) {
```

**14.** Calculate the price of the item, the subtotal, and the total thus far.

```
$price = (empty($row['price'])) ?
→ $row['default_price'] :
→ $row['price'];
$subtotal = $_SESSION['cart']
→ [$row['sw_id']] * $price;
$total += $subtotal;
$subtotal = number_
→ format($subtotal, 2);
```

Remember that the price of an item could be the default price or the specific widget price, if it exists. The ternary operator helps assign the price to use to the $price variable. Then the subtotal is calculated as the price times the quantity. This is added to the $total variable and then formatted (for display purposes).

*continues on next page*

**15.** Print each item in the cart.

```
      echo <<<EOT
<tr>

      <td
align="left">{$row['name']}</td>
      <td
align="left">{$row['size']}</td>
      <td align="left">{$row
→ ['color']}</td>
      <td align="right">\$$price</td>
      <td align="center"><input
→ type="text" size="3"
→ name="qty[{$row['sw_id']}]"
→ value="{$_SESSION['cart'][$row
→ ['sw_id']]}" /></td>
      <td
align="right">\$$subtotal</td>
</tr>\n
EOT;
} // End of the WHILE loop.
```

Because I'm using a mix of HTML and PHP variables here, the heredoc syntax is a good way to print it all out (see Chapter 1 for details). Each record from the query is a row in the table, with the name, size, and color printed as is. Then the price, quantity, and subtotal are printed. Notice that the quantity is printed as an HTML text input, with the current quantity as the value (**Figure 5.35**). This will make it easy for the customer to change the quantities as needed.

**Figure 5.35** Part of the HTML source of the form. For each input, the name is qty[*X*], where *X* is the specific widget ID and the value is preset as the current quantity in the cart.

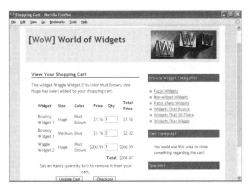

**Figure 5.36** The shopping cart after adding another item.

**Figure 5.37** The shopping cart after updating two quantities and deleting another item (compare with Figure 5.36).

## ✔ Tip

■ Chapter 8, "Real-World OOP," creates a shopping cart class with this same basic functionality. By comparing that code with this code, you can get a glimpse into procedural versus object-oriented programming.

**16.** Complete the table and the form.

```
echo '   <tr>
            <td colspan="5"
→ align="right"><b>Total:<b></td>
            <td align="right">$' .
→ number_format ($total, 2) . '</td>
        </tr>
        <tr>
            <td colspan="6" align=
→ "center">Set an item\'s quantity
→ to 0 to remove it from your
→ cart.</td>
        </tr>
        </table><div align="center">
→ <button type="submit" name=
→ "submit" value="update">Update
→ Cart</button>  
→      
        <a href="checkout.php">
→ <button type="button"
→ name="checkout" value="Checkout">
→ Checkout</button>→ </a></div>
</form>';
```

The table and form conclude with the total being printed. Then instructions show how to remove an item. Finally, the user is given two buttons: one for updating the cart (submitting the form back to this page) and another for checking out.

**17.** Complete the page.

```
    }
} else {
    echo '<p>Your cart is currently
→ empty.</p>';
}
include_once
→ ('./includes/footer.html');
?>
```

**18.** Save the script as cart.php, upload it to your server, and test it in your Web browser (**Figures 5.36** and **5.37**).

# Validating Credit Cards

The next step for the consumer in the e-commerce process would be to check out. It's at this point that the site would take or confirm their name, shipping address, and other information. If using a registration and login system, this information would be pulled out of the database (the `customers` table already allows for it). A checkout page might also apply discounts or gift certificates to an order, allow the customer to specify the shipping method (calculating the shipping accordingly) or choose gift wrapping, and more.

All checkout systems begin the payment process. For some sites, this is a link to PayPal or another online payment handler. For other sites, this is where the credit card information is taken. This next script will be a bare-bones implementation of a checkout page, taking the credit card type, number, and expiration date, and then validating this information. For validating credit cards,

there are certain rules the numbers must abide by. Different types of cards have different lengths and potentially different set numbers (e.g., all Visa cards begin with a 4, all MasterCards with a 5). Every credit card number, no matter the type, must also pass the Luhn/Mod 10 algorithm. It's a complicated little scheme and, coupled with the card type–specific checks, I find it best to use existing card validation code, rather than rolling your own. Toward that end, this next script will use the PEAR Validate_Finance_CreditCard class. Although in alpha stage at this writing, it works just fine. If you can't or don't want to use this PEAR class, just search the Web for other PHP credit card validation code. Note that this, or any similar code, doesn't test if a credit card number is approved for purchases. Rather, it confirms that a number is syntactically correct. The payment gateway (see the accompanying sidebar "Handling Payments") would still have to be used to approve a purchase; this code prevents an attempted purchase using an knowingly invalid card number.

## To validate credit cards:

1. Begin a new PHP script in your text editor or IDE (**Script 5.8**).

```php
<?php # Script 5.8 - checkout.php
require_once ('./includes/
→ config.inc.php');
$page_title = 'Checkout';
include_once ('./includes/
→ header.html');
echo '<h1>Checkout</h1>';
```

*continues on page 228*

**Script 5.8** This, the final script in the chapter, primarily demonstrates one way to validate a credit card number. It uses the PEAR Validate_Finance_CreditCard class.

```php
1    <?php # Script 5.8 - checkout.php
2
3    /*
4     *  This is a bare-bones checkout page.
5     *  For demonstration purposes, this page only
6     *  takes and validates the credit card information.
7     *  The assumption is that other information--
8     *  name, address, etc.
9     *  --would be retrieved from the database after logging in
10    *  and also confirmed on this page.
11    */
12
13   // Require the configuration file before any PHP code:
14   require_once ('./includes/config.inc.php');
15
16   // Include the header file:
17   $page_title = 'Checkout';
18   include_once ('./includes/header.html');
19
20   echo '<h1>Checkout</h1>';
21
22   // Set the time zone:
23   date_default_timezone_set('GMT');
24
25   // Check for form submission.
26   if (isset($_POST['submitted'])) {
27
28       // Validate the credit card...
29
30       // Check the expiration date:
31       $year = (int) $_POST['cc_exp_year'];
```

*(script continues on next page)*

**Script 5.8** *continued*

```
32       $month = (int) $_POST['cc_exp_month'];
33
34       // Get the current date:
35       $today = getdate();
36
37       // Validate the expiration date:
38       if ( ($year > $today['year']) OR
39       ( ($year == $today['year']) AND ($month >= $today['mon']) )
40       ) {
41
42           // Include the class definition:
43           require ('Validate/Finance/CreditCard.php');
44
45           // Create the object:
46           $cc = new Validate_Finance_CreditCard();
47
48           // Validate the card number and type:
49           if ($cc->number($_POST['cc_number'], $_POST['cc_type'])) {
50
51               // Use XXX to process the order!!!
52               // If payment goes through, complete the order!
53               echo '<p>Your order is complete (but not really).</p>';
54               include_once ('./includes/footer.html');
55               exit();
56
57           } else { // Invalid card number or type.
58               echo '<p class="error">Please enter a valid credit card number and type.</p>';
59           }
60
61       } else { // Invalid date.
62           echo '<p class="error">Please enter a valid expiration date.</p>';
63       }
64
65   }
66
67   // Show the form.
68   ?>
69   <form action="checkout.php" method="post">
70   <input type="hidden" name="submitted" value="true" />
71   <table border="0" width="90%" cellspacing="2" cellpadding="2" align="center">
72       <tr>
73           <td align="right">Credit Card Type:</td>
74           <td align="left"><select name="cc_type">
75           <option value="amex">American Express</option>
76           <option value="visa">Visa</option>
77           <option value="mastercard">MasterCard</option>
```

*(script continues on next page)*

**VALIDATING CREDIT CARDS**

**Script 5.8** *continued*

```
78          <option value="diners club">Diners Club</option>
79          <option value="enroute">enRoute</option>
80          </select></td>
81      </tr>
82
83      <tr>
84          <td align="right">Credit Card Number:</td>
85          <td align="left"><input type="text" name="cc_number" maxlength="20" /></td>
86      </tr>
87
88      <tr>
89          <td align="right">Expiration Date:</td>
90          <td align="left"><select name="cc_exp_month">
91          <option value="">Month</option>
92          <option value="1">Jan</option>
93          <option value="2">Feb</option>
94          <option value="3">Mar</option>
95          <option value="4">Apr</option>
96          <option value="5">May</option>
97          <option value="6">Jun</option>
98          <option value="7">Jul</option>
99          <option value="8">Aug</option>
100         <option value="9">Sep</option>
101         <option value="10">Oct</option>
102         <option value="11">Nov</option>
103         <option value="12">Dec</option>
104         </select> <select name="cc_exp_year">
105         <option value="">Year</option>
106         <?php for ($start = date('Y'), $end = date('Y') + 10; $start < $end; $start++) {
107         echo "<option value=\"$start\">$start</option>\n";
108         }
109         ?>
110         </select></td>
111     </tr>
112
113     <tr>
114         <td align="center" colspan="2"><button type="submit" name="submit"
    value="update">Checkout</button></td>
115     </tr>
116 </table>
117 </form>
118
119 <?php
120 // Include the footer file to complete the template:
121 include_once ('./includes/footer.html');
122
123 ?>
```

**2.** Set the default time zone.

```
date_default_timezone_set('GMT');
```

As of PHP 5.1, you should set the time zone using `date_default_timezone_set()` prior to calling a date function. This line could also logically go into the configuration file.

**3.** Check for a form submission.

```
if (isset($_POST['submitted'])) {
```

This page will both display and handle the form.

**4.** Typecast the expiration month and year.

```
$year = (int) $_POST['cc_exp_year'];
$month = (int) $_POST['cc_
→ exp_month'];
```

Even though these values should come from pull-down menus, they should still be typecast as integers for sake of security.

**5.** Make sure the expiration date is in the future.

```
$today = getdate();
if ( ($year > $today['year']) OR
( ($year == $today['year']) AND
→ ($month >= $today['mon']) )
) {
```

This conditional verifies that the expiration year is in the future or, if the year is this year, that the month is not earlier than the current month.

**6.** Create a Validate_Finance_CreditCard object and use its `number()` method.

```
require ('Validate/Finance/
→ CreditCard.php');

$cc = new Validate_Finance_
→ CreditCard();

if ($cc->number($_POST['cc_number'],
→ $_POST['cc_type'])) {
```

See Chapter 6, "Basic Object-Oriented Programming," if you don't understand these lines. You can also refer to Chapter 12, "Using PEAR."

The `number()` function is called, providing the credit card number and type. It returns a Boolean value indicating the validity of that number for that type.

**7.** If the credit card number is valid, complete the checkout process.

```
echo '<p>Your order is complete (but
→ not really).</p>';

include_once ('./includes/
→ footer.html');

exit();
```

Instead of these steps, a real e-commerce site would now connect to the payment gateway (see the sidebar). Here, a simple message is printed, then the footer included, and the script exited.

**8.** Complete the conditionals begun in Steps 2, 5, and 6.

```
} else {
echo '<p
→ class="error">Please enter a valid
→ credit card number and type.</p>';
}
} else {
echo '<p class="error">
→ Please enter a valid expiration
→ date.</p>';
}
}
```

The first `else` applies if the submitted number and type do not pass the `$cc->number()` test. The second applies if the expiration date is in the past or invalid.

**Figure 5.38** The form for taking the credit card information.

**9.** Begin the HTML form.

```
?>
<form action="checkout.php"
→ method="post">
<input type="hidden"
→ name="submitted" value="true" />
```

**10.** Create the form elements for the credit card type and number.

```
<table border="0" width="90%"
→ cellspacing="2" cellpadding="2"
→ align="center">
    <tr>
        <td align="right">Credit
→ Card Type:</td>
        <td align="left"><select
→ name="cc_type">
        <option value="amex">
→ American Express</option>
        <option value="visa">
→ Visa</option>
        <option value=
→ "mastercard">MasterCard</option>
        <option value="diners
→ club">Diners Club</option>
        <option
value="enroute">enRoute</option>
        </select></td>
    </tr>
    <tr>
        <td align="right">Credit
→ Card Number:</td>
        <td align="left"><input
→ type="text" name="cc_number"
→ maxlength="20" /></td>
    </tr>
```

The HTML form is pretty simple (**Figure 5.38**).

*continues on next page*

**11.** Create the form elements for the expiration date.

```
<tr>
    <td align="right">Expiration
→ Date:</td>
    <td align="left"><select
→ name="cc_exp_month">
        <option value="">Month</option>
        <option value="1">Jan</option>
        <option value="2">Feb</option>
        <option value="3">Mar</option>
        <option value="4">Apr</option>
        <option value="5">May</option>
        <option value="6">Jun</option>
        <option value="7">Jul</option>
        <option value="8">Aug</option>
        <option value="9">Sep</option>
        <option value="10">Oct</option>
        <option value="11">Nov</option>
        <option value="12">Dec</option>
    </select> <select name="cc_
→ exp_year">
        <option value="">Year</option>
        <?php for ($start = date('Y'),
→ $end = date('Y') + 10; $start <
→ $end; $start++) {
        echo "<option value=\"$start\">
→ $start</option>\n";
        }
        ?>
    </select></td>
</tr>
```

One thing I like to do with the expiration year is use PHP's date() function to automatically list the next ten years as options (**Figure 5.39**). This way, the HTML will always be correct.

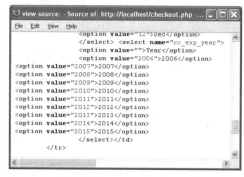

**Figure 5.39** The HTML source code shows the dynamically generated years.

**Figure 5.40** Valid card numbers and types create this result.

**Figure 5.41** Invalid numbers result in an error, with the form redisplayed.

**12.** Complete the HTML form.

```
<tr>
        <td align="center"
→ colspan="2"><button type="submit"
→ name="submit" value="update">
→ Checkout</button></td>
    </tr>
</table>
</form>
```

**13.** Complete the page.

```
<?php
include_once ('./includes/
→ footer.html');
?>
```

**14.** Save the file as checkout.php, place it in your Web directory, and test in your Web browser (**Figures 5.40** and **5.41**). For valid test credit card numbers to use, search the Web.

## ✔ Tip

■ For more information and code to complete this example, see the book's corresponding Web site and supporting forum.

## Handling Payments

Unfortunately it's really impossible to create a complete e-commerce application in a book. The reason is that how the most important aspect—the commerce—is handled varies greatly. This requires some system, called a payment gateway, to get the money from the customer's account to the store's account.

Normally a store creates an account with a chosen gateway. Every gateway I've ever worked with provides an API (application programming interface) for connecting your site to their system. What this really comes down to is submitting a form with certain information—the store's ID, the customer's information, the credit card information, the amount of the transaction, and so on—to the gateway's server. The server processes the information and then returns to the store's site a code indicating the success of the transaction.

When it comes time for you to implement a complete e-commerce solution, you'll need to choose a gateway and then program the final steps of your site to match the gateway's methodologies. It's not at all hard; it's just not something that can really be done in a book.

# BASIC OBJECT-ORIENTED PROGRAMMING

Object-oriented programming (commonly abbreviated OOP) is a relative newcomer to the world of programming. Before the advent of OOP, languages such as Pascal and BASIC solved problems through linear programming. As projects get bigger, perhaps requiring teams of developers, this approach becomes too time-consuming and error-prone. Hence OOP, which allows programmers to more rapidly develop, use, and manage sophisticated applications.

Similarly, OOP is quite new to PHP. Version 3 of the language had rudimentary support, and version 4 made some nice improvements on this front. It's in PHP 5 that OOP support has become closer to what true OOP languages, like Java and C#, offer. Although PHP is still not as strong in its OOP feature set as it could be, object-oriented programming in PHP has a lot going for it. While expert PHP programmers can go through their entire careers without ever using objects without significant limitations on what they can do, most find some knowledge of the subject beneficial.

In this chapter, and the next (Chapter 7, "Advanced OOP"), I will only be using objects as they function in PHP 5 and later. This is very important: *If you're using PHP 4, most of this code will not work!* (And, frankly, compared with PHP 5, objects in PHP 4 aren't even worth learning.) Here, I will use somewhat mundane examples, as the focus of the chapter is more on explaining OOP theory and syntax to the uninitiated. In subsequent chapters, practical, real-world code will be used. Through multiple examples and plenty of explanation, I hope in this book to fully demonstrate not just *how* you do object-oriented programming in PHP but also *when* and *why*.

# OOP Theory

The first thing that you must understand about OOP is that it presents not just new syntax but a new way of thinking about a problem. By far the most common mistake beginning OOP programmers make is to inappropriately apply OOP. PHP will tell you when you make a syntactical mistake, but you'll need to learn how to avoid theoretical mistakes, too.

The two most important terms for OOP are *class* and *object*. A class is a generalized definition of a thing. Think of classes as a blueprint. An object is the implementation of that thing. Think of objects as the house built using the blueprint. To program using OOP, you design your classes and then implement them in your programs as needed.

One of the tenets of OOP is *modularity*: breaking applications into specific subparts. Web sites do many, many things: interact with databases, handle forms, send emails, generate HTML, etc. Each of these things can be a module, which is to say a class. By separating unrelated (albeit interacting) elements, code can be developed independently, maintenance and updates may be less messy, and debugging can be simplified.

Related to modularity is *abstraction*: classes should be defined broadly. This is a common and understandable beginner's mistake. As an example, instead of designing a class for interacting with a MySQL database, you should make one that interacts with a non-specific database. From there, using *inheritance* and *overriding*, you would define a more particular class for MySQL. This class would look and act like the general database class, but some of its functionality would be customized.

Another principle of OOP is *encapsulation*: separating out and hiding how something is accomplished. A properly designed object can do everything you need it to do without your ever knowing how it's being done. Coupled with encapsulation is *access control* or *visibility*, which dictates how accessible aspects of the object are.

Those are the main concepts behind OOP. You'll see how they play out in the many OOP examples in this book. But before getting into the code, I'll talk about OOP's dark side.

First of all, *OOP is not a better way to program*, just a different way. In some cases, it *may be* better and in some cases worse, but OOP is not the Mount Everest of all things programming. And in PHP in particular, you can have a long, happy, and viable programming career without OOP. However, you might have a more productive, easier, and lucrative career using it (emphasis on "might").

As for the technical negatives of OOP, use of objects can (often) be less efficient than a procedural approach (just as defining and invoking your own functions can be less efficient). The performance difference between using an object or not may be imperceptible in some cases, but you should be aware of this potential side effect.

A second issue that arises is what I have already pointed out: misuse and overuse of objects. Making this mistake isn't the end of the world, of course, or even cause for your applications to fail, but like trying to use a screwdriver to drive a nail, it's just not a good thing to do.

True object-oriented programming is smart, purposeful object-oriented programming!

# Defining a Class

OOP programming begins with classes, a class being an abstract definition of a thing: what information must be stored and what functionality must be possible. A philosophical example of a class would be Human. A Human class would be able to store information such as gender, height, weight, birth date, and so forth. The functionality of a Human could be eating, sleeping, working, and more.

Syntactically, a class definition begins with the word class, followed by the name of the class. The class name cannot be a reserved word and is often written in uppercase, as a convention (I always use lowercase for my variables but stick with uppercase classes). After the class name, the class definition is placed within curly braces:

```
class ClassName {

}
```

Classes contain variables and functions, which are referred to as *attributes* (or *properties*) and *methods*, respectively (you'll see other terms, too). Functions are easy to add to classes:

```
class ClassName {
    function function_name() {
        // Function code.
    }
}
```

The methods you define within a class are defined just like functions outside of a class. They can take arguments, have default values, return values, and so on.

*continues on next page*

---

## Design Patterns

A subject you'll hear in correlation to OOP is *patterns* (or *design patterns*). By following the principles of OOP, you'll come up with a class, which is a blueprint for building a thing. Every time you have an application that requires that thing, you use that class. If your application requires a variant of that thing, you use an extension of that class.

The more you program, the more you realize that most applications do the same things (or variants of those things). This is to say that most programs have the same problems that must be solved. With this in mind, design patterns are accepted solutions to common problems. They aren't necessarily specific code implementations but more like a template to apply. Smart people have thought about these issues and come up with the best approach. If you find yourself faced with a common problem, use a design pattern instead of reinventing the wheel.

Attributes within classes are a little different than variables outside of classes. First of all, all attributes must be prefixed with a keyword indicating the variable's *visibility*. The options are: public, private, and protected. Unfortunately these values won't mean anything to you until you understand *inheritance* (in Chapter 7), so until then, just use public:

```
class ClassName {
    public $var1, $var2;
    function function_name() {
        // Function code.
    }
}
```

As shown here, a class's attributes are listed before any method definitions.

The second distinction between attributes and normal variables is that, if an attribute is initialized with a set value, that value must be a constant and not the result of an expression.

```
class GoodClass {
    public $var1 = 123;
    public $var2 = 'string';
    public $var3 = array(1, 2, 3);
}
class BadClass {
    // These won't work!
    public $today = get_date();
    public $square = $num * $num;
}
```

Note that you don't have to initialize the attributes with a value. And, aside from declaring variables, all of a class's code goes within its methods. You could not do this:

```
class BadClass {
    public $num = 2;
    public $square;
    $square = $num * $num; // No!
}
```

With all of this in mind, let's create an easy, almost useless class just to make sure it's all working fine and dandy. Naturally, I'll use a *Hello, world!* example (it's either that or *foo* and *bar*). To make it a little more interesting, this class will be able to say *Hello, world!* in different languages.

**Script 6.1** This simple class will allow you to say *Hello, world!* through the magic of objects! (Okay, so it's completely unnecessary, but it's a fine introductory demonstration.)

```
1    <?php # Script 6.1 - HelloWorld.php
2
3    /*  This page defines the HelloWorld
     class.
4     *  The class says "Hello, world!" in
     different languages.
5     */
6
7    class HelloWorld {
8
9        // This method prints a greeting.
10       // It takes one argument: the
     language to use.
11       // Default language is English.
12       function say_hello ($language =
     'English') {
13
14           // Put the greeting within
     P tags.
15           echo '<p>';
16
```

*(script continues on next page)*

## To define a class:

1. Create a new PHP document in your text editor or IDE (**Script 6.1**).

   `<?php # Script 6.1 - HelloWorld.php`

2. Begin defining the class.

   `class HelloWorld {`

   Using the syntax outlined earlier, start with the keyword `class`, followed by the name of the class, followed by the opening curly brace (which could go on the next line, if you prefer).

   For the class name, I use the "camel" capitalization: initial letters capitalized as are the first letter of new words. This is a pseudo-standardized convention in many OOP languages.

3. Begin defining the first (and only) method.

   ```
   function say_hello ($language =
   → 'English') {
   ```

   This class currently contains no attributes (variables), which would have been declared before the methods. This method is called `say_hello()`. It takes one argument: the language for the greeting.

   For the methods, I normally use all lowercase and separate words with an underscore. This is the same naming scheme I use for functions outside of classes.

4. Start the method's code.

   `echo '<p>';`

   The method will print *Hello, world!* in one of several languages. The message will be wrapped within HTML paragraph tags, begun here.

   *continues on next page*

**5.** Add the method's switch.

```
switch ($language) {
    case 'Dutch':
        echo 'Hello, wereld!';
        break;
    case 'French':
        echo 'Bonjour, monde!';
        break;
    case 'German':
        echo 'Hallo, Welt!';
        break;
    case 'Italian':
        echo 'Ciao, mondo!';
        break;
    case 'Spanish':
        echo '¡Hola, mundo!';
        break;
    case 'English':
    default:
        echo 'Hello, world!';
        break;
}
```

The switch prints different messages based upon the chosen language. English is the default language, both in the switch and as the value of the $language argument (see Step 3). Obviously you can easily expand this switch to include more languages, like non-Western ones.

**Script 6.1** *continued*

```
17          // Print a message specific to a
        language.
18          switch ($language) {
19              case 'Dutch':
20                  echo 'Hello, wereld!';
21                  break;
22              case 'French':
23                  echo 'Bonjour, monde!';
24                  break;
25              case 'German':
26                  echo 'Hallo, Welt!';
27                  break;
28              case 'Italian':
29                  echo 'Ciao, mondo!';
30                  break;
31              case 'Spanish':
32                  echo '¡Hola, mundo!';
33                  break;
34              case 'English':
35              default:
36                  echo 'Hello, world!';
37                  break;
38          } // End of switch.
39
40          // Close the HTML paragraph.
41          echo '</p>';
42
43      } // End of say_hello() function.
44
45  } // End of HelloWorld class.
46
47
48  ?>
```

**6.** Complete the say_hello() method.

```
    echo '</p>';
}
```

You just need to close the HTML paragraph tag.

**7.** Complete the class and the PHP page.

```
}
?>
```

**8.** Save the file as HelloWorld.php.

You've now created your first class. This isn't, to be clear, a good use of OOP, but it starts the process and you'll learn better implementations of the concept in due time.

## ✔ Tips

■ In PHP 4, attributes (class variables) were identified using:

```
var $variable_name;
```

This is still supported in PHP 5, although not recommended unless you need to program for backward compatibility.

■ Class methods can also have a visibility, by preceding the function definition with the appropriate keyword. If not stated, all methods have an assumed definition of

```
public function function_name() {…
```

■ The class stdClass is already in use internally by PHP and cannot be declared in your own code.

# Creating an Object

Using OOP is a two-step process. The first—defining a class—you just did when you wrote the HelloWorld class. The second step is to make use of that class by creating an *object* (or a class instance).

Going back to my Human class analogy, an instance of this class may be called Jude. Jude's attributes are a gender of male, a height of about 50 inches, a weight of 65 pounds, and a birth date of November 15, 1998. Jude is one instance of the Human class and, as you may have noticed, is also a child. A second instance, Kelsey, has a female gender, a height of 5 feet, a weight of 90 pounds, and a birth date of April 11, 1996. Both Jude and Kelsey are separate objects derived from the same class. They are similar in theory, different in actuality.

Creating an object is remarkably easy in PHP once you've defined your class. It involves the keyword new:

```
$object = new ClassName();
```

Now the variable $object exists and is of type ClassName (instead of type string or array).

To call the methods of the class, you use this syntax:

```
$object->method_name();
```

If a method takes arguments, you would use:

```
$object->method_name('value', 32, true);
```

Once you've finished with an object, you can delete it as you would any variable:

```
unset($object);
```

Simple enough! Let's go ahead and quickly make use of the HelloWorld class.

**Script 6.2** In this page, PHP uses the defined class in order to say *Hello, world!* in several different languages.

```
1    <!DOCTYPE html PUBLIC "-//W3C//DTD XHTML
     1.0 Transitional//EN"
2           "http://www.w3.org/TR/xhtml1/DTD/
     xhtml1-transitional.dtd">
3    <html xmlns="http://www.w3.org/1999/
     xhtml" xml:lang="en" lang="en">
4    <head>
5        <meta http-equiv="content-type"
     content="text/html; charset=
     iso-8859-1" />
6        <title>Hello, world!</title>
7    </head>
8    <body>
9    <?php # Script 6.2 - hello_object.php
10
11   /*  This page uses the HelloWorld class.
12    *  This page just says "Hello, world!".
13    */
14
15   // Include the class definition:
16   require_once ('HelloWorld.php');
17
18   // Create the object:
19   $obj = new HelloWorld();
20
21   // Call the say_hello() method:
22   $obj->say_hello();
23
24   // Say hello in different languages:
25   $obj->say_hello('Italian');
26   $obj->say_hello('Dutch');
27   $obj->say_hello('French');
28
29   // Delete the object:
30   unset($obj);
31
32   ?>
33   </body>
34   </html>
```

## To create an object:

**1.** Create a new PHP document in your text editor or IDE, beginning with the standard HTML (**Script 6.2**).

```
<!DOCTYPE html PUBLIC "-//W3C//DTD
→ XHTML 1.0 Transitional//EN"
"http://www.w3.org/TR/xhtml1/DTD/
→ xhtml1-transitional.dtd">
<html xmlns="http://www.w3.org/1999/
→ xhtml" xml:lang="en" lang="en">
<head>
    <meta http-equiv="content-type"
→ content="text/html; charset=iso-
→ 8859-1" />
    <title>Hello, world!</title>
</head>
<body>
<?php # Script 6.2 - hello_object.php
```

The class definition file itself contains no HTML, as it's not meant to be used on its own. This PHP page will include all of the code necessary to make a valid XHTML page.

**2.** Include the class definition.

```
require_once ('HelloWorld.php');
```

In order to create an instance of a class, the PHP script must have access to that class definition. As the definition is stored in a separate file, that file must be included here. By using `require_once()` (as opposed to `include_once()`), the script will stop executing with a fatal error if the file could not be included (and there really is no point in continuing without this file).

*continues on next page*

CREATING AN OBJECT

3. Create the object.

```
$obj = new HelloWorld();
```

This one line of code is all there is to it! You can name the object variable anything you'd like, of course.

4. Invoke the `say_hello()` method.

```
$obj->say_hello();
```

This line of code will call the `say_hello()` method, which is part of the `$obj` object. Since the method is not being given any arguments, the greeting will be in the default language of English.

5. Say hello in a few more languages.

```
$obj->say_hello('Italian');
$obj->say_hello('Dutch');
$obj->say_hello('French');
```

An object's methods can be called multiple times, like any other function. Different arguments are provided to vary the result.

6. Delete the object and complete the page.

```
unset($obj);
?>
</body>
</html>
```

You don't technically have to delete the object, as it will be deleted as soon as the script ends. Still, I think it's better programming form to tidy up like this.

### Analyzing the HelloWorld Example

As I state in the first section of this chapter, OOP is both syntax and theory. For this first example, the HelloWorld class, the emphasis is on the syntax. Hopefully you can already see that this isn't great use of OOP. But why? Well, it's both too specific and too simple. Having an object print one string is a very focused idea, whereas classes should be much more abstract. It also makes absolutely no sense to use all this code—and the extra memory required—for one echo statement. It's nice that the object handles different languages, but still...

The HelloWorld class does succeed in a couple of ways, though. It does demonstrate some of the syntax. And it is reusable: if you have a project that needs to say *Hello, world!* dozens of times, this one object will do it. And if you need to change it to *Hello, World!* (with a capital "W"), edit just the one file and you're golden. Finally, this class kind of reflects the notion of *encapsulation*: you can use the object to say *Hello, world!* in multiple languages without any knowledge of how the class does that.

**Figure 6.1** The resulting Web page (the examples will get better, I promise).

**7.** Save the file as `hello_object.php` and place it in your Web directory, along with `HelloWorld.php`.

You don't have to place both documents in the same directory, but if they are stored separately, you would need to change the `require_once()` line accordingly.

**8.** Test `hello_object.php` by viewing it in your Web browser (**Figure 6.1**).

Note that you should run `hello_object.php`, not `HelloWorld.php` in your Web browser.

### ✔ Tips

- Class names are not case-sensitive. However, object names, like any variable in PHP, are case-sensitive.

- Because function names in PHP are not case-sensitive, the same is true for method names in classes.

# The $this Attribute

The HelloWorld class does actually do something, which is nice, but it's a fairly minimal example. The class does include a method, but it does not contain any attributes (variables).

As I mention in the section "Defining a Class," class attributes:

◆ Are variables

◆ Must be declared as public, private, or protected (I'll use only public in this chapter)

◆ If initialized, must be given a static value (not the result of an expression)

Those are the rules for defining a class's attributes, but using those attributes requires one more piece of information. The problem is that there's no easy way to access a class's attributes within the methods. For example:

```
class MyClass {
    public $var;
    function do() {
        // This won't work:
        print $var;
    }
}
```

The do() method cannot access $var like that. The solution is a special variable called $this. Within a method, you can refer to the instance of a class and its attributes by using the $this->attribute_name syntax.

Rather than over-explaining this concept, it'd be best just to go right into another example putting this new knowledge into action. This next, much more practical, example will define a class representing a rectangle.

**Script 6.3** This class is much more rounded than the HelloWorld example. It contains two attributes—for storing the rectangle's width and height—and four methods.

```
1   <?php # Script 6.3 - Rectangle.php
2
3   /*  This page defines the Rectangle
    class.
4    *  The class contains two attributes:
    width and height.
5    *  The class contains four methods:
6    *  - set_size()
7    *  - get_area()
8    *  - get_perimeter()
9    *  - is_square()
10   */
11
12  class Rectangle {
13
14      // Declare the attributes:
15      public $width = 0;
16      public $height = 0;
17
18      // Method to set the dimensions.
19      function set_size($w = 0, $h = 0) {
20          $this->width = $w;
21          $this->height = $h;
22      }
23
24      // Method to calculate and return the
    area.
25      function get_area() {
26          return ($this->width *
    $this->height);
27      }
28
```

*(script continues on next page)*

**Script 6.3** *continued*

```
29      // Method to calculate and return the
        perimeter.
30      function get_perimeter() {
31          return ( ($this->width +
        $this->height) * 2 );
32      }
33
34      // Method to determine if the
        rectangle
35      // is also a square.
36      function is_square() {
37
38          if ($this->width == $this-
        >height) {
39              return true; // Square
40          } else {
41              return false; // Not a square
42          }
43
44      }
45
46  } // End of Rectangle class.
47
48  ?>
```

## To use the $this variable:

1. Create a new PHP document in your text editor or IDE (**Script 6.3**).

   `<?php # Script 6.3 - Rectangle.php`

2. Begin defining the class.

   `class Rectangle {`

3. Declare the attributes.

   `public $width = 0;`

   `public $height = 0;`

   This class has two attributes: one for the rectangle's width and another for its height. Both are initialized to 0.

4. Create a method for setting the rectangle's dimensions.

   `function set_size($w = 0, $h = 0) {`

   `    $this->width = $w;`

   `    $this->height = $h;`

   `}`

   The set_size() method takes two arguments, corresponding to the width and height. Both have default values of 0, just to be safe.

   Within the method, the class's attributes are given values using the numbers to be provided when this method is called (assigned to $w and $h). Using $this->width and $this->height refers to this class's $width and $height attributes.

*continues on next page*

THE $THIS ATTRIBUTE

**5.** Create a method that calculates and returns the rectangle's area.

```
function get_area() {
      return ($this->width *
→ $this->height);
}
```

This method doesn't need to take any arguments, as it can access the class's attributes via $this. Calculating the area of a rectangle is simple: multiply the width times the height. This value is then returned.

**6.** Create a method that calculates and returns the rectangle's perimeter.

```
function get_perimeter() {
      return ( ($this->width +
→ $this->height) * 2 );
}
```

This method is like get_area(), except it uses a different calculation.

**7.** Create a final method that indicates if the rectangle is also a square.

```
function is_square() {
      if ($this->width ==
→ $this->height) {
            return true;
      } else {
            return false;
      }
}
```

This final method compares the rectangle's dimensions. If they are the same, the Boolean true is returned, indicating the rectangle is a square. Otherwise, false is returned.

**8.** Complete the class and the PHP page.

```
}
?>
```

**9.** Save the file as Rectangle.php.

## To use the Rectangle class:

**1.** Create a new PHP document in your text editor or IDE, beginning with the standard HTML (**Script 6.4**).

```
<!DOCTYPE html PUBLIC "-//W3C//DTD
→ XHTML 1.0 Transitional//EN"
"http://www.w3.org/TR/xhtml1/DTD/
→ xhtml1-transitional.dtd">
<html xmlns="http://www.w3.org/1999/
→ xhtml" xml:lang="en" lang="en">
<head>
      <meta http-equiv="content-type"
→ content="text/html; charset=iso-
→ 8859-1" />
      <title>Rectangle</title>
</head>
<body>
<?php # Script 6.4 - rectangle1.php
```

**2.** Include the class definition.

```
require_once ('Rectangle.php');
```

**3.** Define the necessary variables and print an introduction.

```
$width = 42;
$height = 7;
echo "<h3>With a width of $width and
→ a height of $height...</h3>";
```

*continues on page 248*

THE $THIS ATTRIBUTE

**Script 6.4** The `Rectangle` class is used in this PHP script. The rectangle's dimensions are first assigned to the class's attributes by invoking the `set_size()` method, and then various properties of the rectangle are reported.

```
1    <!DOCTYPE html PUBLIC "-//W3C//DTD XHTML 1.0 Transitional//EN"
2          "http://www.w3.org/TR/xhtml1/DTD/xhtml1-transitional.dtd">
3    <html xmlns="http://www.w3.org/1999/xhtml" xml:lang="en" lang="en">
4    <head>
5        <meta http-equiv="content-type" content="text/html; charset=iso-8859-1" />
6        <title>Rectangle</title>
7    </head>
8    <body>
9    <?php # Script 6.4 - rectangle1.php
10
11   /*  This page uses the Rectangle class.
12    *  This page shows a bunch of information
13    *  about a rectangle.
14    */
15
16   // Include the class definition:
17   require_once ('Rectangle.php');
18
19   // Define the necessary variables:
20   $width = 42;
21   $height = 7;
22
23   // Print a little introduction:
24   echo "<h3>With a width of $width and a height of $height...</h3>";
25
26   // Create a new object:
27   $r = new Rectangle();
28
29   // Assign the rectangle dimensions.
30   $r->set_size($width, $height);
31
32   // Print the area.
33   echo '<p>The area of the rectangle is ' . $r->get_area() . '</p>';
34
35   // Print the perimeter.
36   echo '<p>The perimeter of the rectangle is ' . $r->get_perimeter() . '</p>';
37
38   // Is this a square?
39   echo '<p>This rectangle is ';
40   if ($r->is_square()) {
41       echo 'also';
42   } else {
43       echo 'not';
44   }
45   echo ' a square.</p>';
46
47   // Delete the object:
48   unset($r);
49
50   ?>
51   </body>
52   </html>
```

THE $THIS ATTRIBUTE

**4.** Create the object and assign the rectangle's dimensions.

```
$r = new Rectangle();
$r->set_size($width, $height);
```

The first line creates an object of type Rectangle. The second line assigns the values of the variables in this script— $width and $height—to the object's attributes. The values here are assigned to $w and $h in the set_size() method when it's called, which are then assigned to $this->width and $this->height within that method.

**5.** Print the rectangle's area.

```
echo '<p>The area of the rectangle is
→ ' . $r->get_area() . '</p>';
```

To print the rectangle's area, you only need to have the object tell you what that value is by referring to the get_area() method. As this method returns the area (instead of printing it), it can be used in an echo statement like this.

**6.** Print the rectangle's perimeter.

```
echo '<p>The perimeter of the
→ rectangle is ' .
→ $r->get_perimeter() . '</p>';
```

This is a variation on the code in Step 5.

## Analyzing the Rectangle Example

The Rectangle class as defined isn't perfect, but it's pretty good, if I do say so myself. It encapsulates all the things you might want to do with or know about a rectangle. The methods also only handle calculations and return values; no HTML is used within the class, which is a better way to design.

One criticism may be that the class is too specific. Logically, if you're doing a lot of geometry, the Rectangle class might be an inherited class from a broader Shape.

From the first two examples you can see the benefit of objects: the ability to create your own data type. Whereas a string is a variable type whose only power is to contain characters, the Rectangle is a new, powerful type with all sorts of features.

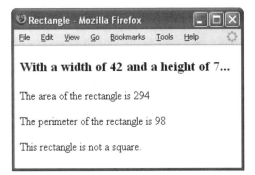

**Figure 6.2** Various attributes for a rectangle are revealed using the `Rectangle` class.

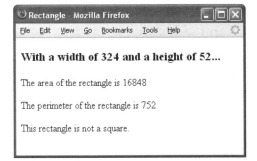

**Figure 6.3** Changing just the `$width` and `$height` values in the script results in all new calculations (compare with Figure 6.2).

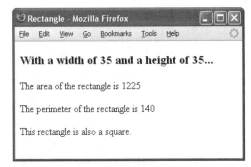

**Figure 6.4** If the width and height are the same, the rectangle is also a square.

**7.** Indicate whether or not this rectangle is also a square.

```
echo '<p>This rectangle is ';
if ($r->is_square()) {
    echo 'also';
} else {
    echo 'not';
}
echo ' a square.</p>';
```

Since the `is_square()` method returns a Boolean value, I can invoke it as a condition. This code will print either *This rectangle is also a square.* or *This rectangle is not a square.*

**8.** Delete the object and complete the page.

```
unset($r);
?>
</body>
</html>
```

**9.** Save the file as `rectangle1.php` and place it in your Web directory, along with `Rectangle.php`.

**10.** Test `rectangle1.php` by viewing it in your Web browser (**Figure 6.2**).

**11.** Change the variables' values in `rectangle1.php` and rerun it in your Web browser (**Figures 6.3** and **6.4**).

*continues on next page*

## ✔ Tips

- Having *get_* and *set_* methods in a class is a common convention. Methods starting with *set_* are used to assign values to class attributes. Methods starting with *get_* are used to return values: either attributes or the results of calculations.

- Methods can call each other, just as they would any other function. To do so, you'll need to use $this again. The following is unnecessary but valid:

```
function get_area() {
    if ($this->is_square()) {
        return ($this->width * 2);
    } else {
        return ($this->width *
        ➝ $this->height);
    }
}
```

- Suppose you do this:

```
$r1 = new Rectangle();
$r1->set_size(10, 25);
$r2 = $r1;
```

Then $r1 and $r2 are objects with the same dimensions. But what if you then do

```
$r2->set_size(8, 40);
```

Then $r2 is an object with different dimensions than $r1, and $r1 retains its original values.

# Creating Constructors

A constructor is a special kind of method that differs from standard ones in two ways:

◆ Its name is always __construct().

◆ It is automatically and immediately called whenever an object of that class is created.

The syntax for defining a constructor is therefore:

```
class ClassName {
    public $var;
    function __construct() {
        // Function code.
    }
}
```

A constructor could be used to connect to a database, set cookies, or establish initial values. Basically you'll use constructors to do whatever should always be done (and done first) when an object of this class is made.

Because the constructor is still just another method, it can take arguments, and values for those arguments can be provided when the object is created:

```
class Human {
    function __construct($name) {
        // Function code.
    }
}
$me = new Human('Henry');
```

The Rectangle class could benefit from having a constructor that assigns the rectangle's dimensions when the rectangle is created.

## To add and use a constructor:

1. Open Rectangle.php (Script 6.3) in your text editor or IDE.

2. After declaring the attributes and before defining the set_size() method, add the constructor (**Script 6.5**).

```
function __construct($w = 0, $h = 0)
{
    $this->width = $w;
    $this->height = $h;
}
```

This method is exactly like the set_size() method, albeit with a different name. Note that constructors are normally the first method defined in a class (but still defined after the attributes).

**Script 6.5** A constructor has been added to the Rectangle class. This makes it possible to assign the rectangle's dimensions when the object is created.

```
1    <?php # Script 6.5 - Rectangle.php
2
3    /*  This page defines the Rectangle
     class.
4     *  The class contains two attributes:
     width and height.
5     *  The class contains four methods:
6     *  - set_size()
7     *  - get_area()
8     *  - get_perimeter()
9     *  - is_square()
10    *  In this new version of the class,
11    *  a constructor is also present.
12    */
13
14   class Rectangle {
15
16       // Declare the attributes:
17       public $width = 0;
18       public $height = 0;
19
20       // Constructor:
21       function __construct($w = 0, $h = 0)
         {
22           $this->width = $w;
23           $this->height = $h;
24       }
25
26       // Method to set the dimensions.
27       function set_size($w = 0, $h = 0) {
28           $this->width = $w;
29           $this->height = $h;
30       }
```

*(script continues on next page)*

**Script 6.5** *continued*

```
      ⊖ ⊖ ⊖              📄 Script
31
32      // Method to calculate and return the
      area.
33      function get_area() {
34          return ($this->width * $this-
      >height);
35      }
36
37      // Method to calculate and return the
      perimeter.
38      function get_perimeter() {
39          return ( ($this->width + $this-
      >height) * 2 );
40      }
41
42      // Method to determine if the
      rectangle
43      // is also a square.
44      function is_square() {
45
46          if ($this->width ==
      $this->height) {
47              return true; // Square
48          } else {
49              return false; // Not a square
50          }
51
52      }
53
54  } // End of Rectangle class.
55
56  ?>
```

**3.** Save the file as `Rectangle.php`.

**4.** Open `rectangle1.php` (Script 6.4) in your text editor or IDE.

*continues on next page*

CREATING CONSTRUCTORS

**5.** If you want, change the values of the
$width and $height variables (**Script 6.6**).

```
$width = 160;
$height = 75;
```

**6.** Change the way the object is created so
that it reads:

```
$r = new Rectangle($width, $height);
```

The object can now be created and the
rectangle assigned its dimensions in
one step.

**Script 6.6** This new version of the script assigns the
rectangle's dimensions when the object is created
(thanks to the constructor).

```
1    <!DOCTYPE html PUBLIC "-//W3C//DTD XHTML
     1.0 Transitional//EN"
2            "http://www.w3.org/TR/xhtml1/DTD/
     xhtml1-transitional.dtd">
3    <html xmlns="http://www.w3.org/1999/
     xhtml" xml:lang="en" lang="en">
4    <head>
5        <meta http-equiv="content-type"
     content="text/html; charset=
     iso-8859-1" />
6        <title>Rectangle</title>
7    </head>
8    <body>
9    <?php # Script 6.6 - rectangle2.php
10
11   /*  This page uses the revised Rectangle
     class.
12    *  This page shows a bunch of
     information
13    *  about a rectangle.
14    */
15
```

**Script 6.6** *continued*

```
16   // Include the class definition:
17   require_once ('Rectangle.php');
18
19   // Define the necessary variables:
20   $width = 160;
21   $height = 75;
22
23   // Print a little introduction:
24   echo "<h3>With a width of $width and a
     height of $height...</h3>";
25
26   // Create a new object:
27   $r = new Rectangle($width, $height);
28
29   // Print the area.
30   echo '<p>The area of the rectangle is ' .
     $r->get_area() . '</p>';
31
32   // Print the perimeter.
33   echo '<p>The perimeter of the rectangle
     is ' . $r->get_perimeter() . '</p>';
34
35   // Is this a square?
36   echo '<p>This rectangle is ';
37   if ($r->is_square()) {
38       echo 'also';
39   } else {
40       echo 'not';
41   }
42   echo ' a square.</p>';
43
44   // Delete the object:
45   unset($r);
46
47   ?>
48   </body>
49   </html>
```

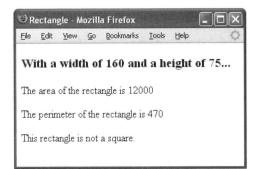

**Figure 6.5** The resulting output is not affected by the incorporation of a constructor in the Rectangle class.

**7.** Delete the invocation of the set_size() method.

This method is still part of the class, though, which makes sense. By keeping it in there, a rectangle object's size can be changed after the object is created.

**8.** Save the file as rectangle2.php, place it in your Web directory along with the new Rectangle.php (Script 6.5), and test in your Web browser (**Figure 6.5**).

## ✔ Tips

■ A constructor like the one just added to the Rectangle class is called a *default constructor*, as it provides default values for its arguments. This means that a Rectangle object can be created using either of these techniques:

```
$r = new Rectangle($width, $height);
$r = new Rectangle();
```

■ You can, although rarely do, call a constructor:

```
$o = new SomeClass();
$o->__construct();
```

With the Rectangle example, this would let you get rid of the set_size() method without losing the ability to resize a rectangle.

■ In PHP 4 and in other programming languages (like C++), a constructor is declared by creating a method whose name is the same as the class itself. So in PHP 4, the Rectangle class would have a constructor named Rectangle().

■ If PHP 5 cannot find a __construct() method in a class, it will then try to find a constructor whose name is the same as the class (the PHP 4 constructor naming scheme).

# Creating Destructors

The corollary to the constructor is the destructor. Whereas a constructor is automatically invoked when an object is created, the destructor is called when the object is destroyed. This may occur when you overtly remove the object:

```
$obj = new ClassName();
unset($obj);
```

Or this may occur when a script ends (at which point PHP releases the memory used by variables).

Being the smart reader that you are, you have probably already assumed that the destructor is created like so:

```
class ClassName {
    function __destruct() {
        // Function code.
    }
}
```

Destructors do differ from constructors and other methods in that they cannot take any arguments.

The Rectangle class used in the last two examples doesn't lend itself to a logical destructor (there's nothing you need to do when you're done with a rectangle). And rather than do a potentially confusing but practical example, I'll run through a dummy example that shows how and when constructors and destructors are called.

**Script 6.7** This script doesn't do anything except best convey when constructors and destructors are called.

```
1    <!DOCTYPE html PUBLIC "-//W3C//DTD XHTML
     1.0 Transitional//EN"
2        "http://www.w3.org/TR/xhtml1/DTD/
     xhtml1-transitional.dtd">
3    <html xmlns="http://www.w3.org/1999/
     xhtml" xml:lang="en" lang="en">
4    <head>
5        <meta http-equiv="content-type"
     content="text/html; charset=
     iso-8859-1" />
6        <title>Constructors and
     Destructors</title>
7    </head>
8    <body>
9    <?php # Script 6.7 - demo.php
10
11   /*  This page defines a Demo class
12    *  and a demo() function.
13    *  Both are used to show when
14    *  constructors and destructors are
     called.
15    */
16
17   // Define the class:
18   class Demo {
19
20       // No attributes.
21
22       // Constructor:
23       function __construct() {
24           echo '<p>In the
     constructor.</p>';
25       }
26
```

*(script continues on next page)*

**Script 6.7** *continued*

```
                          Script
27      // Destructor:
28      function __destruct() {
29          echo '<p>In the destructor.</p>';
30      }
31
32   } // End of Demo class.33
34   // Define a demo() function:
35   function demo () {
36
37      echo '<p>In the function. Creating a
     new object...</p>';
38      $f = new Demo();
39      echo '<p>About to leave the
     function.</p>';
40
41   }
42
43   // Create the object:
44   echo '<p>Creating a new object...</p>';
45   $o = new Demo();
46
47   // Call the demo function:
48   echo '<p>Calling the function...</p>';
49   demo();
50
51   // Delete the object:
52   echo '<p>About to delete the
     object...</p>';
53   unset($o);
54
55   echo '<p>End of the script.</p>';
56   ?>
57   </body>
58   </html>
```

## To create a destructor:

1. Create a new PHP document in your text
   editor or IDE, beginning with the standard HTML (**Script 6.7**).

   ```
   <!DOCTYPE html PUBLIC "-//W3C//DTD
   → XHTML 1.0 Transitional//EN"
   "http://www.w3.org/TR/xhtml1/DTD/
   → xhtml1-transitional.dtd">
   <html xmlns="http://www.w3.org/1999/
   → xhtml" xml:lang="en" lang="en">
   <head>
       <meta http-equiv="content-type"
   → content="text/html; charset=iso-
   → 8859-1" />
       <title>Constructors and
   → Destructors</title>
   </head>
   <body>
   <?php # Script 6.7 - demo.php
   ```

2. Begin defining the class.

   ```
   class Demo {
   ```

   To make this example even simpler, I'll
   define and use the class in the same
   script.

3. Create the constructor.

   ```
   function __construct() {
       echo '<p>In the
   → constructor.</p>';
   }
   ```

   The constructor doesn't do anything but
   print a message indicating that it has
   been invoked. This will allow you to trace
   when the class's automatic methods are
   called.

   *continues on next page*

**4.** Create the destructor.

```
function __destruct() {
    echo '<p>In the
    → destructor.</p>';
}
```

**5.** Complete the class.

```
}
```

It's a very simple class!

**6.** Define a simple function that also creates an object.

```
function demo () {
    echo '<p>In the function.
→ Creating a new object...</p>';
    $f = new Demo();
    echo '<p>About to leave the
→ function.</p>';
}
```

To best illuminate the life of objects, which affects when constructors and destructors are called, I'm adding this simple function. It prints messages and creates its own object, which will be local to this function.

**7.** Create an object of class Demo.

```
echo '<p>Creating a new
→ object...</p>';
$o = new Demo();
```

When this object is created, the constructor will be called. So this script first prints this line (*Creating a new object...*) and will then print *In the constructor*.

**8.** Call the demo() function.

```
echo '<p>Calling the
→ function...</p>';
demo();
```

After printing the first two lines (in Step 7), this third line is printed. Then the function is entered, wherein *In the*

**Figure 6.6** The flow of the two objects' creation and destruction over the execution of the script is revealed by this figure. In particular, you can see how the demo() function's object, $f, lives and dies in the middle of this script.

**Figure 6.7** If you don't forcibly delete the object (demonstrated by Figure 6.6), it will be deleted when the script stops running. This means that the $o object's destructor is called after the final printed message, even after the closing HTML tags (Figure 6.8).

**Figure 6.8** The $o object's destructor is called as the very last script event, when the script stops running. Thus, the *In the destructor.* messages gets sent to the browser after the closing HTML tag.

*function. Creating a new object...* will first be printed. Then, in that function, a new object is created (called $f). Therefore, the constructor will be called again, and the *In the constructor.* message printed.

After the object is created in the function, the *About to leave the function.* message is printed. Then the function is exited, at which point in time the object defined in the function—$f—goes away, thus invoking the $f object's destructor, printing *In the destructor.*

9. Delete the $o object.

    ```
    echo '<p>About to delete the
    → object...</p>';
    unset($o);
    ```

    Once this object is deleted, its destructor is invoked.

10. Complete the page.

    ```
    echo '<p>End of the script.</p>';
    ?>
    </body>
    </html>
    ```

11. Save the file as demo.php and place it in your Web directory, and test by viewing it in your Web browser (**Figure 6.6**).

12. Delete the unset($o) line, save the file, and rerun it in your Web browser (**Figure 6.7**).

    Also check the HTML source code of this page (**Figure 6.8**) to really understand the flow.

## ✔ Tip

■ In C++ and C#, the destructor's name for the class ClassName is ~ClassName, the corollary of the constructor, which is ClassName. Java does not support destructors.

# Autoloading Classes

With OOP, a logical way to modularize the files in an application is to place each class definition in its own file. You've now done this with both the HelloWorld and Rectangle classes. In these examples, the class file has to be required by the script that needs to create an object of that type:

```
require_once('Rectangle.php');
$r = new Rectangle(43, 902);
```

When including just one class file, this isn't much of a hardship, but as your programs use more and more objects, including all the requisite files can become very tedious. The developers behind PHP, big brains that they are, added a simple work-around to the tiresome process of always including class definition files.

PHP 5 supports a special function called __autoload (note that functions in PHP beginning with two underscores are special ones). The __autoload() function is invoked when an object is requested of a class that hasn't yet been defined. You define how this function works in your scripts. In simplest form, this would be:

```
function __autoload ($class) {
    require_once($class . '.php');
}
```

**Script 6.8** An __autoload() function is added to the script so that class definition files, such as Rectangle, don't have to be individually required.

```
1   <!DOCTYPE html PUBLIC "-//W3C//DTD XHTML
    1.0 Transitional//EN"
2           "http://www.w3.org/TR/xhtml1/DTD/
    xhtml1-transitional.dtd">
3   <html xmlns="http://www.w3.org/1999/
    xhtml" xml:lang="en" lang="en">
4   <head>
5       <meta http-equiv="content-type"
    content="text/html; charset=
    iso-8859-1" />
6       <title>Rectangle</title>
7   </head>
8   <body>
9   <?php # Script 6.8 - rectangle3.php
10
11  /*  This page uses the revised Rectangle
    class.
12   *  This page shows a bunch of
    information
13   *  about a rectangle
14   *  This version incorporates
    __autoload().
15   */
16
17  // Define the __autoload() function:
18  function __autoload ($class) {
19      require_once($class . '.php');
20  }
21
22  // Define the necessary variables:
23  $width = 56;
24  $height = 1475;
```

*(script continues on next page)*

**Script 6.8** *continued*

```
                     Script
25
26    // Print a little introduction:
27    echo "<h3>With a width of $width and a
      height of $height...</h3>";
28
29    // Create a new object:
30    $r = new Rectangle($width, $height);
31
32    // Print the area.
33    echo '<p>The area of the rectangle is ' .
      $r->get_area() . '</p>';
34
35    // Print the perimeter.
36    echo '<p>The perimeter of the rectangle
      is ' . $r->get_perimeter() . '</p>';
37
38    // Is this a square?
39    echo '<p>This rectangle is ';
40    if ($r->is_square()) {
41        echo 'also';
42    } else {
43        echo 'not';
44    }
45    echo ' a square.</p>';
46
47    // Delete the object:
48    unset($r);
49
50    ?>
51    </body>
52    </html>
```

For each new object type created in the following code, the function will be invoked:

```
$obj = new Class();
$me = new Human();
$r = new Rectangle();
```

Thanks to the __autoload() function, those three lines will automatically include Class.php, Human.php, and Rectangle.php (within the current directory).

Notice that this __autoload() function is defined outside of any class; instead, it is placed in a script that instantiates the objects.

## To autoload class definition files:

1. Open rectangle2.php (Script 6.6) in your text editor or IDE.

2. Remove the require_once() line (**Script 6.8**).

3. Add the definition of the __autoload() function.

   ```
   function __autoload ($class) {
       require_once($class . '.php');
   }
   ```

4. If you want, change the values of the $width and $height variables.

   ```
   $width = 56;
   $height = 1475;
   ```

   *continues on next page*

5. Save the file as rectangle3.php, place it in your Web directory along with Rectangle.php (Script 6.5), and test in your Web browser (**Figure 6.9**).

### ✔ Tips

- If you store your class definition files in their own directory, change the definition of the __autoload() function to something like:

```
function __autoload ($class) {
    require_once('classes/' .
→ $class . '.php');
}
```

- Although class names in PHP are case-insensitive, some operating systems use case-sensitive file structures. If your class is called MyClass, then you'll be better off naming the file exactly MyClass.php and creating objects using:

```
$obj = new MyClass();
```

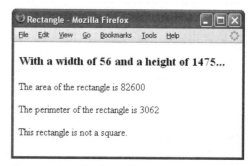

**Figure 6.9** As with other OOP examples, incorporating features like the __autoload() function (see Script 6.8) has no bearing on the end result.

# Advanced OOP

Chapter 6, "Basic Object-Oriented Programming," covers the fundamental concepts of OOP in PHP. Those concepts include: defining a class, creating an object, accessing class attributes (variables) using `$this`, creating constructors, and creating destructors. A fair amount of theory is also discussed there, as that's half the OOP battle. Complete comfort with the contents of that chapter is a prerequisite for this one.

Here, things get more advanced (hence the chapter title!), really getting into the more abstract aspects of OOP. Again, ample time will be given to theory. Almost all of the dozen-ish topics discussed herein involve *inheritance*. Fully understanding inheritance is crucial. Some of the topics get to be rather esoteric, and the need for implementing such features may not be apparent at first. My best recommendation is not to overwhelm yourself with the material in this chapter. Take little bites and chew the material thoroughly. Forging ahead in the hopes that it'll all make sense eventually will only make matters worse (I think) as each new advanced idea is added to the pile. All that being said, don't be too afraid. Advanced object-oriented programming isn't the scariest programming technique you'll encounter, and you can begin to really see the beauty of OOP on this higher level.

# Advanced Theories

I want to begin this chapter with a brief discussion of a few key concepts in advanced OOP. Chapter 6 introduced some of the basic terms: *class*, *object*, *modularity*, and *abstraction*. A few more were also referenced: *inheritance*, *overriding*, *encapsulation*, and *visibility*. Of these latter four notions, all of which arise in this chapter, inheritance is far and away the most important in advanced object-oriented programming.

Object inheritance is where one class is derived from another, just as humans inherit qualities from their parents. Of course, the "qualities" in the object-oriented world are *attributes* (variables) and *methods* (functions). Through inheritance, you can define one class that is born with the same attributes and methods as another (**Figure 7.1**). The inherited child class can even have its own unique qualities that the parent doesn't have (**Figure 7.2**).

But inheritance isn't a simple one-to-one relationship. There's no limit to how many times inheritance can occur: multiple classes can inherit from the same parent (**Figure 7.3**) or a class can be a child of a child (**Figure 7.4**). This speaks to the powerful reusablity of class code.

Once you've defined a class that inherits from another, it doesn't take long to start thinking how nice it'd be if it behaved just slightly differently. You can add new attributes and methods, but what if you wanted to change the behavior of the parent class's methods? It would be wrong to change the definition of the parent class (presumably it works as it should, and besides, other classes might inherit from it too, as shown in Figure 7.3). Instead, you can *override* a parent class's method to customize it for the new class. This is *polymorphism*: where calling the same

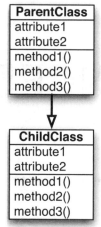

**Figure 7.1** A child class inherits (i.e., has) all of the attributes and methods of its parent class (there can be exceptions to this, but assume this to be true for now).

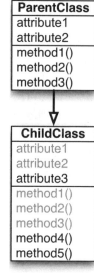

**Figure 7.2** Child classes can add their own members to the ones they inherited. In this way a child can separate itself (functionally speaking) from its parent.

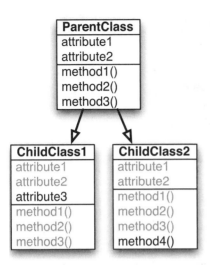

Figure 7.3 A single parent class can have unlimited offspring, each customized in its own way.

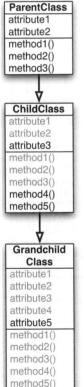

Figure 7.4 Inheritance can theoretically have limitless depth, with each child inheriting all the members of its parent (again, not always so, but...).

method can have different results, depending upon the object type. This probably doesn't mean much yet, but you'll understand in time.

Acknowledging (as I just did) that it's not a good thing for one class to muck around in another, the concept of *visibility* exists. Visibility controls what qualities of a class can be accessed or altered by other classes (or even outside of any class).

As you can tell already, once you introduce inheritance, the OOP world expands exponentially. Just as in the last chapter, I'll attempt to go through this sea of information slowly, to make sure that it really settles in. Some of the examples will be designed for illumination of a concept, rather than real-world implementations (Chapter 8, "Real-World OOP," works toward that end).

## Inheritance Terminology

With class definitions, the main terms are *attributes* and *methods*, meaning variables and functions, respectively. You'll also see *properties* used instead of attributes, but both refer to a class's variables. The combination of attributes and methods make up the *members* of a class.

With inheritance you have a *parent* class and a *child* class: the latter is inherited from the former. You'll also see these described as a *base* class or *superclass* and its *derived* class or *subclass*.

# Inheriting Classes

One of the ways in which objects make programming faster is the ability to use one class definition as the basis for another. From there, the second class can add its own attributes (variables) and methods (functions). This is referred to as *inheritance*.

Going back to the Human example introduced in Chapter 6, if the Human class has the attributes *gender*, *height*, *weight*, and *birth date* and it has the methods *eating* and *sleeping*, you could create another class called Adult that is an extension of Human. Along with the aforementioned variables and functions, an Adult object might also have the attribute of *married* and the method of *working* (**Figure 7.5**).

To make a child class from a parent, you use the extends statement. Assuming you have already defined the ClassName class, you can create a child like so:

```
class ChildClass extends ClassName { }
```

The class ChildClass will possess all the members of its parent, ClassName. Now you can modify this class to adapt it to your specific needs without altering the original class. Ideally, once you've created a solid parent class, you will never need to modify it again and can use child classes to tailor the code to your individual requirements.

For an example implementation of this, I'll start with a silly (but comprehensible) pets example. Say you have two pets: a cat and a dog. Both animals have a name, and they both eat and sleep. Cats differ from dogs in that they can climb trees and dogs differ from cats in that they can fetch. Being able to describe these qualities and relationships in plain language leads to the inheritance structure you would create (**Figure 7.6**).

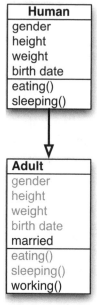

**Figure 7.5** The Adult class can have all the same members as Human, while adding its own.

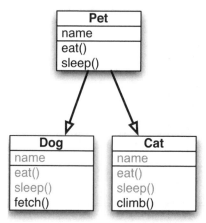

**Figure 7.6** How the pet-cat-dog relationship would be implemented objectively.

## To inherit from a class:

1. Begin a new PHP script in your text editor or IDE, starting with the HTML (**Script 7.1**).

```
<!DOCTYPE html PUBLIC "-//W3C//
→ DTD XHTML 1.0 Transitional//EN"
"http://www.w3.org/TR/xhtml1/DTD/
→ xhtml1-transitional.dtd">
<html xmlns="http://www.w3.org/1999/
→ xhtml" xml:lang="en" lang="en">
<head>
    <meta http-equiv="content-type"
→ content="text/html; charset=iso-
→ 8859-1" />
    <title>Rectangle</title>
</head>
<body>
<?php # Script 7.1 - pets1.php
```

To make things easier, I'm going to put all the class definitions and the usage of these classes in this same script. In a real application, you would separate out your class files from the program files that use them.

*continues on page 269*

**Script 7.1** This example script shows how two classes can be derived from the same parent. Each can access all the members of the parent, and each has defined its own custom method.

```
                                      Script
1    <!DOCTYPE html PUBLIC "-//W3C//DTD XHTML 1.0 Transitional//EN"
2          "http://www.w3.org/TR/xhtml1/DTD/xhtml1-transitional.dtd">
3    <html xmlns="http://www.w3.org/1999/xhtml" xml:lang="en" lang="en">
4    <head>
5        <meta http-equiv="content-type" content="text/html; charset=iso-8859-1" />
6        <title>Pets</title>
7    </head>
8    <body>
9    <?php # Script 7.1 - pets1.php
10
11   /*  This page defines and uses
12    *  the Pet, Cat, and Dog classes.
13    */
14
15   # ***************** #
16   # ***** CLASSES ***** #
17
18   /* Class Pet.
19    *  The class contains one attribute: name.
20    *  The class contains three methods:
21    *  - __construct()
22    *  - eat()
23    *  - go_to_sleep()
24    */
25   class Pet {
26
27       // Declare the attributes:
28       public $name;
29
30       // Constructor assigns the pet's name:
31       function __construct($pet_name) {
32           $this->name = $pet_name;
33       }
34
35       // Pets can eat:
36       function eat() {
```

*(script continues on next page)*

**Script 7.1** *continued*

```
37            echo "<p>$this->name is eating.</p>";
38        }
39
40        // Pets can sleep:
41        function go_to_sleep() {
42            echo "<p>$this->name is sleeping.</p>";
43        }
44
45    } // End of Pet class.
46
47
48    /* Cat class extends Pet.
49     * Cat has additional method: climb().
50     */
51    class Cat extends Pet {
52        function climb() {
53            echo "<p>$this->name is climbing.</p>";
54        }
55    } // End of Cat class.
56
57
58    /* Dog class extends Pet.
59     * Dog has additional method: fetch().
60     */
61    class Dog extends Pet {
62        function fetch() {
63            echo "<p>$this->name is fetching.</p>";
64        }
65    } // End of Dog class.
66
67
68    # ***** END OF CLASSES ***** #
69    # ************************** #
70
71    // Create a dog:
72    $dog = new Dog('Satchel');
73
74    // Create a cat:
75    $cat = new Cat('Bucky');
76
77    // Feed them:
78    $dog->eat();
79    $cat->eat();
80
81    // Nap time:
82    $dog->go_to_sleep();
83    $cat->go_to_sleep();
84
85    // Do animal-specific thing:
86    $dog->fetch();
87    $cat->climb();
88
89    // Delete the objects:
90    unset($dog, $cat);
91
92    ?>
93    </body>
94    </html>
```

**2.** Start declaring the Pet class.

```
class Pet {
    public $name;
```

Pet has one attribute: the pet's name.

**3.** Create the constructor.

```
function __construct($pet_name) {
    $this->name = $pet_name;
}
```

The constructor takes one argument: the name of the pet. This gets assigned to the class's $name attribute.

**4.** Define the eat() method.

```
function eat() {
    echo "<p>$this->name is
→ eating.</p>";
}
```

This method simply reports the name of the animal eating.

**5.** Define the go_to_sleep() method and complete the class.

```
    function go_to_sleep() {
        echo "<p>$this->name is
→ sleeping.</p>";
    }
} // End of Pet class.
```

This function could be named sleep(), but there's already a PHP function with that same name. While no conflict would occur (because this function is built into a class), it's best to avoid confusion.

**6.** Declare the Cat class.

```
class Cat extends Pet {
    function climb() {
        echo "<p>$this->name is
→ climbing.</p>";
    }
} // End of Cat class.
```

The Cat class extends Pet, meaning that it has all the attributes and methods of Pet. Added to those is one new method, climb(). The method can refer to the $name attribute via $this->name because the attribute is also part of this class (thanks to inheritance).

**7.** Declare the Dog class.

```
class Dog extends Pet {
    function fetch() {
        echo "<p>$this->name is
→ fetching.</p>";
    }
} // End of Dog class.
```

**8.** Create two new pets.

```
$dog = new Dog('Satchel');
$cat = new Cat('Bucky');
```

**9.** Make the pets do the things they do.

```
$dog->eat();
$cat->eat();
$dog->go_to_sleep();
$cat->go_to_sleep();
$dog->fetch();
$cat->climb();
```

Each subclass object can invoke the methods in the parent class as well as its own new methods (fetch() and climb()). Note that $dog could not invoke the climb() method, nor could $cat call fetch().

*continues on next page*

INHERITING CLASSES

**10.** Complete the page.

```
unset($dog, $cat);
?>
</body>
</html>
```

You don't have to unset the objects, but it makes for tidier code.

**11.** Save the file as pets1.php, place it in your Web directory, and test in your Web browser (**Figure 7.7**).

## ✔ Tips

■ In this example, you could create an object of type Pet. That object would have a name and could eat() and go_to_sleep(), but it could not fetch() or climb().

■ You cannot create a child class that inherits fewer properties than its parent. In fact, if that was something you were hoping to do, then the design of the child and the parent should be switched. As classes are extended, they should contain more features, never fewer.

■ You can determine the parent class of an object using PHP's get_parent_class() function, a companion to the get_class() function. These two are part of a handful of functions PHP has for getting information about classes.

**Figure 7.7** Two objects are created from different derived classes. Then the various methods are called. Understanding this result and the code in pets1.php is key to the rest of the chapter's material.

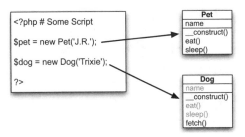

```
<?php # Some Script

$pet = new Pet('J.R.');

$dog = new Dog('Trixie');

?>
```

**Pet**
name
__construct()
eat()
sleep()

**Dog**
name
__construct()
eat()
sleep()
fetch()

**Figure 7.8** When an object is created, PHP will always call the constructor of that object's class type.

# Inheriting Constructors and Destructors

The pets example shows how you can create one class (i.e., Pet) and then derive other classes from it (Dog and Cat). These other classes can have their own methods, unique to themselves, such as climb() and fetch().

Two methods are common to many classes: constructors and destructors (see Chapter 6 for a detailed description). The Pet class has a constructor but no need for a destructor. What would happen, then, if Cat or Dog also had a constructor? By definition, this method is always called __construct(). How does PHP determine which to call when?

As a rule, PHP will always call the constructor for the class just instantiated (**Figure 7.8**). The same rule applies for destructors.

This next, somewhat more practical, example will extend the Rectangle class (Script 6.5, defined in Chapter 6) to create a Square class (because all squares are rectangles but not all rectangles are squares).

## To create subclass constructors:

**1.** Begin a new PHP script in your text editor or IDE, starting with the HTML (**Script 7.2**).

```
<!DOCTYPE html PUBLIC "-//W3C//
→ DTD XHTML 1.0 Transitional//EN"
"http://www.w3.org/TR/xhtml1/DTD/
→ xhtml1-transitional.dtd">
<html xmlns="http://www.w3.org/1999/
→ xhtml" xml:lang="en" lang="en">
```

```
<head>
    <meta http-equiv="content-type"
→ content="text/html; charset=iso-
→ 8859-1" />
    <title>Square</title>
</head>
<body>
<?php # Script 7.2 - square.php
```

*continues on page 274*

**Script 7.2** The Square class is derived from Rectangle but has its own constructor. That constructor, not Rectangle's will be called when an object of type Square is created.

```
1    <!DOCTYPE html PUBLIC "-//W3C//DTD XHTML 1.0 Transitional//EN"
2         "http://www.w3.org/TR/xhtml1/DTD/xhtml1-transitional.dtd">
3    <html xmlns="http://www.w3.org/1999/xhtml" xml:lang="en" lang="en">
4    <head>
5        <meta http-equiv="content-type" content="text/html; charset=iso-8859-1" />
6        <title>Square</title>
7    </head>
8    <body>
9    <?php # Script 7.2 - square.php
10
11   /*  This page declares and uses the Square class
12    *  which is derived from Rectangle (Script 6.5).
13    */
14
15   // Include the class definition:
16   require_once ('Rectangle.php');
17
18   // Create the Square class.
19   // The class only adds its own constructor.
20   class Square extends Rectangle {
21
22       // Constructor takes one argument.
23       // This value is assigned to the
24       // Rectangle width and height attributes.
25       function __construct($side = 0) {
26           $this->width = $side;
27           $this->height = $side;
28       }
29
30   } // End of Square class.
```

*(script continues on next page)*

**Script 7.2** *continued*

```
31
32    // Rectangle dimensions:
33    $width = 21;
34    $height = 98;
35
36    // Print a little introduction:
37    echo "<h3>With a width of $width and a height of $height...</h3>";
38
39    // Create a new rectangle:
40    $r = new Rectangle($width, $height);
41
42    // Print the area.
43    echo '<p>The area of the rectangle is ' . $r->get_area() . '</p>';
44
45    // Print the perimeter.
46    echo '<p>The perimeter of the rectangle is ' . $r->get_perimeter() . '</p>';
47
48    // Square dimensions:
49    $side = 60;
50
51    // Print a little introduction:
52    echo "<h3>With each side being $side...</h3>";
53
54    // Create a new object:
55    $s = new Square($side);
56
57    // Print the area.
58    echo '<p>The area of the square is ' . $s->get_area() . '</p>';
59
60    // Print the perimeter.
61    echo '<p>The perimeter of the square is ' . $s->get_perimeter() . '</p>';
62
63    // Delete the objects:
64    unset($r, $s);
65
66    ?>
67    </body>
68    </html>
```

**2.** Include the Rectangle class.

```
require_once ('Rectangle.php');
```

You'll need to make sure that the Rectangle.php file (Script 6.5) is in the same directory as this script.

**3.** Declare the Square class.

```
class Square extends Rectangle {
    function __construct($side = 0)
    {
        $this->width = $side;
        $this->height = $side;
    }
}
```

The premise is simple: there's no reason to have to pass both a height and a width value to the Rectangle class when you know you're creating a square. So a new constructor is defined that only takes one argument. That value will be assigned, within the constructor, to the parent class's attributes.

Note that in order for this class extension to work, it must be able to access the Rectangle definition (so that file must be included prior to this point).

**4.** Create a rectangle and report on it.

```
$width = 21;
$height = 98;
echo "<h3>With a width of $width and
→ a height of $height...</h3>";
$r = new Rectangle($width, $height);
echo '<p>The area of the rectangle
→ is ' . $r->get_area() . '</p>';
echo '<p>The perimeter of the
→ rectangle is ' . $r-
→ >get_perimeter() . '</p>';
```

This code is also from Chapter 6. It just creates a rectangle and prints its area and perimeter.

## Inheritance Theory

Any time one class inherits from another, the result should be a more specific description of a thing. Hence, I go from Pet to Dog or Cat and from Rectangle to Square. When deciding where to place methods, including constructors and destructors, you have to think about whether that functionality is universal or specific.

In the Pet example, the constructor sets the pet's name, which is universal for all pets. So the Dog and Cat classes don't need their own constructors. In the Rectangle example, its constructor sets the height and width. But a square doesn't have both, so having a new constructor for it is valid.

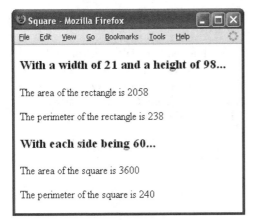

**Figure 7.9** Even though the Square constructor only takes one argument (Script 7.2), the use of the Rectangle methods, and the end result, work just the same.

**5.** Repeat Step 4 for a square.

```
$side = 60;
echo "<h3>With each side being
→ $side...</h3>";
$s = new Square($side);
echo '<p>The area of the square
→ is ' . $s->get_area() . '</p>';
echo '<p>The perimeter of the square
→ is ' . $s->get_perimeter() .
→ '</p>';
```

This code differs from that in Step 4 in that only one value needs to be passed to the Square constructor. Then all the other methods can be called just the same.

**6.** Complete the page.

```
unset($r, $s);
?>
</body>
</html>
```

**7.** Save the file as square.php, place it in your Web directory, and test in your Web browser (**Figure 7.9**).

# Overriding Methods

So far I've covered how one class can inherit from another class and how the child classes can have their own new methods. The last example demonstrated that subclasses can even define their own constructors (and destructors, implicitly), which will be used in lieu of the parent class's constructors and destructors. This same thinking can be applied to the other class methods. This concept is called *overriding* a method.

To achieve this in PHP, the subclass must define a method with the exact same name and number of arguments as the parent class:

```
class SomeClass {
  function scream($count = 1) {
    for ($i = 0; $i < $count; $i++) {
      echo 'Eek!<br />';
    }
  }
}
class SomeOtherClass extends SomeClass{
  function scream($count = 1) {
    for ($i = 0; $i < $count; $i++) {
      echo 'Whohoo!<br />';
    }
  }
}
$obj1 = new SomeClass();
$obj1->scream();
$obj1->scream(2);
$obj2 = new SomeOtherClass();
$obj2->scream();
$obj2->scream(2);
```

**Figure 7.10** shows the result of the preceding code.

Overriding methods is a common and useful feature of advanced object-oriented programming. As a simple example of this, I'll return to the Pet, Dog, and Cat classes. Instead of having separate climb() and fetch() methods, that functionality will be implemented as an overridden play() method.

**Figure 7.10** When related classes have overridden methods, which method is called depends upon the type of the object calling it. Note that for $obj2, the code of the overridden scream() method in SomeOtherClass is used in lieu of the original scream() (hence the different scream in the last three lines).

# To override methods:

1. Open pets1.php (Script 7.1) in your text editor or IDE.

2. Add a play() method to the Pet class (**Script 7.3**).

```
function play() {
    echo "<p>$this->name is
→ playing.</p>";
}
```

This is the method that will be overridden. It just prints the name of the pet that is playing.

3. In the Cat class, change the name of climb() to play().

Now the Pet class's play() method has been overridden in the Cat class.

*continues on page 279*

**Script 7.3** The Cat and Dog classes override the Pet play() method, giving it new functionality. Which version of play() gets called depends upon the type of the object calling it.

```
1    <!DOCTYPE html PUBLIC "-//W3C//DTD XHTML 1.0 Transitional//EN"
2         "http://www.w3.org/TR/xhtml1/DTD/xhtml1-transitional.dtd">
3    <html xmlns="http://www.w3.org/1999/xhtml" xml:lang="en" lang="en">
4    <head>
5        <meta http-equiv="content-type" content="text/html; charset=iso-8859-1" />
6        <title>Pets</title>
7    </head>
8    <body>
9    <?php # Script 7.3 - pets2.php
10
11   /*  This page defines and uses
12    *  the Pet, Cat, and Dog classes.
13    */
14
15   # ****************** #
16   # ***** CLASSES ***** #
17
18   /* Class Pet.
19    *  The class contains one attribute: name.
20    *  The class contains four methods:
21    *  - __construct()
22    *  - eat()
23    *  - go_to_sleep()
24    *  - play()
25    */
26   class Pet {
27
28       // Declare the attributes:
29       public $name;
30
31       // Constructor assigns the pet's name:
32       function __construct($pet_name) {
33           $this->name = $pet_name;
34       }
35
36       // Pets can eat:
37       function eat() {
38           echo "<p>$this->name is eating.</p>";
39       }
40
41       // Pets can sleep:
42       function go_to_sleep() {
43           echo "<p>$this->name is sleeping.</p>";
44       }
```

*(script continues on next page)*

**Script 7.3** *continued*

```
45
46        // Pets can play:
47        function play() {
48            echo "<p>$this->name is playing.</p>";
49        }
50
51    } // End of Pet class.
52
53
54    /* Cat class extends Pet.
55     * Cat overrides play().
56     */
57    class Cat extends Pet {
58        function play() {
59            echo "<p>$this->name is climbing.</p>";
60        }
61    } // End of Cat class.
62
63
64    /* Dog class extends Pet.
65     * Dog overrides play().
66     */
67    class Dog extends Pet {
68        function play() {
69            echo "<p>$this->name is fetching.</p>";
70        }
71    } // End of Dog class.
72
73
74    # ***** END OF CLASSES ***** #
75    # ************************** #
76
77    // Create a dog:
78    $dog = new Dog('Satchel');
79
80    // Create a cat:
81    $cat = new Cat('Bucky');
82
83    // Create an unknown type of pet:
84    $pet = new Pet('Rob');
85
86    // Feed them:
87    $dog->eat();
88    $cat->eat();
89    $pet->eat();
90
91    // Nap time:
92    $dog->go_to_sleep();
93    $cat->go_to_sleep();
94    $pet->go_to_sleep();
95
96    // Have them play:
97    $dog->play();
98    $cat->play();
99    $pet->play();
100
101    // Delete the objects:
102    unset($dog, $cat, $pet);
103
104    ?>
105    </body>
106    </html>
```

4. In the Dog class, change the name of fetch() to play().

5. After the class declarations, create an object of type Pet.

```
$pet = new Pet('Rob');
```

To see the impact of overriding a method, I'll create an object of the parent class as well.

6. Add activities for the Pet object.

```
$pet->eat();
$pet->go_to_sleep();
```

7. Make all three objects play.

```
$dog->play();
$cat->play();
$pet->play();
```

These three lines will reveal which class's method gets called by which object.

8. Delete the calls to $dog->fetch() and $cat->climb().

*continues on next page*

## Final Methods

Most methods in classes can be overridden. The exception is if a function is defined as final:

```
final function myfunc () {…}
```

A final method's definition cannot be altered by any subclass.

A class can also be declared final, meaning that it cannot be extended.

**OVERRIDING METHODS**

**9.** Also unset the $pet object toward the end of the script.

```
unset($dog, $cat, $pet);
```

**10.** Save the file as pets2.php, place it in your Web directory, and test in your Web browser (**Figure 7.11**).

### ✔ Tips

■ The combination of a function's name and its arguments (the number of arguments, specifically) is referred to as the function's *signature*. In PHP 5, except for constructors, any derived class must use the same signature when overriding a method.

■ The Square class could logically override the Rectangle is_square() method. It would be defined as simply:

```
function is_square() {
    return true;
}
```

■ Overriding a method in such a way that it also takes a different number of arguments than the original is referred to as *overloading* a method. This can be accomplished in PHP but not as easily as overriding one. One option is to add dummy (unused) arguments to one method (the original or the derived) so that they both have the same number. The second option is to use PHP's magic __call() method to emulate overloading.

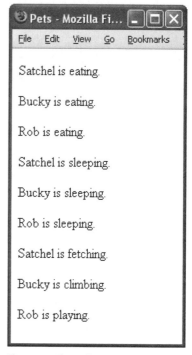

**Figure 7.11** The end result isn't that much different from Figure 7.7, although cat-specific and dog-specific play() methods were introduced. A third object, of type Pet, was also added.

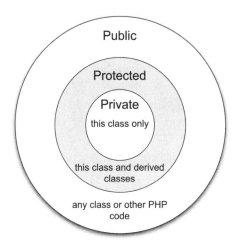

**Figure 7.12** The more restricted the visibility, the smaller the realm where the attribute or method is accessible.

# Access Control

Access control, which is also called *visibility*, dictates how accessible a class's properties and methods are. There are three levels of visibility: public, protected, and private. To establish the visibility of an attribute, prefix the variable's declaration with one of these keywords:

```
class ClassName {
    public $var1 = 'Hello';
    private $var2 = 'world';
    protected $var3 = 234;
}
```

You've already been doing this, in making everything public thus far.

To establish the visibility of a method, prefix the function's declaration with one of these keywords:

```
class ClassName {
    public function my_function() {
        // Function code.
    }
}
```

Methods lacking the accessibility declaration are considered to be public. And because methods often are public, the visibility for them is frequently omitted.

Think of each term as prescribing a more limited circle in which the member can be accessed (**Figure 7.12**). A public member is accessible everywhere: in the class itself, in inherited classes, in other classes, and in scripts without using objects. Protected members can only be accessed within the class and derived subclasses. Private is the most restrictive; those members are only accessible within the class that defines them.

*continues on next page*

As with most concepts in OOP, there are two issues: how it works and how you'd use it. To make clear how access control works, I'll run through a dummy example that just plays around with the accessibility of attributes. How you'd use visibility will become clearer as you see other examples.

## To control member access:

1. Begin a new PHP script in your text editor or IDE, starting with the HTML (**Script 7.4**).

    ```
    <!DOCTYPE html PUBLIC "-//W3C//DTD
    → XHTML 1.0 Transitional//EN"
    "http://www.w3.org/TR/xhtml1/DTD/
    → xhtml1-transitional.dtd">
    <html xmlns="http://www.w3.org/1999/
    → xhtml" xml:lang="en" lang="en">
    <head>
        <meta http-equiv="content-type"
    → content="text/html; charset=iso-
    → 8859-1" />
        <title>Visibility</title>
    </head>
    <body>
    <?php # Script 7.4 - visibility.php
    ```

*continues on page 284*

**Script 7.4** This script demonstrates access control by showing what can and cannot be done with attributes of different visibility.

```
1   <!DOCTYPE html PUBLIC "-//W3C//DTD XHTML 1.0 Transitional//EN"
2          "http://www.w3.org/TR/xhtml1/DTD/xhtml1-transitional.dtd">
3   <html xmlns="http://www.w3.org/1999/xhtml" xml:lang="en" lang="en">
4   <head>
5       <meta http-equiv="content-type" content="text/html; charset=iso-8859-1" />
6       <title>Visibility</title>
7   </head>
8   <body>
9   <?php # Script 7.4 - visibility.php
10
11  /*  This page defines and uses
12   *  the Test and LittleTest classes.
13   */
14
15  # ****************** #
16  # ***** CLASSES ***** #
17
18  /* Class Test.
19   *  The class contains three attributes:
20   *  - public $public
21   *  - protected $protected
22   *  - private $private
23   *  The class defines one method: print_var().
24   */
25  class Test {
26
27      // Declare the attributes:
28      public $public = 'public';
29      protected $protected = 'protected';
30      private $private = 'private';
31
32      // Function for printing a variable's value:
33      function print_var($var) {
34          echo "<p>In Test, \$$var equals '{$this->$var}'.</p>";
35      }
36
37  } // End of Test class.
```

**Script 7.4** *continued*

```
      ┌─────────────────────────────────────────────────────────────────┐
      │ ⊖ ○ ○                          Script                           │
      ├─────────────────────────────────────────────────────────────────┤
38
39
40    /* LittleTest class extends Test.
41     * LittleTest overrides print_var().
42     */
43    class LittleTest extends Test {
44        // Function for printing a variable's value:
45        function print_var($var) {
46            echo "<p>In LittleTest, \$$var equals '{$this->$var}'.</p>";
47        }
48
49    } // End of LittleTest class.
50
51
52    # ***** END OF CLASSES ***** #
53    # ************************* #
54
55    // Create the objects:
56    $parent = new Test();
57    $child = new LittleTest();
58
59    // Print the current value of $public:
60    echo '<h2>Public</h2>';
61    echo '<h3>Initially...</h3>';
62    $parent->print_var('public');
63    $child->print_var('public');
64
65    // Modify $public and reprint:
66    echo '<h3>Modifying $parent->public...</h3>';
67    $parent->public = 'modified';
68    $parent->print_var('public');
69    $child->print_var('public');
70
71    // Print the current value of $protected:
72    echo '<hr /><h2>Protected</h2>';
73    echo '<h3>Initially...</h3>';
74    $parent->print_var('protected');
75    $child->print_var('protected');
76
77    // Attempt to modify $protected and reprint:
78    echo '<h3>Attempting to modify $parent->public...</h3>';
79    $parent->protected = 'modified';
80    $parent->print_var('protected');
81    $child->print_var('protected');
82
83    // Print the current value of $private:
84    echo '<hr /><h2>Private</h2>';
85    echo '<h3>Initially...</h3>';
86    $parent->print_var('private');
87    $child->print_var('private');
88
89    // Attempt to modify $private and reprint:
90    echo '<h3>Attempting to modify $parent->private...</h3>';
91    $parent->private = 'modified';
92    $parent->print_var('private');
93    $child->print_var('private');
94
95    // Delete the objects:
96    unset($parent, $child);
97
98    ?>
99    </body>
100   </html>
```

ACCESS CONTROL

**2.** Begin declaring the Test class.

```
class Test {
    public $public = 'public';
    protected $protected =
→ 'protected';
    private $private = 'private';
```

This class contains three attributes, one of each type. To make things even more obvious, the name and value of each attribute match its visibility.

**3.** Add a print_var() method and complete the class.

```
    function print_var($var) {
        echo "<p>In Test, \$$var
→ equals '{$this->$var}'.</p>";
    }
} // End of Test class.
```

The print_var() method prints the value of a variable whose name it receives as an argument. It will print the attribute's name and value out like this:

```
In Test, $public equals 'public'.
```

The \$$var will end up printing a dollar sign followed by the value of $var (the argument). The $this->$var code will be evaluated as $this->public, $this->protected, and $this->private so that it can access the class attributes.

**4.** Create a class that extends Test.

```
class LittleTest extends Test {
    function print_var($var) {
        echo "<p>In LittleTest,
→ \$$var equals '{$this->$var}'.
→ </p>";
    }
}
```

### The instanceof Keyword

The instanceof keyword can be used to see if a particular object is of a certain class type.

```
if ($obj instanceof SomeClass) { …
```

Notice that you don't put the class's name in quotation marks. Also—and this is important—if the object is not an instance of the given class, the entire script terminates. For a less drastic result, you could use the is_a() function:

```
if (is_a($obj, 'SomeClass')) {…
```

There's also the is_subclass_of() function.

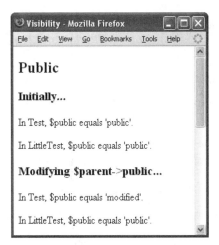

**Figure 7.13** Public variables can be accessed, and modified, anywhere.

The LittleTest class, as an extension of Test, will inherit its own $public and $protected attributes. It will not have the $private attribute, as that variable's visibility is private, meaning it cannot be inherited.

This class will override the print_var() method, changing the printed text slightly.

**5.** Create an object of each type.

```
$parent = new Test();
$child = new LittleTest();
```

**6.** Print the current value of the $public variable by calling the print_var() method.

```
echo '<h2>Public</h2>';
echo '<h3>Initially...</h3>';
$parent->print_var('public');
$child->print_var('public');
```

Because the $public variable is public, it can be accessed by either class's print_var() method.

**7.** Modify the Test $public attribute and reprint.

```
echo '<h3>Modifying $parent-
→ >public...</h3>';
$parent->public = 'modified';
$parent->print_var('public');
$child->print_var('public');
```

Because $public has public visibility, it can be accessed (and therefore modified) anywhere. **Figure 7.13** shows the result of running this script so far. You should note that these lines only change the value of $public in $parent. The $child object's $public variable still has the original value (because the $public attribute is represented as a separate entity in each class).

*continues on next page*

ACCESS CONTROL

8. Repeat Steps 6 and 7 for the protected variable.

```
echo '<hr /><h2>Protected</h2>';
echo '<h3>Initially...</h3>';
$parent->print_var('protected');
$child->print_var('protected');
echo '<h3>Attempting to modify
➞ $parent->public...</h3>';
$parent->protected = 'modified';
$parent->print_var('protected');
$child->print_var('protected');
```

As you'll see when you run this script (**Figure 7.14**), you can access the $protected variable from within either class. But you cannot access it (which also means you cannot modify it) from outside the class. Doing so causes a fatal error.

9. Complete the page.

```
unset($parent, $child);
?>
</body>
</html>
```

Ignore the rest of what you see in Script 7.4 for now, as I'm working you through a process!

**Figure 7.14** Attempting to modify the value of the protected variable using the syntax $obj->var results in a fatal error (which is bad).

**Figure 7.15** Attempting to refer to $this->private within the LittleTest class—which is what happens when you call $child->print_var('private')—creates a notice, as the class does not contain that attribute (because it neither inherited one nor defined one itself). As in Figure 7.14, attempting to refer to $parent->private results in a fatal error.

10. Save the file as `visibility.php`, place it in your Web directory, and test in your Web browser (Figures 7.13 and 7.14).

    This is one of those rare times where I actually want you to see the error, so that you may better understand visibility. A public class member can be accessed anywhere, including outside of a class. A protected member can only be accessed in the class or in derived classes. Attempting to access the member elsewhere results in a fatal error. Thus, a protected class member is more insulated.

11. Comment out this line:

    `$parent->protected = 'modified';`

    This is the line that caused the fatal error, so let's make it inert.

12. Before unsetting the objects, repeat Steps 6 and 7 for the private attribute.

    ```
    echo '<hr /><h2>Private</h2>';
    echo '<h3>Initially...</h3>';
    $parent->print_var('private');
    $child->print_var('private');
    echo '<h3>Attempting to modify
    → $parent->private...</h3>';
    $parent->private = 'modified';
    $parent->print_var('private');
    $child->print_var('private');
    ```

    To finalize this example, let's look at where you can access private class members.

13. Save the file and retest (**Figure 7.15**).

    As you can see in the figure, not even the $child object, which is an instance of the inherited LittleTest class, can access $private. And the script cannot refer to $parent->private, which, again, causes a fatal error.

    *continues on next page*

### ✔ Tips

- Using access control to limit how a class is used is *encapsulation*. Simply put, encapsulation is the hiding of information (actual data or processes). A good class is a usable entity without your necessarily knowing how it works internally.

- Looking at the `Pet` class, its `name` attribute should be made protected. It makes sense for the class and its subclasses to be able to access the name, but you shouldn't be able to do this:

  `$cat->name = 'Fungo';`

  The same applies to the `$width` and `$height` attributes in `Rectangle`.

- As I already mentioned, you can restrict access to methods, but that's less common than restricting access to attributes.

- You should know that the `LittleTest` class doesn't actually need its own `print_var()` method. It can use the (public) `print_var()` in `Test`. Because of inheritance, `LittleTest` would have a `print_var()`, just as it has a `$public` and a `$protected`.

---

### Visibility Suggestions

The `visibility.php` script demonstrates the realms in which variously visible variables can be accessed. It does not, however, demonstrate how you would really use access control in your own classes. You'll see that better in other examples in this chapter and the next. In the meantime, some quick tips:

Start by thinking of access control as a firewall between your class and everything else. Use visibility to prevent bugs and other inappropriate behavior (e.g., being able to change class attributes). Err on the side of making your classes too restrictive! If the restriction ends up being a problem, then adjust. Ask yourself: Are there methods that should only ever get called by the class itself? Then make them protected or private. Also consider that most attributes can be restricted, as the class's methods can be used to access them.

---

**ACCESS CONTROL**

# Using the Scope Resolution Operator

The scope resolution operator is the combination of two colons together (::). It's used to specify to which class a member belongs (and avoiding confusion is often necessary with inherited classes that have the same attributes and methods).

Outside of a class, assuming the method is not protected or private, you could call a method directly using:

`ClassName::method_name();`

The scope resolution operator can also be used within a class to refer to its own properties and members. In that case, you would use the keyword self:

```
class SomeClass {
    function __construct() {
        self::do();
    }
    protected function do() {
        echo 'do!';
    }
}
```

In that code, `self::do()` is the same as using `$this->do()`.

To refer to a member of a parent class, use the keyword parent:

```
class SomeOtherClass extends SomeClass{
    function __construct() {
        parent::do();
    }
}
```

(As a side note on understanding visibility, the do() function defined in SomeClass can only be called by other methods within SomeClass or by methods within inherited classes, because do() is defined as protected.)

For the most part, you'll use the scope resolution operator to access overridden members. You'll also use it with static and constant members, two topics yet to be discussed. As a simple demonstration of how you might use this, I'll touch up the Pet, Dog, and Cat classes.

*continues on next page*

## To use the scope resolution operator:

1. Open pets2.php (Script 7.3) in your text editor or IDE.

2. Modify the Pet constructor so that the animals immediately sleep (**Script 7.5**).

```
function __construct($pet_name) {
    $this->name = $pet_name;
    self::go_to_sleep();
}
```

It seems that many animals go to sleep as one of the first things they do (and there is no go_to_bathroom() method!). By placing this new line in the constructor, the go_to_sleep() method will be called as soon as the object is created.

*continues on page 293*

**Script 7.5** The scope resolution operator makes it easy to refer to overridden methods.

```
1    <!DOCTYPE html PUBLIC "-//W3C//DTD XHTML 1.0 Transitional//EN"
2        "http://www.w3.org/TR/xhtml1/DTD/xhtml1-transitional.dtd">
3    <html xmlns="http://www.w3.org/1999/xhtml" xml:lang="en" lang="en">
4    <head>
5        <meta http-equiv="content-type" content="text/html; charset=iso-8859-1" />
6        <title>Pets</title>
7    </head>
8    <body>
9    <?php # Script 7.5 - pets3.php
10
11   /*   This page defines and uses
12    *   the Pet, Cat, and Dog classes.
13    */
14
15   # ****************** #
16   # ***** CLASSES ***** #
17
18   /* Class Pet.
19    *  The class contains one attribute: name.
20    *  The class contains four methods:
21    *  - __construct()
22    *  - eat()
23    *  - go_to_sleep()
24    *  - play()
25    */
26   class Pet {
27
28       // Declare the attributes:
29       public $name;
30
31       // Constructor assigns the pet's name:
32       function __construct($pet_name) {
33           $this->name = $pet_name;
34           self::go_to_sleep();
35       }
36
```

*(script continues on next page)*

**Script 7.5** *continued*

```
37        // Pets can eat:
38        function eat() {
39        echo "<p>$this->name is eating.</p>";
40        }
41
42        // Pets can sleep:
43        function go_to_sleep() {
44            echo "<p>$this->name is sleeping.</p>";
45        }
46
47        // Pets can play:
48        function play() {
49            echo "<p>$this->name is playing.</p>";
50        }
51
52    } // End of Pet class.
53
54
55    /* Cat class extends Pet.
56     * Cat overrides play().
57     */
58    class Cat extends Pet {
59        function play() {
60
61        // Call the Pet::play() method:
62        parent::play();
63
64        echo "<p>$this->name is climbing.</p>";
65
66        }
67    } // End of Cat class.
68
69
70    /* Dog class extends Pet.
71     * Dog overrides play().
72     */
73    class Dog extends Pet {
74        function play() {
75
76        // Call the Pet::play() method:
77        parent::play();
78
79            echo "<p>$this->name is fetching.</p>";
80        }
81    } // End of Dog class.
82
83
84    # ***** END OF CLASSES ***** #
85    # ************************** #
86
87    // Create a dog:
88    $dog = new Dog('Satchel');
```

*(script continues on next page)*

**Script 7.5** *continued*

```
89
90   // Create a cat:
91   $cat = new Cat('Bucky');
92
93   // Create an unknown type of pet:
94   $pet = new Pet('Rob');
95
96   // Feed them:
97   $dog->eat();
98   $cat->eat();
99   $pet->eat();
100
101  // Nap time:
102  $dog->go_to_sleep();
103  $cat->go_to_sleep();
104  $pet->go_to_sleep();
105
106  // Have them play:
107  $dog->play();
108  $cat->play();
109  $pet->play();
110
111  // Delete the objects:
112  unset($dog, $bucky, $pet);
113
114  ?>
115  </body>
116  </html>
```

**Figure 7.16** The modified code (Script 7.5) now calls the Pet play() method each time a Cat or Dog plays.

■ In Dog and Cat, you could also use the code Pet::play(). But by using parent::play(), you minimize the chance of future problems should the class definitions change.

■ You will often see documentation use the *ClassName*::*method_name*() syntax. When you see this, it's not suggesting that you *should* call the method this way, but rather that method_name() is part of ClassName.

**3.** Modify the Cat play() method so that it calls Pet play().

```
function play() {
    parent::play();
    echo "<p>$this->name is
→ climbing.</p>";
}
```

The play() method in the Pet and Cat classes do slightly different things. The Pet method says that the object is playing. The Cat method says specifically what kind of play. To have the functionality of both methods, call parent::play() within the Cat method.

**4.** Repeat Step 3 for the Dog class.

```
function play() {
    parent::play();
    echo "<p>$this->name is
→ fetching.</p>";
}
```

**5.** Save the file as pets3.php, place it in your Web directory, and test in your Web browser (**Figure 7.16**).

## ✔ Tips

■ In the Pet class it would be more common to see $this->go_to_sleep() than self::go_to_sleep(), but I was trying to demonstrate self:: versus parent::.

■ In PHP 4, you could access any class member without objects using the scope resolution operator:

*ClassName*::*method_name*();

This worked in PHP 4 in part because it did not employ the concept of visibility. In PHP 5, only static members (a concept discussed next) can be referred to this way.

# Creating Static Members

Static class attributes are the class equivalent of static function variables (see Chapter 1, "Advanced PHP Techniques"). A static function variable remembers its value each time a function is called:

```
function test () {
    static $n = 1;
    echo "$n<br />";
    $n++;
}
test();
test();
test();
```

**Figure 7.17** A static variable in a function retains its value over multiple calls (in the same script).

As **Figure 7.17** shows, each call of the test() function increments the value of $n by one. If $n was not declared as static, each call to the function would print the number 1.

With static class attributes, the concept is just the same except that a static variable is remembered across all instances of that class (across all objects based upon the class). To declare a static attribute, use the static keyword after the visibility:

```
class SomeClass {
    public static $var = 'value';
}
```

Static variables differ from standard attributes in that you cannot access them within the class using `$this`. Instead, you'll use `self`, followed by the scope resolution operator (`::`), followed by the variable name, *with its initial dollar sign*:

```
class SomeClass {
    public static $counter = 0;
    function __construct() {
        self::$counter++
    }
}
```

The preceding code creates a counter for how many objects of this class exist. Each time a new object is created:

```
$obj = new SomeClass();
```

`$counter` goes up by one.

Static methods are created in much the same way:

```
class SomeClass {
    public static function do() {
        // Code.
    }
}
```

But once defined, static methods cannot be called using an object. You could never execute:

```
$obj = new SomeClass();
$obj->do(); // NO!
```

Instead you would have to use:

```
SomeClass::do();
```

To play this out, let's create a new `Pet` class that uses a static attribute and a static method. The attribute will be used to count the number of pets in existence. The static method will return the number of pets. As this is a demonstration, no other methods will be created.

## Class Constants

Class constants are like static attributes in that they are accessible to all instances of that class (or derived classes). But as with any other constant, the value can never change. Class constants are created using the `const` keyword, followed by the name of the constant (without a dollar sign), followed by the assignment operator and the constant's value:

```
class SomeClass {
    const PI = 3.14;
}
```

Constants can only be assigned a value like in that example. The value cannot be based upon another variable, and it can't be the result of an expression or a function call.

Constants, like static attributes, also cannot be accessed through the object. You cannot do:

```
$obj->PI
```

or

```
$obj::PI
```

But you can use *ClassName::constant_name* (e.g., `SomeClass::PI`) anywhere. You can also use `self::constant_name` within the class's methods.

## To create static members:

1. Begin a new PHP script in your text editor or IDE, starting with the HTML (**Script 7.6**).

   ```
   <!DOCTYPE html PUBLIC "-//W3C//
   → DTD XHTML 1.0 Transitional//EN"
   "http://www.w3.org/TR/xhtml1/DTD/
   → xhtml1-transitional.dtd">
   <html xmlns="http://www.w3.org/1999/
   → xhtml" xml:lang="en" lang="en">
   <head>
       <meta http-equiv="content-type"
   → content="text/html; charset=iso-
   → 8859-1" />
       <title>Pets</title>
   </head>
   <body>
   <?php # Script 7.6 - static.php
   ```

   *continues on page 298*

**Script 7.6** A static attribute and a static method are used to count the number of pets created in this script.

```
1    <!DOCTYPE html PUBLIC "-//W3C//DTD XHTML 1.0 Transitional//EN"
2           "http://www.w3.org/TR/xhtml1/DTD/xhtml1-transitional.dtd">
3    <html xmlns="http://www.w3.org/1999/xhtml" xml:lang="en" lang="en">
4    <head>
5        <meta http-equiv="content-type" content="text/html; charset=iso-8859-1" />
6        <title>Pets</title>
7    </head>
8    <body>
9    <?php # Script 7.6 - static.php
10
11   /*  This page defines and uses
12    *  the Pet, Cat, and Dog classes.
13    */
14
15   # ****************** #
16   # ***** CLASSES ***** #
17
18   /* Class Pet.
19    *  The class contains two attributes:
20    *  - protected name
21    *  - private static count
22    *  The class contains three methods:
23    *  - __construct()
24    *  - __destruct()
25    *  - public static get_count()
26    */
27   class Pet {
28
29       // Declare the attributes:
30       protected $name;
31
32       private static $count = 0;
33
34       // Constructor assigns the pet's name
35       // and increments the counter.
36       function __construct($pet_name) {
37
38           $this->name = $pet_name;
39
40           // Increment the counter:
41           self::$count++;
42
43       }
44
```

**Script 7.6** *continued*

```
45        // Destructor decrements the counter:
46        function __destruct() {
47            self::$count--;
48        }
49
50        // Static method for returning the counter:
51        public static function get_count() {
52            return self::$count;
53        }
54
55    } // End of Pet class.
56
57
58    /* Cat class extends Pet. */
59    class Cat extends Pet {
60    } // End of Cat class.
61
62    /* Dog class extends Pet. */
63    class Dog extends Pet {
64    } // End of Dog class.
65
66    /* Ferret class extends Pet. */
67    class Ferret extends Pet {
68    } // End of Ferret class.
69
70    /* PygmyMarmoset class extends Pet. */
71    class PygmyMarmoset extends Pet {
72    } // End of PygmyMarmoset class.
73
74
75    # ***** END OF CLASSES ***** #
76    # ************************** #
77
78    // Create a dog:
79    $dog = new Dog('Old Yeller');
80
81    // Print the number of pets:
82    echo '<p>After creating a Dog, I now have ' . Pet::get_count() . ' pet(s).</p>';
83
84    // Create a cat:
85    $cat = new Cat('Bucky');
86    echo '<p>After creating a Cat, I now have ' . Pet::get_count() . ' pet(s).</p>';
87
88    // Create another pet:
89    $ferret = new Ferret('Fungo');
90    echo '<p>After creating a Ferret, I now have ' . Pet::get_count() . ' pet(s).</p>';
91
92    // Tragedy strikes!
93    unset($dog);
94    echo '<p>After tragedy strikes, I now have ' . Pet::get_count() . ' pet(s).</p>';
95
96    // Pygmy Marmosets are so cute:
97    $pygmymarmoset = new PygmyMarmoset('Toodles');
98    echo '<p>After creating a Pygmy Marmoset, I now have ' . Pet::get_count() . ' pet(s).</p>';
99
100   // Delete the objects:
101   unset($cat, $ferret, $pygmymarmoset);
102
103   ?>
104   </body>
105   </html>
```

**2.** Begin declaring the `Pet` class.

```
class Pet {
    protected $name;
    private static $count = 0;
```

The class still has the `$name` attribute, but it's now marked as `protected` so that only this and derived classes can access it. The `$count` variable, which is initialized as 0, is both private and static. By making it private, only this class can access it, which is smart, because you don't want anything else to be able to adjust the counter. By making `$count` static, it retains its value for all instances of `Pet` or any derived classes.

**3.** Create the constructor.

```
function __construct($pet_name) {
    $this->name = $pet_name;
    self::$count++;
}
```

The constructor still assigns the name to the `$name` attribute, but now it also increments the counter. Note the unique syntax for referring to a static attribute.

Every time an object of type `Pet` or of a derived type is created, this constructor gets called. So for every qualifying object, `$count` is incremented.

**4.** Create the destructor.

```
function __destruct() {
    self::$count--;
}
```

Just as the constructor should increase the value of `$count`, the destructor should decrease it. Every time an object of a qualifying type (`Pet` or a derived class) is destroyed, this destructor is called.

**5.** Create the static method and complete the class.

```
    public static function
→ get_count() {
        return self::$count;
    }
} // End of Pet class.
```

The `get_count()` method is public and static. This means that it's available to be called anywhere but cannot be called through an object. It returns the value of `$count`.

**6.** Create a `Cat` class.

```
class Cat extends Pet {
}
```

Since the focus here is on the static members, the derived classes don't need to do anything.

**7.** Create a couple more subclasses.

```
class Dog extends Pet {
}
class Ferret extends Pet {
}
class PygmyMarmoset extends Pet {
}
```

**8.** Create a new object and print the number of pets.

```
$dog = new Dog('Old Yeller');
echo '<p>After creating a Dog, I now
→ have ' . Pet::get_count() . '
→ pet(s).</p>';
```

When `$dog` is created, the `Pet` constructor is called, incrementing `$count` to 1. To return this value, refer to `Pet::get_count()`.

To avoid confusion, I'll point out that the `Pet` constructor is called when making an object of `Dog` type because `Dog` does not have its own constructor.

**Figure 7.18** As the Pet class contains a static attribute, it can be used to count the number of objects created from derived classes.

## ✔ Tips

■ If you did want to have overridden constructors and destructors in the derived classes in this example (Cat, Dog, et al.), you would need them to call the Pet constructor and destructor in order to properly manage the page count. You would do so by adding parent::__construct() and parent::__destruct() to them.

■ Static methods are almost always public because they can't be called through an object.

**9.** Create a couple more pets.

```
$cat = new Cat('Bucky');
echo '<p>After creating a Cat, I now
→ have ' . Pet::get_count() . '
→ pet(s).</p>';
$ferret = new Ferret('Fungo');
echo '<p>After creating a Ferret, I
→ now have ' . Pet::get_count() . '
→ pet(s).</p>';
```

**10.** Have the unthinkable happen (my condolences).

```
unset($dog);
echo '<p>After tragedy strikes, I
→ now have ' . Pet::get_count() . '
→ pet(s).</p>';
```

When the Dog (or any other subclass) object is destroyed (here using unset()), the Pet destructor is invoked, subtracting 1 from $count. (Again, the Pet destructor is called because no derived class has its own destructor.)

**11.** Recover by getting another pet.

```
$pygmymarmoset = new
PygmyMarmoset('Toodles');
echo '<p>After creating a Pygmy
→ Marmoset, I now have ' .
→ Pet::get_count() . ' pet(s).</p>';
```

**12.** Complete the page.

```
unset($cat, $ferret,
→ $pygmymarmoset);
?>
</body>
</html>
```

**13.** Save the file as static.php, place it in your Web directory, and test in your Web browser (**Figure 7.18**).

# Abstract Classes and Methods

To wrap up the chapter, I'm going to introduce abstract classes and methods. Abstract classes are template versions of a parent class. By defining an abstract class, you can indicate the general behavior of a class. It starts with the keyword `abstract`:

```
abstract class ClassName {

}
```

Abstract classes differ from normal classes in that attempting to create an object of an abstract class's type results in a fatal error (**Figure 7.19**). Instead, abstract classes are meant to be extended, and then you create an instance of that extended class.

Abstract classes often have abstract methods. These are defined like so:

```
abstract function function_name();

abstract function function_name($var1,
→ $var2);
```

That's it! You do not define the functionality of the method; instead, that functionality will be determined by the class that extends the abstract class. If you want to add visibility to the definition, add the corresponding keyword after the word abstract:

```
abstract public function
function_name();
```

The implementation of the abstract method in the extended class must abide by the same visibility or weaker. If the abstract function is `public`, the extended version must also be `public`. The implemented version of the method must also have the same number of arguments as the abstract definition.

To put this into action, let's return to geometry examples, like `Rectangle`. That class could be an extension of a more generic `Shape` class. **Figure 7.20** shows just part of the `Shape` family tree. Let's institute the `Shape` abstract class and its child, `Triangle`.

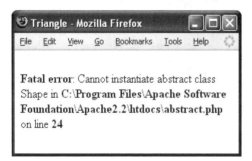

**Figure 7.19** The fatal error created by trying to make an object of an abstract class.

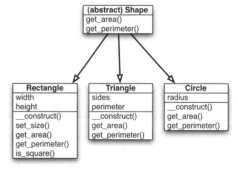

**Figure 7.20** The abstract Shape class can be the parent to many types of (two-dimensional) shapes.

**Script 7.7** The abstract Shape class, with two abstract methods, will be the template for more specific shapes, like Triangle (Script 7.8).

```
1    <?php # Script 7.7 - Shape.php
2
3    /*  This page defines the Shape abstract
     class.
4     *   The class contains no attributes.
5     *   The class contains two abstract
     methods:
6     *   - get_area()
7     *   - get_perimeter()
8     */
9
10   abstract class Shape {
11
12       // No attributes to declare.
13
14       // No constructor or destructor
     defined here.
15
16       // Method to calculate and return the
     area.
17       abstract protected function
     get_area();
18
19       // Method to calculate and return the
     perimeter.
20       abstract protected function
     get_perimeter();
21
22   } // End of Shape class.
23
24   ?>
```

## To create abstract classes and methods:

**1.** Begin a new PHP script in your text editor or IDE (**Script 7.7**).

```
<?php # Script 7.7 - Shape.php
```

**2.** Start defining the Shape class.

```
abstract class Shape {
```

Remember that when a class is abstract, it means you'll never create an object of that type. So you wouldn't make an abstract Rectangle class because you do need to occasionally make rectangles.

**3.** Define the first abstract method.

```
abstract protected function
→ get_area();
```

This line says that any class that extends Shape needs to define a get_area() method. Furthermore, this method should not take any arguments and have either public or protected visibility (the same visibility or weaker). Defining this as an abstract method makes sense, as every two-dimensional shape should have the ability to calculate its own area (three-dimensional shapes have volumes, not areas).

**4.** Define the second abstract method.

```
abstract protected function
→ get_perimeter();
```

**5.** Complete the class and the page.

```
} // End of Shape class.
?>
```

**6.** Save the file as Shape.php and place it in your Web directory.

**ABSTRACT CLASSES AND METHODS**

## To create the Triangle class:

1. Begin a new PHP script in your text editor or IDE (**Script 7.8**).

   ```
   <?php # Script 7.8 - Triangle.php
   ```

**Script 7.8** The Triangle class is an extension of Shape. It is therefore responsible for defining how the get_area() and get_perimeter() methods work.

```
● ● ●                                    📄 Script
1    <?php # Script 7.8 - Triangle.php
2
3    /*  This page defines the Triangle class.
4     *  The class contains two attributes:
5     *  - private $sides (array)
6     *  - private $perimeter (number)
7     *  The class contains three methods:
8     *  - __construct()
9     *  - get_area()
10    *  - get_perimeter()
11    */
12
13   class Triangle extends Shape {
14
15       // Declare the attributes:
16       private $sides = array();
17       private $perimeter = NULL;
18
19       // Constructor:
20       function __construct($s0 = 0, $s1 = 0, $s2 = 0) {
21
22           // Store the values in the array:
23           $this->sides[] = $s0;
24           $this->sides[] = $s1;
25           $this->sides[] = $s2;
26
27           // Calculate the perimeter:
28           $this->perimeter = array_sum($this->sides);
29
30       } // End of constructor.
31
32       // Method to calculate and return the area:
33       public function get_area() {
34
35           // Calculate and return the area:
36           return (SQRT(
37           ($this->perimeter/2) *
38           (($this->perimeter/2) - $this->sides[0]) *
39           (($this->perimeter/2) - $this->sides[1]) *
40           (($this->perimeter/2) - $this->sides[2])
41           ));
42
43       } // End of get_area() method.
44
45       // Method to return the perimeter:
46       public function get_perimeter() {
47           return $this->perimeter;
48       } // End of get_perimeter() method.
49
50   } // End of Triangle class.
51
52   ?>
```

**2.** Begin declaring the Triangle class.

```
class Triangle extends Shape {
```

**3.** Declare the attributes.

```
private $sides = array();
private $perimeter = NULL;
```

The first attribute will store the size of the three sides (you could make three separate variables instead). The second will store the perimeter. I'm only adding this one because the perimeter will be used in calculating the area (a lot), so it's nice to have it in a variable instead of retrieving it through a method call.

All the attributes are `private`, as they shouldn't be accessed outside of any class and I can't imagine how a `Triangle` class would be inherited (in which case they may need to be `protected`).

**4.** Define the constructor.

```
function __construct($s0 = 0, $s1 =
→ 0, $s2 = 0) {
    $this->sides[] = $s0;
    $this->sides[] = $s1;
    $this->sides[] = $s2;
    $this->perimeter =
→ array_sum($this->sides);
}
```

The constructor takes three arguments for the three sides of the triangle. Those values are placed in the `$sides` array, and then the perimeter is calculated. The `array_sum()` function adds up all the elements of an array.

*continues on next page*

ABSTRACT CLASSES AND METHODS

**5.** Create the get_area() method.

```
public function get_area() {
    return (SQRT(
    ($this->perimeter/2) *
    (($this->perimeter/2) -
→ $this->sides[0]) *
    (($this->perimeter/2) -
→ $this->sides[1]) *
    (($this->perimeter/2) -
→ $this->sides[2])
    ));
}
```

If you remember your geometry, you know that the area of a triangle is equal to one-half the base times the height (**Figure 7.21**). Of course, to make that calculation, the class would need to determine the base (the longest side, not a problem) and the height (requiring trigonometry, yikes!). So instead I'll use the formula in **Figure 7.22**. This code implements that formula in PHP.

**6.** Create the get_perimeter() method.

```
public function get_perimeter() {
    return $this->perimeter;
}
```

This is the second of the abstract methods in Shape that must be implemented here. For this example, it simply returns the perimeter attribute. Had I not created a perimeter attribute, this method would instead return array_sum($this->sides).

**7.** Complete the class and the page.

```
} // End of Triangle class.
?>
```

**8.** Save the file as Triangle.php and place it in your Web directory.

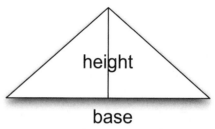

**Figure 7.21** To calculate the area of a triangle the easy way, you would need to know the height value.

$$area = \sqrt{z\,(z - a)\,(z - b)\,(z - c)}$$

**Figure 7.22** Heron's Formula says that the area of a triangle is equal to the square root of z times z minus a times z minus b times z minus c, where z is half the perimeter and a, b, and c are the three sides. (And no, I didn't know this offhand, Mr. Friendly Internet helped out.)

## To use the Triangle class:

**1.** Begin a new PHP script in your text editor or IDE, starting with the HTML (**Script 7.9**).

```
<!DOCTYPE html PUBLIC "-//W3C//
→ DTD XHTML 1.0 Transitional//EN"
"http://www.w3.org/TR/xhtml1/DTD/
→ xhtml1-transitional.dtd">
<html xmlns="http://www.w3.org/1999/
→ xhtml" xml:lang="en" lang="en">
```

```
<head>
    <meta http-equiv="content-type"
→ content="text/html; charset=iso-
→ 8859-1" />
    <title>Triangle</title>
</head>
<body>
<?php # Script 7.9 - abstract.php
```

*continues on next page*

**Script 7.9** This script makes an object of type Triangle, which is derived from the abstract Shape class.

```
1   <!DOCTYPE html PUBLIC "-//W3C//DTD XHTML 1.0 Transitional//EN"
2          "http://www.w3.org/TR/xhtml1/DTD/xhtml1-transitional.dtd">
3   <html xmlns="http://www.w3.org/1999/xhtml" xml:lang="en" lang="en">
4   <head>
5       <meta http-equiv="content-type" content="text/html; charset=iso-8859-1" />
6       <title>Triangle</title>
7   </head>
8   <body>
9   <?php # Script 7.9 - abstract.php
10
11  /*  This page uses the Triangle class (Script 7.8)
12   *  which is derived from Shape (Script 7.7).
13   */
14
15  // Define the __autoload() function:
16  function __autoload ($class) {
17      require_once($class . '.php');
18  }
19
20  // Set the triangle's sides:
21  $side1 = 5;
22  $side2 = 12;
23  $side3 = 13;
24
25  // Print a little introduction:
26  echo "<h3>With sides of $side1, $side2, and $side3...</h3>";
27
28  // Create a new triangle:
29  $t = new Triangle($side1, $side2, $side3);
30
31  // Print the area.
32  echo '<p>The area of the triangle is ' . $t->get_area() . '</p>';
33
34  // Print the perimeter.
35  echo '<p>The perimeter of the triangle is ' . $t->get_perimeter() . '</p>';
36
37  // Delete the object:
38  unset($t);
39
40  ?>
41  </body>
42  </html>
```

**2.** Define the __autoload() function.

```
function __autoload ($class) {
    require_once($class . '.php');
}
```

As discussed at the end of Chapter 6, this function will automatically load files when an object is created for a type that's not defined. In this script, it will load both Triangle.php and Shape.php.

**3.** Set the sides of the triangle.

```
$side1 = 5;
$side2 = 12;
$side3 = 13;
```

Technically a valid triangle abides by a certain rule regarding the three sides: the sum of any two sides has to be greater than the third side (I seriously brushed up on my geometry skills for this).

**4.** Print an introduction and create a new triangle.

```
echo "<h3>With sides of $side1,
→ $side2, and $side3...</h3>";
$t = new Triangle($side1, $side2,
→ $side3);
```

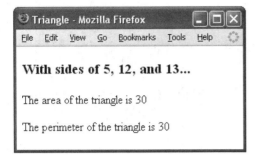

**Figure 7.23** The use of the Triangle class.

**5.** Print the area.

```
echo '<p>The area of the triangle is
→ ' . $t->get_area() . '</p>';
```

This code is much like the Square and Rectangle examples already demonstrated (usage redundancy is a hallmark of OOP).

**6.** Print the perimeter.

```
echo '<p>The perimeter of the
→ triangle is ' . $t->get_perimeter()
→ . '</p>';
```

**7.** Complete the page.

```
unset($t);
?>
</body>
</html>
```

**8.** Save the file as abstract.php, place it in your Web directory, and test in your Web browser (**Figures 7.23**).

### ✔ Tips

■ If a class has even one abstract method, the class itself must be abstract.

■ Similar in theory to abstract classes are interfaces. Interfaces have an added advantage of allowing a derived class to inherit from multiple parent classes.

## Where to Go from Here

In this chapter I focus on the most important aspects of so-called advanced object-oriented programming. It all starts with inheritance, which is what you really need to master.

Although I formally discussed seven topics and included sidebars on many others, another entire chapter could be dedicated to "more advanced object-oriented programming." But I strongly believe that you can't go from little-to-no OOP knowledge to advanced OOP in just a few chapters or even an entire book.

If you are interested in expanding your OOP skills, you'll need to practice, practice, practice. Also look at how existing classes are defined, in particular looking at some of the PEAR stuff. Keep reading, keep experimenting, but start slow and really think things through! If you get stuck or confused, feel free to make use of my supporting forum (www.DMCInsights.com.com/phorum/).

# REAL-WORLD OOP

The preceding two chapters each discuss object-oriented programming, as it pertains specifically to version 5 of PHP (which has a drastically new object model and syntax). The majority of the examples in those chapters tend to be more demonstrative than practical (the Rectangle, Square, Shape, and Triangle classes are useful, though, but only if you're doing geometric work). Philosophical examples are best for teaching OOP, I believe, but real-world object-oriented programming hammers the points home.

In this chapter I focus on two popular uses of OOP: exception handling and a shopping cart. The first subject is new to PHP 5 and worth knowing, even if you don't regularly do object-based programming. The shopping cart example will be an alternative to the procedural method implemented in Chapter 5, "E-Commerce Techniques." My hope is that by having both the procedural and objective implementations of this example, you'll be best able to grasp the OOP concepts.

# Catching Exceptions

One of the OOP additions in PHP 5 is the ability to handle errors using `try` and `catch` statements. The premise is that you *try* to do certain things in your PHP code, specifically the kinds of things that might fail (like connecting to a database or including a file). If an error occurs, you then *throw* an exception. Your code will then *catch* the exception and respond accordingly. Simply put, an *exception* is when something other than what you expected happens.

The basic syntax is

```
try {
    // Do something.
    // Throw an exception on error.
} catch (exception) {
    // Do whatever now.
}
```

This is a more sophisticated version of

```
if (/* Do something. */) {
} else {
    /* Do whatever because a problem
→ occurred. */
}
```

The benefit that the exception handling has over the conditional is that it further separates the functionality and logic from the error handling. Furthermore, multiple errors can be handled without having to use lots of nested conditionals.

There are two ways exceptions might be thrown. The first is to forcibly throw an exception, using the syntax

```
throw new Exception('error message');
```

## Exceptions vs. Error Handling

Catching exceptions, like all object-oriented programming, shouldn't be used just because you can or know how. Exceptions can be overused, cluttering up code with unnecessary `try…catch` blocks. Exception handling also introduces a new potential problem: any exception that's not caught results in a fatal error. A third concern is that every time you create an object, including an `Exception` object, quite a bit of server overhead is required.

You'll see in this book that I tend to use exception handling most frequently when using secondary libraries. For example, in later chapters, `try…catch` blocks will be used when working with COM (Chapter 10, "PHP and the Server") and the PDFlib (download the free bonus chapter, "Creating PDFs," from www.peachpit.com/title/0321376013.).

This code throws an object of type `Exception`, a class defined in PHP. To catch this exception, you would have:

```
catch (Exception $e)
```

where `$e` is an object of the `Exception` type.

The `Exception` class contains the methods (functions) indicated in **Table 8.1**, which you can use to access information about the error. A `try…catch` example might therefore look like:

```
try {
    // Do something.
} catch (Exception $e) {
    echo $e->getMessage();
}
```

You should note that any code after an executed `throw` will never run. Conversely, if no exception ever occurs, the code in the `catch` block will never be executed.

The second way an exception might be thrown is if the `try` block is executing code that throws exceptions itself. You'll see this later in the chapter. For this first example, some sample data will be written to a text file.

**Table 8.1** These methods are all part of the `Exception` class and will be necessary to properly handle exceptions that occur.

| Exception Class Methods | |
| --- | --- |
| NAME | RETURNS |
| getCode() | The code received, if any |
| getMessage() | The message received, if any |
| getFile() | The name of the file where the exception occurred |
| getLine() | The line number from which the exception was thrown |
| getTrace() | An array of information, like the file name, line number, and so on |
| getTraceAsString() | The same information as getTrace() but as a string |
| __toString() | All of the preceding information as a string |

## To use exception handling:

1. Begin a new PHP script in your text editor or IDE, starting with the HTML (**Script 8.1**).

```
<!DOCTYPE html PUBLIC "-//W3C//DTD
XHTML → 1.0 Transitional//EN"
"http://www.w3.org/TR/xhtml1/DTD/
→ xhtml1-transitional.dtd">
<html xmlns="http://www.w3.org/1999/
→ xhtml" xml:lang="en" lang="en">
<head>
    <meta http-equiv="content-type"
→ content="text/html; charset=iso-
→ 8859-1" />
    <title>Handling
Exceptions</title>
</head>
<body>
<?php # Script 8.1 -
write_to_file.php
```

*continues on page 314*

Script 8.1 If any of three different steps in this code cannot be completed, exceptions are thrown, to be handled by the catch.

```
1    <!DOCTYPE html PUBLIC "-//W3C//DTD XHTML 1.0 Transitional//EN"
2          "http://www.w3.org/TR/xhtml1/DTD/xhtml1-transitional.dtd">
3    <html xmlns="http://www.w3.org/1999/xhtml" xml:lang="en" lang="en">
4    <head>
5        <meta http-equiv="content-type" content="text/html; charset=iso-8859-1" />
6        <title>Handling Exceptions</title>
7    </head>
8    <body>
9    <?php # Script 8.1 - write_to_file.php
10
11   /*  This page attempts to write some data
12    *  to a text file.
13    *  Errors are handled using try...catch.
14    */
15
16   // Identify the file:
17   $file = 'data.txt';
18
```

*(script continues on next page)*

**Script 8.1** *continued*

```
 ⊖ ⊙ ⊖                                    📄 Script
19    // Data to be written:
20    $data = "This is a line of data.\n";
21
22    // Start the try...catch block:
23    try {
24
25        // Open the file:
26        if (!$fp = @fopen($file, 'w')) {
27            throw new Exception('could not open the file.');
28        }
29
30        // Write to the file:
31        if (!@fwrite($fp, $data)) {
32            throw new Exception('could not write to the file.');
33        }
34
35        // Close the file:
36        if (!@fclose($fp)) {
37            throw new Exception('could not close the file.');
38        }
39
40        // If we got this far, everything worked!
41        echo '<p>The data has been written.</p>';
42
43    } catch (Exception $e) {
44        echo '<p>The process could not be completed because the script ' . $e->getMessage() . '</p>';
45    }
46
47    echo '<p>This is the end of the script.</p>';
48
49    ?>
50    </body>
51    </html>
```

**2.** Identify the file used for storing the data and the data to be written.

```
$file = 'data.txt';
$data = "This is a line of data.\n";
```

The $file variable should store the full path (relative or absolute) to the text file. This code is outside of a **try...catch** structure and will therefore always be executed, like any other PHP code.

**3.** Begin a **try** block.

```
try {
```

The bulk of the functionality of the script will go within this block.

**4.** Attempt to open the file.

```
if (!$fp = @fopen($file, 'w')) {
    throw new Exception('could not
→ open the file.');
}
```

Opening a file for writing is a common cause of problems, most likely because the file doesn't exist, the file's name and path are incorrect, or the file does not have the proper permissions. If the file could not be opened in writing mode, an exception is thrown with the message *could not open the file*.

Any errors generated by the function calls will be suppressed by @ (the error suppression operator).

**5.** Attempt to write data to the file.

```
if (!@fwrite($fp, $data)) {
    throw new Exception('could not
→ write to the file.');
}
```

This piece of code will only be executed if no exception was thrown by the code in Step 4. Logically, if the file could be opened for writing, the script should be able to use **fwrite()** here. But, just as an example, if you accidentally coded

```
!fwrite($file, $data)
```

here, that mistake would be caught, too.

**6.** Attempt to close the file.

```
if (!@fclose($fp)) {
    throw new Exception('could not
→ close the file.');
}
```

Each exception thrown within the **try** block is of the **Exception** type, but each has a unique message.

**7.** Print a message indicating success of the operation.

```
echo '<p>The data has been
→ written.</p>';
```

This line of code will be executed only if no exceptions were thrown prior to this point.

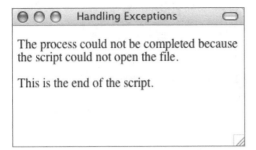

**Figure 8.1** Although it may not be apparent in the end result, this script uses a try...catch block to throw, and then catch, an object of Exception type.

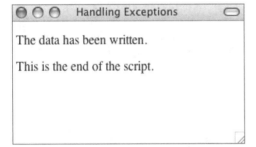

**Figure 8.2** If no problems occurred, this is the end result.

**8.** Catch, and handle, the exception.

```
} catch (Exception $e) {
    echo '<p>The process could not
→ be completed because the
→ script ' . $e->getMessage() .
→ '</p>';
}
```

The variable $e will be an object of Exception type, matching the kinds of exceptions thrown. Within this block, the received message is printed (by calling the getMessage() method) within context.

**9.** Print another message.

```
echo '<p>This is the end of the
→ script.</p>';
```

This code, outside of the try...catch block, will always be executed, even if exceptions occur.

**10.** Complete the page.

```
?>
</body>
</html>
```

**11.** Save the file as write_to_file.php, place it in your Web directory, and test in your Web browser (**Figure 8.1**).

Without first creating a text file called data.txt, with the proper permissions, Figure 8.1 shows the result.

**12.** Create a file called data.txt in the same directory as write_to_file.php, and adjust its permissions if necessary. Then rerun the PHP page in your Web browser (**Figure 8.2**).

*continues on next page*

## ✔ Tips

- To see the other exception error messages (**Figures 8.3** and **8.4**), you'll need to introduce errors into the code. For example, changing the `fopen()` mode to *r* will create the result in Figure 8.3. Changing `!fclose($fp)` to `!fclose($Fp)` will create the result in Figure 8.4.

- Failure to catch a thrown exception results in a fatal error (**Figure 8.5**).

- Every `try` statement requires at least one `catch`. You can have multiple `catch` statements, each catching a different exception type. You'll see this in the next example.

- The `Exception` class's constructor can take anywhere from zero to two arguments. The first argument is an error message, and the second is an error code.

- A `catch` block can also throw an exception to be caught by a later `catch` block. The object thrown can be new or the current exception object:

```
try {
    // Code.
} catch (Exception $e) {
    // Do whatever.
    throw $e;
} catch (Exception $e) {
    // Now do this.
}
```

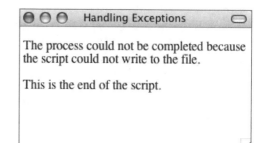

**Figure 8.3** If the script could not write to the data file, an exception with a different message is thrown (compare with Figures 8.1 and 8.4).

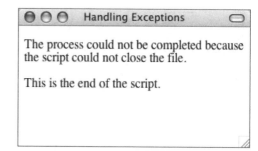

**Figure 8.4** An inability to close the opened file generates this result.

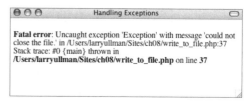

**Figure 8.5** When using `try`, you must ensure that all exceptions are caught, lest you're left with ugly fatal errors like this one.

# Extending the Exception Class

The preceding example demonstrates basic usage of a try…catch block, using the built-in Exception class. This class is very basic, designed to be extended so that you can add, or change, functionality as needed. **Script 8.2** shows the basic outline of this class.

Extending the Exception class is accomplished just like extending any class (see Chapter 7, "Advanced OOP"):

class MyException extends Exception {…

*continues on next page*

**Script 8.2** This code, which comes from the PHP manual, shows the basic definition of the Exception class.

```php
1   <?php
2   class Exception
3   {
4       protected $message = 'Unknown exception';   // exception message
5       protected $code = 0;                         // user defined exception code
6       protected $file;                             // source filename of exception
7       protected $line;                             // source line of exception
8
9       function __construct($message = null, $code = 0);
10
11      final function getMessage();                  // message of exception
12      final function getCode();                     // code of exception
13      final function getFile();                     // source filename
14      final function getLine();                     // source line
15      final function getTrace();                    // an array of the backtrace()
16      final function getTraceAsString();            // formatted string of trace
17
18      /* Overrideable */
19      function __toString();                        // formatted string for display
20  }
21  ?>
```

Note that only the Exception constructor and __toString() methods can be overridden, because the others are all defined as final.

To use your extended class, you would change the try...catch block to:

```
try {
    // Some code.
    throw new MyException('error
→ message');
} catch (MyException $e) {
}
```

Thanks to object type hinting (see the sidebar), you can catch different kinds of exceptions from the same try block:

```
try {
    // Some code.
    throw new MyException1('error
→ message');
    // Some more code.
    throw new MyException2('error
→ message');
} catch (MyException1 $e) {
} catch (MyException2 $e) {
}
```

In the preceding section of the chapter I mention the two ways exceptions are normally thrown: forcibly in the try code or by using code that throws exceptions itself. I'll demonstrate this other method in the next example. This script will do the same thing as the preceding example—write data to a file—but will use an object to do so. This object will throw exceptions of a specific class. To save time and book space, both new classes and the code that uses them will be put into this one file. In a real application, you'd likely want to separate the code into three distinct files.

## Object Type Hinting

Not discussed in Chapter 7 but more of an advanced topic is object type hinting. This is accomplished by preceding a variable with a class name, as in a `catch` block:

```
catch (ClassName $e)
```

You'll also come across type hinting in functions or methods that must take a specific type of object as an argument:

```
function my_func (ClassName $e) {…
```

The intent of type hinting is to only accept a value if it's of the proper type (or class, when it comes to objects). PHP's loosely typed nature is fine for numbers and strings, as you can treat variables of these types just the same without complaint. But thinking you have an object of a certain class when you don't will be a real problem when you go to invoke the object's class-specific methods. Object type hinting prevents this from being an issue.

The last thing to know about type hinting is that it matches a class or any derived class. The code

```
catch (Exception $e)
```

will catch exceptions thrown of type `MyException` or `Exception` (given that `MyException` is derived from `Exception`). If your code might catch both kinds of exceptions, you would want to catch the derived types first:

```
try {
    // Code
} catch (MyException $me) {
} catch (Exception $e) {
}
```

In that code, any exception of type `MyException` will be caught by the first `catch`.

EXTENDING THE EXCEPTION CLASS

## To extend the Exception class:

**1.** Begin a new PHP script in your text editor or IDE, starting with the HTML (**Script 8.3**).

```
<!DOCTYPE html PUBLIC "-//W3C//DTD
→ XHTML 1.0 Transitional//EN"
"http://www.w3.org/TR/xhtml1/DTD/
→ xhtml1-transitional.dtd">
<html xmlns="http://www.w3.org/1999/
→ xhtml" xml:lang="en" lang="en">
<head>
    <meta http-equiv="content-type"
→ content="text/html; charset=iso-
→ 8859-1" />
    <title>Handling Exceptions, Part
→ 2</title>
</head>
<body>
<?php # Script 8.3 - write_to_
→ file2.php
```

*continues on page 324*

**Script 8.3** This script first extends the Exception class to create a more specific type of exception handler. Then it defines and uses a WriteToFile class, which throws exceptions of type FileException.

```
1   <!DOCTYPE html PUBLIC "-//W3C//DTD XHTML 1.0 Transitional//EN"
2          "http://www.w3.org/TR/xhtml1/DTD/xhtml1-transitional.dtd">
3   <html xmlns="http://www.w3.org/1999/xhtml" xml:lang="en" lang="en">
4   <head>
5       <meta http-equiv="content-type" content="text/html; charset=iso-8859-1" />
6       <title>Handling Exceptions, Part 2</title>
7   </head>
8   <body>
9   <?php # Script 8.3 - write_to_file2.php
10
11  /*  This page attempts to write some data
12   *  to a text file.
13   *  A special class is used for this purpose.
14   *  An extended exception class is used for errors.
15   */
16
17  # ****************** #
18  # ***** CLASSES ***** #
```

*(script continues on next page)*

**Script 8.3** *continued*

```
19
20   // Define the extended exception class...
21   // This class adds a get_detail() method.
22   class FileException extends Exception {
23
24       // Define the get_details() method...
25       // Method takes no arguments and
26       // returns a detailed message.
27       function get_details() {
28
29           // Return a different message based
30           // upon the code:
31           switch ($this->code) {
32               case 0:
33                   return 'No filename was provided';
34                   break;
35               case 1:
36                   return 'The file does not exist.';
37                   break;
38               case 2:
39                   return 'The file is not a file.';
40                   break;
41               case 3:
42                   return 'The file is writable.';
43                   break;
44               case 4:
45                   return 'An invalid mode was provided.';
46                   break;
47               case 5:
48                   return 'The data could not be written.';
49                   break;
50               case 6:
51                   return 'The file could not be closed.';
52                   break;
53               default:
54                   return 'No further information is available.';
55                   break;
56           } // End of SWITCH.
57
58       } // End of get_details() function.
59
60   } // End of FileException class.
61
62
63   // Create a class for writing to a file...
64   // Class has one attribute for storing the file pointer.
65   // Class has a constructor, that performs validation
66   // and assigns the pointer.
67   // Class has a write() method for writing data.
68   // Class has a close() method to close the pointer.
```

*(script continues on next page)*

**Script 8.3** *continued*

```
69    class WriteToFile {
70
71        // Attributes:
72        private $fp = null;
73        private $message = '';
74
75        // Constructor:
76        function __construct($file = null, $mode = 'w') {
77
78            // Assign the file name and mode
79            // to the message attribute:
80            $this->message = "File: $file Mode: $mode";
81
82            // Make sure a file name was provided:
83            if (empty($file)) {
84                throw new FileException($this->message, 0);
85            }
86
87            // Make sure the file exists:
88            if (!file_exists($file)) {
89                throw new FileException ($this->message, 1);
90            }
91
92            // Make sure the file is a file:
93            if (!is_file($file)) {
94                throw new FileException ($this->message, 2);
95            }
96
97            // Make sure the file is writable:
98            if (!is_writable($file) ) {
99                throw new FileException ($this->message, 3);
100           }
101
102           // Validate the mode:
103           if (!in_array($mode, array('a', 'a+', 'w', 'w+'))) {
104               throw new FileException($this->message, 4);
105           }
106
107           // Open the file:
108           $this->fp = fopen($file, $mode);
109
110       } // End of constructor.
111
112       // Method for writing the data:
113       function write($data = null) {
114
115           if (!fwrite($this->fp, $data)) {
116               throw new FileException($this->message . " Data: $data", 5);
117           }
118
```

*(script continues on next page)*

**Script 8.3** *continued*

```
119        } // End of write() method.
120
121        // Method for closing the file:
122        function close() {
123
124            if (!fclose($this->fp)) {
125                throw new FileException($this->message, 6);
126                }
127
128            $this->fp = null;
129
130        } // End of close() method.
131
132    } // End of WriteToFile class.
133
134    # ***** END OF CLASSES ***** #
135    # ************************** #
136
137    // Identify the file:
138    $file = 'data.txt';
139
140    // Data to be written:
141    $data = "This is a line of data.\n";
142
143    // Start the try...catch block:
144    try {
145
146        $fp = new WriteToFile($file);
147        $fp->write($data);
148        $fp->close();
149
150        // If we got this far, everything worked!
151        echo '<p>The data has been written.</p>';
152
153    } catch (FileException $fe) {
154
155        echo '<p>The process could not be completed. Debugging information:<br />' .
        $fe->getMessage() . '<br />' . $fe->get_details() . '</p>';
156
157    }
158
159
160    ?>
161    </body>
162    </html>
```

2. Begin defining an extension to the Exception class.

```
class FileException extends
→ Exception {
```

This class, called FileException, will specifically handle file opening, writing, and closing errors. It will add one method to the inherited Exception methods.

3. Begin defining the get_details() method.

```
function get_details() {
    switch ($this->code) {
        case 0:
            return 'No
→ filename was provided';
            break;
```

Any time an exception occurs, up to two arguments can be passed to the Exception class: the message and the error code. The WriteToFile class, to be written shortly, will generate its own error codes. This class, FileException, will associate those error codes with more specific error messages. This get_details() method returns the message that goes with each code, using a switch.

4. Complete the switch.

```
        case 1:
            return 'The file does
→ not exist.';
            break;
        case 2:
            return 'The file is not
→ a file.';
            break;
        case 3:
```

```
            return 'The file is not
→ writable.';
            break;
        case 4:
            return 'An invalid mode
→ was provided.';
            break;
        case 5:
            return 'The data could
→ not be written.';
            break;
        case 6:
            return 'The file could
→ not be closed.';
            break;
        default:
            return 'No further
→ information is available.';
            break;
    } // End of SWITCH.
```

Each of these messages will mean more once you see the WriteToFile class.

5. Complete the get_details() method and the FileException class.

```
    } // End of get_details()
→ function.
} // End of FileException class.
```

6. Begin defining the WriteToFile class.

```
class WriteToFile {
    private $fp = null;
    private $message = '';
```

This class is going to wrap up under one umbrella all the validation and code required for writing to a file. It has two attributes, the first of which will be the file pointer. The second attribute will be assigned an error message. Both attributes are private, as they should not be accessible outside of this class.

**7.** Begin defining the constructor.

```
function __construct($file = null,
→ $mode = 'w') {
    $this->message = "File: $file
→ Mode: $mode";
```

The constructor is called when a new `WriteToFile` object is created. It takes two arguments: the file and the mode, whose default value is *w*. The purpose of the constructor is to confirm that the file exists and is writable, and then to open that file for writing. The constructor also helps build the error message, which, for debugging purposes, will contain the filename and the mode.

**8.** Make sure that a filename was provided.

```
if (empty($file)) {
    throw new FileException
→ ($this->message, 0);
}
```

The first validation routine checks that some filename was passed to the class. If not, an exception of type `FileException` is thrown, using the default message and an error code of 0. This error code matches the more specific message in the `FileException` `get_details()` method.

**9.** Make sure that the file exists and that it is a file.

```
if (!file_exists($file)) {
    throw new FileException
→ ($this->message, 1);
}
if (!is_file($file)) {
    throw new FileException
→ ($this->message, 2);
}
```

The `file_exists()` function will return `TRUE` even if provided with a directory name, so the second check is also necessary. If either check fails, an exception is thrown, providing different error codes accordingly.

**10.** Confirm that the file is writable.

```
if (!is_writable($file) ) {
    throw new FileException
→ ($this->message, 3);
}
```

**11.** Confirm that a valid mode was used.

```
if (!in_array($mode, array('a',
→ 'a+', 'w', 'w+'))) {
    throw new FileException
→ ($this->message, 4);
}
```

As I don't want to try to open the file in an invalid mode, this check is necessary. I've omitted some valid modes (like *ab*) and all reading modes (because I'm creating a write-specific class) to keep it simple.

**12.** Open the file and complete the constructor.

```
    $this->fp = fopen($file,
→ $mode);
} // End of constructor.
```

If all of the validation tests were passed, the file is opened in the given mode, assigning the result to the `$fp` attribute.

**13.** Create the method for writing data to the file.

```
function write($data = null) {
    if (!fwrite($this->fp, $data))
{
        throw new
→ FileException($this->message . "
→ Data: $data", 5);
    }
} // End of write() method.
```

This method has its own validation test and throws an exception with its own error code.

*continues on next page*

**14.** Create the method for closing the file.

```
function close() {
    if (!fclose($this->fp)) {
        throw new
FileException($this->message, 6);
    }
    $this->fp = null;
} // End of close() method.
```

**15.** Complete the `WriteToFile` class.

```
} // End of WriteToFile class.
```

**16.** Identify the file to use and the data to write.

```
$file = 'data.txt';
$data = "This is a line of data.\n";
```

**17.** Create a try block that uses the `WriteToFile` class.

```
try {
    $fp = new WriteToFile($file);
    $fp->write($data);
    $fp->close();
    echo '<p>The data has been
written.</p>';
```

Because all of the validation resides in the `WriteToFile` class, using this class is remarkably simple. Compare this code with that in `write_to_file.php` (Script 8.1).

**18.** Catch the exceptions.

```
} catch (FileException $fe) {
    echo '<p>The process could not
be completed. Debugging
information:<br />' .
$fe->getMessage() . '<br />' .
$fe->get_details() . '</p>';
}
```

This `catch` expects exceptions of type `FileException`, which will be thrown by the `WriteToFile` object. Within the `catch`, debugging information is printed using both the `Exception` `getMessage()` method (which should print the file, mode, and possibly data) and the `FileException` `get_details()` method.

## Analyzing the WriteToFile Class

The focus in this section of the chapter is on extending the `Exception` class, but I do want to take a minute to analyze the `WriteToFile` class, as part of my ongoing attempt to convey good OOP theory. The class is good in that it puts everything involved with writing to a file in one place. It also has a ton of validation built in, which makes using the class really easy (see Script 8.3). Tying the class to an extended `Exception` class also works nicely.

The class is a bit too specific, though. In reality, you'd probably want to create a `FileIO` class, that handles both writing and reading. I would probably, in hindsight, place the code that closes the file in the destructor instead of a separate `close()` method.

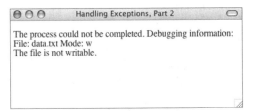

**Figure 8.6** The result if the file exists but is not writable. The first line of debugging information comes from the Exception getMessage() class. The rest comes from FileException get_details().

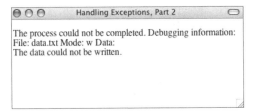

**Figure 8.7** If the data cannot be written to the file, the debugging information also shows what data was received (here, nothing).

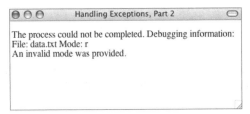

**Figure 8.8** Attempting to open the file in reading mode will also fail.

**19.** Complete the page.

```
?>
</body>
</html>
```

**20.** Save the file as `write_to_file2.php`, place it in your Web directory, and test in your Web browser (**Figures 8.6**, **8.7**, and **8.8**).

This example really emphasizes two things. First, it shows how you can extend the Exception class to make your error handling as detailed as possible (the default errors you might encounter when opening, writing to, and closing files are generally not very informative). Second, it shows how much of an application's functionality can be stored in a class, making the rest of the code quite simple. This is just one of the benefits of object-oriented programming.

### ✔ Tips

■ Because PHP generates an ugly error should an uncaught exception occur, you can create your own exception handler to handle this situation more gracefully:

```
function my_exception_handler
(Exception $e) {
    // Do whatever.
}
set_exception_handler('my_exception_
→ handler');
```

■ If your extended class has its own constructor, it should also call the Exception constructor using `parent::__construct()`.

# Creating a Shopping Cart Class

For the second "real-world" use of object-oriented programming, I want to implement as a class the shopping cart system created in Chapter 5, "E-Commerce Techniques." If you look back at cart.php (Script 5.7), you'll see that the one page does several things:

◆ Adds items to the cart

◆ Updates the quantities in the cart

◆ Removes items from the cart (when the user enters a quantity of 0)

◆ Displays the shopping cart in an HTML form

In an object-oriented structure, this can be implemented in many ways. You could start with an abstract ShoppingCart class that is then extended by a more specific WidgetShoppingCart class. I'm going to keep this simple and just go with the WidgetShoppingCart, but check out the Shape and Triangle classes in Chapter 7 for how an inherited abstract class would work.

For this class, each of the preceding features can be turned into a method. Only one attribute, which will store an array of items in the cart, will be required. Unlike the session variable in Chapter 5, which only stored the product IDs and their respective quantities, this cart will store everything about each product: ID, name, color, size, quantity, and price.

## To create a shopping cart class:

1. Begin a new PHP script in your text editor or IDE (**Script 8.4**).

   ```
   <?php # Script 8.4 -
   → WidgetShoppingCart.php
   ```

*continues on page 333*

**Script 8.4** The WidgetShoppingCart class implements all of the shopping cart functionality required by the "World of Widgets" e-commerce store.

```
1    <?php # Script 8.4 - WidgetShoppingCart.php
2
3    /*  This page defines the WidgetShoppingCart class.
4     *  The class contains one attribute: an array called $items.
5     *  The class contains five methods:
6     *  - is_empty()
7     *  - add_item()
8     *  - update_item()
9     *  - delete_item()
10    *  - display_cart()
11    */
12
13   class WidgetShoppingCart {
14
15       // Attribute:
16       protected  $items = array();
17
18
19       // Method that returns a Boolean
20       // value indicating if the cart is empty:
21       public function is_empty() {
22           if (empty($this->items)) {
23               return true;
24           } else {
25               return false;
26           }
27       }
28
29
30       // Method for adding an item to a cart.
31       // Takes two arguments: the item ID and an array of info.
32       public function add_item($id, $info) {
33
34           // Is it already in the cart?
35           if (isset($this->items[$id])) {
36
37               // Call the update_item() method:
```

*(script continues on next page)*

**Script 8.4** *continued*

```
38              $this->update_item($id, $this->items[$id]['qty'] + 1);
39
40         } else {
41
42             // Add the array of info:
43             $this->items[$id] = $info;
44
45             // Add the quantity.
46             $this->items[$id]['qty'] = 1;
47
48             // Print a message:
49             echo "<p>The widget '{$info['name']}' in color {$info['color']}, size {$info['size']}
    has been added to your shopping cart.</p>\n";
50
51         }
52
53     } // End of add_item() method.
54
55
56     // Method for updating an item in the cart.
57     // Takes two arguments: the item ID and the quantity.
58     public function update_item($id, $qty) {
59
60         // Delete if $qty equals 0:
61         if ($qty == 0) {
62
63             $this->delete_item($id);
64
65         } elseif ( ($qty > 0) && ($qty != $this->items[$id]['qty'])) {
66
67             // Update the quantity:
68             $this->items[$id]['qty'] = $qty;
69
70             // Print a message:
71             echo "<p>You now have $qty copy(ies) of the widget '{$this->items[$id]['name']}' in
    color {$this->items[$id]['color']}, size {$this->items[$id]['size']} in your shopping
    cart.</p>\n";
72
73         }
74
75     } // End of update_item() method.
76
77
78     // Method for deleting an item in the cart.
79     // Takes one argument: the item ID.
80     public function delete_item($id) {
81
82         // Confirm that it's in the cart:
83         if (isset($this->items[$id])) {
84
```

*(script continues on next page)*

**Script 8.4** *continued*

```
85          // Print a message:
86          echo "<p>The widget '{$this->items[$id]['name']}' in color {$this-
      >items[$id]['color']}, size {$this->items[$id]['size']}} has been removed from your shopping
      cart.</p>\n";
87
88          // Remove the item:
89          unset($this->items[$id]);
90
91      }
92
93    } // End of delete_item() method.
94
95
96    // Method for displaying the cart.
97    // Takes one argument: a form action value.
98    public function display_cart($action = false) {
99
100       // Print a table:
101       echo '<table border="0" width="90%" cellspacing="2" cellpadding="2" align="center">
102       <tr>
103           <td align="left" width="20%"><b>Widget</b></td>
104           <td align="left" width="15%"><b>Size</b></td>
105           <td align="left" width="15%"><b>Color</b></td>
106           <td align="right" width="15%"><b>Price</b></td>
107           <td align="center" width="10%"><b>Qty</b></td>
108           <td align="right" width="15%"><b>Total Price</b></td>
109       </tr>
110       ';
111
112       // Print form code, if appropriate.
113       if ($action) {
114           echo '<form action="' . $action . '" method="post">
115       <input type="hidden" name="do" value="update" />
116       ';
117       }
118
119       // Initialize the total:
120       $total = 0;
121
122       // Loop through each item:
123       foreach ($this->items as $id => $info) {
124
125           // Calculate the total and subtotals:
126           $subtotal = $info['qty'] * $info['price'];
127           $total += $subtotal;
128           $subtotal = number_format($subtotal, 2);
129
130           // Determine how to show the quantity:
131           $qty = ($action) ? "<input type=\"text\" size=\"3\" name=\"qty[$id]\"
      value=\"{$info['qty']}\" />" :  $info['qty'];
```

*(script continues on next page)*

**Script 8.4** *continued*

```
132
133            // Print the row:
134            echo <<<EOT
135    <tr>
136       <td align="left">{$info['name']}</td>
137       <td align="left">{$info['size']}</td>
138       <td align="left">{$info['color']}</td>
139       <td align="right">\${$info['price']}</td>
140       <td align="center">$qty</td>
141            <td align="right">\$$subtotal</td>
142         </tr>\n
143    EOT;
144
145         } // End of FOREACH loop.
146
147         // Complete the table:
148         echo '   <tr>
149            <td colspan="5" align="right"><b>Total:<b></td>
150            <td align="right">$' . number_format ($total, 2) . '</td>
151         </tr>';
152
153         // Complete the form, if appropriate:
154         if ($action) {
155            echo '<tr>
156            <td colspan="6" align="center">Set an item\'s quantity to 0 to remove it from your
       cart.</td>
157         </tr>
158    <tr>
159       <td colspan="6" align="center"><button type="submit" name="submit" value="update">Update
       Cart</button></td>
160       </tr>
161       </form>';
162         }
163
164         echo '</table>';
165
166    } // End of display_cart() method.
167
168    } // End of WidgetShoppingCart class.
169
170    ?>
```

**2.** Start defining the class.

```
class WidgetShoppingCart {
    protected $items = array();
```

The class contains only the one attribute. By making it protected, it cannot be manipulated outside of WidgetShoppingCart (or derived) type objects.

**3.** Define the is_empty() method.

```
public function is_empty() {
    if (empty($this->items)) {
        return true;
    } else {
        return false;
    }
}
```

This method returns a Boolean value indicating whether or not the cart is empty. It'll be used by scripts to know whether or not the cart should be displayed.

**4.** Begin defining the add_item() method.

```
public function add_item($id,
→ $info) {
    if (isset($this->items[$id])) {
        $this->update_item($id,
→ $this->items[$id]['qty'] + 1);
```

This method receives two arguments: the item ID and an array of information. The ID will be the index in the $items array. The array of information will contain the product's name, color, size, and price, to which will be added the quantity.

The method starts by checking if the item is already in the cart. If so, the update_item() method is called, sending it the item ID and the new quantity (which is the current quantity plus 1). Although the item's quantity could be updated within this method, since the other method with the appropriate functionality already exists, it's best not to replicate that functionality here (creating redundancies).

*continues on next page*

**CREATING A SHOPPING CART CLASS**

**5.** Complete the add_item() method.

```
        } else {

                $this->items[$id] =
→ $info;

                $this->items[$id]['qty']
→ = 1;

                echo "<p>The widget
→ '{$info['name']}' in color
→ {$info['color']}, size
→ {$info['size']} has been added to
→ your shopping cart.</p>\n";

        }

} // End of add_item() method.
```

The else clause applies if the item is not already in the cart. In that case, the item is put into the virtual cart by adding a new element to the $items array. The $info variable will be sent to this method as an array, defined like so:

```
$info = array (

'name' => $name,

'color' => $color,

'size' => $size,

'price' => $price);
```

To this array, a fifth element is added: a quantity of 1, indexed at *qty*.

Finally, this method prints a message indicating what just happened (**Figure 8.9**).

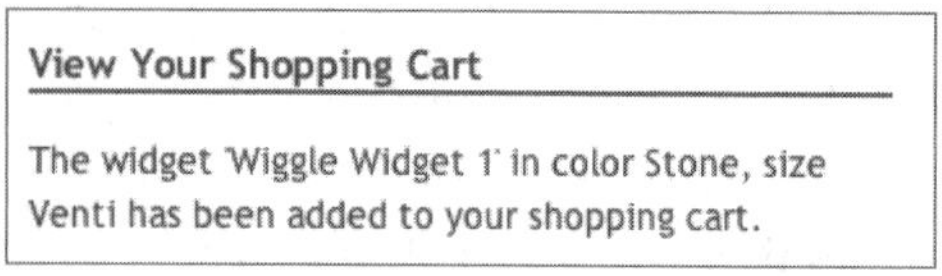

**View Your Shopping Cart**

The widget 'Wiggle Widget 1' in color Stone, size Venti has been added to your shopping cart.

**Figure 8.9** The message generated when a new item is added to the shopping cart.

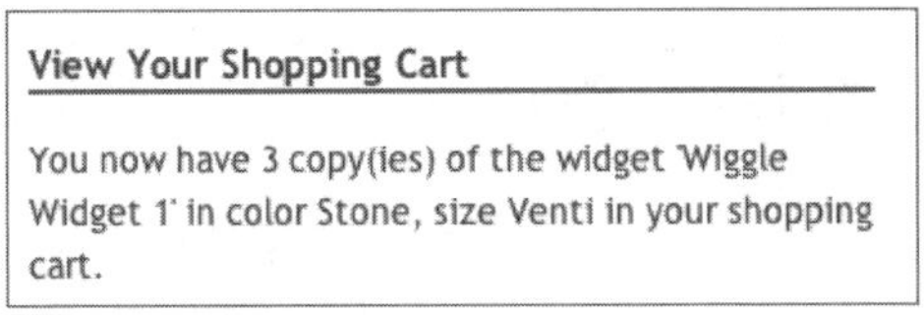

**View Your Shopping Cart**

You now have 3 copy(ies) of the widget 'Wiggle Widget 1' in color Stone, size Venti in your shopping cart.

**Figure 8.10** When the quantity of an item in the cart is updated, a message like this is printed.

6. Create a method for updating an item.

```
public function update_item($id,
$qty) {
        if ($qty == 0) {
                $this->delete_item($id);
        } elseif ( ($qty > 0) && ($qty
→ != $this->items[$id]['qty'])) {
                $this->items[$id]['qty']
→ = $qty;
                echo "<p>You now have
→ $qty copy(ies) of the widget
→ '{$this->items[$id]['name']}' in
→ color {$this->items[$id]['color']},
→ size {$this->items[$id]['size']} in
→ your shopping cart.</p>\n";
        }
} // End of update_item() method.
```

The first check sees if the new quantity is 0, in which case the item should be deleted. To do so, the delete_item() method is called, which contains that functionality. Otherwise, as long as the quantity is positive and it's not the same as the current quantity (because that wouldn't be an update, would it?), the quantity in the cart will be updated. Again, a message reports on what just happened (**Figure 8.10**).

*continues on next page*

CREATING A SHOPPING CART CLASS

**7.** Create a method for deleting an item.

```
public function delete_item($id) {
    if (isset($this->items[$id])) {
        echo "<p>The widget
→ '{$this->items[$id]['name']}' in
→ color {$this->items[$id]['color']},
→ size {$this->items[$id]['size']}
→ has been removed from your shopping
→ cart.</p>\n";
        unset($this->items
→ [$id]);
    }
} // End of delete_item() method.
```

The only thing this method should do is confirm that the item is in the cart prior to unsetting it. A message indicating what just happened is also printed (**Figure 8.11**). Note that you have to print the message before unsetting the item or else you won't be able to refer to $this->items[$id]['name'], etc.

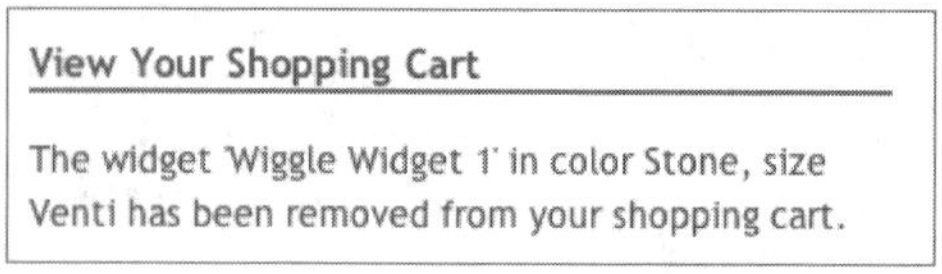

**Figure 8.11** Unlike the cart in Chapter 5, this version now indicates what item(s) are removed when the user sets a quantity to zero.

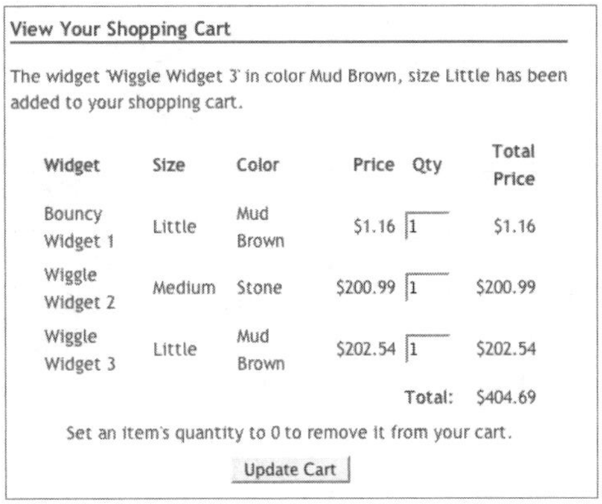

View Your Shopping Cart

The widget 'Wiggle Widget 3' in color Mud Brown, size Little has been added to your shopping cart.

| Widget | Size | Color | Price | Qty | Total Price |
|---|---|---|---|---|---|
| Bouncy Widget 1 | Little | Mud Brown | $1.16 | 1 | $1.16 |
| Wiggle Widget 2 | Medium | Stone | $200.99 | 1 | $200.99 |
| Wiggle Widget 3 | Little | Mud Brown | $202.54 | 1 | $202.54 |
| | | | | Total: | $404.69 |

Set an item's quantity to 0 to remove it from your cart.

Update Cart

**Figure 8.12** The cart viewed as an HTML form so that the user can update the quantities.

View Your Shopping Cart

| Widget | Size | Color | Price | Qty | Total Price |
|---|---|---|---|---|---|
| Bouncy Widget 1 | Little | Mud Brown | $1.16 | 1 | $1.16 |
| Wiggle Widget 2 | Medium | Stone | $200.99 | 1 | $200.99 |
| Wiggle Widget 3 | Little | Mud Brown | $202.54 | 1 | $202.54 |
| | | | | Total: | $404.69 |

**Figure 8.13** The cart viewed without the HTML form, so it is uneditable. This feature might be used on the final checkout page.

8. Begin the method for displaying the cart's contents.

```
public function display_cart($action
→ = false) {
    echo '<table border="0"
→ width="90%" cellspacing="2"
→ cellpadding="2" align="center">
        <tr>
            <td align="left"
→ width="20%"><b>Widget</b></td>
            <td align="left"
→ width="15%"><b>Size</b></td>
            <td align="left"
→ width="15%"><b>Color</b></td>
            <td align="right"
→ width="15%"><b>Price</b></td>
            <td align="center"
→ width="10%"><b>Qty</b></td>
            <td align="right"
→ width="15%"><b>Total Price</b></td>
        </tr>
';
        if ($action) {
            echo '<form action="' .
→ $action . '" method="post">
        <input type="hidden" name="do"
→ value="update" />
        ';
        }
```

I want this method to display the cart either as part of an HTML form (**Figure 8.12**) or not (**Figure 8.13**). To distinguish between these two modes, the method takes an optional $action argument. If provided, this should be the name of the file to which the form should be submitted.

The method begins by printing a table and its header. If an action was received, the initial form tags are generated.

*continues on next page*

**9.** Initialize a total variable and begin looping through each item in the cart.

```
$total = 0;
foreach ($this->items as $id =>
→ $info) {
    $subtotal = $info['qty'] *
→ $info['price'];
    $total += $subtotal;
    $subtotal =
→ number_format($subtotal, 2);
```

The first thing that happens within the loop is the calculation of the subtotals and total. This code is similar to that in the original script.

**10.** Determine how the item's quantity should be displayed.

```
$qty = ($action) ? "<input
→ type=\"text\" size=\"3\"
→ name=\"qty[$id]\"
→ value=\"{$info['qty']}\" />" :
→ $info['qty'];
```

If the cart is being displayed as a form, then the quantities should be shown as an input box with a preset value (**Figure 8.14**). Otherwise, the quantity should just be the quantity. The ternary operator helps makes this decision, using the $action variable. This is the equivalent of writing:

```
if ($action) {
    $qty = "<input type=\"text\"
→ size=\"3\" name=\"qty[$id]\"
→ value=\"{$info['qty']}\" />";
} else {
    $qty = $info['qty'];
}
```

**Figure 8.14** The HTML source code of the form shows how each item's quantity is a text input.

**11.** Print the item and complete the foreach loop.

```
    echo <<<EOT
<tr>
    <td
→ align="left">{$info['name']}</td>
    <td align="left">{$info['size']}
→ </td>
    <td align="left">{$info
→ ['color']}</td>
    <td align="right">\${$info
→ ['price']}</td>
    <td align="center">$qty</td>
                <td
align="right">\$$subtotal</td>
        </tr>\n
EOT;
} // End of FOREACH loop.
```

Because this code involves both variables and HTML, I use the heredoc syntax, as described in Chapter 1, "Advanced PHP Techniques."

**12.** Print the order total.

```
echo '      <tr>
    <td colspan="5"
→ align="right"><b>Total:<b></td>
    <td align="right">$' .
→ number_format ($total, 2) . '</td>
</tr>';
```

**13.** Complete the form, if necessary.

```
if ($action) {
    echo '<tr>
    <td colspan="6"
→ align="center">Set an item\'s
→ quantity to 0 to remove it from
→ your cart.</td>
</tr>
<tr>
    <td colspan="6"
→ align="center"><button
→ type="submit" name="submit"
→ value="update">Update
→ Cart</button></td>
</tr>
</form>';
}
```

If this cart is being displayed as part of a form, it must also inform the user how to delete an item, and create a submit button.

**14.** Complete the method.

```
    echo '</table>';
} // End of display_cart() method.
```

**15.** Complete the class and the page.

```
} // End of WidgetShoppingCart
→ class.
?>
```

**16.** Save the file as `WidgetShoppingCart.php` and place it in your Web directory.

# Using the Cart Class

Having created the WidgetShoppingCart class, a script now has to be made that uses an object of that type. This next script will replace cart.php (Script 5.7), doing everything the original file did, but using OOP for the cart management. However, the page must still uses sessions, because any created object will still only exist for the life of the page. Therefore, this script will now store the object in the session at the end of the script and refer to that session-stored object at the beginning of the script, if it exists. Other than that, much of the basic functionality of this page will mimic that in the original file.

## To use the WidgetShoppingCart class:

1. Create a new PHP document in your text editor or IDE (**Script 8.5**).

   ```php
   <?php # Script 8.5 - cart.php
   require_once ('./includes/
   → config.inc.php');
   $page_title = 'Shopping Cart';
   include_once ('./includes/
   → header.html');
   echo '<h1>View Your Shopping
   → Cart</h1>';
   ```

*continues on page 343*

**Script 8.5** The cart.php page handles all cart management through an object of type WidgetShoppingCart. The object must be serialized and stored in the session in order to be available over multiple page views.

```php
1    <?php # Script 8.5 - cart.php
2
3    /*
4     *  This is the shopping cart page.
5     *  This page has two modes:
6     *  - add a product to the cart
7     *  - update the cart
8     *  The page shows the cart as a form for updating quantities.
9     *  The cart is an object of WidgetShoppingCart type,
10    *  which is stored in a session.
11    */
12
13   // Require the configuration file before any PHP code:
14   require_once ('./includes/config.inc.php');
15
16   // Include the header file:
17   $page_title = 'Shopping Cart';
18   include_once ('./includes/header.html');
19
20   echo '<h1>View Your Shopping Cart</h1>';
21
22   // Create the shopping cart:
23   require_once('WidgetShoppingCart.php');
24   if (isset($_SESSION['cart'])) {
25       $cart = unserialize($_SESSION['cart']);
```

*(script continues on next page)*

**Script 8.5** *continued*

```
26    } else {
27        $cart = new WidgetShoppingCart();
28    }
29
30    // This page will either add to or update the
31    // shopping cart, based upon the value of $_REQUEST['do'];
32    if (isset($_REQUEST['do']) && ($_REQUEST['do'] == 'add') ) { // Add new item.
33
34        if (isset($_GET['sw_id'])) { // Check for a product ID.
35
36            // Typecast to an integer:
37            $sw_id = (int) $_GET['sw_id'];
38
39            // If it's a positive integer,
40            // get the item information:
41            if ($sw_id > 0) {
42
43                // Define and execute the query:
44                $q = "SELECT name, color, size, default_price, price FROM general_widgets LEFT JOIN
     specific_widgets USING (gw_id) LEFT JOIN colors USING (color_id) LEFT JOIN sizes USING (size_id)
     WHERE sw_id=$sw_id";
45                $r = mysqli_query($dbc, $q);
46
47                if (mysqli_num_rows($r) == 1) {
48
49                    // Get the information:
50                    $row = mysqli_fetch_array($r, MYSQLI_ASSOC);
51
52                    // Determine the price:
53                    $price = (empty($row['price'])) ? $row['default_price'] : $row['price'];
54
55                    // Add to the cart:
56                    $cart->add_item($sw_id, array('name' => $row['name'], 'color' => $row['color'],
     'size' => $row['size'], 'price' => $price));
57
58                } // End of mysqli_num_rows() IF.
59
60            } // End of ($sw_id > 0) IF.
61
62        } // End of isset($_GET['sw_id']) IF.
63
64    } elseif (isset($_REQUEST['do']) && ($_REQUEST['do'] == 'update')) {
65
66        // Change any quantities...
67        // $k is the product ID.
68        // $v is the new quantity.
69        foreach ($_POST['qty'] as $k => $v) {
70
```

*(script continues on next page)*

**Script 8.5** *continued*

```
71          // Must be integers!
72          $pid = (int) $k;
73          $qty = (int) $v;
74
75          // Update the cart:
76          $cart->update_item($pid, $qty);
77
78     } // End of FOREACH.
79
80     // Print a message:
81     echo '<p>Your shopping cart has been updated.</p>';
82
83  } // End of $_REQUEST IF-ELSE.
84
85  // Show the shopping cart if it's not empty:
86  if (!$cart->is_empty()) {
87     $cart->display_cart('cart.php');
88  } else {
89     echo '<p>Your cart is currently empty.</p>';
90  }
91
92  // Store the cart in the session:
93  $_SESSION['cart'] = serialize($cart);
94
95  // Include the footer file to complete the template:
96  include_once ('./includes/footer.html');
97
98  ?>
```

**2.** Create the shopping cart object.

```
require_once('WidgetShoppingCart.
→ php');
if (isset($_SESSION['cart'])) {
    $cart = unserialize
→ ($_SESSION['cart']);
} else {
    $cart = new
→ WidgetShoppingCart();
}
```

To create the object, the class definition file must first be included. Next, the script checks to see if the cart object exists in the session (which is to say that the user has accessed this page before). If so, the $cart variable will be assigned the unserialized version of $_SESSION['cart']. You have to use the unserialize() function to access it, as the cart object will be serialized prior to storing it in the session.

If $_SESSION['cart'] does not exist, a new object of type WidgetShoppingCart() will be created.

**3.** Check for a $_REQUEST['do'] variable.

```
if (isset($_REQUEST['do']) &&
→ ($_REQUEST['do'] == 'add') ) {
```

When an item is added to the cart by clicking the link on the products page, $_GET['do'] will have a value of *add*.

**4.** Validate the specific widget ID.

```
if (isset($_GET['sw_id'])) {
    $sw_id = (int) $_GET['sw_id'];
    if ($sw_id > 0) {
```

Just to be safe, you should make sure that the specific widget ID is a positive integer.

*continues on next page*

**5.** Retrieve the product information from the database.

```
$q = "SELECT name, color, size,
→ default_price, price FROM
→ general_widgets LEFT JOIN
→ specific_widgets USING (gw_id) LEFT
→ JOIN colors USING (color_id) LEFT
→ JOIN sizes USING (size_id) WHERE
→ sw_id=$sw_id";
$r = mysqli_query($dbc, $q);
if (mysqli_num_rows($r) == 1) {
```

In order both to confirm that a valid product ID was received and to be able to add it to the shopping cart, this query is necessary. It performs a join across four tables in order to get the general widget name as well as the specific widget's color and size (**Figure 8.15**).

Because a widget could have a default price or a specific price (which overrides the default), both prices are selected. Code in Step 6 will determine which price to use.

**6.** Update the cart.

```
$row = mysqli_fetch_array($r,
→ MYSQLI_ASSOC);
$price = (empty($row['price'])) ?
→ $row['default_price'] :
→ $row['price'];
$cart->add_item($sw_id, array('name'
→ => $row['name'], 'color' =>
→ $row['color'], 'size' =>
→ $row['size'], 'price' => $price));
```

First, the record is retrieved from the database. Second, the correct price is determined by checking if `$row['price']` has a value. If so, this new price should be used; otherwise, the default price is correct.

Then, the item is added to the cart using the `add_item()` method. The first argument should be the item ID, which is `$sw_id`. The second argument is an array of information.

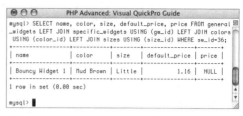

**Figure 8.15** The query retrieves all the required information for an individual product.

**7.** Complete the conditionals started in Steps 5 and 4, and then check to see if $_REQUEST['do'] equals *update*.

```
                    } // End of
→ mysqli_num_rows() IF.
                } // End of ($sw_id > 0)
→ IF.
        } // End of
→ isset($_GET['sw_id']) IF.
} elseif (isset($_REQUEST['do']) &&
→ ($_REQUEST['do'] == 'update')) {
```

$_REQUEST['do'] will have a value of *update* when the user updates their cart by submitting the form. At this point the shopping cart should attempt to update every quantity.

**8.** Update the cart quantities.

```
foreach ($_POST['qty'] as $k => $v) {
    $pid = (int) $k;
    $qty = (int) $v;
    $cart->update_item($pid, $qty);
}
```

This is pretty simple. Both the key, which is the product ID, and the value, which is the quantity, are first typecast to integers. Then the update_item() method is called. That method will only update the quantity if it has a positive value different from the current quantity (see WidgetShoppingCart.php, Script 8.4). The method also removes any items whose quantity is set to 0.

**9.** Print a message and complete the $_REQUEST if-else.

```
    echo '<p>Your shopping cart has
→ been updated.</p>';
} // End of $_REQUEST IF-ELSE.
```

*continues on next page*

## The Standard PHP Library

More "real-world" object-oriented programming can be found in PEAR (see Chapter 12, "Using PEAR") or in the Standard PHP Library (SPL). The Standard PHP Library (no doubt inspired by the very popular Standard C++ Library) contains class definitions and other code meant to address common problems. For more information see www.php.net/spl.

**10.** Show the cart contents, if it's not empty.

```
if (!$cart->is_empty()) {
    $cart->display_cart
→ ('cart.php');
} else {
    echo '<p>Your cart is currently
→ empty.</p>';
}
```

Invoking the `display_cart()` method is all that's required to show the cart. By passing this method one argument with a value of `cart.php`, the method will create a form that is submitted back to this page.

**11.** Store the cart object in a session.

```
$_SESSION['cart'] =
→ serialize($cart);
```

The cart must be stored in the session, or else the cart will be empty each time the user comes to the page.

**12.** Complete the page.

```
include_once ('./includes/
→ footer.html');
?>
```

**13.** Save the script as `cart.php`, upload it to your server (in the same directory as all of the Chapter 5 files), and test it in your Web browser (**Figures 8.16**, **8.17** and **8.18**).

## ✔ Tip

- Even if the cart object being used by the script is stored in a session, the script still has to include the object's class definition file. This is true for all objects, as PHP would otherwise have no way of accessing a class's methods.

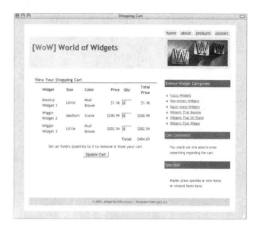

**Figure 8.16** These values will update the cart's contents (Figure 8.17) upon submitting the form.

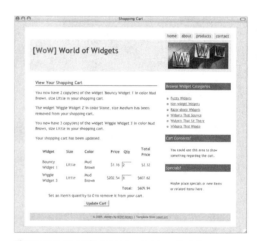

**Figure 8.17** Specific messages show what changes were made to the cart's contents.

**Figure 8.18** If the `WidgetShoppingCart` `is_empty()` function returns a value of `true`, the cart will not be displayed.

# NETWORKING WITH PHP

The vast bulk of what PHP is used to do is based upon taking information from the server (like a database or a text file) and sending it to the client (the end user's Web browser) or vice versa. But PHP also supports a slew of features for the purpose of interacting with other Web sites, communicating with other servers, and even FTP'ing files. In this chapter, I'll discuss and demonstrate a couple of network-related PHP functions and capabilities.

In the first example, you'll see how to read data from another Web site as if it were any old text file. In the second, a URL validator will be created (a tool for checking if a link is still good). In the third section of the chapter, you'll learn how to identify from what country a user is connecting to your server. And finally, you'll get a quick introduction to cURL, a powerful networking utility.

# Accessing Other Web Sites

Even though PHP itself is normally used to create Web sites, it can also access and interact with Web pages on its own. This can be useful for retrieving information, writing spiders (applications that scour the Internet for particular data), and more. Surprisingly, you can access other Web sites in much the same way you would access a text file on your hard drive: by using `fopen()`.

```
fopen ('http://www.example.com/', 'r');
```

The `fopen()` function used for opening files can also open Web pages because they are, after all, just files on a server. The parameters for using `fopen()` are the same (r, w, and a), although you will be limited to opening a file only for reading unless the file's permissions are open (which hopefully they are not).

One caveat, though, is that you must use a trailing slash after a directory because `fopen()` will not support redirects. The preceding example and this one are fine:

```
fopen ('http://www.example.com/
→ index.php', 'r');
```

But this will fail:

```
fopen ('http://www.example.com/
→ dir', 'r');
```

(Many people are unaware that the URL www.example.com/dir is redirected to www.example.com/dir/.)

Once you have opened a file, you can treat it as you otherwise would, using `file()`, `fgets()`, etc., to retrieve (or place) the data.

I'll demonstrate this concept by making use of Yahoo!'s financial pages to return New York Stock Exchange quotes for different stocks.

Before proceeding, I should state that the legality of retrieving information from another Web site is an issue you would want to investigate before permanently implementing something like this. Most sites contain copyrighted information, and using it without permission would be a violation. This demonstration with Yahoo! is just a demonstration, not a suggestion that you make a habit of this!

### To read a Web site with PHP:

1. Create a new PHP document in your text editor or IDE, beginning with the HTML (**Script 9.1**):

```
<!DOCTYPE html PUBLIC "-//W3C//DTD
→ XHTML 1.0 Transitional//EN"
"http://www.w3.org/TR/xhtml1/DTD/
→ xhtml1-transitional.dtd">
<html xmlns="http://www.w3.org/1999/
→ xhtml" xml:lang="en" lang="en">
<head>
    <meta http-equiv="content-type"
→ content="text/html; charset=
→ iso-8859-1" />
    <title>Get Stock Quotes</title>
    <style type="text/css"
→ title="text/css" media="all">
.error {
    color: #F30;
}
.quote {
    font-weight : bold;
}
</style>
</head>
<body>
<?php # Script 9.1 - get_quote.php
```

*continues on page 351*

**Script 9.1** The code in this example will retrieve stock quotes by opening up Yahoo!'s quote page and parsing the data therein.

```
1    <!DOCTYPE html PUBLIC "-//W3C//DTD XHTML 1.0 Transitional//EN"
2          "http://www.w3.org/TR/xhtml1/DTD/xhtml1-transitional.dtd">
3    <html xmlns="http://www.w3.org/1999/xhtml" xml:lang="en" lang="en">
4    <head>
5        <meta http-equiv="content-type" content="text/html; charset=iso-8859-1" />
6        <title>Get Stock Quotes</title>
7        <style type="text/css" title="text/css" media="all">
8    .error {
9        color: #F30;
10    }
11    .quote {
12        font-weight : bold;
13    }
14    </style>
15    </head>
16    <body>
17    <?php # Script 9.1 - get_quote.php
18
19    /*  This page retrieves a stock price from Yahoo!.
20     */
21
22    if (isset($_GET['symbol']) && !empty($_GET['symbol'])) { // Handle the form.
23
24        // Identify the URL:
25        $url = sprintf('http://quote.yahoo.com/d/quotes.csv?s=%s&f=nl1', $_GET['symbol']);
26
27        // Open the "file".
28        $fp = @fopen ($url, 'r') or die ('<div align="center" class="error">Cannot access
     Yahoo!</div></body></html>');
29
30        // Get the data:
31        $read = fgetcsv ($fp);
32
33        // Close the "file":
34        fclose ($fp);
35
36        // Check the results for improper symbols:
```

*(script continues on next page)*

**Script 9.1** *continued*

```
37        if (strcasecmp($read[0], $_GET['symbol']) != 0) {

38

39            // Print the results:

40            echo '<div align="center">The latest value for <span class="quote">' . $read[0] .
   '</span> (<span class="quote">' . $_GET['symbol'] . '</span>) is $<span class="quote">' .
   $read[1] . '</span>.</div><br />';

41

42        } else {

43            echo '<div align="center" class="error">Invalid symbol!</div>';

44        }

45

46    }

47

48    // Show the form:

49    ?>

50    <form action="get_quote.php" method="get">

51    <table border="0" cellspacing="2" cellpadding="2" align="center">

52        <tr align="center" valign="top">

53            <td align="center" valign="top" colspan="2">Enter a NYSE stock symbol to get the
   latest price:</td>

54        </tr>

55        <tr align="center" valign="top">

56            <td align="right" valign="top">Symbol:</td>

57            <td align="left" valign="top"><input type="text" name="symbol" size="5" maxlength="5"
   /></td>

58        </tr>

59        <tr>

60            <td align="center" valign="top" colspan="2"><input type="submit" name="submit"
   value="Fetch the Quote!" /></td>

61        </tr>

62    </table>

63    </form>

64    </body>

65    </html>
```

You'll notice here that I've thrown in a little CSS to format the results. There are two classes: error and quote.

2. Check if the form has been submitted.

```
if (isset($_GET['symbol']) &&
→ !empty($_GET['symbol'])) {
```

This page will both display and handle a form. The form itself takes just one input: the symbol for a stock. As the form uses the GET method, the handling PHP code checks for the presence of a $_GET['symbol'].

3. Define the URL to be opened.

```
$url = sprintf('http://
→ quote.yahoo.com/d/quotes.csv?s=
→ %s&f=nl1', $_GET['symbol']);
```

The most important consideration when accessing and reading other Web pages is to know exactly what data will be there and in what form. In other words, unless you are merely copying the entire contents of a file, you'll need to develop some system for gleaning the parts of the page you want according to how the data is structured.

In this example, a URL such as http://quote.yahoo.com/d/quotes.csv takes two arguments: the stock (or stocks) to check and the formatting parameters. It will then return a CSV (comma-separated value) file.

For this example, I want to know the stock's name and the latest price, so the formatting would be nl1 (see www.gummy-stuff.org/Yahoo-data.htm for the options and what they mean). Throw in the ticker symbol and the result will be in the format (where *XX.XX* is the price):

```
"STOCK NAME",XX.XX
```

*continues on next page*

Once I know that this is a comma-delineated list of the stock's name and its latest price, I can then parse exactly what I am looking for. More complex Web pages might require use of regular expressions to retrieve the particular pieces you want.

4. Open the Web page and read in the data.

```
$fp = @fopen ($url, 'r') or die
→ ('<div align="center"
→ class="error">Cannot access
→ Yahoo!</div></body></html>');
$read = fgetcsv ($fp);
fclose ($fp);
```

Now that the URL is defined, I can open the "file" for reading. Since I know that the returned data is in CSV form, I can use fgetcsv() to read it. This function will automatically turn the line it reads into an array, using commas as the delimiter. Then I close the file pointer. Note that if the URL were a proper HTML document (this one is not), the first line read would be something like <!DOCTYPE html PUBLIC "-//W3C/.

If the URL could not be opened, an error message is printed and the script terminated (**Figure 9.1**).

5. Validate that a legitimate stock symbol was used.

```
if (strcasecmp($read[0],
→ $_GET['symbol']) != 0) {
```

If an invalid stock symbol is used, then the Yahoo! page will return that symbol as the stock name and $0.00 as the price. To weed these instances out, check if the returned name is the same as the symbol. I use the strcasecmp() function to perform a case-insensitive equality check between them. If they are the same, the function will return 0. If they are not the same, a nonzero value is returned, meaning it's safe to print the result.

**Figure 9.1** The result if the URL could not be opened.

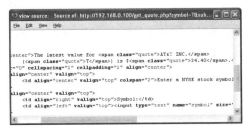

**Figure 9.2** The resulting HTML, including the CSS references.

**6.** Print the stock's value.

```
echo '<div align="center">The latest
→ value for <span class="quote">' .
→ $read[0] . '</span> (<span
→ class="quote">' . $_GET['symbol'] .
→ '</span>) is <span class="quote">
→ '. $read[1] . '</span>.</div>
→ <br />';
```

The code in Step 4 takes the information retrieved (e.g., *"STOCK NAME",24.34*) and turns it into an array. The first element in the array is the stock's name, and the second is the current stock value. Both are printed, along with the stock's symbol, within some CSS formatting (**Figure 9.2**). Note that the fgetcsv() function will strip the quotes from around the stock's name.

**7.** Complete the strcasecmp() conditional.

```
} else {
            echo '<div align=
→ "center" class="error">Invalid
→ symbol!</div>';
    }
}
```

**8.** Complete the $_GET['symbol'] conditional and the PHP section.

```
}
?>
```

**9.** Create the HTML form.

```
<form action="get_quote.php"
→ method="get">
<table border="0" cellspacing="2"
→ cellpadding="2" align="center">
    <tr align="center" valign="top">
            <td align="center"
→ valign="top" colspan="2">Enter a
→ NYSE stock symbol to get the latest
→ price:</td>
    </tr>
    <tr align="center" valign="top">
```

*continues on next page*

```
                <td align="right"
→ valign="top">Symbol:</td>
                <td align="left"
→ valign="top"><input type="text"
→ name="symbol" size="5"
→ maxlength="5" /></td>
        </tr>
        <tr>
                <td align="center"
→ valign="top" colspan="2"><input
→ type="submit" name="submit"
→ value="Fetch the Quote!" /></td>
        </tr>
    </table>
    </form>
```

The form takes just one input: a text box for the stock's symbol (**Figure 9.3**).

**10.** Complete the page.

```
    </body>
    </html>
```

**11.** Save the file as get_quote.php, place it in your Web directory, and test in your Web browser (**Figures 9.4**, **9.5**, and **9.6**).

## ✔ Tips

- PEAR (PHP Extension and Application Repository) contains dozens of networking-related classes. See Chapter 12, "Using PEAR," and the Web site http://pear.php.net for more.

- The Zend Framework (http://framework.zend.com) has some network-related classes as well. At the time of this writing, there are ones specifically for connecting to Amazon, Flickr, and Yahoo!.

**Figure 9.3** The form takes just a stock symbol from the user.

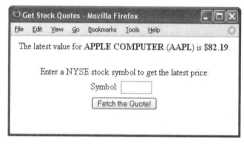

**Figure 9.4** The script has determined, by accessing the Yahoo! page, that Apple Computer is currently at $82.19.

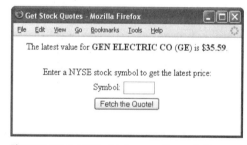

**Figure 9.5** General Electric is currently worth $35.59.

**Figure 9.6** The result if an invalid ticker symbol is entered.

**Table 9.1** These are just the most popular of the 60,000+ ports computers can use for communication.

| Common Ports | |
|---|---|
| **NUMBER** | **PRIMARY PURPOSE** |
| 21 | FTP |
| 22 | SSH |
| 23 | Telnet |
| 25 | SMTP |
| 80 | Web |
| 81 | Web (alternate) |
| 110 | POP |
| 143 | IMAP |
| 389 | LDAP |
| 443 | SSL |

# Working with Sockets

The fopen() function is one way to access Web pages, but a more sophisticated method would be to use sockets. A socket, in case you are not familiar, is a channel through which two computers can communicate with each other. To open a socket in PHP, use fsockopen():

$fp = fsockopen ($url, $port, $error_
→ number, $error_string, $timeout);

You use fsockopen() to establish a file pointer as you would use fopen(). The parameters the function takes are the URL, the port, an error number variable, an error string variable, and the timeout (only the first argument is required).

In layman's terms, a *port* is the door through which different protocols (methods of communication) go. For Web pages, the port is normally 80 (see **Table 9.1**). The error number and string variables are interesting in that they are not really sent to the function (as they have no value initially) so much as they are returned by the function should an error occur. Finally, the timeout simply states for how many seconds the function should try to connect.

Once the file has been successfully opened, you can again use fwrite(), fgets(), and so forth to manipulate the data.

Another function I'll explain before writing the fsockopen() example is parse_url(). This function takes a URL and turns it into an associative array by breaking the structure into its parts:

$url_pieces = parse_url ($url);

*continues on next page*

*continues on next page*

**WORKING WITH SOCKETS**

The primary pieces of the URL will be *scheme*, *host*, *port*, *path*, and *query*. **Table 9.2** shows how the URL

```
http://www.example.com/view.php?week=1
```

would be broken down by `parse_url()`.

The `parse_url()` function can be handy in all sorts of instances. I'll demonstrate one example in the following script. The code developed there will run through a list of URLs and check each to make sure they are still valid. To do so, a user-defined function will take a provided URL, parse it, and then use `fsockopen()` to connect to it. The server's HTTP response code will indicate the validate of that link. (**Table 9.3** lists some common HTTP status codes, which you can also find by searching the Web.)

## To use fsockopen():

1. Create a new PHP document in your text editor or IDE, beginning with the HTML (**Script 9.2**):

```
<!DOCTYPE html PUBLIC "-//W3C//DTD
→ XHTML 1.0 Transitional//EN"
"http://www.w3.org/TR/xhtml1/DTD/
→ xhtml1-transitional.dtd">
<html xmlns="http://www.w3.org/1999/
→ xhtml" xml:lang="en" lang="en">
<head>
    <meta http-equiv="content-type"
    → content="text/html; charset=
    → iso-8859-1" />
    <title>Validate URLs</title>
    <style type="text/css" title=
    → "text/css" media="all">
.bad {
    color: #F30;
}
.good {
```

*continues on page 359*

**Table 9.2** How `parse_url()` breaks down a sample URL. The *fragment* value corresponds to anything after a #. The *user* and *pass* values would exist if the URL were of the format `http://username:password@www.example.com`.

| parse_url() Example | |
|---|---|
| INDEX | VALUE |
| scheme | http |
| host | www.example.com |
| port | 80 |
| user | |
| pass | |
| path | view.php |
| query | week=1 |
| fragment | |

**Table 9.3** Every requested server page returns an HTTP status code. For URL validation purposes, 200 is the preferred code to see.

| Common HTTP Status Codes | |
|---|---|
| CODE | MEANING |
| 200 | OK |
| 204 | No content |
| 400 | Bad request |
| 401 | Unauthorized |
| 403 | Forbidden |
| 404 | Not found |
| 408 | Timeout |
| 500 | Internal server error |

WORKING WITH SOCKETS

**Script 9.2** By making a socket connection, this script can quickly check if a given URL is still valid.

```
1    <!DOCTYPE html PUBLIC "-//W3C//DTD XHTML 1.0 Transitional//EN"
2            "http://www.w3.org/TR/xhtml1/DTD/xhtml1-transitional.dtd">
3    <html xmlns="http://www.w3.org/1999/xhtml" xml:lang="en" lang="en">
4    <head>
5        <meta http-equiv="content-type" content="text/html; charset=iso-8859-1" />
6        <title>Validate URLs</title>
7        <style type="text/css" title="text/css" media="all">
8    .bad {
9        color: #F30;
10   }
11   .good {
12       color: #0C0;
13   }
14   </style>
15   </head>
16   <body>
17   <?php # Script 9.2 - check_urls.php
18
19   /*  This page validates a list of URLs.
20    *  It uses fsockopen() and parse_url() to do so.
21    */
22
23   // This function will try to connect to a URL:
24   function check_url ($url) {
25
26       // Break the URL down into its parts:
27       $url_pieces = parse_url ($url);
28
29       // Set the $path and $port:
30       $path = (isset($url_pieces['path'])) ? $url_pieces['path'] :  '/';
31       $port = (isset($url_pieces['port'])) ? $url_pieces['port'] : 80;
32
33       // Connect using fsockopen():
34       if ($fp = @fsockopen ($url_pieces['host'], $port, $errno, $errstr, 30)) {
35
36           // Send some data:
37           $send = "HEAD $path HTTP/1.1\r\n";
38           $send .= "HOST: {$url_pieces['host']}\r\n";
39           $send .= "CONNECTION: Close\r\n\r\n";
40           fwrite($fp, $send);
41
42           // Read the response:
43           $data = fgets ($fp, 128);
44
45           // Close the connection:
46           fclose($fp);
47
```

*(script continues on next page)*

**Script 9.2** *continued*

```
48        // Return the response code:
49        list($response, $code) = explode (' ', $data);
50
51        if ($code == 200) {
52            return array($code, 'good');
53        } else {
54            return array($code, 'bad');
55        }
56
57    } else { // No connection, return the error message:
58        return array($errstr, 'bad');
59    }
60
61  } // End of check_url() function.
62
63  // Create the list of URLs:
64  $urls = array (
65  'http://zirzow.dyndns.org/php-general/NEWBIE/',
66  'http://video.google.com/videoplay?docid=-5137581991288263801&q=loose+change',
67  'http://www.securephpwiki.com/index.php/Email_Injection/',
68  'http://www.uic.rsu.ru/doc/web/php_coding_standard.html',
69  'http://nfl.dmcinsights.com/MadminY/',
70  'http://seagull.phpkitchen.com/'
71  );
72
73  // Print a header:
74  echo '<h2>Validating URLs</h2>';
75
76  // Kill the PHP time limit:
77  set_time_limit(0);
78
79  // Validate each URL:
80  foreach ($urls as $url) {
81
82      list($code, $class) = check_url ($url);
83      echo "<p><a href=\"$url\" target=\"_new\">$url</a> (<span class=\"$class\">$code</span>)
      </p>\n";
84
85  }
86  ?>
87  </body>
88  </html>
```

```
      color: #0C0;
}
</style>
</head>
<body>
<?php # Script 9.2 - check_urls.php
```

As with get_quote.php (Script 9.1), I've thrown in two CSS classes to format the results.

2. Begin defining the check_url() function.

```
function check_url ($url) {
```

The function takes one argument: the URL to be validated.

3. Parse the URL.

```
$url_pieces = parse_url ($url);
```

4. Set the proper path and port values.

```
$path = (isset($url_pieces['path']))
→ ? $url_pieces['path'] :  '/';
$port = (isset($url_pieces['port']))
→ ? $url_pieces['port'] : 80;
```

I want to make sure that I've got the right path and port when testing the connection later on, so I set the $path variable to be either the existing path, if any, or a slash, as the default. For the URL www.example.com/dir, the path would be /dir. For www.example.com, the path would be /.

The same treatment is given to the $port, with the default as 80.

5. Attempt to connect using fsockopen().

```
if ($fp = @fsockopen ($url_
→ pieces['host'], $port, $errno,
→ $errstr, 30)) {
```

*continues on next page*

**6.** If a connection is established, write some data to the server.

```
$send = "HEAD $path HTTP/1.1\r\n";
$send .= "HOST: {$url_
→ pieces['host']}\r\n";
$send .= "CONNECTION: Close\r\n\r\n";
fwrite($fp, $send);
```

These lines may seem confusing, but what they are essentially doing is sending a series of HTTP headers to the server to initiate communication. The type of request being made is HEAD. Such a request is like GET, except that the server will only return a response and not the entire page (compare **Figures 9.7** and **9.8**). The fsockopen() line connects to the server; the HEAD $path line here requests a specific page. This could be just / or /somefolder/somepage.php.

The \r\n code is required for properly formatting the request.

**7.** Retrieve the response code.

```
$data = fgets ($fp, 128);
fclose($fp);
list($response, $code) = explode
→ (' ', $data);
```

Once the URL has been hit with a header, it will respond with its own HTTP headers. The code will read in the first 128 characters of the response and then break this down into an array. The second element returned will be the HTTP code. Table 9.3 lists some of the possible response codes, and Figure 9.7 shows a sample response.

**Figure 9.7** A HEAD request only returns the basic headers for a page.

**Figure 9.8** A normal (GET) request returns the entire page (this figure just shows the first few lines of the HTML source code returned).

8. Return the code and a class message.

```
if ($code == 200) {
    return array($code, 'good');
} else {
    return array($code, 'bad');
}
```

This function should indicate, via its return values, what code was received and whether that code is good or bad (these strings match up to the CSS classes). An HTTP status code of 200 is considered normal (OK, technically); anything else indicates some sort of problem.

9. Finish the conditional begun in Step 5 and the function.

```
    } else {
            return array($errstr,
'bad');
    }
} // End of check_url() function.
```

If a socket connection was not made, the returned error message will be sent back from the check_urls() function.

10. Create a list of URLs.

```
$urls = array (
'http://zirzow.dyndns.org/
→ php-general/NEWBIE/',
'http://video.google.com/videoplay?
→ docid=-5137581991288263801&q=
→ loose+change',
'http://www.securephpwiki.com/
→ index.php/Email_Injection/',
'http://www.uic.rsu.ru/doc/web/
→ php_coding_standard.html',
'http://nfl.dmcinsights.com/
→ MadminY/',
'http://seagull.phpkitchen.com/'
);
```

*continues on next page*

WORKING WITH SOCKETS

For sake of simplicity, I'm creating an array of hard-coded URLs. You might retrieve your own URLs from a database or file instead.

**11.** Print a header and adjust the PHP scripts' time limit.

```
echo '<h2>Validating URLs</h2>';
set_time_limit(0);
```

Making these socket connections can take some time, especially if you have a lot of URLs to validate. By calling the set_time_limit() function with a value of 0, the PHP script is given limitless time to do its thing.

**12.** Validate each URL.

```
foreach ($urls as $url) {
    list($code, $class) = check_url
→ ($url);
    echo "<p><a href=\"$url\"
→ target=\"_new\">$url</a> (<span
→ class=\"$class\">$code</span>)
→ </p>\n";
}
```

The foreach loop goes through each URL in the array. Then the check_url() function is called. It returns two values: the code (or an error message) and the CSS class name to use (either good or bad). Then the URL is printed, as a link, followed by the code or error message (**Figure 9.9**).

**13.** Finish the PHP and the HTML.

```
?>
</body>
</html>
```

**14.** Save the file as check_urls.php, place it in your Web directory, and test in your Web browser (**Figure 9.10**).

**Figure 9.9** Part of the resulting HTML source code after validating the links.

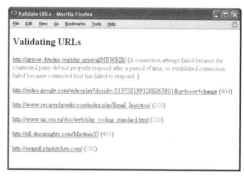

**Figure 9.10** How the validation panned out for the provided five URLs.

## ✔ Tips

- Another benefit that fsockopen() has over the fopen() method used in the first section of the chapter is that the fopen() technique will fail unless PHP's allow_url_fopen setting is true.

- This is just one example of using sockets in PHP. You can create your own socket server using PHP and the socket functions. If you don't already know why you might want to do this, you'll likely never need to touch these functions. But for more information, see www.php.net/sockets.

# Performing IP Geolocation

One of the questions that I commonly see in my support forums (www.dmcinsights.com/phorum/) or in the PHP newsgroups is how to identify what country a user resides in. Although the server where PHP is located could be anywhere in the world and the user could be located anywhere in the world, it is possible to make a geographic match. The premise is this:

Every computer must have an IP address to have Internet access (or to connect to any network). An Internet service provider (ISP) assigns a computer an IP address from a pool of valid addresses only they have access to. By knowing a computer's IP address, which PHP puts in $_SERVER['REMOTE_ADDR'], one can know the ISP and therefore, the country. Hence, the name *IP geolocation*. New GeoIP databases can even predict the city and state, although with less accuracy.

The easiest way to implement this is to use the PEAR Net_Geo class. It uses online services to retrieve the information for a provided IP address. This class has its downsides, which I discuss in the sidebar.

This next example will make use of another network-related PHP function. The gethostbyname() function returns the IP address for a given domain name.

## Choosing an IP Geolocation Option

Unfortunately the online resources used by the Net_Geo PEAR class aren't that up-to-date, so its accuracy could fade over time. In the interest of most readily demonstrating the IP geolocation concept, I think it's a fine enough option.

A more accurate option is to use the Net_GeoIP PEAR class. Unfortunately, this is still in beta form at the time of this writing and relies upon a commercial database for best accuracy and information. In fact, as a rule of thumb, if you're writing an application that relies upon IP geolocation, you'll want to pay someone for a commercial database, which is likely to be most accurate.

## To find a user's location:

1. Create a new PHP script in your text editor or IDE, beginning with the HTML (**Script 9.3**).

   ```
   <!DOCTYPE html PUBLIC "-//W3C//DTD
   → XHTML 1.0 Transitional//EN"

   "http://www.w3.org/TR/xhtml1/DTD/
   → xhtml1-transitional.dtd">

   <html xmlns="http://www.w3.org/
   → 1999/xhtml" xml:lang="en"
   → lang="en">

   <head>

       <meta http-equiv="content-type"
       → content="text/html; charset=
       → iso-8859-1" />

       <title>PEAR::Net_Geo</title>

   </head>

   <body>

   <?php # Script 9.3 - net_geo.php
   ```

2. Include the class definition and create the object.

   ```
   require_once('Net/Geo.php');

   $net_geo = new Net_Geo();
   ```

   This is standard PEAR and OOP. See Chapter 6, "Basic Object-Oriented Programming," and Chapter 12, "Using PEAR," for more.

3. Get the user's IP address.

   ```
   $ip = $_SERVER['REMOTE_ADDR'];
   ```

4. Fetch the information.

   ```
   $results = $net_geo->getRecord($ip);
   ```

   The class's getRecord() method does all the work, returning an associative array of values (**Figure 9.11**).

*continues on page 366*

```
Array
(
    [TARGET] => 69.251.82.126
    [NAME] => IANA-NETBLOCK-69
    [NUMBER] => 69.0.0.0 - 69.255.255.255
    [COUNTRY] => AU
    [LAT] => -25.00
    [LONG] => 135.00
    [LAT_LONG_GRAN] => Country
    [NIC] => APNIC
    [LOOKUP_TYPE] => Block Allocation
    [DOMAIN_GUESS] => apnic.net
    [STATUS] => OK
    [RAWDATA] => Array
        (
            [TARGET] => 69.251.82.126
            [NAME] => IANA-NETBLOCK-69
            [NUMBER] => 69.0.0.0 - 69.255.255.255
            [COUNTRY] => AU
            [LAT] => -25.00
            [LONG] => 135.00
            [LAT_LONG_GRAN] => Country
            [NIC] => APNIC
            [LOOKUP_TYPE] => Block Allocation
            [DOMAIN_GUESS] => apnic.net
            [STATUS] => OK
        )

)
```

**Figure 9.11** The array of data returned by the getRecord() method.

**Script 9.3** The PEAR Net_Geo class is used to provide geographic location information based upon IP addresses.

```
1    <!DOCTYPE html PUBLIC "-//W3C//DTD XHTML 1.0 Transitional//EN"
2            "http://www.w3.org/TR/xhtml1/DTD/xhtml1-transitional.dtd">
3    <html xmlns="http://www.w3.org/1999/xhtml" xml:lang="en" lang="en">
4    <head>
5        <meta http-equiv="content-type" content="text/html; charset=iso-8859-1" />
6        <title>PEAR::Net_Geo</title>
7    </head>
8    <body>
9    <?php # Script 9.3 - net_geo.php
10
11   /*   This page uses the PEAR Net_Geo class
12    *   to retrieve a user's geographic location.
13    */
14
15   // Include the class definition:
16   require_once('Net/Geo.php');
17
18   // Create the object:
19   $net_geo = new Net_Geo();
20
21   // Get the client's IP address:
22   $ip = $_SERVER['REMOTE_ADDR'];
23
24   // Get the information:
25   $results = $net_geo->getRecord($ip);
26
27   // Print whatever about the user:
28   echo "<p>Our spies tell us the following information about you:<br />
29   IP Address: $ip<br />
30   Country: {$results['COUNTRY']}<br />
31   City, State: {$results['CITY']}, {$results['STATE']}<br />
32   Latitude: {$results['LAT']}<br />
33   Longitude: {$results['LONG']}</p>";
34
35   // Print something about a site:
36   $url = 'www.entropy.ch';
37
38   // Get the IP address:
39   $ip = gethostbyname($url);
40
41   // Get the information:
42   $results = $net_geo->getRecord($ip);
43
44   // Print whatever about the URL:
45   echo "<p>Our spies tell us the following information about the URL $url:<br />
46   IP Address: $ip<br />
47   Country: {$results['COUNTRY']}<br />
48   City, State: {$results['CITY']}, {$results['STATE']}</p>";
49   ?>
50   </body>
51   </html>
```

**PERFROMING IP GEOLOCATION**

**5.** Print the results.

```
echo "<p>Our spies tell us the
→ following information about
→ you:<br />
IP Address: $ip<br />
Country: {$results['COUNTRY']}<br />
City, State: {$results['CITY']},
→ {$results['STATE']}<br />
Latitude: {$results['LAT']}<br />
Longitude: {$results['LONG']}</p>";
```

Looking at the array in Figure 9.11, you can see the options available. For the first IP address (the user's), the script will print the country, city, state, and—why not?—the latitude and longitude.

**6.** Identify a URL to report upon and get its IP address.

```
$url = 'www.entropy.ch';
$ip = gethostbyname($url);
```

While playing around, the script will fetch the information for a Web site, which is to say where the server it's running on is located. In this case, I'm choosing Marc Liyanage's invaluable site, `www.entropy.ch`.

**7.** Retrieve the information and report upon the results.

```
$results = $net_geo->getRecord($ip);
echo "<p>Our spies tell us the
→ following information about the URL
→ $url:<br />
IP Address: $ip<br />
Country: {$results['COUNTRY']}<br />
City, State: {$results['CITY']},
→ {$results['STATE']}</p>";
```

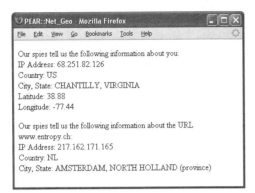

**Figure 9.12** The IP geolocation results for my IP address and the URL www.entropy.ch.

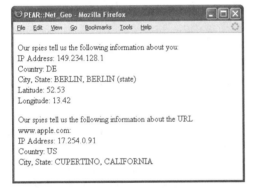

**Figure 9.13** Running the script again, after flying to Berlin, Germany. I also changed the URL to www.apple.com to see those results.

8. Complete the page.

```
?>
</body>
</html>
```

9. Save the file as net_geo.php, place it in your Web directory, and test in your Web browser (**Figure 9.12**).

10. Hop into a plane, train, or automobile, travel to another country, get online, and retest the script in your Web browser (**Figure 9.13**).

## ✔ Tips

- One resource I found suggested that IP geolocation is very accurate on the country level, probably close to 95 percent. On the city and state level, that accuracy may dip down to 50–80 percent, depending upon the database being used. In my case, it did not accurately pick the city but suggested one about 20 miles away (in another state). As I suggest in the sidebar, using a commercial database would garner more accurate results.

- If you have need to find out the host name of associated with an IP address, use the corresponding gethostbyaddr() function.

- If a URL might be on multiple servers, the gethostbyname1() function returns all the possible IP addresses. You can then check one or every IP.

**PERFROMING IP GEOLOCATION**

# Using cURL

The last network-related topic to be discussed in this chapter is a technology called cURL. This utility, which stands for *client URLs* (and is also written as just *curl* or *Curl*), is a command-line tool for working with URLs. With cURL you can access Web sites, FTP files, and do much, much more. PHP can use cURL via the `shell_exec()` and other system functions. But PHP also supports libcurl, a cURL library.

The process starts by using `curl_init()`, providing this function the name of the URL being accessed:

`$curl = curl_init('www.example.com');`

The value returned by the function should be assigned to a variable, which will act as a pointer or a handle to the transaction.

Next, the `curl_setopt()` function is used (a lot) to set any options. The syntax is:

`curl_setopt($curl, CONSTANT, value);`

Unfortunately, there are way too many options to even provide a subset here. In the following example I'll highlight a handful of them. If you take to cURL, check out the PHP manual for the full list of settings.

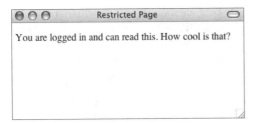

**Figure 9.14** After the user logs in (providing a valid username/password combination, of course), they're rewarded with this impressive result.

**Figure 9.15** Until a user successfully logs in, this is what they see.

After setting all the options (and note that you can set them in any order), use `curl_exec()` to execute the transaction:

`$result = curl_exec($curl);`

You should assign the result of the `curl_exec()` command to a variable, in case you need to print the result.

Finally, close the connection:

`curl_close($curl);`

The great thing about cURL is that it could also do everything that the other examples in the chapter accomplish. But for this next example, let's use it for something that `fopen()`, `fsockopen()`, and the rest can't do: open a Web page and post data to it (as if it submitted a form). In Chapter 4, "Security Techniques," the PEAR `Auth` module is used to add a database-driven username/password restriction to a Web page. After a user submits a valid username/password combination, they can access the page (**Figure 9.14**). Otherwise, they'll get a message indicating the need to log in (**Figure 9.15**).

## To use cURL:

1. Create a new PHP script in your text editor or IDE, beginning with the HTML (**Script 9.4**).

```
<!DOCTYPE html PUBLIC "-//W3C//DTD
→ XHTML 1.0 Transitional//EN"
"http://www.w3.org/TR/xhtml1/DTD/
→ xhtml1-transitional.dtd">
<html xmlns="http://www.w3.org/1999/
→ xhtml" xml:lang="en" lang="en">
<head>
    <meta http-equiv="content-type"
→ content="text/html; charset=
→ iso-8859-1" />
    <title>Using cURL</title>
</head>
<body>
<?php # Script 9.4 - curl.php
```

2. Begin the cURL transaction.

```
$url = 'http://localhost/login.php';
$curl = curl_init($url);
```

You don't have to assign the URL to use to a variable prior to the `curl_init()` line, of course. But do make sure you change this URL to point to the `login.php` script you made (and put in your Web directory) in Chapter 4. If you haven't done that yet, get thyself over to Chapter 4 and do so before continuing.

3. Tell cURL to fail if an error occurs.

```
curl_setopt($curl, CURLOPT_
→ FAILONERROR, 1);
```

The first of the options is `CURLOPT_FAILONERROR`. By setting this to `true` (or 1), you tell cURL to stop the process if an error occurs (rather than continuing on).

4. Tell cURL to allow for redirects.

```
curl_setopt($curl, CURLOPT_
→ FOLLOWLOCATION, 1);
```

This second option sets whether or not redirections (think of a PHP `header` (`'Location: somepage.php'`) call) should stop the transaction or if redirections should be followed.

5. Opt to assign the returned data to a variable.

```
curl_setopt($curl, CURLOPT_
→ RETURNTRANSFER,1);
```

If you'll not use the data that would be returned by a cURL request, then you don't need to enable this option. In this script, that data will be printed for verification, so this value is set to 1.

6. Set the timeout.

```
curl_setopt($curl, CURLOPT_
→ TIMEOUT, 5);
```

This is the maximum amount of time to attempt the transaction, in seconds.

7. Tell cURL to use the POST method.

```
curl_setopt($curl, CURLOPT_POST, 1);
```

In this example, data will be posted to the page (`http://localhost/login.php`) as if a form were submitted.

8. Set the POST data.

```
curl_setopt($curl, CURLOPT_
→ POSTFIELDS, 'username=me&password=
→ mypass');
```

The `CURLOPT_POSTFIELDS` option is where you set the POST data. The syntax is a series of *name=value* pairs, separated by ampersands. The values you use here should match those registered in the database back in Chapter 4.

9. Execute the transaction.

```
$r = curl_exec($curl);
```

10. Close the connection.

```
curl_close($curl);
```

*continues on page 372*

**Script 9.4** The cURL library is used by PHP to post data to a page that requires logging in for access.

```
1    <!DOCTYPE html PUBLIC "-//W3C//DTD XHTML 1.0 Transitional//EN"
2        "http://www.w3.org/TR/xhtml1/DTD/xhtml1-transitional.dtd">
3    <html xmlns="http://www.w3.org/1999/xhtml" xml:lang="en" lang="en">
4    <head>
5        <meta http-equiv="content-type" content="text/html; charset=iso-8859-1" />
6        <title>Using cURL</title>
7    </head>
8    <body>
9    <?php # Script 9.4 - curl.php
10
11   /*  This page uses cURL to post a usernamme/password
12    *  combination to a password-protected Web page.
13    */
14
15   // Identify the URL:
16   $url = 'http://localhost/login.php';
17
18   // Start the process:
19   $curl = curl_init($url);
20
21   // Tell cURL to fail if an error occurs:
22   curl_setopt($curl, CURLOPT_FAILONERROR, 1);
23
24   // Allow for redirects:
25   curl_setopt($curl, CURLOPT_FOLLOWLOCATION, 1);
26
27   // Assign the returned data to a variable:
28   curl_setopt($curl, CURLOPT_RETURNTRANSFER,1);
29
30   // Set the timeout:
31   curl_setopt($curl, CURLOPT_TIMEOUT, 5);
32
33   // Use POST:
34   curl_setopt($curl, CURLOPT_POST, 1);
35
36   // Set the POST data:
37   curl_setopt($curl, CURLOPT_POSTFIELDS, 'username=me&password=mypass');
38
39   // Execute the transaction:
40   $r = curl_exec($curl);
41
42   // Close the connection:
43   curl_close($curl);
44
45   // Print the results:
46   echo '<h2>cURL Results:</h2><pre>' . htmlentities($r) . '</pre>';
47
48   ?>
49   </body>
50   </html>
```

USING CURL

**11.** Print the results.

```
echo '<h2>cURL Results:</h2><pre>' .
→ htmlentities($r) . '</pre>';
```

Everything returned by the request is assigned to the $r variable. I want to print this, but since I know it's a bunch of HTML, I'll print it within the preformatted tags, and apply the htmlentities() function. The end result will be the other page's HTML shown as the HTML tags.

**12.** Complete the page.

```
?>
</body>
</html>
```

**13.** Save the file as curl.php, place it in your Web directory, and test in your Web browser (**Figure 9.16**).

**14.** Change the POST data to an invalid username/password combination and retest in your Web browser (**Figure 9.17**).

## ✔ Tips

- If a page is protected by HTTP authentication, use this option:
  ```
  curl_setopt($curl, CURLOPT_USERPWD,
  → 'username:password');
  ```

- The curl_getinfo() function, which must be called prior to closing the connection, returns an array of information about the transaction (**Figure 9.18**).

- The cURL utility can also be used to send and receive cookies, handle file uploads, work over SSL connections, even FTP files.

- Use the curl_errno() and curl_error() functions to retrieve the error number and message, should one occur.

**Figure 9.16** The cURL request was able to successfully log in.

**Figure 9.17** The cURL request was not able to log in.

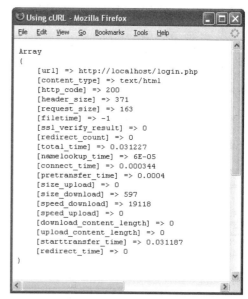

**Figure 9.18** The array returned by the curl_getinfo() function.

# PHP AND
# THE SERVER

Most of the chapters in this book focus on creating dynamic Web sites with PHP, which is, after all, the original intention of the language. Chapter 9, "Networking with PHP," approaches some behind-the-scenes features of the language, specifically toward the goal of communicating between servers. Continuing along this vein, there's plenty to discuss when it comes to PHP interacting with, or just how it runs on, the server itself.

A lot of very standard PHP actions, such as communicating with databases and sending emails, actually occur between applications on the server and PHP. As PHP is increasingly used for advanced purposes and not simply to generate Web content, its ability to manipulate and use the features the server has to offer becomes more important.

This chapter will show you how to better take advantage of the other services and applications that your server may have. Starting off is a demonstration of how to compress files using PHP. The second example takes off into a whole new world: creating graphical programs using PHP-GTK. The third and fourth topics are related to each other: how to automatically run your PHP scripts, first using cron on Unix (and Mac OS X), then using Scheduled Tasks on Windows. In the final example, COM is used on Windows to create an Excel spreadsheet.

# Compressing Files

Most users are familiar with client-based GUI compression utilities such as WinZip or StuffIt, which will compress and decompress files. Thanks to zlib, available from www.zlib.net, you can have PHP automatically compress files as well. The zlib library was written by two of the major compression/decompression developers as a patent-free, lossless data-compression tool. Zlib is available on every major platform (even for Palm handhelds!) and is frequently built into a server's configuration. I would be surprised if a Unix brand of operating system did not include zlib, and you can use a dynamic link library (DLL) version of the library on Windows. In fact, PHP has built-in support for zlib ever since version 4.3.

Once zlib is installed and PHP is made to support it (**Figure 10.1**), you can use it for writing to or reading from compressed files. Most of the functions work exactly like the standard file functions (fopen(), fwrite(), fclose(),...). You start by opening a file, indicating the mode:

$fp = gzopen('filename.gz', 'mode');

The modes, shown in **Table 10.1**, are the same as those used with fopen(). Added to this can be a compression level on a scale of 1 (least compressed) to 9 (most). With an open file, you can then write data to it:

$fp = gzopen('filename.gz', 'w5');

gzwrite($fp, 'data');

Finally, close the file:

gzclose($fp);

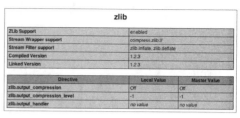

**Figure 10.1** Before attempting to use the zlib functions, run a phpinfo() script to confirm PHP's support for the library.

**Table 10.1** Use these letters to set the mode when opening a file. For gzopen(), you can also set the level of compression from 1 to 9 and indicate f, h, and b to further modify the mode.

## File Open Modes

| MODE | OPEN FOR… |
|------|-----------|
| r | Reading only, starting at the beginning of the file. |
| r+ | Reading and writing, starting at the beginning of the file. |
| w | Writing only, starting at the beginning of the file; empty the file if it exists, create it if it doesn't. |
| w+ | Reading and writing, starting at the beginning of the file; empty the file if it exists, create it if it doesn't. |
| a | Writing only, starting at the end of the file; create the file if it doesn't exist. |
| a+ | Reading and writing, starting at the end of the file; create the file if it doesn't exist. |
| x | Writing only, starting at the beginning of the file; create the file if it doesn't exist, indicate failure if it does. |
| x | Reading and writing, starting at the beginning of the file; create the file if it doesn't exist, indicate failure if it does. |
| f | Filtered data |
| h | Huffman-only compression |
| b | Binary mode |

COMPRESSING FILES

Reading from files can be even easier. You can use `readgzfile()`, which reads in a compressed file, decompresses the data, and sends it to the output. There is also the `gzfile()` function, which reads in compressed file, decompresses it, and returns it as an array (one element for each line in the file).

In this next example I'll have PHP create a compressed file on the fly. The PHP script itself will retrieve all of the data stored in a named database and will create files listing said data in comma-delineated format. In short, this PHP script will create a compressed backup of a database's records.

## To compress a file:

1. Create a new PHP document in your text editor or IDE, beginning with the standard HTML (**Script 10.1**).

   ```
   <!DOCTYPE html PUBLIC "-//W3C//DTD
   → XHTML 1.0 Transitional//EN"
   "http://www.w3.org/TR/xhtml1/DTD/
   → xhtml1-transitional.dtd">
   <html xmlns="http://www.w3.org/1999/
   → xhtml" xml:lang="en" lang="en">
   <head>
       <meta http-equiv="content-type"
   → content="text/html; charset=
   → iso-8859-1" />
       <title>Database Backup</title>
   </head>
   <body>
   <?php # Script 10.1 - db_backup.php
   ```

2. Set the name of the database.

   ```
   $db_name = 'test';
   ```

   First, I set a variable with the name of the database to be backed up. I do so mostly because the database name will be referenced several times over in this script and I want to make changes easily.

*continues on page 378*

**Script 10.1** This very useful script will back up a database, table by table, to a compressed, comma-separated text file.

```php
1    <!DOCTYPE html PUBLIC "-//W3C//DTD XHTML 1.0 Transitional//EN"
2         "http://www.w3.org/TR/xhtml1/DTD/xhtml1-transitional.dtd">
3    <html xmlns="http://www.w3.org/1999/xhtml" xml:lang="en" lang="en">
4    <head>
5        <meta http-equiv="content-type" content="text/html; charset=iso-8859-1" />
6        <title>Database Backup</title>
7    </head>
8    <body>
9    <?php # Script 10.1 - db_backup.php
10
11   /*  This page retrieves all the data from a database
12    *  and writes that data to a text file.
13    *  The text file is then compressed using zlib.
14    */
15
16   // Establish variables and setup:
17   $db_name = 'test';
18
19   // Backup directory:
20   $dir = "backups/$db_name";
21
22   // Make the database-specific directory, if it doesn't exist.
23   if (!is_dir($dir)) {
24       if (!@mkdir($dir)) {
25           die ("<p>The backup directory--$dir--could not be created.</p>\n</body>\n</html>\n");
26       }
27   }
28
29   // Get the current time for using in all filenames:
30   $time = time();
31
32   // Connect to the database:
33   $dbc = @mysqli_connect ('localhost', 'username', 'password', $db_name) OR die ("<p>The
     database--$db_name--could not be backed up.</p>\n</body>\n</html>\n");
34
35   // Retrieve the tables:
36   $q = 'SHOW TABLES';
37   $r = mysqli_query($dbc, $q);
38
39   // Back up if at least one table exists:
40   if (mysqli_num_rows($r) > 0) {
41
42       // Indicate what is happening:
43       echo "<p>Backing up database '$db_name'.</p>\n";
44
45       // Fetch each table name.
46       while (list($table) = mysqli_fetch_array($r, MYSQLI_NUM)) {
```

*(script continues on next page)*

**Script 10.1** *continued*

```
47
48         // Get the records for this table:
49         $q2 = "SELECT * FROM $table";
50         $r2 = mysqli_query($dbc, $q2);
51
52         // Back up if records exist:
53         if (mysqli_num_rows($r2) > 0) {
54
55             // Attempt to open the file:
56             if ($fp = gzopen ("$dir/{$table}_{$time}.sql.gz", 'w9')) {
57
58                 // Fetch all the records for this table:
59                 while ($row = mysqli_fetch_array($r2, MYSQLI_NUM)) {
60
61                     // Write the data as a comma-delineated row:
62                     foreach ($row as $value) {
63
64                         gzwrite ($fp, "'$value', ");
65                     }
66
67                     // Add a new line to each row:
68                     gzwrite ($fp, "\n");
69
70                 } // End of WHILE loop.
71
72                 // Close the file:
73                 gzclose ($fp);
74
75                 // Print the success:
76                 echo "<p>Table '$table' backed up.</p>\n";
77
78             } else { // Could not create the file!
79                 echo "<p>The file--$dir/{$table}_{$time}.sql.gz--could not be opened for
    writing.</p>\n";
80                 break; // Leave the WHILE loop.
81             } // End of gzopen() IF.
82
83         } // End of mysqli_num_rows() IF.
84
85     } // End of WHILE loop.
86
87 } else {
88     echo "<p>The submitted database--$db_name--contains no tables.</p>\n";
89 }
90
91 ?>
92 </body>
93 </html>
```

**3.** Make sure that the backup directory exists.

```
$dir = "backups/$db_name";
if (!is_dir($dir)) {
    if (!@mkdir($dir)) {
        die ("<p>The backup
→ directory--$dir--could not be
→ created.</p>\n</body>\n</html>\n");
    }
}
```

The backups will be stored in a directory called *backups*. Within this directory, each database will have its own directory. First, a variable is given the value of the final destination. Next, the script checks to see if that directory already exists. If not, the script attempts to create it. The script terminates if the directory could not be created (**Figure 10.2**), as there'd be no point in continuing.

One assumption here is that an existing directory is already writable, something you could easily check for (using the `is_writable()` function). This section of the code, which is secondary to what's really being taught, assumes you already understand what permissions must exist for PHP to write to directories.

**4.** Get the current time.

```
$time = time();
```

This value will be used in each table backup's filename. Because every file should have the same time, I assign this to a variable once, instead of invoking the function once for each file.

**5.** Connect to the database.

```
$dbc = @mysqli_connect ('localhost',
→ 'username', 'password', $db_name)
→ OR die ("<p>The database--$db_
→ name--could not be backed
→ up.</p>\n</body>\n</html>\n");
```

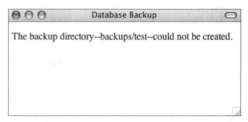

**Figure 10.2** The result if the destination directory could not be created.

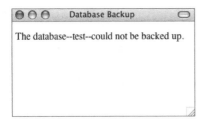

**Figure 10.3** The result if a database connection could not be made.

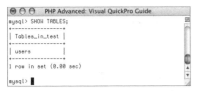

**Figure 10.4** Running the same query that the script runs (the first of two) using the mysql client.

**Figure 10.5** The main query, the results of which will be written to a file.

The script attempts to connect to the named database. If it can't, a message indicating a problem is displayed in the Web browser (**Figure 10.3**), and the HTML page is concluded. You can change the error message to incorporate a MySQL error function, if you want a more informative response.

Note, also, that I'm using the Improved MySQL extension functions, available as of PHP 5 and MySQL 4.1. If your setup doesn't support them, switch to the older MySQL functions instead (changing all the code in the script as needed).

**6.** Retrieve the tables in this database.

```
$q = 'SHOW TABLES';
$r = mysqli_query($dbc, $q);
```

This query will return a list of every table in the current database (**Figure 10.4**).

**7.** Confirm that at least one record was returned and print a message.

```
if (mysqli_num_rows($r) > 0) {
    echo "<p>Backing up database
→ '$db_name'.</p>\n";
```

No need to back up an empty database!

**8.** Create a loop that fetches each table name.

```
while (list($table) = mysqli_
→ fetch_array($r, MYSQLI_NUM)) {
```

**9.** Retrieve all the records for this table.

```
$q2 = "SELECT * FROM $table";
$r2 = mysqli_query($dbc, $q2);
```

Since this query is run within a while loop for another query, you have to use a different result variable ($r2 here instead of $r), or else you'll overwrite the first query's results. **Figure 10.5** shows the result of this query based upon the results in Figure 10.4.

**10.** If the table contains some records, open the text file for writing.

```
if (mysqli_num_rows($r2) > 0) {

    if ($fp = gzopen
("$dir/{$table}_{$time}.sql.gz",
→ 'w9')) {
```

Each table will be backed up to its own file, the name of which is derived from the table name ($table), the current time stamp ($time), and a .sql.gz extension. All of the files will be written to a database-specific folder within a backup folder. Both directories must have appropriate permissions for PHP to write to them.

The gzopen() function takes two parameters: the filename and the mode of opening. The modes correspond directly to fopen()'s modes (w, r, a along with b for writing binary data) but can also indicate a level of compression. The acceptable compression levels are on a scale from 1 (minimal compression) to 9 (maximum) with a trade-off between compression and performance. For relatively small files like these text documents, maximum compression is fine.

**11.** Retrieve all of the table's data, and write it to the file.

```
while ($row = mysqli_fetch_array
→ ($r2, MYSQLI_NUM)) {

    foreach ($row as $value) {
        gzwrite ($fp, "'$value',
→ ");
    }
    gzwrite ($fp, "\n");
}
```

This loop will take every row out of the table and write that to a text file in the format *'value',*[SPACE]. Instead of using the fwrite() function that you may be familiar with, there is gzwrite(), which works just the same (except that it writes to a compressed file).

**12.** Close the file and print a message to the browser.

```
gzclose ($fp);
echo "<p>Table '$table' backed
→ up.</p>\n";
```

**13.** Complete the conditionals.

```
        } else {
            echo
→ "<p>The file--$dir/{$table}_
→ {$time}.sql.gz--could not be
→ opened for writing.</p>\n";
            break;
        }
    }
}
} else {
    echo "<p>The submitted database-
→ -$db_name--contains no
→ tables.</p>\n";
}
```

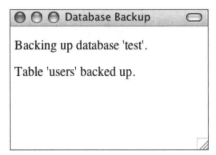

**Figure 10.6** What the Web page shows after successfully backing up the one table found within the test database.

**14.** Complete the page.

```
}
?>
</body>
</html>
```

**15.** Save the file as db_backup.php and place it in your Web directory.

**16.** Create a folder called backups, in the same directory as db_backup.php, and change its permissions (if necessary).

How you do this depends upon your operating system, which I assume, as an experienced PHP developer, you've already discovered. If you don't know how to change a directory's permissions, search the Web or check out the book's corresponding support forum (www.DMCInsights.com/phorum/).

**17.** Test the PHP script in your Web browser (**Figure 10.6**).

**18.** Change the code to use another database (also changing the MySQL connection parameters, if necessary) and rerun the script in your Web browser (**Figures 10.7** and **10.8**).

### ✔ Tips

- For security purposes, you'd likely want to place the backups folder outside of the Web directory (considering its open permissions.)

- The zlib functions can also work with compressed binary files. (Windows makes a distinction between binary and plain text files, but Unix and Mac OS X do not.) Binary files offer the advantage of being able to read from, and write to, the file in a nonlinear fashion.

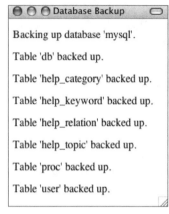

Database Backup

Backing up database 'mysql'.

Table 'db' backed up.

Table 'help_category' backed up.

Table 'help_keyword' backed up.

Table 'help_relation' backed up.

Table 'help_topic' backed up.

Table 'proc' backed up.

Table 'user' backed up.

**Figure 10.7** The browser will display what tables were backed up by the db_backup.php script.

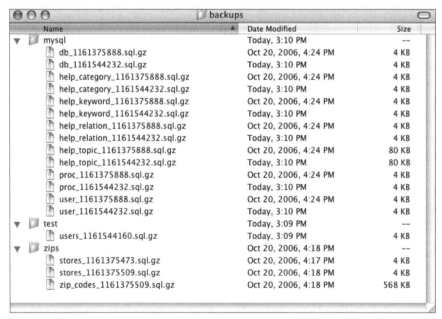

| Name | Date Modified | Size |
|---|---|---|
| ▼ 📁 mysql | Today, 3:10 PM | -- |
| db_1161375888.sql.gz | Oct 20, 2006, 4:24 PM | 4 KB |
| db_1161544232.sql.gz | Today, 3:10 PM | 4 KB |
| help_category_1161375888.sql.gz | Oct 20, 2006, 4:24 PM | 4 KB |
| help_category_1161544232.sql.gz | Today, 3:10 PM | 4 KB |
| help_keyword_1161375888.sql.gz | Oct 20, 2006, 4:24 PM | 4 KB |
| help_keyword_1161544232.sql.gz | Today, 3:10 PM | 4 KB |
| help_relation_1161375888.sql.gz | Oct 20, 2006, 4:24 PM | 4 KB |
| help_relation_1161544232.sql.gz | Today, 3:10 PM | 4 KB |
| help_topic_1161375888.sql.gz | Oct 20, 2006, 4:24 PM | 80 KB |
| help_topic_1161544232.sql.gz | Today, 3:10 PM | 80 KB |
| proc_1161375888.sql.gz | Oct 20, 2006, 4:24 PM | 4 KB |
| proc_1161544232.sql.gz | Today, 3:10 PM | 4 KB |
| user_1161375888.sql.gz | Oct 20, 2006, 4:24 PM | 4 KB |
| user_1161544232.sql.gz | Today, 3:10 PM | 4 KB |
| ▼ 📁 test | Today, 3:09 PM | -- |
| users_1161544160.sql.gz | Today, 3:09 PM | 4 KB |
| ▼ 📁 zips | Oct 20, 2006, 4:18 PM | -- |
| stores_1161375473.sql.gz | Oct 20, 2006, 4:17 PM | 4 KB |
| stores_1161375509.sql.gz | Oct 20, 2006, 4:18 PM | 4 KB |
| zip_codes_1161375509.sql.gz | Oct 20, 2006, 4:18 PM | 568 KB |

**Figure 10.8** The db_backup.php script has created compressed backup files of the databases and stored them in the backups folder.

**COMPRESSING FILES**

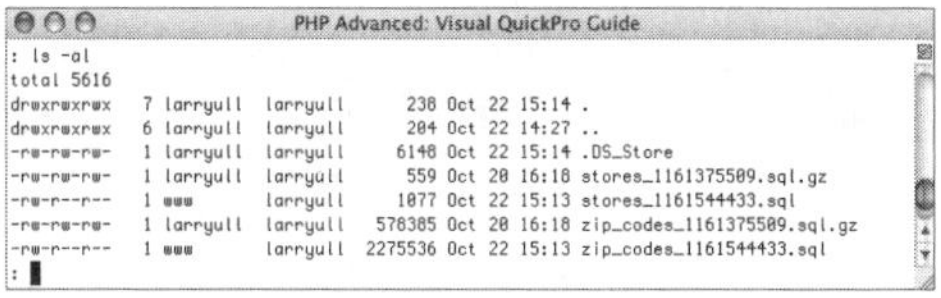

**Figure 10.9** The benefits of compression in small tables, like stores, are negligible (559 bytes vs. 1,077). But in large tables, like zip_codes, the benefits can be huge (approximately 568 KB vs. 2.2 MB!).

■ To see the effect that compression has on your file, rewrite backup_db.php to use fopen(), fwrite(), and fclose() instead (**Script 10.2**). On one table that contained about 150 rows of 6 columns each, the compressed file was 40 percent of the size of the noncompressed form (**Figure 10.9**).

**Script 10.2** To tell how much impact compression has on a file's size, rewrite Script 10.1 like so, and then compare the results.

```
1    <!DOCTYPE html PUBLIC "-//W3C//DTD XHTML 1.0 Transitional//EN"
2        "http://www.w3.org/TR/xhtml1/DTD/xhtml1-transitional.dtd">
3    <html xmlns="http://www.w3.org/1999/xhtml" xml:lang="en" lang="en">
4    <head>
5        <meta http-equiv="content-type" content="text/html; charset=iso-8859-1" />
6        <title>Database Backup</title>
7    </head>
8    <body>
9    <?php # Script 10.2 - db_backup2.php
10
11   /*  This page retrieves all the data from a database
12    *  and writes that data to a text file.
13    *  The text file is NOT compressed.
14    */
15
16   // Establish variables and setup:
17   $db_name = 'test';
18
19   // Backup directory:
20   $dir = "backups/$db_name";
21
22   // Make the database-specific directory, if it doesn't exist.
23   if (!is_dir($dir)) {
24       if (!@mkdir($dir)) {
25           die ("<p>The backup directory--$dir--could not be created.</p>\n</body>\n</html>\n");
26       }
27   }
28
29   // Get the current time for using in all filenames:
30   $time = time();
31
32   // Connect to the database:
33   $dbc = @mysqli_connect ('localhost', 'username', 'password', $db_name) OR die ("<p>The
     database--$db_name--could not be backed up.</p>\n</body>\n</html>\n");
34
35   // Retrieve the tables:
36   $q = 'SHOW TABLES';
37   $r = mysqli_query($dbc, $q);
38
39   // Back up if at least one table exists:
```

*(script continues on next page)*

**Script 10.2** *continued*

```
40    if (mysqli_num_rows($r) > 0) {
41
42        // Indicate what is happening:
43        echo "<p>Backing up database '$db_name'.</p>\n";
44
45        // Fetch each table name.
46        while (list($table) = mysqli_fetch_array($r, MYSQLI_NUM)) {
47
48            // Get the records for this table:
49            $q2 = "SELECT * FROM $table";
50            $r2 = mysqli_query($dbc, $q2);
51
52            // Back up if records exist:
53            if (mysqli_num_rows($r2) > 0) {
54
55                // Attempt to open the file:
56                if ($fp = fopen ("$dir/{$table}_{$time}.sql", 'w')) {
57
58                    // Fetch all the records for this table:
59                    while ($row = mysqli_fetch_array($r2, MYSQLI_NUM)) {
60
61                        // Write the data as a comma-delineated row:
62                        foreach ($row as $value) {
63
64                            fwrite ($fp, "'$value', ");
65                        }
66
67                        // Add a new line to each row:
68                        fwrite ($fp, "\n");
69
70                    } // End of WHILE loop.
71
72                    // Close the file:
73                    fclose ($fp);
74
75                    // Print the success:
76                    echo "<p>Table '$table' backed up.</p>\n";
77
78                } else { // Could not create the file!
79                    echo "<p>The file--$dir/{$table}_{$time}.sql--could not be opened for
      writing.</p>\n";
80                    break; // Leave the WHILE loop.
81                } // End of fopen() IF.
82
83            } // End of mysqli_num_rows() IF.
84
85        } // End of WHILE loop.
86
87    } else {
88        echo "<p>The submitted database--$db_name--contains no tables.</p>\n";
89    }
90
91    ?>
92    </body>
93    </html>
```

# PHP-GTK

GTK+, which stands for GIMP Tool Kit (GIMP being the GNU Image Manipulation Program), is an open-source toolkit that works on multiple platforms. This resource makes it easy for programmers to generate graphical elements—windows, buttons, and so on—for their applications. The GTK home page, www.gtk.org, describes the system's origins and usage but from a C programming perspective (GTK, like PHP, is written in C).

The PHP-GTK Web site, http://gtk.php.net (**Figure 10.10**), discusses how GTK can be used with PHP. To do so, you need a binary version of PHP, GTK+, and the php_gtk module. You can download and configure all of these for a Unix (Linux, etc.) system or retrieve preconfigured binaries for Windows. The Web site Gnope (www.gnope.org) provides a lot of help in this area.

GTK is way too deep to thoroughly discuss in just a few pages or even a whole chapter. But I can provide you with a taste of how it works and then develop a practical, real-world application with only a little bit of know-how.

GTK uses *widgets* to make applications. A widget can be anything from a window to a button to a table to a text label. To build an application, you create new instances of widgets (PHP uses an OOP interface to GTK) and then apply different properties by calling that widget's methods. There are special widgets called *containers* that are used as parents for other widgets. The primary container will be a window. The entire application will exist within this window.

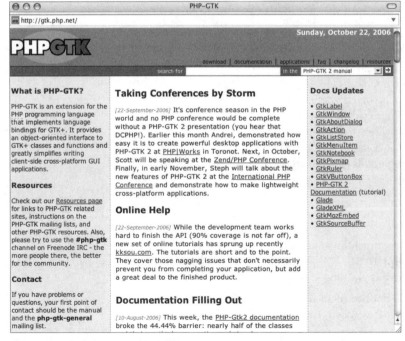

**Figure 10.10** The home page of PHP-GTK.

Besides creating widgets that make up an application, you associate user-defined PHP functions with different widgets so that, for example, when this button is clicked, this function is invoked. A widget listens for signals—user events—and then enacts a callback—the function that gets called upon for that event. You assign a function to an event using the `connect_simple()` method.

```php
$widget->connect_simple('event',
→ 'function_name');
```

The primary event I'll demonstrate is *clicked*, indicating that the mouse button was clicked on the widget.

You can pass a value to the callback function by adding it as a parameter to the `connect_simple()` call.

```php
$widget->connect_simple('event',
→ 'function_name', $var);
```

These are just the basics of how you'll use GTK with PHP. Every widget has its own methods and attributes, and GTK includes dozens upon dozens of widgets. I'll explain in more detail in this example, a simple graphical calculator (**Figure 10.11**). For each action that takes place in the calculator—entering a number, selecting an operator, clicking clear, and clicking equals—a user-defined function must exist. Those will be written first. These functions will work with the three main variables the calculator requires: two numbers for the operands (the numbers used in the math) and one variable storing the selected operator.

## To use PHP-GTK:

1. Begin a new PHP document in your text editor or IDE (**Script 10.3**).

   ```php
   <?php # Script 10.3 - calculator.php
   ```

   Since this page will not be accessed via a Web browser, there is no need to use any HTML.

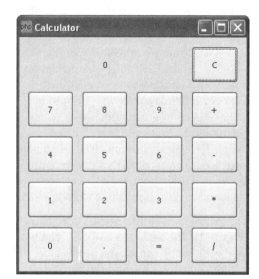

**Figure 10.11** This calculator is actually a PHP script that uses PHP-GTK.

*continues on page 391*

**Script 10.3** This PHP script makes use of PHP-GTK in order to make a graphical calculator.

```php
1    <?php # Script 10.3 - calculator.php
2
3    /*  This page uses GTK to create
4     *  a graphical calculator.
5     */
6
7    // Make sure that the GTK module has been loaded:
8    if (!class_exists('gtk')) die('The PHP-Gtk2 module has not been loaded!');
9
10   // Function for resetting the calculator:
11   function clear () {
12
13       // Reset the vars:
14       global $n1, $n2, $operator;
15       $n1 = false;
16       $n2 = false;
17       $operator = false;
18
19       // Clear the display:
20       set_display ();
21
22   } // End of clear() function.
23
24   // Function for displaying value in the calculator 'window':
25   function set_display ($value = 0) {
26       global $display;
27       $display->set_text ($value);
28   } // End of set_display() function.
29
30   // The calculate() function does the actual math:
31   function calculate () {
32
33       global $n1, $n2, $operator;
34
35       // Set initial value, just in case:
36       $value = $n1;
37
38       // What mathematical operation?
39       switch ($operator) {
40           case 'add':
41               $value = $n1 + $n2;
42               break;
43           case 'subtract':
44               $value = $n1 - $n2;
45               break;
46           case 'multiply':
47               $value = $n1 * $n2;
48               break;
49           case 'divide':
50               $value = $n1 / $n2;
51               break;
52       }
53
54       // Display the calculated value:
55       set_display ($value);
56
```

*(script continues on next page)*

**Script 10.3** *continued*

```
 57        // Reset the values:
 58        $n1 = $value;
 59        $operator = false;
 60        $n2 = false;
 61
 62     } // End of calculate() function.
 63
 64     // Function for assigning the operator being used:
 65     function set_operator ($which) {
 66        global $operator;
 67
 68        // If the $operator is already set,
 69        // calculate using the current values.
 70        if ($operator) calculate();
 71
 72        $operator = $which;
 73
 74     } // End of set_operator() function.
 75
 76     // Function for assigning values:
 77     function set_number ($value) {
 78
 79        global $n1, $n2, $operator;
 80
 81        // Concatenate to either the $n1 or $n2 value:
 82        if (!$operator) {
 83            $n1 .= $value;
 84            set_display($n1);
 85        } else {
 86            $n2 .= $value;
 87            set_display($n2);
 88        }
 89     }
 90
 91     // ******************
 92     // End of Functions
 93     // ******************
 94
 95     // Define the main variables:
 96     $n1 = false;
 97     $n2 = false;
 98     $operator = false;
 99
100     // Create a new window:
101     $window = new GtkWindow();
102     $window->set_title ('Calculator');
103     $window->set_default_size (320, 320);
104
105     // Create another container:
106     $box = new GtkVBox();
107     $window->add($box);
108
109     // Make a table:
110     $table = new GtkTable(5, 6);
111     $table->set_row_spacings(2);
112     $table->set_col_spacings(2);
113     $table->set_border_width(5);
```

PHP-GTK

**Script 10.3** *continued*

```
114
115    // Put the table into the box:
116    $box->pack_start($table);
117
118    // Make a display:
119    $display = new GtkLabel('display');
120    $table->attach($display, 1, 4, 1, 2);
121
122    // Make the 0-9 buttons.
123    for ($i = 0; $i <= 9; $i++) {
124
125        // Determine the table coordinates
126        // for each number:
127        switch ($i) {
128            case 0:
129                $x = 1;
130                $y = 5;
131                break;
132            case 1:
133                $x = 1;
134                $y = 4;
135                break;
136            case 2:
137                $x = 2;
138                $y = 4;
139                break;
140            case 3:
141                $x = 3;
142                $y = 4;
143                break;
144            case 4:
145                $x = 1;
146                $y = 3;
147                break;
148            case 5:
149                $x = 2;
150                $y = 3;
151                break;
152            case 6:
153                $x = 3;
154                $y = 3;
155                break;
156            case 7:
157                $x = 1;
158                $y = 2;
159                break;
160            case 8:
161                $x = 2;
162                $y = 2;
163                break;
164            case 9:
165                $x = 3;
166                $y = 2;
167                break;
168        }
169
```

*(script continues on next page)*

PHP-GTK

**Script 10.3** *continued*

```
170      // Make the button for the number:
171      $button = new GtkButton($i);
172      $button->connect_simple ('clicked', 'set_number', $i);
173      $table->attach($button, $x, ($x+1), $y, ($y+1));
174
175  } // End of 0-9 FOR loop.
176
177
178  // Place the remaining buttons...
179
180  // Decimal point:
181  $decimal = new GtkButton('.');
182  $decimal->connect_simple ('clicked', 'set_number', '.');
183  $table->attach($decimal, 2, 3, 5, 6);
184
185  // Equals sign:
186  $equals = new GtkButton('=');
187  $equals->connect_simple ('clicked', 'calculate');
188  $table->attach($equals, 3, 4, 5, 6);
189
190  // Clear:
191  $clear = new GtkButton('C');
192  $clear->connect_simple ('clicked', 'clear');
193  $table->attach($clear, 4, 5, 1, 2);
194
195  // Plus sign:
196  $add = new GtkButton('+');
197  $add->connect_simple ('clicked', 'set_operator', 'add');
198  $table->attach($add, 4, 5, 2, 3);
199
200  // Minus sign:
201  $subtract = new GtkButton('-');
202  $subtract->connect_simple ('clicked', 'set_operator', 'subtract');
203  $table->attach($subtract, 4, 5, 3, 4);
204
205  // Multiplication sign:
206  $multiply = new GtkButton('*');
207  $multiply->connect_simple ('clicked', 'set_operator', 'multiply');
208  $table->attach($multiply, 4, 5, 4, 5);
209
210  // Division sign:
211  $divide = new GtkButton('/');
212  $divide->connect_simple ('clicked', 'set_operator', 'divide');
213  $table->attach($divide, 4, 5, 5, 6);
214
215  // Reset the calculator to start:
216  clear();
217
218  // Connect the quit function:
219  $window->connect_simple ('destroy', array('Gtk', 'main_quit'));
220
221  // Show everything:
222  $window->show_all();
223
224  // Start the application:
225  Gtk::main();
226  ?>
```

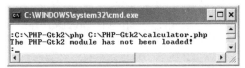

**Figure 10.12** The calculator is started from the command line. If the GTK module isn't supported, it won't even try to run.

**2.** Make sure that the GTK module has been loaded.

```
if (!class_exists('gtk')) die('The
→ PHP-Gtk2 module has not been
→ loaded!');
```

With GTK2 and PHP 5, you cannot load the library dynamically using the dl() function. Instead, you must be using a version of PHP with built-in support for the library. This line checks that the GTK class has been defined, killing the script otherwise (**Figure 10.12**).

**3.** Create a function for clearing the calculator.

```
function clear () {
    global $n1, $n2, $operator;
    $n1 = false;
    $n2 = false;
    $operator = false;
    set_display ();
}
```

This function will reset the three main global variables. The first two—$n1 and $n2—store the two numbers used in any calculation (even if you add 30 numbers together, that's really just adding two numbers at a time, repeatedly). The third variable, $operator, will store a string indicating what operation was selected. Finally, this function calls the user-defined set_display() function, which sets the value of the calculator's display (the default value being 0).

**4.** Write the function that will set the value of the display window.

```
function set_display ($value = 0) {
    global $display;
    $display->set_text ($value);
}
```

*continues on next page*

**PHP-GTK**

The global $display variable refers to the widget that is the calculator's display window. The widget itself is a label, which is merely a display of text. The set_text() method will place a string (or, in this case, a number) on that label. Anytime a number is entered or a calculation is made, this function will be called so that the resulting number is shown in the display.

**5.** Begin the calculate() function.

```
function calculate () {
    global $n1, $n2, $operator;
    $value = $n1;
```

The calculate() function will do the actual math. It uses three global variables—the $n1 number, the $n2 number, and the $operator. This function is called when the equals sign is clicked or when a second operator is selected. For example, if a user clicks 10 + 9 + 8 =, the calculate() function is called twice (once after the second plus, to add 10 + 9, and again after the equals, to add 19 + 8).

The $value variable is used internally by this function. It's initialized as $n1.

**6.** Create the main switch.

```
switch ($operator) {
    case 'add':
        $value = $n1 + $n2;
        break;
    case 'subtract':
        $value = $n1 - $n2;
        break;
    case 'multiply':
        $value = $n1 * $n2;
        break;
    case 'divide':
        $value = $n1 / $n2;
        break;
}
```

This calculator performs four kinds of calculations, depending upon the value of $operator.

**7.** Complete the function.

```
    set_display ($value);
    $n1 = $value;
    $operator = false;
    $n2 = false;
} // End of calculate() function.
```

After doing the math, the determined value will be shown in the calculator display via the set_display() function. Then the $n1 value is assigned the value of the current $value, allowing for a continued calculation. An entry of 2 + 3 + 4 is really 2 + 3 = 5 (which is assigned to $n1), plus 4.

**8.** Write a function for assigning the operator.

```
function set_operator ($which) {
    global $operator;
    if ($operator) calculate();
    $operator = $which;
}
```

This function is called whenever one of the four operators—+, −, *, /—is clicked. It assigns the string version of that operator to the global $operator variable. Before doing so, it will check if a calculation should be made. To explain…

The $operator variable starts with a value of false (also the case when the calculator is cleared). If a user clicks 2 + 3 + 4, then $n1 is assigned the value of 2 (in the set_number() function, written next), $operator is assigned the value of *add*, and then $n2 is assigned the value of 3. When the user clicks the next +, set_operator() is called again. This function sees that $operator already has a value and knows that the calculations thus far must be completed (because the calculator only stores two numbers at a time).

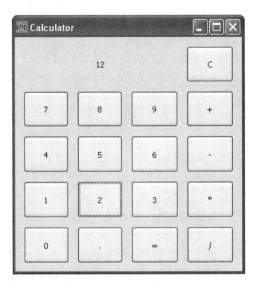

**Figure 10.13** Allowing for multidigit numbers, like 12, requires a little thought. My trick is to track the $operator variable.

**9.** Make a function for building up numbers.

```
function set_number ($value) {
    global $n1, $n2, $operator;
    if (!$operator) {
        $n1 .= $value;
        set_display($n1);
    } else {
        $n2 .= $value;
        set_display($n2);
    }
}
```

When any of the number buttons are clicked, along with the decimal point, the calculator will need to keep track of the $n1 and $n2 values (which will be used for the calculations). If, for example, the user clicks 1 and then 2, that should be 12. To accomplish this, the function works like so: It receives the $value every time a number or the decimal is clicked. If the $operator variable is equal to false, which means that it has been reset or has no value, then the user is building up the $n1 number and the new value should be concatenated to the old. If $operator has a value such as *add* or *subtract*, then the user has stopped entering the $n1 number and is working on entering the $n2 number.

The number that the user is making will be displayed in the calculator window (**Figure 10.13**).

*continues on next page*

**10.** Make the global variables.

```
$n1 = false;
$n2 = false;
$operator = false;
```

All of the functions have been written, so now it's into the heart of the code. These are the three global variables used by the functions. Initializing them like so isn't strictly necessary but is good programming form.

**11.** Make the window widget.

```
$window = new GtkWindow();
$window->set_title ('Calculator');
$window->set_default_size (320,
→ 320);
```

The `$window` variable is the first and most important of all the widgets. It acts as a container for everything. The `GtkWindow()` widget has multiple methods, including `set_title()`, which ends up in the taskbar (**Figure 10.14**), and `set_default_size()`.

**12.** Make a secondary container.

```
$box = new GtkVBox();
$window->add($box);
```

The box is another container widget into which I'll place the calculator. I could have multiple boxes within my window, should I choose (perhaps another box would contain a *Close* button). I use the window's `add()` method to physically place the box in the window.

**13.** Create a table.

```
$table = new GtkTable(5, 6);
$table->set_row_spacings(2);
$table->set_col_spacings(2);
$table->set_border_width(5);
$box->pack_start($table);
```

Making tables with GTK is slightly trickier than it is with HTML. I first make a new table object, setting the number of

**Figure 10.14** The window widget's title value applies when the operating system refers to the application, as in the taskbar.

rows and columns I intend to use. The tricky part is that although I want my table to have four rows and five columns, I need to add one extra of each. This is because elements are placed from, say, row 1 to row 2 and column 1 to column 2. Thus, an element in the fourth row will go from row 4 to row 5.

The final line in this section of code—

`$box->pack_start($table);`

—says to place the table just created onto the box made earlier.

**14.** Create a display window.

```
$display = new GtkLabel('display');
$table->attach($display, 1, 4, 1,
→ 2);
```

The display window of the calculator is a label—a simple noneditable text field. After creating the label (whose name is *display*), it should be placed on, or attached to, the table.

The attach() method takes the following arguments: the widget being attached, the x starting point, the x stopping point, the y starting point, and the y stopping point. I want the label to go from 1 to 4 along the x-axis (i.e., across three columns) and from 1 to 2 on the y (just one row).

**15.** Place all of the number buttons.

```
for ($i = 0; $i <= 9; $i++) {
    switch ($i) {
        case 0:
            $x = 1;
            $y = 5;
            break;
        case 1:
            $x = 1;
            $y = 4;
            break;
        case 2:
            $x = 2;
            $y = 4;
            break;
        case 3:
            $x = 3;
            $y = 4;
            break;
        case 4:
            $x = 1;
            $y = 3;
            break;
        case 5:
            $x = 2;
            $y = 3;
            break;
        case 6:
            $x = 3;
            $y = 3;
            break;
        case 7:
            $x = 1;
            $y = 2;
            break;
        case 8:
            $x = 2;
            $y = 2;
            break;
        case 9:
            $x = 3;
            $y = 2;
            break;
    }
    $button = new GtkButton($i);
    $button->connect_simple
→ ('clicked', 'set_number', $i);
    $table->attach($button, $x,
→ ($x+1), $y, ($y+1));
} // End of 0-9 FOR loop.
```

*continues on next page*

To make these ten buttons, I loop through the numbers 0 through 9. I then determine the x- and y-coordinates of each on my table (use Figure 10.11 as a reference). Once I know the coordinates, I can create a new button.

The button will then be told to watch for when the user clicks it, by attaching the `set_number()` function to the *clicked* event. When that occurs, I also want to pass the value of the button, which is the number (`$i`), to the function as well.

Looking back at the `set_number()` function written earlier, you will see that it receives a `$value`, which is this `$i` value here.

The final step is to place this button on the table, using the predetermined x- and y-coordinates.

**16.** Create the decimal button.

```
$decimal = new GtkButton('.');
$decimal->connect_simple ('clicked',
→ 'set_number', '.');
$table->attach($decimal,
→ 2, 3, 5, 6);
```

The decimal point has a value of a period. When clicked, the `set_number()` function should be called, so that the decimal is concatenated to the operand.

**17.** Create the equals button.

```
$equals = new GtkButton('=');
$equals->connect_simple ('clicked',
→ 'calculate');
$table->attach($equals, 3, 4, 5, 6);
```

This button differs from the decimal button in that the calculate function should be called when it is clicked. It passes no values to that function.

**18.** Create the clear button.

```
$clear = new GtkButton('C');
$clear->connect_simple ('clicked',
→ 'clear');
$table->attach($clear, 4, 5, 1, 2);
```

This button just calls the `clear()` function when clicked.

**19.** Create the operator buttons.

```
$add = new GtkButton('+');
$add->connect_simple ('clicked',
→ 'set_operator', 'add');
$table->attach($add, 4, 5, 2, 3);
$subtract = new GtkButton('-');
$subtract->connect_simple
→ ('clicked', 'set_operator',
→ 'subtract');
$table->attach($subtract,
→ 4, 5, 3, 4);
$multiply = new GtkButton('*');
$multiply->connect_simple
→ ('clicked', 'set_operator',
→ 'multiply');
$table->attach($multiply,
→ 4, 5, 4, 5);
$divide = new GtkButton('/');
$divide->connect_simple ('clicked',
→ 'set_operator', 'divide');
$table->attach($divide, 4, 5, 5, 6);
```

Each of these operator buttons is linked to the `set_operator()` function. They pass a string value to it: *add, subtract, multiply, divide.*

**20.** Call the `clear()` function to reset the calculator.

```
clear();
```

If you look at the code in Step 3, you will see that this function voids out any value for `$n1` and `$n2` and resets the `$operator`. It also sets the value of the display window to 0 (by calling the `set_display()` function).

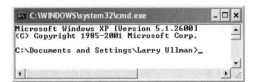

**Figure 10.15** The calculator will need to be started through a command-line interface. I'm using Windows here; see Chapter 11, "PHP's Command-Line Interface," for more on Windows or Unix command-line operations.

**21.** Finish the script.

```
$window->connect_simple ('destroy',
→ array('Gtk', 'main_quit'));
$window->show_all();
Gtk::main();
?>
```

One of the events you will want to watch for is when the user quits or closes the application. At that time, the GTK's `main_quit()` method should be called. The line of code that associates `main_quit()` with a destroy event is something you'll have verbatim in every PHP-GTK application.

Next, I call the `show_all()` method, which reveals every element—the box, the table, the buttons, and the label—within the window. The opposite of `show_all()` (or `show()` for a specific widget) is `hide()`, which makes a widget invisible without destroying it.

Finally, I call the `main()` method, the most important line of all. This function starts a loop in which the application will watch for user events. Unlike a standard PHP script, which does nothing else once it has completed running, this script will continue to be active until the user quits the application. It's the `main()` method that gives it this dimension.

**22.** Save the file as `calculator.php` and load it on your computer or server that supports PHP-GTK.

**23.** Access the command-line interface on your server/computer (**Figure 10.15**).

Because this script will not be run through a Web browser, you need to start it through a direct command.

*continues on next page*

**PHP-GTK**

**24.** Type in the location of your PHP binary followed by the location of the script (**Figure 10.16**).

```
C:\PHP-Gtk2\php C:\PHP-Gtk2\
→ calculator.php
```

The is the standard command-line method for running a file with an application.

Figure 10.16 Make sure you run the script using a version of PHP with support for GTK.

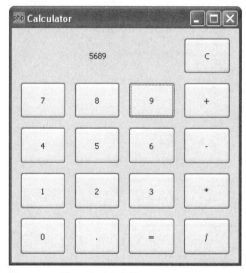

Figure 10.17 The calculator allows me to enter multiple-digit numbers for addition, subtraction, multiplication, and division.

**25.** Test the calculator that appears (**Figures 10.17** and **10.18**).

Hopefully this script has given you the know-how to make your own improvements to it, should you desire. It would not be that hard to add, for example, memory buttons (M+, M–, MC, MR) or to create a second window that shows a "paper tape" of the calculations.

## ✔ Tips

■ The calculator as created relies upon the clicking of the buttons using the mouse. There is also a way to tie specific keys to specific buttons, allowing for use of the calculator with just the keyboard.

■ When creating programs that use PHP-GTK, you can still use the `print()` or `echo()` functions to send text to the command-line window. This will give you a way to debug your scripts.

■ You can connect multiple callback functions to a single widget using multiple `$widget->connect_simple()` lines. The callback functions will be called in order when the event signal is sent.

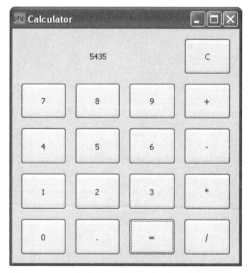

Figure 10.18 Calculations are made when the equals button is clicked (or when repeated operators are clicked).

# Establishing a cron

A cron is a service on Unix servers that allows tasks to be scheduled and executed automatically. The cron application runs constantly and will, according to instructions, carry out its orders. These orders are stored in a file called crontab. This file is a to-do list that contains lines that might look like this:

```
30 22 * * * lynx --dump http://
→ www.DMCinsights.com > /dev/null
```

The crontab format dictates that each line contain six fields separated by spaces or tabs. The first five fields represent, in order, minutes, hours, days, months, and day of the week (from 0 to 6, with 0 being Sunday). Notice that you can specify the day of operation as either a day of the month (1–31) or a day of the week (Sunday through Saturday), the latter being date-indifferent.

An asterisk as one of the first five parameters means that value is not limited (i.e., it always applies). In the preceding example, the instruction is to be carried out at 10:30 P.M. (22 being 10 P.M. on the 24-hour clock) every day of the month, every month of the year.

You can also set ranges using the hyphen (1–6 for the month field would mean that the job applies to the first six months of the year) or list elements separated by comma (1, 3, 5 for Monday, Wednesday, Friday). The sixth field on each line is the task itself.

Looking at the preceding example, the actual command is to open the URL www.DMCinsights.com with Lynx, a text-based Web browser built into Unix. The --dump and > /dev/null tell Lynx to close itself after viewing the site and not to store the information accessed.

Another example would be:

```
0 1 * * 1-5 mail -s 'Howdy'
→ phpvqp2@DMCinsights.com
```

This line states that from Monday through Friday (1–5), at 1 A.M. (0 minutes, 1 hour) every day of the month and every month of the year (* *) it will send me an email (apparently I like email).

To use cron to run a PHP script, you have a couple of options. The first is to use the server's own Web browser—like Lynx or Wget—to run a PHP script. Another would be to use the server's installation of cURL. This program works very well with URLs, although it's not a Web browser, per se. A final option is to run the PHP script using the Command-Line Interface (see Chapter 11, "PHP's Command-Line Interface").

For this example, I'll run the db_backup.php script (Script 10.1) created earlier in the chapter, using cURL. The syntax for using cURL is easy:

```
curl yourURLhere
```

So:

```
curl http://www.example.com/page.php
```

To add an item to the crontab file, you can manually edit it by typing crontab -e in a command prompt. This will allow you to edit the file using your default command-line text editor. Unfortunately, if you don't know how to already use said text editor—a surprisingly daunting task—this does you no good. So instead I'll show you another method....

## To establish a cron for a PHP file:

1. Access your server via a command-line interface.

   For Mac OS X and other Unix users, this likely means opening the Terminal application.

2. Test the command (**Figure 10.19**).

   `curl http://localhost/db_backup.php`

   It's always best to test the command you'll have cron execute so that you know that it works. Do so just by entering the command within the Terminal application. You'll obviously need to change your URL to match where you put your copy of db_backup.php. In this case, it's running on the same server.

3. View the current contents of the crontab file.

   `crontab -l`

   This command will show you the current crontab, which you should be careful with, as the following steps will replace any existing instructions. If you've never worked with the crontab before, it's probably blank, but better safe than sorry!

4. Create a new document in your text editor or IDE (**Script 10.4**).

   `1 0 * * 5 curl http://localhost/`
   `→ db_backup.php`

   First you'll write a dummy cronjob file, and then you'll install this into the actual crontab. This file should contain the entire command. Make sure you press Enter/Return once at the end of the line.

   The command itself says that cURL should be invoked with that URL every Friday (5) at 12:01 A.M.

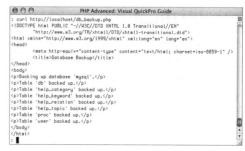

**Figure 10.19** Before entering the command into the crontab file, I test it once to confirm the results.

**Script 10.4** The cronjob1 file lists the command to be added to crontab.

```
1    1 0 * * 5 curl http://localhost/
     db_backup.php
```

ESTABLISHING A CRON

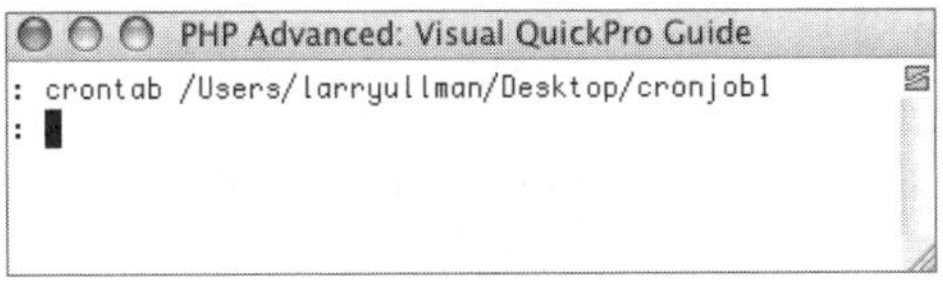

**Figure 10.20** Adding the new instruction to the crontab file.

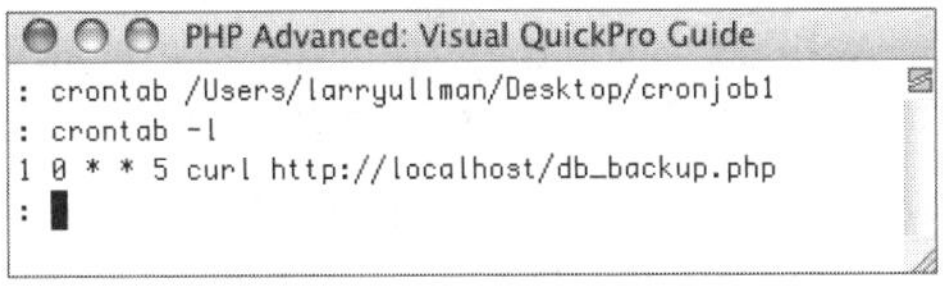

**Figure 10.21** Confirming the contents of the crontab file.

- A couple more helpful cURL options...
  The -o option lets you specify a text file where the output will be written:

  ```
  curl -o /path/to/filename.txt
  → http://www.example.com
  ```

  The -s option runs cURL in silent mode (so it doesn't return the results):

  ```
  curl -s http://www.example.com
  ```

  The -retry option tells cURL to attempt to access the URL *X* number of times (if it fails):

  ```
  curl -retry X http://www.example.com
  ```

- To see more information about using cron, type man cron or man crontab in the command line.

5. If Step 3 revealed anything in the current crontab, add it to the text document begun in Step 4.

   Just copy-paste whatever was returned in Step 3 to the text document. Each task should be on its own line.

6. Save this file as cronjob1 (without any extension) and upload it to the server in a convenient location (not necessarily within the Web document root).

7. Within your server's command prompt, enter the following code and then press Enter/Return once:

   ```
   crontab /path/to/cronjob1
   ```

   In my example (**Figure 10.20**), cronjob1 is stored on the desktop of user *larryullman*. The full path is therefore /Users/larryullman/Desktop/cronjob1. Replace that part of the code with the applicable location of your cronjob1 file on the server.

8. Confirm the cron task list by viewing the crontab file (**Figure 10.21**).

   ```
   crontab -l
   ```

## ✔ Tips

- If you are using a hosted Web site, the hosting company will often provide a Web-based interface to the cron utility.

- The crontab is unique for each user on the server. This also means that the instructions in the crontab file will run as that user, so permissions conflicts may arise.

ESTABLISHING A CRON

# Scheduling Tasks on Windows

The cron utility works on Unix for scheduling tasks, but it is not present on Windows. Windows users can instead work with Scheduled Tasks. The operating system provides a wizard for easily adding a task, which I'll run through in the following steps. The specific task to be scheduled will be the execution of the db_backup.php script.

### To schedule a task on Windows:

1. Click Start menu > All Programs > Accessories > System Tools > Scheduled Tasks (**Figure 10.22**).

2. In the resulting window (**Figure 10.23**), double-click Add Scheduled Task.

3. In the first window of the Scheduled Task Wizard, click Next.

4. In the next window (**Figure 10.24**), click Browse.

5. Using the Select Program to Schedule window, select the PHP script to execute (**Figure 10.25**), and then click Open.

6. In the next window (**Figure 10.26**), enter a name for this task, choose when the task should run, and click Next.

   The running options are: Daily, Weekly, Monthly, One time only, When my computer starts, and When I log on.

**Figure 10.22** Begin by navigating to the Scheduled Tasks window.

**Figure 10.23** The Scheduled Tasks window.

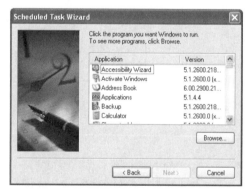

**Figure 10.24** In this prompt, you select which application should be scheduled.

**Figure 10.25** Find the PHP script that you want to run.

**7.** Fine-tune how and when the task runs.

The choice made in Step 6 will dictate what options appear. **Figure 10.27** shows the weekly scheduling options. If in Step 6 you chose either of the last two options, you'll go straight to Step 8.

**8.** Enter the username and password of the user for whom the task should run, and then click Next (**Figure 10.28**).

**9.** In the last window, click Finish.

## ✔ Tips

- This method of directly running a PHP script in Windows assumes that you have already configured Windows to run PHP scripts using the PHP executable. This is discussed in Chapter 11.

- To edit an existing task, follow Step 1, and then double-click the name of the task listed in the window (under Add Scheduled Task).

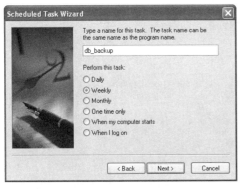

**Figure 10.26** Tasks can be given a descriptive name and scheduled in all sorts of ways.

**Figure 10.28** Tasks can be run under different users.

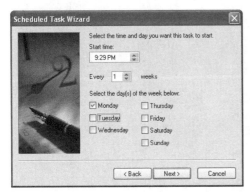

**Figure 10.27** Setting the specific details for a weekly scheduled task.

# Using COM with PHP

Added in PHP 4 is support for COM on Windows operating systems. COM, which stands for Component Object Module, is a technology developed by Microsoft to control its applications via a programming language, notably Visual Basic. It is related to other Microsoft technologies such as OLE (Object Linking and Embedding) and ActiveX.

Microsoft has defined every function and attribute that an application—such as Word or Excel—has as an object with methods and properties. Using the proper notation, you can then control the application with Visual Basic or, in this case, PHP. You begin by creating a new object using the name of the application and PHP's com() function.

```
$word = new COM('word.application');
```

You can set the application to run either visibly on the computer or invisibly by setting the Visible value (this step is not required).

```
$word->Visible = 1; // Visible
```

Once the application is running, you begin by creating a new document.

```
$word->Documents->Add();
```

Now, in the case of a Word document, you can start adding text to the page.

```
$word->Selection->
→ TypeText('mmmm…COM...');
```

Finally, save the document and quit Word.

```
$word->Documents[1]->SaveAs('com.doc');
$word->Quit();
```

USING COM WITH PHP

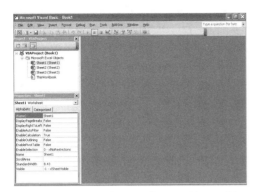

**Figure 10.29** The Visual Basic editor provides useful tools for working with COM elements.

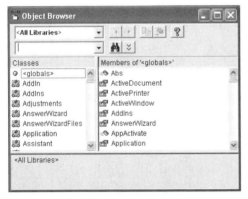

**Figure 10.30** The Object Browser lists all the properties and methods of existing objects.

As you can see from those lines, accessing COM with PHP is fairly simple and direct; the most complicated issue will be understanding what objects are available in an application and how exactly you should refer to them. You have several options:

◆ Pick up a book that covers COM for the specific application you are using.

◆ Learn Visual Basic, which will help with knowing the different objects available.

◆ Use the Visual Basic Help aspect of the application itself.

◆ Search the Internet!

I've taken all of these steps, and still, understanding how to do certain things can be a challenge. But if you work with Windows a lot, mastering this skill can be very useful.

For some assistance, once you have opened an application, like Word or Excel, press Alt+F11 to bring up the Visual Basic editor (**Figure 10.29**). Then press F2 to view the Object Browser (**Figure 10.30**). By clicking and viewing the different elements in the Object Browser, you can see how the different objects, methods, and attributes you'll need relate. To get a jump-start on understanding COM for an application, use the Visual Basic Help application.

As an example of using COM technology with PHP, I'll write a script similar to db_backup.php. Instead of creating a CSV file, this version will create an Excel spreadsheet containing the database's data.

Note that support for COM is built into PHP but that it only exists on Windows. You should also have some familiarity with OOP before proceeding, as COM is entirely object-based.

**USING COM WITH PHP**

## To use COM with PHP:

1. Create a new PHP document in your text editor or IDE, beginning with the HTML (**Script 10.5**).

```
<!DOCTYPE html PUBLIC "-//W3C//DTD
→ XHTML 1.0 Transitional//EN"
"http://www.w3.org/TR/xhtml1/DTD/
→ xhtml1-transitional.dtd">
<html xmlns="http://www.w3.org/1999/
→ xhtml" xml:lang="en" lang="en">
<head>
    <meta http-equiv="content-type"
→ content="text/html; charset=
→ iso-8859-1" />
    <title>Excel Backup</title>
</head>
<body>
<?php # Script 10.5 -
excel_backup.php
```

2. Increase the allowable time limit for script execution.

```
set_time_limit(300);
```

The `set_time_limit()` function determines, in seconds, at what point the script has taken too long. Because this script will need to open, write to, save, and quit an application, the default time limit—probably 30 seconds, depending on the setting in your `php.ini` file—needs to be increased. Five minutes should be adequate, but there would be little harm in doubling or tripling that value, depending on the complexity of the script.

*continues on page 410*

**Script 10.5** This PHP script makes use of COM to back up a MySQL database to an Excel spreadsheet. Each table in the database will be represented in its own Excel worksheet.

```
1    <!DOCTYPE html PUBLIC "-//W3C//DTD XHTML 1.0 Transitional//EN"
2            "http://www.w3.org/TR/xhtml1/DTD/xhtml1-transitional.dtd">
3    <html xmlns="http://www.w3.org/1999/xhtml" xml:lang="en" lang="en">
4    <head>
5        <meta http-equiv="content-type" content="text/html; charset=iso-8859-1" />
6        <title>Excel Backup</title>
7    </head>
8    <body>
9    <?php # Script 10.5 - excel_backup.php
10
11   /*  This page uses COM to back up
12    *  a MySQL database to an Excel file.
13    */
14
15   // Increase the PHP time limit:
16   set_time_limit(300);
17
18   // Load the COM:
19   $excel = new COM ("excel.application") or die ("Cannot start Excel.</body></html>");
20
21   echo "<p>Loaded Excel Version $excel->Version</p>\n";
22
23   try {
24
25       // Don't show the application:
26       $excel->Visible = 0;
27
28       // Connect to the database:
29       $db_name = 'mysql';
30       $dbc = @mysqli_connect ('localhost', 'username', 'password', $db_name) OR die ("<p>The
     database--$db_name--could not be backed up.</p>\n</body>\n</html>\n");
31
32       // Retrieve the tables:
33       $q = 'SHOW TABLES';
34       $r = mysqli_query($dbc, $q);
35
36       // Back up if at least one table exists:
37       if (mysqli_num_rows($r) > 0) {
38
39           // Indicate what is happening:
40           echo "<p>Backing up database '$db_name'.</p>\n";
41
42           // Create a new workbook:
43           $workbook = $excel->Workbooks->Add();
44
```

*(script continues on next page)*

**Script 10.5** *continued*

```
45        // Go ahead and save the file:
46        $workbook->SaveAs("C:\Documents and Settings\Larry Ullman\Desktop\db_backup.xls");
47
48        // Each table gets its own sheet:
49        $sheet_number = 1;
50
51        // Fetch each table name.
52        while (list($table) = mysqli_fetch_array($r, MYSQLI_NUM)) {
53
54            // Get the records for this table:
55            $q2 = "SELECT * FROM $table";
56            $r2 = mysqli_query($dbc, $q2);
57
58            // Back up if records exist:
59            if (mysqli_num_rows($r2) > 0) {
60
61                // Add the sheet:
62                $sheet = 'Sheet' . $sheet_number;
63                if ($sheet_number > 3) $workbook->Sheets->Add;
64                $worksheet = $workbook->Worksheets($sheet);
65                $worksheet->Activate;
66                $worksheet->Name = $table;
67
68                // Start at row 1 for each table:
69                $excel_row = 1;
70
71                // Fetch all the records for this table:
72                while ($row = mysqli_fetch_array($r2, MYSQLI_NUM)) {
73
74                    // Each record starts in the first column:
75                    $excel_col = 1;
76
77                    // Write the data to the spreadsheet:
78                    foreach ($row as $value) {
79
80                        // Reference the cell:
81                        $cell = $worksheet->Cells($excel_row,$excel_col);
82
83                        // Need to change the formatting if
84                        // the data isn't numeric:
85                        if (is_numeric($value)) {
86                            $cell->Value = $value;
87                        } else {
88                            $cell->NumberFormat = '@';
89                            $cell->Value = $value;
90                        }
91
```

**Script 10.5** *continued*

```
 92                        // Increase the column:
 93                        $excel_col++;
 94
 95                    } // End of FOREACH.
 96
 97                    // Increase the row:
 98                    $excel_row++;
 99
100                } // End of table WHILE loop.
101
102                // Print the success:
103                echo "<p>Table '$table' backed up.</p>\n";
104
105                // Increase the sheet number:
106                $sheet_number++;
107
108                // Save the workbook:
109                $workbook->Save();
110
111            } // End of mysqli_num_rows() IF.
112
113        } // End of WHILE loop.
114
115        // Quit the application.
116        $excel->Quit();
117
118    } else { // No tables to backup!
119        echo "<p>The submitted database--$db_name--contains no tables.</p>\n";
120    }
121
122 } catch (com_exception $e) { // Catch COM exceptions.
123     echo "<p>$e</p>";
124 } catch (exception $e) { // Catch other exceptions.
125     echo '<p>' . $e->getMessage() . '</p>';
126 }
127
128 ?>
129 <body>
130 <html>
```

**3.** Create an instance of the COM object.

```
$excel = new COM
("excel.application") or die ("Cannot
→ start Excel.</body></html>");
echo "<p>Loaded Excel Version
→ $excel->Version</p>\n";
```

You may need to change the name of the application if your system has trouble with *excel.application*. (I am running this script on a server with Windows XP and Office 2003.) Just for the heck of it, I'm going to print the version of Excel loaded to the Web browser so that I know it's working (**Figure 10.31**).

If the COM object cannot be created, the script terminates immediately.

The script may function differently on your computer, but in my case, each creation of a new COM object will open up a new copy of that application, so be careful not to overburden the server when using COM.

**4.** Begin a `try…catch` block and set the visibility of the application.

```
try {
    $excel->Visible = 0;
```

By using `try` and `catch`, I can easily handle any COM errors that occur (see Chapter 8, "Real-World OOP," for more on this concept). I set the `Visible` property to 0 so that Excel is opened in an invisible manner.

**Figure 10.31** The PHP script starts by reporting to the Web browser the version of Excel being used.

**5.** Connect to the database and fetch all the tables.

```
$db_name = 'mysql';
$dbc = @mysqli_connect ('localhost',
→ 'username', 'password', $db_name)
→ OR die ("<p>The database--$db_
→ name--could not be backed
→ up.</p>\n</body>\n</html>\n");
$q = 'SHOW TABLES';
$r = mysqli_query($dbc, $q);
if (mysqli_num_rows($r) > 0) {
      echo "<p>Backing up database
→ '$db_name'.</p>\n";
```

This code is all very basic and exactly like that in the original db_backup.php (Script 10.1).

**6.** Create a new workbook and save the document.

```
$workbook = $excel->Workbooks->Add();
$workbook->SaveAs("C:\Documents and
→ Settings\Larry Ullman\Desktop\
→ db_backup.xls");
```

The first line creates a workbook, which Excel itself would normally do if it were opened as a regular application. Then I immediately save the file to the computer. You'll need to provide a valid full pathname and a unique filename for your server.

**7.** Set the initial sheet number.

```
$sheet_number = 1;
```

An Excel document is called a *workbook* and is made up of *sheets*. For backing up a MySQL database, I'll want to put one table on each sheet, so I need to track the number of sheets to reference them.

*continues on next page*

**8.** Fetch each table name and fetch the data in that table.

```
while (list($table) = mysqli_fetch_
→ array($r, MYSQLI_NUM)) {
      $q2 = "SELECT * FROM $table";
$r2 = mysqli_query($dbc, $q2);
if (mysqli_num_rows($r2) > 0) {
```

**9.** Create a new sheet for each table.

```
$sheet = 'Sheet' . $sheet_number;
if ($sheet_number > 3)
→ $workbook->Sheets->Add;
$worksheet =
→ $workbook->Worksheets($sheet);
$worksheet->Activate;
$worksheet->Name = $table;
```

This is starting to get a little complicated. First, understand that Excel, by default, creates a workbook with three sheets, called *Sheet1*, *Sheet2*, and *Sheet3* (**Figure 10.32**). So to reference a sheet by name, I use the syntax *SheetX*, which is why I want to track the sheet number. For the first three tables, I can use these first three sheets. The last three lines of code here select a sheet, assigning it to **$worksheet**, make it active, and then rename it to the table name (**Figure 10.33**). But if a database has more than three tables, extra sheets are necessary. In those cases, a new sheet is added (line 2 of this step's code).

**Figure 10.32** Excel starts off with three sheets.

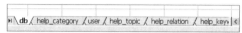

**Figure 10.33** The sheet names will reflect the MySQL table names.

**10.** Initialize a row value.

```
$excel_row = 1;
```

Each table's data should begin in the first row, so I set a variable to this value for each table.

**11.** Fetch all the records and initialize a column counter.

```
while ($row =
mysqli_fetch_array($r2,
→ MYSQLI_NUM)) {
    $excel_col = 1;
```

Each record of each table should start in the first column, so I initialize another variable inside of this loop.

**12.** Place the data into the Excel spreadsheet.

```
foreach ($row as $value) {
    $cell = $worksheet-
→ >Cells($excel_row,$excel_col);
    if (is_numeric($value)) {
        $cell->Value = $value;
    } else {
        $cell->NumberFormat
→ = '@';
        $cell->Value = $value;
    }
    $excel_col++;
}
```

The foreach loop will loop through each record returned, accessing a single column's value at a time. This value should be placed in a column of the spreadsheet.

Within the loop, the cell is identified using the $excel_row and $excel_col variables, going from 1, 1 to *X*, *Y*, where *X* is the number of rows in the MySQL table and *Y* is the number of columns.

Once you've identified the column, you can put some data there by referring to $cell->Value. Unfortunately, if the value being stored has certain characters in it (if, for instance, it starts with an equals sign), it'll cause errors. So I first check if the value is numeric, in which case it can just be written to the spreadsheet. Otherwise, I change the formatting of the cell to text, and then set the value.

Finally, the column count is increased so that the next MySQL column goes into the next spreadsheet column.

It is possible to define a range of cells and place all of the data at once, but I'm trying to keep this as straightforward as possible.

**13.** Complete the while loop, print a message to the browser, increase the sheet count, and save the file.

```
    $excel_row++;
} // End of table WHILE loop.
echo "<p>Table '$table' backed
→ up.</p>\n";
$sheet_number++;
$workbook->Save();
```

The while loop closed here is the one that returned all the records for a single table. Within the while loop, the row variable needs to be increased (so that the next record is placed on the next row of the spreadsheet). After that, a message is printed in the browser and the sheet count is increased (because each sheet matches a table). To be safe, the spreadsheet is then saved.

**14.** Complete the control structures begun in Step 8.

```
    } // End of mysqli_num_rows()
→ IF.
} // End of WHILE loop.
```

*continues on next page*

USING COM WITH PHP

**15.** Quit the application.

```
$excel->Quit();
```

**16.** Complete the conditional begun in Step 5.

```
} else {
    echo "<p>The submitted
→ database--$db_name--contains no
→ tables.</p>\n";
}
```

**17.** Catch the exceptions.

```
} catch (com_exception $e) {
    echo "<p>$e</p>";
} catch (exception $e) {
    echo '<p>' . $e->getMessage() .
'</p>';
}
```

The `com_exception` class is for any COM exceptions. I find it to be rather unhelpful for debugging purposes (**Figure 10.34**), but you should catch them anyway.

**18.** Complete the page.

```
?>
<body>
<html>
```

**19.** Save the file as `excel_backup.php`, place it in your Web directory, and test in your Web browser (**Figure 10.35**).

**20.** Open the generated spreadsheet in Excel (**Figure 10.36**).

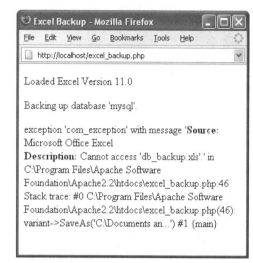

**Figure 10.34** An example of the awkward and often uninformative COM exceptions.

**Figure 10.35** The resulting Web page.

| | A | B | C | D | E | F | G | H | I | J | K | |
|---|---|---|---|---|---|---|---|---|---|---|---|---|
| 1 | % | test | username | Y | Y | Y | Y | Y | Y | Y | Y | |
| 2 | % | information | username | Y | Y | Y | Y | Y | Y | Y | Y | |
| 3 | % | mysql | username | Y | Y | Y | Y | Y | Y | Y | Y | |
| 4 | | | | | | | | | | | | |
| 5 | | | | | | | | | | | | |

**Figure 10.36** The generated Excel spreadsheet.

**USING COM WITH PHP**

## Running Server Commands

Another server-related topic not discussed in this chapter is how to run commands on the server. There are many PHP functions available for executing server commands. For starters, there is exec():

exec(*command*, $output);

This function takes a command and assigns to $output an array where each element is a line of the generated output.

There is also system(), which just returns the output (so that it could be immediately sent to the Web browser):

system(*command*);

The passthru() function is similar, but it can also return binary output:

passthru(*command*);

Finally, you could use shell_exec() or the backticks, both of which just return the output:

$var = shell_exec(*command*);

$var = `*command*`;

For security purposes, you should use escapeshellarg() or escapeshellcmd() to sanctify any command that isn't hard-coded.

### ✔ Tips

- Within the Unix family of operating systems you can connect to other applications using popen() and pclose(), which create pipes—avenues of communication.

- Another way to see what COM properties you'll need is to record a macro in the application that does what you intend to do. Then view this macro in the macro editor to see what terminology it uses.

- There are already COM classes available such as the Excel class at http://sourceforge.net/projects/psxlsgen.

- PHP 5 also supports interactions with .NET objects.

USING COM WITH PHP

# PHP's Command-Line Interface

PHP is known and loved as one of the best technologies for generating dynamic Web sites. Inevitably, developers started asking: If I can use PHP for Web pages, why can't I use it for other things, too? Why not, indeed! The people behind PHP came around to this way of thinking circa PHP 4.2, and PHP CLI (Command Line Interface) was born. As of PHP 4.3, it's part of the default configuration for all installations. Now you can do the equivalent of *shell scripting* (command-line programming) using your favorite language, PHP.

PHP CLI lets you run PHP scripts and even snippets of PHP code outside of a Web browser. On Windows, the action takes place within a DOS prompt (aka a console or command window). On Unix and Mac OS X, you'll use Terminal (or a similar program). The CLI is best used for:

- Quickly testing bits of PHP code
- Performing routine maintenance
- Creating your own system utilities
- Making installers for your PHP applications

In this chapter I'll cover what you need to know to accomplish these tasks. As an understanding of PHP itself is assumed, the focus will be on the fundamentals of using this new interface.

# Testing Your Installation

To get the ball rolling, the first thing you'll need to do is confirm that you have an available PHP CLI and to see what version you have (see the sidebar "CLI vs. CGI"). Hopefully, this is just a matter of:

1. Opening a command-line interface.

2. Typing `php -v` and pressing Return or Enter.

If the CLI version of PHP is installed and is in your PATH (a list of locations on your computer where the operating system is likely to find executable files), this should work. Worst-case scenario—assuming PHP CLI is installed, you'll need to use the full path to the CLI executable or move into the PHP directory first.

Along with the -v option, there are three others to point out up front:

◆ -i reveals information about the PHP installation.

◆ -h accesses the help file.

◆ -m lists the modules compiled into this PHP installation.

I'll formally run through these steps for both Windows and Unix/Mac OS X users.

---

## CLI vs. CGI

There are two versions of PHP that can be used for command-line scripting. The older version is the CGI (Common Gateway Interface). It's intended for Web pages but could also be used for shell scripts. The only drawback is that it needs to be told to behave differently or else it's likely to clutter up the command-line interface.

The CLI version is really a pared-down CGI, lacking GET and POST variables. It also does not send out MIME headers, which are needed for Web pages but not for consoles. The CLI version also does not use HTML in its errors, and it has no maximum execution time.

Figure 11.1 My Start menu; the Run option appears in the second column.

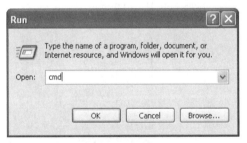

Figure 11.2 The Run prompt.

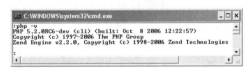

Figure 11.3 The command php -v shows the version of PHP CLI installed.

## To test your installation on Windows XP:

1. Click the Start menu.

2. In the Start menu, click Run (**Figure 11.1**).

3. At the Run prompt, type cmd (**Figure 11.2**) and click OK (or press Enter).

4. In the console window, type php -v and press Enter (**Figure 11.3**).

   This should show you the PHP and CLI versions installed.

5. Still in the console window, type php -i and press Enter to learn more about the installation.

   This is the equivalent of running a phpinfo() script within a Web browser. There's a ton of information available here, although you'll need to scroll back to view it all (and possibly increase the console's buffer size before running this command).

   *continues on next page*

TESTING YOUR INSTALLATION

**6.** (Having not left the console window...) Type php -m and press Enter to see what modules are installed (**Figure 11.4**).

This lists the extensions that the PHP installation supports.

**7.** (Where else but...) In the console window, type php -h and press Enter to see the help menu.

The help file, should you need...um...help, is mostly just a listing of the few basic options.

**8.** In the console window, type exit and press Enter to close the window.

## ✔ Tips

■ My Windows console window may not look like yours, so don't be alarmed. I've tried to "pretty it up" by changing from the default colors to black text on a white background. To do so, click the icon in the upper-left corner, and then click *Properties*.

■ Another change I make in my console window is that I change the prompt from the default (which is the current directory followed by >) to a simple colon. To do so, type prompt *X* and press Enter, where *X* is whatever you want the prompt to be.

■ At the time of this writing, the next version of Windows after XP—Vista—hasn't yet been released. Regardless, the early reviews suggest that Vista will still have a Start menu, within which you can access the Run prompt. So these instructions *should* continue to work when Windows Vista finally hits the scene.

**Figure 11.4** The list of modules built into this PHP CLI installation.

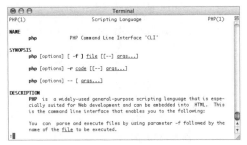

```
●●●         PHP Advanced: Visual QuickPro Guide
: php -v
PHP 5.2.0 (cli) (built: Nov  8 2006 19:56:23)
Copyright (c) 1997-2006 The PHP Group
Zend Engine v2.2.0, Copyright (c) 1998-2006 Zend Technologies
: ▊
```

**Figure 11.5** The command php -v shows the version of PHP CLI installed.

```
●●●                    Terminal
: php -h
Usage: php [options] [-f] <file> [--] [args...]
       php [options] -r <code> [--] [args...]
       php [options] [-B <begin_code>] -R <code> [-E <end_code>] [--] [args...]
       php [options] [-B <begin_code>] -F <file> [-E <end_code>] [--] [args...]
       php [options] -- [args...]
       php [options] -a

  -a               Run interactively
  -c <path>|<file> Look for php.ini file in this directory
  -n               No php.ini file will be used
  -d foo[=bar]     Define INI entry foo with value 'bar'
  -e               Generate extended information for debugger/profiler
  -f <file>        Parse <file>.
  -h               This help
  -i               PHP information
  -l               Syntax check only (lint)
  -m               Show compiled in modules
  -r <code>        Run PHP <code> without using script tags <?..?>
  -B <begin_code>  Run PHP <begin_code> before processing input lines
  -R <code>        Run PHP <code> for every input line
  -F <file>        Parse and execute <file> for every input line
  -E <end_code>    Run PHP <end_code> after processing all input lines
  -H               Hide any passed arguments from external tools.
  -s               Display colour syntax highlighted source.
  -v               Version number
  -w               Display source with stripped comments and whitespace.
  -z <file>        Load Zend extension <file>.

  args...          Arguments passed to script. Use -- args when first argument
                   starts with - or script is read from stdin

  --rf <name>      Show information about function <name>.
  --rc <name>      Show information about class <name>.
  --re <name>      Show information about extension <name>.

: ▊
```

**Figure 11.6** The PHP CLI help file.

```
●●●                    Terminal
PHP(1)              Scripting Language              PHP(1)

NAME
     php            PHP Command Line Interface 'CLI'

SYNOPSIS
     php [options] [ -f ] file [[--] args...]

     php [options] -r code [[--] args...]

     php [options] -- [ args...]

DESCRIPTION
     PHP is a widely-used general-purpose scripting language that is espe-
     cially suited for Web development and can be embedded into HTML. This
     is the command line interface that enables you to the following:

     You can parse and execute files by using parameter -f followed by the
     name of the file to be executed.
:▊
```

**Figure 11.7** The PHP CLI man page, quite similar to the help file (Figure 11.6).

## To test your installation on Unix and Mac OS X:

**1.** Open your Terminal application.

Most flavors of Unix that I'm familiar with as well as Mac OS X provide an application called Terminal, which is used for command-line operations. It's likely present in your Applications folder, or wherever your OS keeps its programs.

**2.** In the console window, type php -v and press Enter (**Figure 11.5**).

This should show you the PHP and CLI versions installed.

**3.** Still in the console window, type php -i and press Enter to learn more about the installation.

This is the equivalent of running a phpinfo() script within a Web browser. There's a ton of information available here, although you'll need to scroll back to catch it all (and possibly increase the console's buffer size).

**4.** (Having not left the console window...) Type php -m and press Enter to see what modules are installed.

This lists the extensions that the PHP installation supports.

**5.** (Where else but...) In the console window, type php -h and press Enter to see the help menu (**Figure 11.6**).

The help file, should you need...um...help, is mostly just a listing of the few basic options.

**6.** In the console window, type exit and press Enter to close the window.

## ✔ Tip

■ There is, on Unix and Mac OS X, a manual page installed for the PHP CLI. To access it, type man php (**Figure 11.7**).

# Executing Bits of Code

One of the first uses I find for PHP CLI is to be able to test snippets of code without going through the process of:

1. Writing a formal PHP script.

2. Placing it in a Web directory.

3. Running it in a Web browser.

You can test small sections of code using this syntax:

```
php -r 'php_code_here'
```

For a predictable example:

```
php -r 'echo "Hello, world!";'
```

A couple of things to memorize with this syntax: First, using PHP tags will cause parse errors (**Figure 11.8**). Second, it's safest to use single quotes around the code block. Without getting too deep into the reasons why, if you have variables in your code and use double quotation marks for the whole block, you'll get wonky results (**Figure 11.9**).

Finally, you should end each statement in PHP with a semicolon, just as you would in a script.

**Figure 11.8** Do not use PHP tags with the `php -r` option.

**Figure 11.9** It's best not to use double quotation marks around your PHP code, or else any variables used might create parse errors or worse.

## Using a Remote Server

If you want to work with PHP CLI on a remote server instead of a local one, that may also be an option. To do so, you must first make sure that the server's administrator—be it an ISP, hosting company, or whoever—allows remote logins. If so, they should provide you with a username and password.

Next, you need an SSH application to connect to that server (SSH provides a secure connection between two computers). If running Unix or Mac OS X, you can use SSH within a Terminal, typing

```
ssh -l username address
```

After the lowercase "L", enter your username. For the address, this can be either a URL—www.example.com—or an IP address (123.123.123.123). You'll then be prompted for the password.

For Windows users, I recommend PuTTY (search the Web for the current URL). This simple and free application provides a graphical interface along with the SSH and Telnet clients.

Once connected to the remote server, you can follow the other steps in this chapter.

**Figure 11.10** Among its many benefits, PHP CLI provides yet another way to say *Hello, world!*

**Figure 11.11** Using two lines of PHP code, I can print a formatted version of a file's last modification date.

**Figure 11.12** Thanks to the printed newlines, the command prompt no longer appears immediately after the result of the code (compare with Figure 11.10).

### ✔ Tip

■ In truth, what PHP CLI offers is a way for PHP programmers to do things they might otherwise do using Perl, awk, or shell scripts. Or in some cases, PHP CLI might replicate what is already possible using built-in utilities that you're unfamiliar with. This is fine, of course, as the benefit of PHP CLI is having a new way to use the knowledge you already possess.

### To use PHP CLI for code blocks:

1. Follow the steps in the first section of this chapter so that you can access PHP CLI.

   By this I just mean: open a Terminal application (Mac OS X and Unix), bring up a DOS prompt (Windows), or connect to your remote server.

2. Test an echo() statement (**Figure 11.10**).

   `php -r 'echo "Hello, world!";'`

   The PHP code being tested is

   `echo "Hello, world!";`

   This is wrapped within single quotes and placed after `php -r` to execute it.

3. Print the modification date of a file (**Figure 11.11**).

   `php -r '$ts =`
   `filemtime("/Users/larryullman/Desktop`
   `→ /php/number.php");`

   `echo date ("F j Y H:i:s", $ts);'`

   Here I'm actually executing two lines of PHP code. In the first line, the `$ts` variable is assigned the timestamp value of the last time the `number.php` file was modified. In the second line, that timestamp is formatted using the `date()` function, and printed. Because of the single quotes surrounding the entire PHP code block, I can enter this over multiple lines (see the figure).

   Obviously you'll need to change the path to the file so that it's appropriate for a file—any file—on your server.

4. Add a newline or two to the printed result (**Figure 11.12**).

   `php -r 'echo "Hello, world! \n\n"; '`

   By printing newline characters, I can add spacing to the output.

# Creating a Command-Line Script

Being able to test little bits of PHP code from the command line is nice, but it won't take you far. What you'll really want to do is run entire PHP scripts from the command-line interface. Such scripts could perform file or database maintenance, run updates for your Web sites, and more.

A PHP script to be used by PHP CLI is different from a Web script in three ways:

1. It won't use or create any HTML.

2. It doesn't need to use the .php extension (although it's fine if it does).

3. The very first line of the script will be:

   `#!/usr/bin/php`

You can use HTML, if you like, but it'll just clutter up the result in the console window. As for the file's extension, how the script is run will change (covered in the next section of the chapter), so you could literally use anything. But .php is still a fine idea. Or you could use a different extension to differentiate your Web PHP scripts from the command-line ones (or no extension at all!). But of the three rules, only the last one matters (and, frankly, it only matters on Unix and Mac OS X).

---

### The CLI php.ini

Most PHP installations will end up with two or more usable command-line versions of PHP. The one I'm focusing on in this chapter is CLI. But there are probably other PHPs lingering on your server, like the one used by Apache or IIS for handling Web pages.

One interesting point about PHP CLI is that it uses a different php.ini file than the Web PHP module. This file, of course, is where you dictate how PHP behaves. So it's important to remember that PHP CLI may run differently than you're used to. (For that matter, your PHP CLI installation may support different modules than your Web installation.)

In this same vein, you can, when invoking PHP CLI, use options to change the php.ini behavior:

♦ -c tells PHP CLI where to look for a php.ini file.

♦ -n tells PHP CLI not to use a php.ini.

♦ -d sets a php.ini value for PHP CLI.

**Figure 11.13** Text outside of the PHP tags is revealed in the console.

That line of code is called the *shebang* line. It tells the operating system where to find the executable that should be used to run this script. For Unix and Mac OS X, that executable should have been installed in /usr/bin. If you know that PHP CLI was installed elsewhere, change the shebang line accordingly. For Windows, this line is ignored, but you should keep it in there for cross-platform reliability.

After that line, all PHP code goes within the normal PHP tags. Anything outside of the PHP tags is sent to the standard output just like Web-based PHP scripts (**Figure 11.13**):

```
#!/usr/bin/php
<?php
// Do whatever.
?>
This text is also displayed.
<?php
// Do whatever.
?>
```

As the first implementation of this concept, I'll create a script that reads in a text file and reprints it, numbering the lines along the way.

## To create a command-line script:

1. Create a new PHP script in your text editor or IDE, beginning with the shebang line (**Script 11.1**).

   ```
   #!/usr/bin/php
   <?php # Script 11.1 - number.php
   ```

   Remember that the first line is the most important and that you might need to change it if PHP CLI was installed in a place other than /usr/bin. And although Windows users can skip this line, it's best to leave it in there.

   Finally, you still need to use the PHP tags.

2. Identify what file will be numbered.

   ```
   $file = 'number.php';
   ```

   Later in the chapter you'll see how to write this script so that this information can be assigned when the script is run. As for number.php, I'm actually having this script number itself. You can use any plain text file, like another PHP script from the book.

3. Print an introductory message.

   ```
   echo "\nNumbering the file named
   → '$file'...
   ------------------\n\n";
   ```

4. Read in the file.

   ```
   $data = file($file);
   ```

   The file() function reads an entire file into an array. Each line becomes one array element. You could use fopen() and the other file functions instead, if you prefer.

**Script 11.1** This PHP script will be run from the command line. It reads in a text file and prints it out, line by line, with the lines numbered.

```
1   #!/usr/bin/php
2   <?php # Script 11.1 - number.php
3
4   /* This page reads in a file.
5    * It then reprints the file, numbering
        the lines.
6    * This script is meant to be used with
        PHP CLI.
7    */
8
9   // The file to number:
10  $file = 'number.php';
11
12  // Print an intro message:
13  echo "\nNumbering the file named
        '$file'...
14  ------------------\n\n";
15
16  // Read in the file:
17  $data = file($file);
18
19  // Line number counter:
20  $n = 1;
21
22  // Print each line:
23  foreach ($data as $line) {
24
25      // Print number and line:
26      echo "$n  $line";
27
28      // Increment line number:
29      $n++;
30
31  } // End of FOREACH loop.
32
33  echo "\n------------------
34  End of file '$file'.\n";
35  ?>
```

**5.** Print each line with its number.

```
$n = 1;
foreach ($data as $line) {
    echo "$n  $line";
    $n++;
}
```

To start, a counter is initialized so that the first line is numbered at 1. Then a `foreach` loop goes through the array. Within the loop, each line is printed, prefixed by the line number and a couple of spaces. You do not need to print a newline here, as the line read in from the original file retained that newline. Finally, the counter is incremented.

**6.** Print a closing message.

```
echo "\n-------------------
End of file '$file'.\n";
```

**7.** Complete the PHP script.

```
?>
```

**8.** Save the file as `number.php`.

## ✔ Tips

■ PHP CLI can be used in combination with PHP-GTK to create stand-alone applications. Check out Chapter 10, "PHP and the Server," or `http://gtk.php.net` for more information.

■ The original CGI version of the command-line PHP would send out HTTP headers as part of its duties (as it was meant to work with Web servers). To avoid that step, it could be invoked using `-q`, which stands for quiet mode. This is no longer required with PHP CLI, but you'll sometimes see that flag used anyway, like so:

```
#!/usr/bin/php -q
```

# Running a Command-Line Script

Now that you've written a script especially meant for a command-line execution (and wasn't it nice not to mess with all that pesky HTML?), it's time to learn how to run it. There are two methods:

The first is to directly invoke PHP CLI, as you did when executing a bit of code, this time providing it with the name of a script to execute:

```
php scriptname.php
```

You'll also see the -f flag used. It stands for *file*, and whether you use it or not makes no difference on the end result:

```
php -f scriptname.php
```

This method should work just fine, as long as php is in your PATH and you are in the same directory as *scriptname*.php. Variations to circumvent these limitations might be:

```
/usr/bin/php scriptname.php
```

```
php /path/to/scriptname.php
```

```
C:\php\php.exe scriptname.php
```

The second method for executing PHP scripts is to treat the script as if it were an application in its own right:

```
scriptname.php (Windows)
```

```
./scriptname.php (Unix and Mac OS X)
```

This method, which is preferred, can have some tricks to it, so I'll run through the details in the following steps.

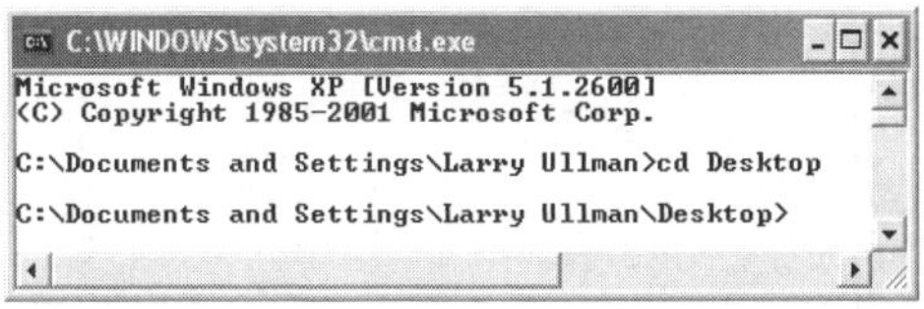

**Figure 11.14** Start by moving into the same directory where the PHP script you want to execute is located.

**Figure 11.15** The execution of the number.php script.

## To run a command-line script in Windows:

1. Use the instructions outlined earlier in the chapter to access a DOS prompt.

2. Move into the directory where number.php was saved (**Figure 11.14**).

   cd C:\path\to\directory

   In my case, this was a matter of just typing cd Desktop, as the file was saved on my Desktop.

3. Run the file using the php scriptname.php syntax (**Figure 11.15**).

   php number.php

   Hopefully this should work for you. If you get an error message, it's most likely because php is not in your PATH. If you don't know how to change your PATH, either search the Web for tutorials or turn to my support forums (www.dmcinsights.com/phorum/).

*continues on next page*

**RUNNING A COMMAND-LINE SCRIPT**

**4.** Run the file using the *scriptname*.php syntax.

`number.php`

If this doesn't immediately work, it's because you'll need to tell Windows what program to use for running .php scripts (**Figure 11.16**). To do so:

**a.** Choose *Select the program from a list* and click OK.

**b.** Click Browse in the Open With prompt (**Figure 11.17**).

**c.** Find and select the php executable (**Figure 11.18**), and then click Open.

From here on out, all .php scripts will run just fine from the command-line interface (assuming that you kept the *Always use the selected program to open this kind of file* box checked. See Figure 11.17.)

**Figure 11.16** If Windows doesn't know what program to run the script in, you'll see a prompt like this.

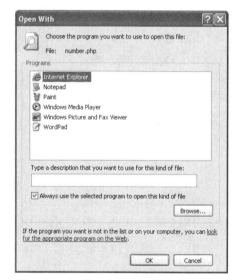

**Figure 11.17** You'll need to tell Windows what application to use for your scripts. The php executable will not likely come up as an option.

**Figure 11.18** Find the installed php executable to finish the association.

RUNNING A COMMAND-LINE SCRIPT

```
● ● ●               Terminal
: cd ~/Desktop
: php number.php

Numbering the file named 'number.php'...
-------------------

1  #!/usr/bin/php
2  <?php # Script 11.1 - number.php
3
4  /*   This page reads in a file.
5   *   It then reprints the file, numbering the lines.
6   *   This script is meant to be used with PHP CLI.
7   */
8
9  // The file to number:
10 $file = 'number.php';
11
12 // Print an intro message:
13 echo "\nNumbering the file named '$file'...
14 -------------------\n\n";
15
16 // Read in the file:
17 $data = file($file);
18
19 // Line number counter:
20 $n = 1;
21
22 // Print each line:
23 foreach ($data as $line) {
24
25     // Print number and line:
26     echo "$n  $line";
27
28     // Increment line number:
29     $n++;
30
31 } // End of FOREACH loop.
32
33 echo "\n-------------------
34 End of file '$file'.\n";
35 ?>

-------------------
End of file 'number.php'.
: █
```

**Figure 11.19** The first method for running the PHP script.

```
● ● ●               Terminal
: chmod +x number.php
: ./number.php

Numbering the file named 'number.php'...
-------------------

1  #!/usr/bin/php
2  <?php # Script 11.1 - number.php
```

**Figure 11.20** Executables can be run using the `./thing` syntax, assuming you are in the same directory as the thing to be run.

## To run a command-line script in Unix and Mac OS X:

1. Use the instructions outlined earlier in the chapter to access a command-line prompt.

2. Move into the directory where `number.php` was saved.

   cd `/path/to/directory`

   In my case, this was a matter of just typing cd `~/Desktop`, as the file was saved on my Desktop.

3. Run the file using the php `scriptname.php` syntax (**Figure 11.19**).

   php `number.php`

   Hopefully this should work for you. If you get an error message, it's most likely because php is not in your PATH. If you don't know how to change your PATH, either search the Web for tutorials or turn to my support forums (www.dmcinsights.com/phorum/).

4. Make the file executable.

   chmod +x `number.php`

   If you're not familiar with chmod, it's a utility for changing the properties of files and directories. The +x code says to add executable status to `number.php`.

5. Run the file using the `./scriptname.php` syntax (**Figure 11.20**).

   ./number.php

## ✔ Tip

■ You can use php -l `scriptname.php` to have PHP check a script's syntax, without actually running it. The only caveats are that this doesn't work with the -r option (for testing bits of code) and it doesn't check for fatal errors.

**RUNNING A COMMAND-LINE SCRIPT**

# Working with Command-Line Arguments

The number.php example (Script 11.1) is a reasonable-enough application of PHP CLI. The script provides a viable service but has one limitation: the file to be numbered is hard-coded into the script. It'd be better to set that value when the application is used. This can be easily achieved by rewriting the script so that it uses command-line arguments.

Command-line arguments are values passed to an application when it is run. For example, the PHP CLI takes several configuration options, the name of a script to be run, or some code to be executed. Arguments are passed to the invoked application by adding them after the application's name:

*scriptname.php arg1 arg2…*

In your PHP script, you can then access these arguments by referring to $argv and $argc (or the more formal $_SERVER['argv'] and $_SERVER['argc']. The $argv array stores every argument provided; $argc stores the number of arguments provided. The only catch to using these is that the name of the script itself is the first listed argument ($_SERVER['argv'][0]). To get a better understanding of this, **Figure 11.21** shows the execution of this code:

```
#!/usr/bin/php

<?php
echo "\n{$_SERVER['argc']} arguments
→ received. They are...\n";
foreach ($_SERVER['argv'] as $k => $v) {
    echo "$k: $v\n";
}
?>
```

Let's write a new number.php script so that it accepts an argument: the name of the script to number.

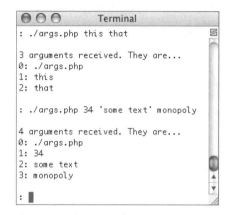

**Figure 11.21** The args.php script just prints out the number and values of the arguments used when calling it. Notice that the script name itself is always the first received argument.

## To use command-line arguments:

**1.** Create a new PHP script in your text editor or IDE, beginning with the shebang line (**Script 11.2**).

```
#!/usr/bin/php
<?php # Script 11.2 - number2.php
```

*continues on page 435*

**Script 11.2** This PHP script expects to receive the name of the file to number as a command-line argument.

```
1   #!/usr/bin/php
2   <?php # Script 11.2 - number2.php
3
4   /*  This page reads in a file.
5    *  It then reprints the file, numbering the lines.
6    *  This script is meant to be used with PHP CLI.
7    *  This script expects one argument (plus the script's name):
8    *  the name of the file to number.
9    */
10
11  // Check that a filename was provided:
12  if ($_SERVER['argc'] == 2) {
13
14      $file = $_SERVER['argv'][1];
15
16      // Make sure the file exists and is a file.
17      if (file_exists($file) && is_file($file)) {
18
19          // Read in the file.
20          if ($data = file($file)) {
21
22              // Print an intro message:
23              echo "\nNumbering the file named '$file'...\n------------------\n\n";
24
25              // Line number counter:
26              $n = 1;
27
28              // Print each line:
29              foreach ($data as $line) {
30
31                  // Print number and line:
32                  echo "$n  $line";
33
34                  // Increment line number:
35                  $n++;
```

*(script continues on next page)*

WORKING WITH COMMAND-LINE ARGUMENTS

**Script 11.2** *continued*

```
36
37              } // End of FOREACH loop.
38
39              echo "\n-------------------\nEnd of file '$file'.\n";
40
41          } else {
42              echo "The file could not be read.\n";
43              return 1;
44          }
45
46      } else {
47          echo "The file does not exist.\n";
48          return 1;
49      }
50
51  } else {
52
53      // Print the usage:
54      echo "\nUsage: number2.php <filename>\n\n";
55
56      // Kill the script, indicate error.
57      return 1;
58  }
59
60  ?>
```

**2.** Check that a filename was provided.

```
if ($_SERVER['argc'] == 2) {
```

Since the script will receive the script's name as its first argument, it would need to receive two arguments to be properly used. This conditional checks for that.

**3.** Make sure that the file exists.

```
$file = $_SERVER['argc'][1];
if (file_exists($file) &&
→ is_file($file)) {
```

First, the name of the file is identified as the second argument provided (the arguments list being an array, the indexing begins at 0). Then two conditionals confirm that the given file does exist and is a file (because a directory would pass the first test). You'd likely want to add code restricting the files to a certain directory, for security purposes.

**4.** Read in the file and print each line.

```
if ($data = file($file)) {
    echo "\nNumbering the file named
→ '$file'...\n-------------------
→ \n\n";
    $n = 1;
    foreach ($data as $line) {
        echo "$n  $line";
        $n++;
    }
    echo "\n-------------------\nEnd
→ of file '$file'.\n";
```

This code matches that in number.php, except for reading the file's contents as a conditional.

**5.** Complete the conditional started in Step 4.

```
} else {
    echo "The file could not be
→ read.\n";
    return 1;
}
```

If the file couldn't be read for some reason, likely a permissions issue, a message should be printed. The return 1 line is used to indicate a problem. Returning a nonzero number when a problem occurs is a convention for command-line applications (see the sidebar "Creating an Interface" later in this chapter).

**6.** Complete the conditional started in Step 3.

```
} else {
    echo "The file does not
→ exist.\n";
    return 1;
}
```

*continues on next page*

7. Complete the conditional started in Step 2.

```
} else {
    echo "\nUsage: number2.php
→ <filename>\n\n";
    return 1;
}
```

If the script was not invoked with the proper number of arguments, how it should be used is indicated (**Figure 11.22**). This is a command-line convention, also discussed in the sidebar.

8. Complete the PHP script.

```
?>
```

9. Save the file as number2.php.

10. Run the script (**Figures 11.23** and **11.24**). Note that on Windows, you'll need to use this syntax:

php number2.php *filename*

If you use

number2.php *filename*

the script will only recognize one argument (with a value of *number2.php*).

## ✔ Tip

■ To get really professional with your command-line arguments, check out the PEAR Console_Getargs and Console_Getopt packages. They both help establish and manage the list of long and short options that your program will accept.

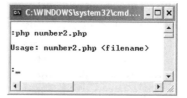

**Figure 11.22** If no filename is provided, the utility's proper usage is shown.

**Figure 11.23** The args.php script is numbered by number2.php.

**Figure 11.24** If the script cannot find the given file, an error is displayed.

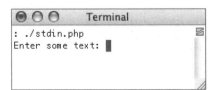

**Figure 11.25** Any function that attempts to read from the standard input will create a prompt where the user can type.

# Taking Input

An alternative to using command-line arguments is to request input from the user (although you could use both techniques in combination). By doing so, you can create an interactive application, where it prompts the user for information and does something with what is entered.

Strange as it may seem, taking input in a command-line application is exactly like reading in data from a file. But in this case, instead of using a file handle (a pointer to an opened file), you'll use a special constant, STDIN. This stands for *standard input*, which would be the keyboard by default. One easy way to read in standard input would be to use the fgets() function:

$data = fgets(STDIN);

This line of code creates a prompt (**Figure 11.25**). Anything typed there is assigned to $data.

To be more precise with input, I like to use the fscanf() function. Like printf() and sprintf(), discussed in Chapter 1, "Advanced PHP Techniques," this function takes formatting parameters to handle specific types of data. By using this function, instead of a more generic one, some basic validation as to the type of data read in can take place. In this next example, fscanf() will be used to create an application that converts temperatures between degrees Fahrenheit and Celsius (in either direction).

## Creating an Interface

Using PHP in a command-line situation opens up a whole new world that PHP for Web development doesn't have: the user interface. Sure, presentation and usage of Web pages is a vitally important HTML issue, but on the command line it's a different beast.

For starters, most command-line applications indicate how the command is to be used, should it be used incorrectly. Type php -varmit and you'll see what I mean. The number2.php script does this a little bit (showing the usage) but commands normally do more, like offer help if *commandname* -h or *commandname* --help is entered.

Finally, command-line applications often return a code indicating how successful the operation was. The number 0 is returned to indicate no problems, and some nonzero number otherwise. In number2.php, the integer 1 is returned when things go wrong (you could also write it as exit(1) in your PHP code).

## To take user input:

1. Create a new PHP script in your text editor or IDE, beginning with the shebang line (**Script 11.3**).

   ```
   #!/usr/bin/php
   <?php # Script 11.3 - temperature.php
   ```

2. Prompt the user for the input.

   ```
   echo "\nEnter a temperature and
   → indicate if it's Fahrenheit or
   → Celsius [##.# C/F]: ";
   ```

   The prompt (**Figure 11.26**) clearly indicates to the user what information is expected and in what format. Because there is no newline character printed at the end of this text, the user will be able to type immediately after the colon.

3. Read in a floating-point number and a string.

   ```
   if (fscanf (STDIN, "%f %s", $temp_i,
   → $which_i) == 2) {
   ```

   There's a lot going on in this one line. First, the fscanf() function will attempt to read in, from the standard input, one floating-point number and one string. These should match up to the temperature (e.g., 98.6) and the indicator as to the current temperature type (*C* or *F*). There is no "character" format with fscanf(), so the %s for string will have to do. If fscanf() can read in exactly these two data types in that order, they'll be assigned to the variables $temp_i and $which_i.

   The last bit of trickery is that the fscanf() function can return the number of values it assigned to variables. So if it reads in two values, assigned to $temp_i and $which_i, the conditional knows that the proper data was entered.

*continues on page 440*

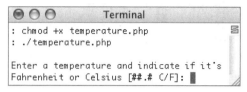

**Figure 11.26** The initial prompt.

**Script 11.3** User input is requested when this script runs. The input is read in from STDIN and validated; if proper, a temperature conversion occurs.

```php
1    #!/usr/bin/php
2    <?php # Script 11.3 - temperature.php
3
4    /*  This page convers temperatures between
5     *  Fahrenheit and Celsius.
6     *  This script is meant to be used with PHP CLI.
7     *  This script requests input from the user.
8     */
9
10   // Prompt the user:
11   echo "\nEnter a temperature and indicate if it's Fahrenheit or Celsius [##.# C/F]: ";
12
13   // Read the input as a conditional:
14   if (fscanf (STDIN, "%f %s", $temp_i, $which_i) == 2) {
15
16       // Make the conversion based upon $which_i:
17       switch (trim($which_i)) {
18
19           // Celsius, convert to Fahrenheit:
20           case 'C':
21           case 'c':
22               $temp_o = ($temp_i * (9.0/5.0)) + 32;
23               $which_o = 'F';
24               $which_i = 'C';
25               break;
26
27           // Fahrenheit, convert to Celsius:
28           case 'F':
29           case 'f':
30               $temp_o = ($temp_i - 32) * (5.0/9.0);
31               $which_o = 'C';
32               $which_i = 'F';
33               break;
34
35           // Problem: neither C nor F entered, set $which_o to FALSE:
36           default:
37               $which_o = FALSE;
38               break;
39
40       } // End of SWITCH.
41
42       // Print the results:
43       if ($which_o) {
44           printf ("%0.1f %s is %0.1f %s.\n", $temp_i, $which_i, $temp_o, $which_o);
45       } else {
46           echo "You failed to enter C or F to indicate the current temperature.\n";
47       }
48
49   } else { // Didn't enter the right input.
50
51       echo "You failed to use the proper syntax.\n";
52
53   } // End of main IF.
54   ?>
```

**TAKING INPUT**

**4.** Make the appropriate conversion.

```
switch (trim($which_i)) {
    case 'C':
    case 'c':
            $temp_o = ($temp_i *
            → (9.0/5.0)) + 32;
            $which_o = 'F';
            $which_i = 'C';
            break;
    case 'F':
    case 'f':
            $temp_o = ($temp_i - 32)
            → * (5.0/9.0);
            $which_o = 'C';
            $which_i = 'F';
            break;
    default:
            $which_o = FALSE;
            break;
} // End of SWITCH.
```

The `switch` checks to see if degrees Celsius is being converted to Fahrenheit or vice versa. If the second piece of input submitted is not C, c, F, or f, no conversion takes place.

## Taking CLI Further

This chapter covers what you need to know about running PHP code from a command-line interface. For the most part this just means that you'll take what you already know how to do with PHP and execute it in a non-Web interface. That alone is perfect for many automated tasks that you might want to do.

On a more sophisticated level, PHP CLI can be used to really interact with the operating system on a low level. One thing to look into is the `pcntl` (process control) extension. The extension, which isn't available when using PHP for Web pages, lets you *fork* your processes (split them off). From there you can go on to the concept of signals. If you don't know what these things are, that's fine: you probably shouldn't be messing with them in PHP anyway. But if you do understand these concepts, knowing that you can work with them in PHP is a welcome bit of news.

Finally, with PHP CLI you can use the backticks, `exec()`, `system()`, and similar functions to call system utilities. Using these functions with PHP CLI doesn't really differ from using them in a Web script, but your need to use them might increase.

TAKING INPUT

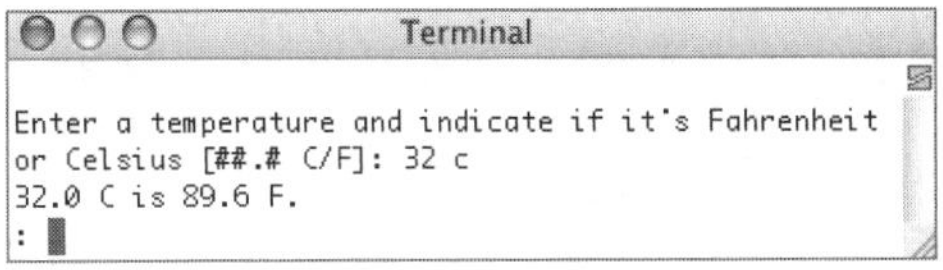

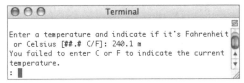

**Figure 11.27** The result of the calculation is printed as a floating-point number with one decimal.

```
Enter a temperature and indicate if it's Fahrenheit
or Celsius [##.# C/F]: 240.1 m
You failed to enter C or F to indicate the current
temperature.
:
```

**Figure 11.28** One of the possible error messages if the script is not used properly.

**5.** Print the results.

```
if ($which_o) {
        printf ("%0.1f %s is %0.1f
→ %s.\n", $temp_i, $which_i,
→ $temp_o, $which_o);
} else {
        echo "You failed to enter C or F
→ to indicate the current
→ temperature.\n";
}
```

If $which_o is equal to *C* or *F*, then the conditional is true and the conversion is printed, using the printf() function to handle the formatting (**Figure 11.27**). Otherwise, a default message is printed (**Figure 11.28**).

*continues on next page*

**TAKING INPUT**

**6.** Complete the conditional started in Step 3.

```
} else {
    echo "You failed to use the
    → proper syntax.\n";
}
```

This `else` clause applies if the `fscanf()` function does not return the number 2, meaning it didn't read in two values (**Figure 11.29**). In neither this case nor the `else` clause in Step 5 did I return a number indicating a problem, but that could be added.

**7.** Complete the PHP script.

```
?>
```

**8.** Save the file as `temperature.php`.

**9.** Run the script (**Figure 11.30**).

## ✔ Tips

- This script could have been simplified by taking the temperature and the temperature type as two separate inputs. But doing so would have been far less cool than using just one prompt and showing off what `fscanf()` can do.

- Any of PHP's file functions can be used on `STDIN`. This means, for example, that you could use `fgetc()` to retrieve just a single character or `fgetcsv()` to retrieve and parse an entire line.

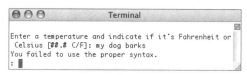

**Figure 11.29** The second of the possible error messages for misuse.

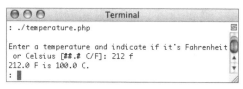

**Figure 11.30** Successfully converting from Fahrenheit to Celsius.

TAKING INPUT

# Using PEAR

One part of my definition of "advanced" PHP is simply: Do the things you already do but better and faster. Toward this end, PEAR is a miraculous tool. PEAR, the PHP Extension and Application Repository (`http://pear.php.net`), is a shared library of PHP code that you can use to develop your own applications. The library is made up of *packages*, each package providing functionality within a specific area.

In some other chapters, I have either mentioned related PEAR packages or outright used them (because why reinvent the wheel, right?). In this chapter I am going to demonstrate three more PEAR packages, which did not fit in elsewhere. These packages address common problems PHP programmers encounter, and frequently asked questions on my support forums.

A couple last words on PEAR: as much as it's great, it has some limitations. How current and how well documented a package is varies greatly (both being good indicators as to the package's usability). And installation can be troublesome. But you can also learn a lot from PEAR: it's an excellent model of object-oriented design (see Chapter 6, "Basic Object-Oriented Programming," and Chapter 7, "Advanced OOP"). By looking at PEAR source code, you can learn much about defining classes, documenting your work, extending classes, or even how to use an otherwise undocumented package. I will be using OOP terminology in this chapter, so an understanding of those fundamentals (again, see Chapter 6) will help comprehension of this material.

# Using Benchmark

The first of the PEAR packages to discuss in this chapter is Benchmark. As the name implies, this is a simple class for benchmarking code. Benchmarking, in case you're not familiar, is the process of timing how long code blocks, entire scripts, or whole applications take to run. Doing so can be a useful tool for finding bottlenecks in your sites and improving performance.

In this next section I'll run through two uses of the Benchmark package. The first will time three different ways of printing text in PHP, because which method is fastest is a common question. The second will show how fast PHP executes a particular user-defined function.

I'll say up front that the Benchmark class is nice and simple, but the documentation for it is lacking. There is simply no end-user documentation available. But through these next two pages, and by looking at the class definitions in the downloadable files, you'll be able to start benchmarking your scripts.

## Understanding Benchmarks

In the first two examples of this chapter, I benchmark some PHP code. While the results of the benchmarks are clear and easy to understand, they are not universal. For the first example, several executions of this script show that using single quotes is faster, *for that exact example on my computer*. This is not to say that single quotes are *always* faster.

Benchmarking is a good way to give you an understanding of *execution tendencies*: is it generally better to do this or that? When it comes time to really fine-tune your applications, you should benchmark your exact code (i.e., what you've written versus alternative methods) on the server it will run on. Only then will you know for certain that you've got the best performance possible.

It should also be remembered that the benchmarking itself affects a script's performance. Because of the extra memory required by the Benchmark object, and the extra processing required by calling its methods, any benchmarked script will perform worse than its unbenchmarked version (not that there's a way to test for that, of course).

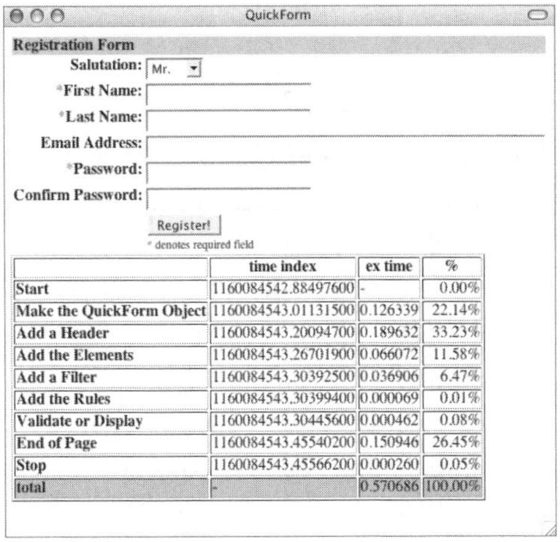

**Figure 12.1** The benchmark results for timing the execution of a script (this being a QuickForm example developed later in the chapter) are revealed using the `display()` method.

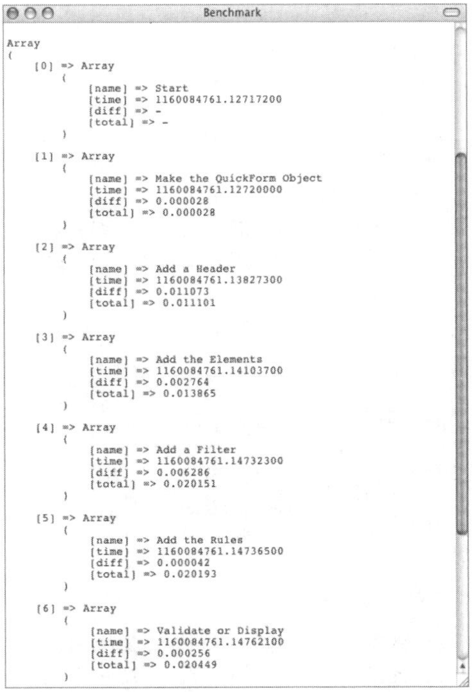

**Figure 12.2** Part of the structure of the array returned by the `getProfiling()` method.

# Benchmarking some code

To simply benchmark some sections of code in a PHP script, use the Benchmark `Timer` class. Start by including the file and creating the object:

```
require ('Benchmark/Timer.php');
$timer = new Benchmark_Timer();
```

Once you have a timer object, you can start the timer at any point:

```
$timer->start();
```

Stopping the timer is a matter of:

```
$timer->stop();
```

Commonly, you'll want to see how long specific parts of your code take to run. You can set place markers using:

```
$timer->setMarker('Marker Name');
```

When you're done doing whatever, you can easily report on the results by invoking the `display()` method (**Figure 12.1**):

```
$timer->display();
```

Or you can manually access the intervals between points using:

```
$timer->timeElapsed('Marker1',
→ 'Marker2')
```

A final option is to get an array of results via:

```
$profile = $timer->getProfiling();
```

This array (see **Figure 12.2**) can then be used however you see fit.

As a practical example, I'm going to run a test to see what the execution difference is between using echo with single quotes, double quotes, or the heredoc syntax (if you're not familiar with the heredoc syntax, see Chapter 1, "Advanced PHP Techniques"). Because PHP has to look for variables to be extrapolated within double quotes and heredoc, the performance difference is often questioned.

## To benchmark your code:

1. Create a new PHP script in your text editor or IDE, beginning with the standard HTML (**Script 12.1**).

```
<!DOCTYPE html PUBLIC "-//W3C//DTD
→ XHTML 1.0 Transitional//EN"
"http://www.w3.org/TR/xhtml1/DTD/
→ xhtml1-transitional.dtd">
<html xmlns="http://www.w3.org/1999/
→ xhtml" xml:lang="en" lang="en">
<head>
    <meta http-equiv="content-type"
→ content="text/html; charset=
→ iso-8859-1" />
    <title>Benchmarking Code</title>
</head>
<body>
<?php # Script 12.1 - timer.php
```

2. Define at least one variable.

```
$data = 'This is some text.';
```

To really test the performance difference, I want to print some HTML and a variable.

3. Include the Timer class definition.

```
require ('Benchmark/Timer.php');
```

Assuming that you've installed the Benchmark package and that the PEAR directory is in your include path, this one line is all you need to use the class.

*continues on page 448*

## Installing PEAR Packages

One PEAR-related thing I do not discuss in this book is the installation process, for two good reasons. First, with the variations of available operating systems, it's too tough to nail down comprehensive instructions for all potential readers. Second, experience tells me that many users are on hosted servers, where they cannot directly install anything.

Still, installing PEAR is not impossibly hard, and once you master the installation of a single package, installing more is a snap. If you want to try your hand at installing PEAR packages, start by checking out the PEAR manual, which has instructions (you have to set up the installer first). If you're still not clear as to what you should do, search the Web for articles on the subject and/or post a question in the book's supporting forum, where I'll be happy to assist.

Some installation tips up front:

- You may need to invoke the `pear` installer as a superuser (or using sudo).

- Make sure that the location of your PEAR directory is in your PHP include path.

- If using PHP 5, you may want to set error reporting below `E_STRICT`, as not all PEAR packages have been upgraded to the new object model.

- Run the command `pear help install` to see what options are available.

If you are on a hosted server, the hosting company should be willing to install PEAR packages for you (which benefit every user on the server). If they won't do that, you ought to consider a different hosting company (seriously). Barring that, for some PEAR classes, you can just download a package from the PEAR site, copy its files onto your server, and include them as if they were any other class definition files.

**Script 12.1** How long it takes PHP to execute three different echo() statements is benchmarked in this script.

```
1    <!DOCTYPE html PUBLIC "-//W3C//DTD XHTML
     1.0 Transitional//EN"
2            "http://www.w3.org/TR/xhtml1/DTD/
     xhtml1-transitional.dtd">
3    <html xmlns="http://www.w3.org/1999/
     xhtml" xml:lang="en" lang="en">
4    <head>
5        <meta http-equiv="content-type"
     content="text/html; charset=
     iso-8859-1" />
6        <title>Benchmarking Code</title>
7    </head>
8    <body>
9    <?php # Script 12.1 - timer.php
10
11   /*   This page performs benchmarks on
     three
12    *   different types of echo() statements.
13    *   This page requires the PEAR Benchmark
     package.
14    */
15
16   // Some dummy data to be printed:
17   $data = 'This is some text.';
18
19   // Include the Timer class definition:
20   require ('Benchmark/Timer.php');
21
22   // Create and start a timer:
23   $timer = new Benchmark_Timer();
24   $timer->start();
25
26   // Time a single-quote example:
27   $timer->setMarker('echo1');
28   echo '<h1>echo() with single quotes</h1>
29   <table border="0" width="90%"
     cellspacing="3" cellpadding="3"
     align="center">
30       <tr>
31           <td>' . $data . '</td>
32           <td>' . $data . '</td>
33           <td>' . $data . '</td>
34       </tr>
35       <tr>
36           <td>' . $data . '</td>
```

**Script 12.1** *continued*

```
37           <td>' . $data . '</td>
38           <td>' . $data . '</td>
39       </tr>
40   </table>
41   <p>End of echo() with single quotes.</p>
42   ';
43
44   // Time a double-quote example:
45   $timer->setMarker('echo2');
46   echo "<h1>echo() with double quotes</h1>
47   <table border=\"0\" width=\"90%\"
     cellspacing=\"3\" cellpadding=\"3\"
     align=\"center\">
48       <tr>
49           <td>$data</td>
50           <td>$data</td>
51           <td>$data</td>
52       </tr>
53       <tr>
54           <td>$data</td>
55           <td>$data</td>
56           <td>$data</td>
57       </tr>
58   </table>
59   <p>End of echo() with double quotes.</p>
60   ";
61
62   // Time a heredoc example:
63   $timer->setMarker('heredoc');
64   echo <<<EOT
65   <h1>heredoc Syntax</h1>
66   <table border="0" width="90%"
     cellspacing="3" cellpadding="3"
     align="center">
67       <tr>
68           <td>$data</td>
69           <td>$data</td>
70           <td>$data</td>
71       </tr>
72       <tr>
73           <td>$data</td>
74           <td>$data</td>
75           <td>$data</td>
76       </tr>
77   </table>
78   <p>End of heredoc syntax.</p>
```

*(script continues on next page)*

USING BENCHMARK

**4.** Create and start a timer.

```
$timer = new Benchmark_Timer();
$timer->start();
```

**5.** Time a single-quote example.

```
$timer->setMarker('echo1');
echo '<h1>echo() with single
→ quotes</h1>
<table border="0" width="90%"
→ cellspacing="3" cellpadding="3"
→ align="center">
    <tr>
            <td>' . $data . '</td>
            <td>' . $data . '</td>
            <td>' . $data . '</td>
    </tr>
    <tr>
            <td>' . $data . '</td>
            <td>' . $data . '</td>
            <td>' . $data . '</td>
    </tr>
</table>
<p>End of echo() with single
→ quotes.</p>
';
```

I begin by setting a marker; any name is fine for it. Then I print out, using echo(), some HTML. Within the HTML, a variable will be concatenated several times over.

**6.** Time a double-quote example.

```
$timer->setMarker('echo2');
echo "<h1>echo() with double
→ quotes</h1>
<table border=\"0\" width=\"90%\"
→ cellspacing=\"3\" cellpadding=\"3\"
→ align=\"center\">
    <tr>
```

**Script 12.1** *continued*

```
79    EOT;
80
81    // Set a final marker and stop the timer:
82    $timer->setMarker('end');
83    $timer->stop();
84
85    // Print the results:
86    echo '<hr /><h1>Results:</h1>';
87
88    echo '<p>Time required for the single
      quote echo(): ' . $timer->timeElapsed
      ('echo1', 'echo2') . '</p>';
89
90    echo '<p>Time required for the double
      quote echo(): ' . $timer->timeElapsed
      ('echo2', 'heredoc') . '</p>';
91
92    echo '<p>Time required for the heredoc
      echo(): ' . $timer->timeElapsed
      ('heredoc', 'end') . '</p>';
93
94    // Delete the object:
95    unset($timer);
96    ?>
97    </body>
98    </html>
```

```
        <td>$data</td>
        <td>$data</td>
        <td>$data</td>
    </tr>
    <tr>
        <td>$data</td>
        <td>$data</td>
        <td>$data</td>
    </tr>
</table>
<p>End of echo() with double
→ quotes.</p>
";
```

This is a variation on the code in Step 5, except that double quotes are used. This means that all double quotes in the HTML must be escaped but that the variables can be kept within the string (and not concatenated).

**7.** Time a heredoc example.

```
$timer->setMarker('heredoc');
echo <<<EOT
<h1>heredoc Syntax</h1>
<table border="0" width="90%"
→ cellspacing="3" cellpadding="3"
→ align="center">
    <tr>
        <td>$data</td>
        <td>$data</td>
        <td>$data</td>
    </tr>
    <tr>
        <td>$data</td>
        <td>$data</td>
        <td>$data</td>
    </tr>
```

```
</table>
<p>End of heredoc syntax.</p>
EOT;
```

This is the heredoc syntax, discussed in Chapter 1. Variables can be kept in the string, but double quotation marks do not need to be escaped.

**8.** Set a final marker and stop the timer.

```
$timer->setMarker('end');
$timer->stop();
```

So that the timing of each code block is consistent, I set a marker and then stop the timer. This way each chunk begins and ends with a setMarker() call.

**9.** Print the results.

```
echo '<hr /><h1>Results:</h1>';
echo '<p>Time required for the
→ single quote echo(): ' . $timer-
→ >timeElapsed('echo1', 'echo2') .
→ '</p>';
echo '<p>Time required for the
→ double quote echo(): ' . $timer-
→ >timeElapsed('echo2', 'heredoc') .
→ '</p>';
echo '<p>Time required for the
→ heredoc echo(): ' . $timer-
→ >timeElapsed('heredoc', 'end') .
→ '</p>';
```

To find out how long each section of code took to execute, invoke the timeElapsed() method, providing two markers as the start and stop points.

**10.** Delete the object and complete the page.

```
unset($timer);
?>
</body>
</html>
```

*continues on next page*

**11.** Save the file as `timer.php`, place it in your Web directory, and test in your Web browser (**Figure 12.3**).

**12.** Run the page several times to confirm the results (**Figures 12.4** and **12.5**).

### ✔ Tips

■ As I mention in the introduction to this section of the chapter, the Benchmark package does not come with much in the way of documentation. But if you download the package files and view the class definitions, you'll find some sample code and, what is more important, be able to see what each method does. Doing so only requires an understanding of basic object-oriented programming (see Chapter 6).

■ If you do this when creating a new timer:

```
$timer = new Benchmark_Timer(true);
```

then the timer will automatically be started at that point. The timer will also automatically stop at the end of the script (or when the variable is deleted) with the results shown as in Figure 12.1.

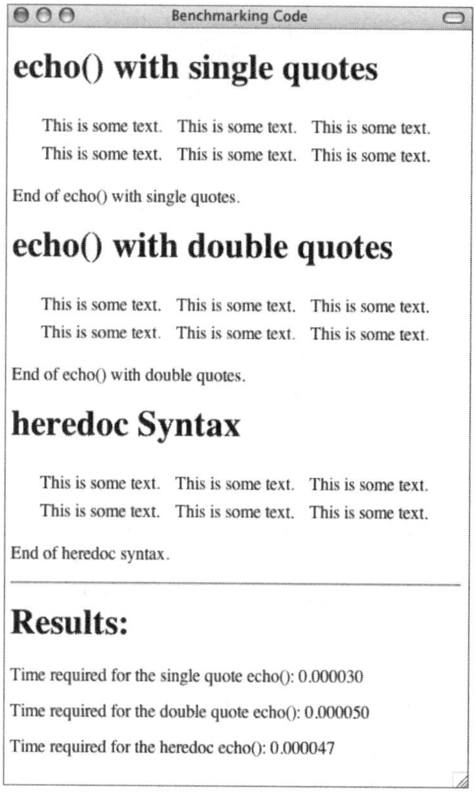

**Figure 12.3** The first part of the page is the tested code: three different ways to achieve the same result. The bottom of the page shows how long, in seconds, each code block took to execute.

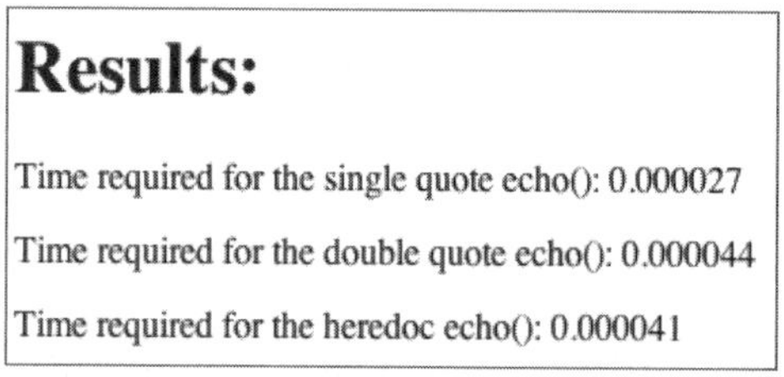

**Figure 12.4** Rerun the same page (compare with Figures 12.3 and 12.5) multiple times to confirm and compare the benchmarking numbers.

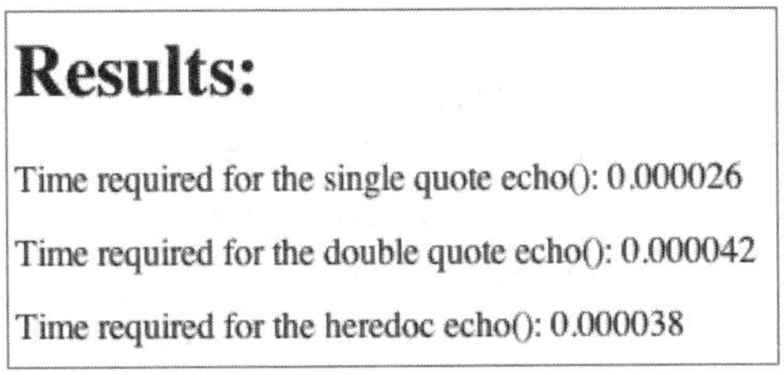

## Results:

Time required for the single quote echo(): 0.000026

Time required for the double quote echo(): 0.000042

Time required for the heredoc echo(): 0.000038

**Figure 12.5** Using echo() with single quotes is consistently the fastest option, followed by the heredoc syntax, and finally, double quotes.

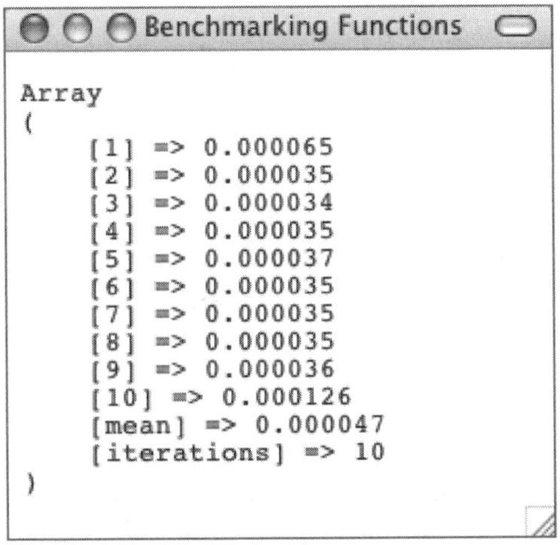

```
● ○ ○   Benchmarking Functions   ⊂⊃

Array
(
    [1]  => 0.000065
    [2]  => 0.000035
    [3]  => 0.000034
    [4]  => 0.000035
    [5]  => 0.000037
    [6]  => 0.000035
    [7]  => 0.000035
    [8]  => 0.000035
    [9]  => 0.000036
    [10] => 0.000126
    [mean]  => 0.000047
    [iterations]  => 10
)
```

**Figure 12.6** The array returned by the get() method of the Benchmark_Iterate class.

# Benchmarking functions

The previous example uses the Timer class to perform a simple timing operation on some code. The drawback of those tests is that they represent a single execution. Part of the Benchmark package is the Benchmark_Iterate class, which can test the performance of functions by invoking them for a repeated number of times. To use it, create an object of type Benchmark_Iterate:

```
require ('Benchmark/Iterate.php');
$b = new Benchmark_Iterate();
```

Then, just tell the object what function to run and how many times:

```
$b->run($iterations, 'function_name');
```

Finally, invoke the get() method to retrieve all the results.

```
$r = $b->get();
```

The returned data is an associative array, listing the time taken by each iteration of the function, plus the mean and a confirmation of the number of iterations (**Figure 12.6**).

## To benchmark a function:

1. Create a new PHP script in your text editor or IDE, beginning with the standard HTML (**Script 12.2**).

```
<!DOCTYPE html PUBLIC "-//W3C//DTD
→ XHTML 1.0 Transitional//EN"
"http://www.w3.org/TR/xhtml1/DTD/
→ xhtml1-transitional.dtd">
<html xmlns="http://www.w3.org/1999/
→ xhtml" xml:lang="en" lang="en">
<head>
    <meta http-equiv="content-type"
→ content="text/html; charset=
→ iso-8859-1" />
    <title>Benchmarking
→ Functions</title>
</head>
<body>
<?php # Script 12.2 - iterate.php
```

2. Define the function to test.

```
function dummy() {
    $data = 'This is some text.';
    echo '<!--<h1>echo() with single
→ quotes</h1>
    <table border="0" width="90%"
→ cellspacing="3" cellpadding="3"
→ align="center">
        <tr>
            <td>' . $data .
→ '</td>
            <td>' . $data .
→ '</td>
            <td>' . $data .
→ '</td>
        </tr>
        <tr>
            <td>' . $data .
→ '</td>
            <td>' . $data .
→ '</td>
            <td>' . $data .
→ '</td>
        </tr>
    </table>
    <p>End of echo() with single
→ quotes.</p>-->';
}
```

*continues on page 454*

**Script 12.2** A dummy function is benchmarked in this script. By increasing the number of times the function is executed, you'll get a more accurate sense of the function's performance.

```
1    <!DOCTYPE html PUBLIC "-//W3C//DTD XHTML 1.0 Transitional//EN"
2         "http://www.w3.org/TR/xhtml1/DTD/xhtml1-transitional.dtd">
3    <html xmlns="http://www.w3.org/1999/xhtml" xml:lang="en" lang="en">
4    <head>
5        <meta http-equiv="content-type" content="text/html; charset=iso-8859-1" />
6        <title>Benchmarking Functions</title>
7    </head>
8    <body>
9    <?php # Script 12.2 - iterate.php
10
11   /*  This page performs benchmarks on a function.
12    *  This page requires the PEAR Benchmark package.
13    */
14
15   // Function to be tested:
16   function dummy() {
17       $data = 'This is some text.';
18       echo '<!--<h1>echo() with single quotes</h1>
19       <table border="0" width="90%" cellspacing="3" cellpadding="3" align="center">
20           <tr>
21               <td>' . $data . '</td>
22               <td>' . $data . '</td>
23               <td>' . $data . '</td>
24           </tr>
25           <tr>
26               <td>' . $data . '</td>
27               <td>' . $data . '</td>
28               <td>' . $data . '</td>
29           </tr>
30       </table>
31       <p>End of echo() with single quotes.</p>-->';
32   }
33
34   // Include the Iterate class definition:
35   require ('Benchmark/Iterate.php');
36
37   // Create and start an iteration:
38   $b = new Benchmark_Iterate();
39   $b->run(100, 'dummy');
40
41   // Get the results:
42   $r = $b->get();
43
44   // Print the results:
45   echo "<h1>Results: {$r['iterations']} iterations of the dummy() function took an average of
       {$r['mean']} seconds.</h1>";
46
47   // Delete the object:
48   unset($b);
49   ?>
50   </body>
51   </html>
```

**USING BENCHMARK**

I know what you're thinking: this really isn't a very good use of user-defined functions. True. But to demonstrate the performance hit between straight-up executing a bit of code (Script 12.1 and Figures 12.3 through 12.5) and having a function do the same thing, I want to repeat the single-quotes echo() statement. I have made one alteration: the data is being written within HTML comments so that it doesn't all appear in the Web browser (**Figure 12.7**).

**3.** Include the Iterate class definition.

```
require ('Benchmark/Iterate.php');
```

**4.** Create and start an iteration of the dummy() function.

```
$b = new Benchmark_Iterate();
$b->run(100, 'dummy');
```

I'll invoke this function 100 times and average the results of using it.

**5.** Fetch the results.

```
$r = $b->get();
```

**6.** Print the results.

```
echo "<h1>Results: {$r['iterations']}
→ iterations of the dummy() function
→ took an average of {$r['mean']}
→ seconds.</h1>";
```

In the array returned by get() (see Figure 12.6) the number of iterations can be found indexed at *iterations* and the mean result at *mean*.

**7.** Delete the object and complete the page.

```
unset($b);
?>
</body>
</html>
```

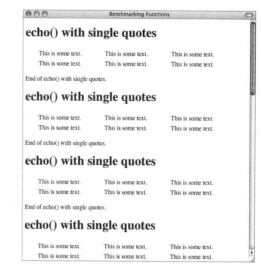

**Figure 12.7** When using the Benchmark_Iterate class, remember that the function is being executed, so whatever that function does, like print some HTML, will happen X number of times.

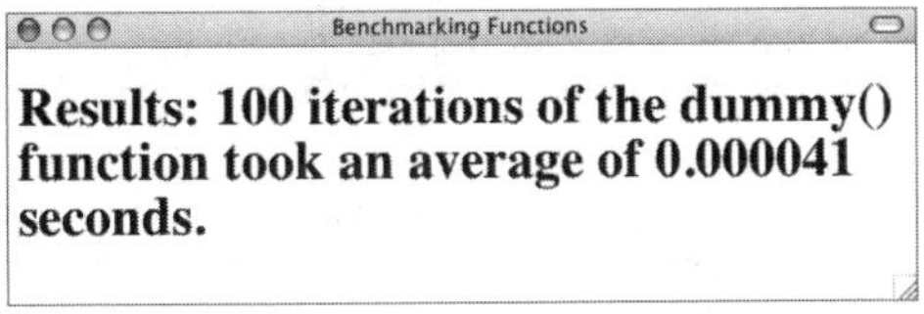

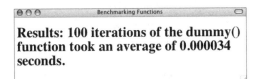

**Figure 12.8** The first 100 executions of the function each took an average of .000041 seconds.

Results: 100 iterations of the dummy() function took an average of 0.000034 seconds.

**Figure 12.9** The second 100 executions of the dummy() function took slightly less time (compare with Figure 12.8).

**8.** Save the file as `iterate.php`, place it in your Web directory, and test in your Web browser (**Figure 12.8**).

**9.** Run the page several times to confirm the results (**Figure 12.9**).

### ✔ Tips

■ You can provide arguments to the function being called by adding them as arguments to the run() method.

```
$b->run($iterations, 'function_name',
→ 21, 'value');
```

■ You can even use the Benchmark_Iterate class to test methods defined in classes.

■ Not to put too much stock in these examples, but the results suggest that executing the same bit of code in your own function (`iterate.php`, Script 12.2) is slightly slower than executing it outside of a function (`timer.php`, Script 12.1). This does make sense.

USING BENCHMARK

# Using HTML_QuickForm

Of the several hundred PEAR packages available, HTML_QuickForm may well be my favorite. And with great reason: it helps you create and process HTML forms. Even after all these years working with PHP, displaying and then handling an HTML form is the overwhelming majority of what I do with the language.

I could write a whole book (maybe a small book) on the subject, and it breaks my heart to know that there isn't room here to discuss everything I love about this package. But I can provide you with enough real-world code to whet your appetite and start you down the path of HTML_QuickForm adulation.

One of the reasons that QuickForm is so usable and successful is that it places all of the form-related events—creating the form, filtering the form data, validating the form, and processing the form data—into one object and one PHP page. This ensures consistency and a minimum of code, two hallmarks of the advanced PHP programmer.

## ✔ Tip

- At the time of this writing, HTML_QuickForm2 is just in the works, without any releases. This is going to be a PHP 5 rewrite of the HTML_QuickForm package. I expect it will function exactly the same as the original, albeit using the PHP 5 object model behind the scenes.

**Table 12.1** The HTML_QuickForm class starts by accepting all of the standard HTML form element types.

| Standard HTML Element Types | |
|---|---|
| **Name** | **Creates a(n)…** |
| button | button |
| checkbox | single check box |
| file | file upload prompt |
| hidden | hidden input |
| image | image input |
| password | password input |
| radio | radio button |
| reset | reset button |
| select | select menu |
| submit | submit button |
| text | text input |
| textarea | textarea field |

**Table 12.2** The HTML_QuickForm class improves upon the standard HTML form element types by creating some of its own.

| Custom QuickForm Element Types | |
|---|---|
| **Name** | **Creates a…** |
| advcheckbox | smarter type of check box |
| autocomplete | JavaScript-enhanced text box |
| date | series of select menus for the month, day, and year |
| group | group of related elements |
| header | label |
| hiddenselect | hidden select menu of set values |
| hierselect | two chained select inputs, the second controlled by the first |
| link | URL link |
| static | block of text |

# Creating a basic form

Like all PEAR classes, QuickForm uses an objective interface. Begin by creating the object:

```
require_once ('HTML/QuickForm.php');
$form = new HTML_QuickForm();
```

When creating this object, you can pass parameters to the constructor, giving the form a name, choosing a method other than POST (the default), setting a target, and so on.

From there you want to add elements to the form. There are many element types, from the standard HTML ones with which you are accustomed (**Table 12.1**) to useful ones defined by QuickForm (**Table 12.2**). The syntax for adding a form element is:

```
$form->addElement('type', 'name',
→ 'prompt', $options);
```

These lines create the inputs seen in **Figures 12.10** and **12.11**:

```
$form->addElement('text', 'email',
→ 'Email Address: ', array('size' => 30,
→ 'maxlength' => 100));

$form->addElement('hidden', 'secret',
→ 'hidden data');

$form->addElement('radio', 'gender',
→ 'Gender: ', 'Male', 'M');

$form->addElement('radio', 'gender',
→ NULL, 'Female', 'F');

$form->addElement('submit', 'submit',
→ 'Submit!');
```

Once you've added all the elements, you show the form using

```
$form->display();
```

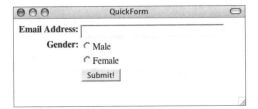

**Figure 12.10** The form contains five elements: one text input, one hidden input, two radio buttons, and a submit button.

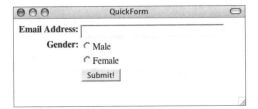

**Figure 12.11** The HTML source of the page (see Figure 12.10) reveals the code generated by the QuickForm class, including an HTML table.

**USING HTML_QUICKFORM**

## To make a registration form:

**1.** Create a new PHP script in your text editor or IDE, beginning with the standard HTML (**Script 12.3**).

```
<!DOCTYPE html PUBLIC "-//W3C//DTD
→ XHTML 1.0 Transitional//EN"
"http://www.w3.org/TR/xhtml1/DTD/
→ xhtml1-transitional.dtd">
<html xmlns="http://www.w3.org/1999/
→ xhtml" xml:lang="en" lang="en">
<head>
    <meta http-equiv="content-type"
→ content="text/html; charset=
→ iso-8859-1" />
    <title>QuickForm</title>
</head>
<body>
<?php # Script 12.3 - quickform.php
```

**2.** Create the QuickForm object.

```
require_once ('HTML/QuickForm.php');
$form = new HTML_QuickForm();
```

**3.** Add a header.

```
$form->addElement('header', NULL,
→ 'Registration Form');
```

The *header* element type is a QuickForm invention. It adds a label to the top of the form.

**4.** Add the elements for the person's name.

```
$form->addElement('select',
→ 'salutation', 'Salutation: ',
→ array(
    'Mr.' => 'Mr.',
    'Miss' => 'Miss',
    'Mrs.' => 'Mrs.',
    'Dr.' => 'Dr.')
);
$form->addElement('text',
→ 'first_name', 'First Name: ');
$form->addElement('text',
→ 'last_name', 'Last Name: ');
```

The person's name will require three inputs. The first is a select menu called *salutation*. The prompt for this item is *Salutation:* and its possible values are *Mr., Miss, Mrs.,* and *Dr.* The next two elements are simple text boxes.

**5.** Add an element for an email address.

```
$form->addElement('text', 'email',
→ 'Email Address: ', array('size' =>
→ 30, 'maxlength' => 100));
```

This is another text box, like those for the person's name, but the box's dimensions are set as well.

*continues on page 460*

**Script 12.3** The HTML_QuickForm class is used to make a registration form.

```
1    <!DOCTYPE html PUBLIC "-//W3C//DTD XHTML 1.0 Transitional//EN"
2         "http://www.w3.org/TR/xhtml1/DTD/xhtml1-transitional.dtd">
3    <html xmlns="http://www.w3.org/1999/xhtml" xml:lang="en" lang="en">
4    <head>
5        <meta http-equiv="content-type" content="text/html; charset=iso-8859-1" />
6        <title>QuickForm</title>
7    </head>
8    <body>
9    <?php # Script 12.3 - quickform.php
10
11   /*  This page creates a registration form.
12    *  This page requires the PEAR HTML_QuickForm package.
13    */
14
15   // Include the class definition:
16   require_once ('HTML/QuickForm.php');
17
18   // Create the form object:
19   $form = new HTML_QuickForm();
20
21   // Add a header:
22   $form->addElement('header', NULL, 'Registration Form');
23
24   // Ask for the person's name:
25   $form->addElement('select', 'salutation', 'Salutation: ',  array(
26       'Mr.' => 'Mr.',
27       'Miss' => 'Miss',
28       'Mrs.' => 'Mrs.',
29       'Dr.' => 'Dr.')
30   );
31   $form->addElement('text', 'first_name', 'First Name: ');
32   $form->addElement('text', 'last_name', 'Last Name: ');
33
34   // Ask for an email address:
35   $form->addElement('text', 'email', 'Email Address: ', array('size' => 30, 'maxlength' => 100));
36
37   // Ask for a password:
38   $form->addElement('password', 'pass1', 'Password: ');
39   $form->addElement('password', 'pass2', 'Confirm Password: ');
40
41   // Add the submit button:
42   $form->addElement('submit', 'submit', 'Register!');
43
44   // Display the form:
45   $form->display();
46
47   // Delete the object:
48   unset($form);
49   ?>
50   </body>
51   </html>
```

**6.** Add two elements for the passwords.

```
$form->addElement('password',
→ 'pass1', 'Password: ');
$form->addElement('password',
→ 'pass2', 'Confirm Password: ');
```

The inputs are both of type password. I think it's best to take passwords twice, since what is typed is not visible to the end user (**Figure 12.12**).

**7.** Add a submit button.

```
$form->addElement('submit',
→ 'submit', 'Register!');
```

**8.** Display the form.

```
$form->display();
```

If you don't include this line, the form will never appear.

**9.** Delete the object and complete the page.

```
unset($form);
?>
</body>
</html>
```

**10.** Save the file as `quickform.php`, place it in your Web directory, and test in your Web browser (**Figure 12.13**).

**11.** View the HTML source of the page to see what QuickForm created (**Figure 12.14**).

## ✔ Tip

■ Naturally, you can tweak how forms are displayed. Check out the discussion of *renderers* in the QuickForm manual.

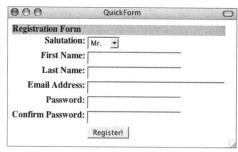

**Figure 12.13** The simple HTML form.

**Figure 12.12** What's typed in a password input is replaced by stars (or other characters) in the Web browser (but you probably already knew that).

**Figure 12.14** The HTML generated by QuickForm.

## Filtering and validating form data

In the `quickform.php` example (Script 12.3), I show how to start using QuickForm to create an HTML form. Those steps generate the HTML required to make the elements. But that's just a drop in the bucket as for what QuickForm can do.

Commonly you'll want to apply some sort of filter to your form data. The `applyFilter()` method does this, taking the name of the element to which this should be applied and the function to apply as its arguments:

```
$form->applyFilter('element_name',
→ 'function_name');
```

To have an element's submitted data trimmed, use:

```
$form->applyFilter('email', 'trim');
```

Or you might want to apply nl2br() to a text area field:

```
$form->applyFilter('comments', 'nl2br');
```

To apply a filter to every element, use the special identifier __ALL__:

```
$form->applyFilter('__ALL__',
→ 'function_name');
```

Along with filters, you can add rules to form elements. Rules can apply validation techniques to the form data. The `addRule()` method is used here:

```
$form->addRule('element_name', 'error
→ message', 'rule_type');
```

*continues on next page*

---

### Setting Default Form Values

If you need to establish default values for your form inputs, rest assured that doing so is possible and stunningly simple. Begin by defining an array whose keys are the element names and whose values are the default values:

```
$defaults = array ('username' =>
→ 'jellyhead',
'age' => 8,
'email' => 'jellyhead@thejelly.org'
);
```

Then invoke the `setDefaults()` method:

```
$form->setDefaults($defaults);
```

All there is to it!

Often the default form values will be based upon data stored in a database. In such a case, if your database columns have the same names as your form elements (which is a good idea anyway), using this data as the default values is a snap:

```
$q = 'SELECT username, age, email
→ FROM users WHERE user_id=3453';
$r = mysql_query($q);
// Check that a row was returned.
$defaults = mysql_fetch_array($r,
→ MYSQL_ASSOC);
$form->setDefaults($defaults);
```

Table 12.3 lists the available rule types. To make a field required, use:

$form->addRule('city', 'Enter your
→ city.', 'required');

If a rule, like *maxlength*, takes another argument, that would come after the rule type:

$form->addRule('age', 'Please enter your
→ age.', 'rangelength', array(1, 120));

Better yet, you can have QuickForm perform not only server-side validation (using PHP) but also client-side (by generating the necessary JavaScript). Just add the word *client* as the fifth argument:

$form->addRule('city', 'Enter your
→ city.', 'required', NULL, 'client');

$form->addRule('age', 'Please enter your
→ age.', 'rangelength', array(1, 120) ,
→ 'client');

## To filter and validate form data:

1. Open quickform.php (Script 12.3) in your text editor or IDE, if it is not already.

2. After adding all the elements but before displaying the form, apply a trim() filter (**Script 12.4**).

   $form->applyFilter('__ALL__',
   → 'trim');

   This one line will run all of the submitted data through PHP's trim() function. Although it may be overkill to do so to the select menu (the salutation) and the submit button, the convenience of trimming all form data through this one line of code more than makes up for the potential performance hit.

*continues on page 464*

**Table 12.3** These rule types are used in the *addRule()* method to add validation routines to a form.

| QuickForm Validation Rules | |
|---|---|
| **NAME** | **MEANING** |
| required | Some value required |
| maxlength | Cannot have more characters than |
| minlength | Must be at least this many characters |
| rangelength | Within a range |
| regex | Matches a regular expression pattern |
| email | Is a valid email address |
| emailorblank | Is a valid email address or is empty |
| lettersonly | Only uses letters |
| alphanumeric | Only uses letters and numbers |
| numeric | Only uses numbers |
| nopunctuation | Anything but punctuation |
| nonzero | A number not starting with zero |
| compare | Compare two or more elements |
| uploadedfile | Element must contain an uploaded file |
| maxfilesize | Uploaded file cannot be bigger than this value |
| mimetype | Uploaded file must be of this type (or types) |
| filename | Uploaded file must have a certain filename |

**Script 12.4** The form (started in Script 12.3) is improved upon by applying one filter and four validation rules.

```
1    <!DOCTYPE html PUBLIC "-//W3C//DTD XHTML 1.0 Transitional//EN"
2            "http://www.w3.org/TR/xhtml1/DTD/xhtml1-transitional.dtd">
3    <html xmlns="http://www.w3.org/1999/xhtml" xml:lang="en" lang="en">
4    <head>
5        <meta http-equiv="content-type" content="text/html; charset=iso-8859-1" />
6        <title>QuickForm</title>
7    </head>
8    <body>
9    <?php # Script 12.4 - quickform.php
10
11   /*   This page creates a registration form.
12    *   This page requires the PEAR HTML_QuickForm package.
13    *   This version adds a filter and validation rules.
14    */
15
16   // Include the class definition:
17   require_once ('HTML/QuickForm.php');
18
19   // Create the form object:
20   $form = new HTML_QuickForm();
21
22   // Add a header:
23   $form->addElement('header', NULL, 'Registration Form');
24
25   // Ask for the person's name:
26   $form->addElement('select', 'salutation', 'Salutation: ', array(
27       'Mr.' => 'Mr.',
28       'Miss' => 'Miss',
29       'Mrs.' => 'Mrs.',
30       'Dr.' => 'Dr.')
31   );
32   $form->addElement('text', 'first_name', 'First Name: ');
33   $form->addElement('text', 'last_name', 'Last Name: ');
34
35   // Ask for an email address:
36   $form->addElement('text', 'email', 'Email Address: ', array('size' => 30, 'maxlength' => 100));
37
38   // Ask for a password:
39   $form->addElement('password', 'pass1', 'Password: ');
40   $form->addElement('password', 'pass2', 'Confirm Password: ');
41
42   // Add the submit button:
43   $form->addElement('submit', 'submit', 'Register!');
44
45   // Apply the filter:
46   $form->applyFilter('__ALL__', 'trim');
47
48   // Add the rules:
49   $form->addRule('first_name', 'Please enter your first name.', 'required', NULL, 'client');
50   $form->addRule('last_name', 'Please enter your last name.', 'required', NULL, 'client');
51   $form->addRule('email', 'Please enter your email address.', 'email', NULL, 'client');
```

*(script continues on next page)*

**3.** Add rules requiring the name fields.

```
$form->addRule('first_name', 'Please
→ enter your first name.',
→ 'required', NULL, 'client');

$form->addRule('last_name', 'Please
→ enter your last name.', 'required',
→ NULL, 'client');
```

The first argument should be the name of the element to which the rule applies. The second is the error message that should appear if the rule isn't obeyed. The message could show in a JavaScript alert window (**Figure 12.15**) or in the HTML page (**Figure 12.16**).

**4.** Add a rule for the email address.

```
$form->addRule('email', 'Please enter
→ your email address.', 'email',
→ NULL, 'client');
```

This rule is of type *email*, meaning that the entered value must be a valid email address.

**Figure 12.15** The client-side validation will use alert windows to warn of rule violations.

**Figure 12.16** If the client's JavaScript is disabled, then the error messages will be printed when PHP handles the form.

**Script 12.4** *continued*

```
52   $form->addRule('pass1', 'Please enter a password.', 'required', NULL, 'client');
53   $form->addRule(array('pass1', 'pass2'), 'Please make sure the two passwords are the same.',
     'compare', NULL, 'client');
54
55   // Display the form:
56   $form->display();
57
58   // Delete the object:
59   unset($form);
60   ?>
61   </body>
62   </html>
```

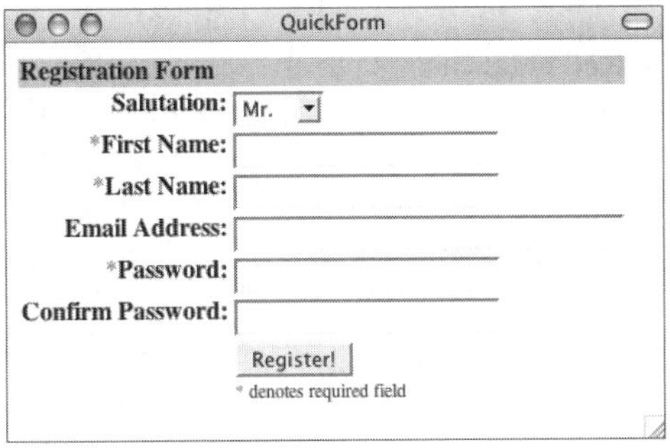


**Figure 12.17** Required fields are automatically marked by QuickForm.

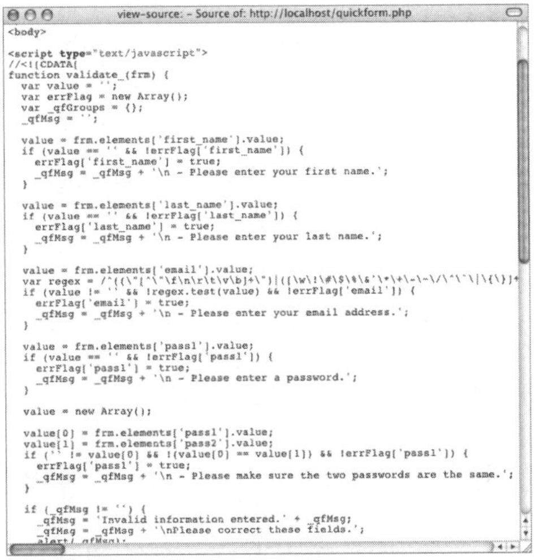

```
view-source: - Source of: http://localhost/quickform.php
<body>

<script type="text/javascript">
//<![CDATA[
function validate_(frm) {
  var value = '';
  var errFlag = new Array();
  var _qfGroups = {};
  _qfMsg = '';

  value = frm.elements['first_name'].value;
  if (value == '' && !errFlag['first_name']) {
    errFlag['first_name'] = true;
    _qfMsg = _qfMsg + '\n - Please enter your first name.';
  }

  value = frm.elements['last_name'].value;
  if (value == '' && !errFlag['last_name']) {
    errFlag['last_name'] = true;
    _qfMsg = _qfMsg + '\n - Please enter your last name.';
  }

  value = frm.elements['email'].value;
  var regex = /^((\"[^\"\f\n\r\t\v\b]+\")|([\w\!\#\$\%\&'\*\+\-\~\/\^\`\|\{\}]+
  if (value != '' && !regex.test(value) && !errFlag['email']) {
    errFlag['email'] = true;
    _qfMsg = _qfMsg + '\n - Please enter your email address.';
  }

  value = frm.elements['pass1'].value;
  if (value == '' && !errFlag['pass1']) {
    errFlag['pass1'] = true;
    _qfMsg = _qfMsg + '\n - Please enter a password.';
  }

  value = new Array();

  value[0] = frm.elements['pass1'].value;
  value[1] = frm.elements['pass2'].value;
  if ('' != value[0] && !(value[0] == value[1]) && !errFlag['pass1']) {
    errFlag['pass1'] = true;
    _qfMsg = _qfMsg + '\n - Please make sure the two passwords are the same.';
  }

  if (_qfMsg != '') {
    _qfMsg = 'Invalid information entered.' + _qfMsg;
    _qfMsg = _qfMsg + '\nPlease correct these fields.';
```

**Figure 12.18** QuickForm generates a slew of JavaScript to perform the client-side validation.

5. Add rules to validate the passwords.

```
$form->addRule('pass1', 'Please enter
→ a password.', 'required', NULL,
→ 'client');
$form->addRule(array('pass1',
→ 'pass2'), 'Please make sure the two
→ passwords are the same.',
→ 'compare', NULL, 'client');
```

Two rules are required to validate the passwords. The first makes sure that something is entered for the first password field. The second checks if the two password fields have the same value. This is accomplished using the *compare* rule, whose default comparison is equality. This particular rule takes as its first argument an array of the elements to be compared.

6. Save the file, place it in your Web directory, and test in your Web browser (**Figure 12.17**).

7. Check the HTML source of the page to see the generated JavaScript (**Figure 12.18**).

## ✔ Tips

- You can create your own validation rules and then declare them for use using `registerRule()`. This could be used, for example, to make sure that a username or email address has not already been registered. The function involved would check your database for that name or address's presence.

- Constants in the form of *__NAME__* (like `__ALL__` in the QuickForm class) are called "magic" constants.

## Processing form data

The final step in the whole form dance is to do something with the form data. QuickForm provides a method that returns a Boolean value indicating if the form passes the server-side validation (if the form fails client-side validation, it'll never get to the server side). This method can be used in a conditional:

```
if ($form->validate()) {
    // Good to go!
}
```

The form data will pass the validate() test if every form element passes all of the applicable rules you've established.

To then access the form values, refer to $form->exportValue('*element_name*'). This method returns the "safe" version of the submitted data: the results after running the data through the filters. You can also fetch all the safe form data as an associative array using:

```
$form->exportValues();
```

To wrap up the QuickForm example, the submitted form data will be displayed if it passes validation.

### To process a QuickForm:

1. Open quickform.php (Script 12.4) in your text editor or IDE, if it is not already.

2. Remove the current invocation of the display() method (**Script 12.5**).

   I will change when this method is called.

*continues on page 468*

**Script 12.5** The final step in the form process is to do something with the submitted data. A conditional added here lists all the submitted data if the form passes validation, and shows the form otherwise.

```
1    <!DOCTYPE html PUBLIC "-//W3C//DTD XHTML 1.0 Transitional//EN"
2         "http://www.w3.org/TR/xhtml1/DTD/xhtml1-transitional.dtd">
3    <html xmlns="http://www.w3.org/1999/xhtml" xml:lang="en" lang="en">
4    <head>
5        <meta http-equiv="content-type" content="text/html; charset=iso-8859-1" />
6        <title>QuickForm</title>
7    </head>
8    <body>
9    <?php # Script 12.5 - quickform.php
10
11   /*  This page creates a registration form.
12    *  This page requires the PEAR HTML_QuickForm package.
13    *  This is the final version of the page.
14    */
15
16   // Include the class definition:
17   require_once ('HTML/QuickForm.php');
18
19   // Create the form object:
20   $form = new HTML_QuickForm();
21
22   // Add a header:
23   $form->addElement('header', NULL, 'Registration Form');
```

*(script continues on next page)*

**Script 12.5** *continued*

```
24
25    // Ask for the person's name:
26    $form->addElement('select', 'salutation', 'Salutation: ', array(
27        'Mr.' => 'Mr.',
28        'Miss' => 'Miss',
29        'Mrs.' => 'Mrs.',
30        'Dr.' => 'Dr.')
31    );
32    $form->addElement('text', 'first_name', 'First Name: ');
33    $form->addElement('text', 'last_name', 'Last Name: ');
34
35    // Ask for an email address:
36    $form->addElement('text', 'email', 'Email Address: ', array('size' => 30, 'maxlength' => 100));
37
38    // Ask for a password:
39    $form->addElement('password', 'pass1', 'Password: ');
40    $form->addElement('password', 'pass2', 'Confirm Password: ');
41
42    // Add the submit button:
43    $form->addElement('submit', 'submit', 'Register!');
44
45    // Apply the filter:
46    $form->applyFilter('__ALL__', 'trim');
47
48    // Add the rules:
49    $form->addRule('first_name', 'Please enter your first name.', 'required', NULL, 'client');
50    $form->addRule('last_name', 'Please enter your last name.', 'required', NULL, 'client');
51    $form->addRule('email', 'Please enter your email address.', 'email', NULL, 'client');
52    $form->addRule('pass1', 'Please enter a password.', 'required', NULL, 'client');
53    $form->addRule(array('pass1', 'pass2'), 'Please make sure the two passwords are the same.',
          'compare', NULL, 'client');
54
55    // Display or handle the form:
56    if ($form->validate()) { // Handle
57
58        // Just print out the received data:
59        echo '<h1>The following information has been received:</h1>';
60        $data = $form->exportValues();
61        foreach ($data as $k => $v) {
62        echo "<p><em>$k</em> $v</p>\n";
63        }
64
65    } else { // Show
66        $form->display();
67    }
68
69    // Delete the object:
70    unset($form);
71    ?>
72    </body>
73    </html>
```

**3.** Just before deleting the object, begin a conditional that checks if the form passes validation.

```
if ($form->validate()) {
```

This conditional checks if the form passes all the validation tests. If so, the form data should be handled in some way.

**4.** Print out the filtered data.

```
echo '<h1>The following information
→ has been received:</h1>';
$data = $form->exportValues();
foreach ($data as $k => $v) {
    echo "<p><em>$k</em> $v</p>\n";
}
```

In all likelihood you'll want to store this data in a database, send it in an email, or whatever, but for demonstration purposes, it'll be reprinted in the Web browser.

**5.** Complete the conditional.

```
} else {
    $form->display();
}
```

**6.** Save the file, place it in your Web directory, and test in your Web browser (**Figures 12.19** and **12.20**).

### ✔ Tip

■ Another way to handle the form is to establish a function to process the data:

```
function process_data($data) {
    // Do something with $data.
    // Use $data['element_name'].
}
$form->process('process_data');
```

---

### Escaping Data for Databases

For any incoming data that will be used in a query, I like to make sure it's safe by using a database-specific escaping function, like `mysql_real_escape_string()` for MySQL. I wrap this function call inside of my own function, which will also strip any existing slashes if Magic Quotes is on. My resulting function looks like:

```
function escape_data ($data) {
    global $dbc;
    if (get_magic_quotes_gpc()) $data = stripslashes($data);
    return mysql_real_escape_string (trim ($data), $dbc);
}
```

Having defined this function, I can apply it to all form data using `applyFilter()`:

```
$form->applyFilter('__ALL__', 'escape_data');
```

Now all of the form data will be safe to use in a query. Because this function also trims the data, I don't need to apply that as a filter.

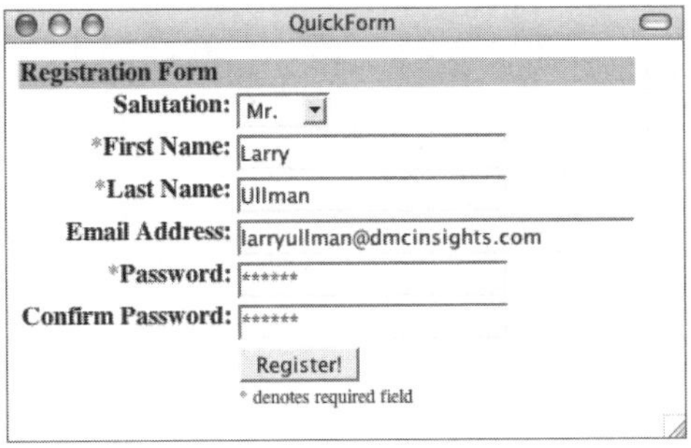

**Figure 12.19** The complete HTML form. The data entered here is validated, filtered, and then redisplayed (Figure 12.20).

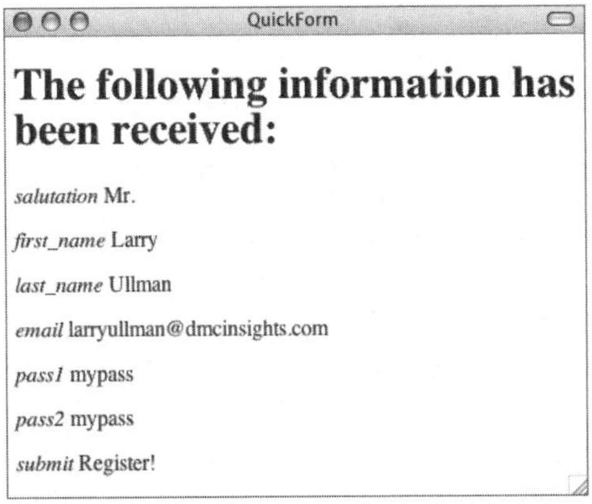

**Figure 12.20** The processed form data.

# Using Mail_Mime

Next up on my march through PEAR is the Mail_Mime package (and, ever so slightly, Mail). PHP's built-in mail() function is simple to use, but it does have its shortcomings. For starters, you cannot use it with an SMTP server that requires authentication. Second, it's not very easy to use it for sending HMTL email or email with attachments. A solution is to use PEAR's Mail and Mail_Mime classes. The documentation for both is slight, but I can provide you with more than enough functional knowledge.

As a preview to what you'll see in the next two examples, the Mail_Mime class is used to create the proper email code (there are pages and pages of documentation as to how emails are formatted). In layman's terms, Mail_Mime turns the information you need to send—be it HTML or attachments—into the proper syntax for an email message. The Mail class is then used to send that message.

## Sending HTML email

To start, you'll need to include two class definitions (after having installed both PEAR packages, of course):

```
require_once ('Mail.php');
require_once ('Mail/mime.php');
```

You'll also want to establish your message body. For HTML emails, you should create a plain text and an HTML equivalent. For the HTML content, it should be a complete HTML document:

```
$text = 'Plain text version';
$html = '<!DOCTYPE html…

</body>
</html>';
```

Now create a new Mail_Mime object:

```
$mime = new Mail_Mime();
```

*continues on next page*

USING MAIL_MIME

Using the object's methods, set the email's body for both the plain text and the HTML versions:

```
$mime->setTXTBody($text);
```

```
$mime->setHTMLBody($html);
```

Before sending the email, the extra headers have to be generated: who the email is from and what the subject is. There are separate methods for each:

```
$mime->setFrom('this@address.com');
```

```
$mime->setSubject('Your Email Subject');
```

You can also use addCc() and addBcc() to carbon copy and blind carbon copy other addresses.

Now that all this information has been stored in the object, use the get() and headers() methods to fetch the generated code for use with the Mail class:

```
$body = $mime->get();
```

```
$headers = $mime->headers();
```

Note that you must call these two functions in this order as the headers() method partly uses the result of the get() method.

## Using SMTP with Mail

One of the features of the Mail class is that it can send an email using three different methods: PHP's mail() function, the server's sendmail application, or an SMTP server. PHP's mail() function can also use an SMTP server, but not if that server requires authentication.

If running PHP on your own computer, you can install a free SMTP server or just tap into one likely provided by your Internet provider or Web host. To do so, first create an array containing the SMTP server address and your authentication information:

```
$smtp['host'] = 'smtp.hostname.com';
```

```
$smtp['auth'] = true;
```

```
$smtp['username'] =
→ 'username@hostname.com';
```

```
$smtp['password'] = 'password';
```

The *auth* element just indicates that authentication should be used. Now use this array as the second parameter in the Mail factory() method:

```
$mail =& Mail::factory('smtp',
→ $smtp);
```

**Figure 12.21** Aside from the all-capital *BODY* and *HEADERS*, this is the code generated by the `Mail_Mime` class.

The result is two pieces of data that can be used in an email (print their values to see the end result, **Figure 12.21**). Finally, the `Mail` class can be used to send the actual email.

To do so, you don't actually create an object of type `Mail` but rather invoke the class's `factory()` method directly:

`$mail =& Mail::factory($backend);`

For the `$backend` value, this can be: *mail* (PHP's built-in `mail()` function); *sendmail* (if installed on the server); or *smtp* (to use an SMTP server). Assuming you can use the `mail()` function or sendmail on the server already, either of those options is fine. To use an SMTP server, see the sidebar "Using SMTP with Mail."

The final step is to send the email, providing the *to* address, the headers, and the body:

`$mail->send('to@address.com', $headers,`
`→ $body);`

## To send HTML email:

**1.** Create a new PHP script in your text editor or IDE, starting with the standard HTML (**Script 12.6**).

```
<!DOCTYPE html PUBLIC "-//W3C//DTD
→ XHTML 1.0 Transitional//EN"
"http://www.w3.org/TR/xhtml1/DTD/
→ xhtml1-transitional.dtd">
<html
xmlns="http://www.w3.org/1999/xhtml"
→ xml:lang="en" lang="en">
```

```
<head>
    <meta http-equiv="content-type"
content="text/html; charset=iso-8859-
1" />
    <title>Sending HTML
Email</title>
</head>
<body>
<?php # Script 12.6 - mail_html.php
```

*continues on page 474*

**Script 12.6** This sequence of potentially confusing code simplifies the complex process of sending HTML email (Figure 12.23).

```
                                          Script
1    <!DOCTYPE html PUBLIC "-//W3C//DTD XHTML 1.0 Transitional//EN"
2            "http://www.w3.org/TR/xhtml1/DTD/xhtml1-transitional.dtd">
3    <html xmlns="http://www.w3.org/1999/xhtml" xml:lang="en" lang="en">
4    <head>
5        <meta http-equiv="content-type" content="text/html; charset=iso-8859-1" />
6        <title>Sending HTML Email</title>
7    </head>
8    <body>
9    <?php # Script 12.6 - mail_html.php
10
11   /*  This page sends an HTML email.
12    *  This page requires the PEAR Mail and Mail_Mime packages.
13    */
14
15   // Include the class definitions:
16   require_once ('Mail.php');
17   require_once ('Mail/mime.php');
18
19   // Define the data to use in the email body:
20   $text = 'Testing HTML Email
21   ----------
22   Just some simple HTML.';
23
24   $html = '<!DOCTYPE html PUBLIC "-//W3C//DTD XHTML 1.0 Transitional//EN"
25            "http://www.w3.org/TR/xhtml1/DTD/xhtml1-transitional.dtd">
26   <html xmlns="http://www.w3.org/1999/xhtml" xml:lang="en" lang="en">
27   <head>
28       <meta http-equiv="content-type" content="text/html; charset=iso-8859-1" />
29       <title>Testing HTML Email</title>
```

**Script 12.6** *continued*

```
        ⊖ ⊖ ⊖                          📄 Script
30    </head>
31    <body>
32    <h1>Testing HTML Email</h1>
33    <hr />
34    <p>Just some <em>simple</em> HTML.</p>
35    </body>
36    </html>';
37
38    // Create the Mail_Mime object:
39    $mime = new Mail_Mime();
40
41    // Set the email body:
42    $mime->setTXTBody($text);
43    $mime->setHTMLBody($html);
44
45    // Set the headers:
46    $mime->setFrom('me@address.com');
47    $mime->setSubject('Testing HTML Email');
48
49    // Get the formatted code:
50    $body = $mime->get();
51    $headers = $mime->headers();
52
53    // Invoke the Mail class's factory() method:
54    $mail =& Mail::factory('mail');
55
56    // Send the email.
57    $mail->send('you@address.com', $headers, $body);
58
59    // Delete the objects:
60    unset($mime, $mail);
61
62    // Print a message, if you want.
63    echo '<p>The mail has been sent (hopefully).</p>';
64    ?>
65    </body>
66    </html>
```

**2.** Include the class definitions.

```
require_once ('Mail.php');
require_once ('Mail/mime.php');
```

**3.** Define the email body, in both plain text and HTML formats.

```
$text = 'Testing HTML Email
----------
Just some simple HTML.';
$html = '<!DOCTYPE html PUBLIC "-
→ //W3C//DTD XHTML 1.0
→ Transitional//EN"
"http://www.w3.org/TR/xhtml1/DTD/
→ xhtml1-transitional.dtd">
<html xmlns="http://www.w3.org/1999/
→ xhtml" xml:lang="en" lang="en">
<head>
    <meta http-equiv="content-type"
→ content="text/html; charset=
→ iso-8859-1" />
    <title>Testing HTML
→ Email</title>
</head>
<body>
<h1>Testing HTML Email</h1>
<hr />
<p>Just some <em>simple</em>
→ HTML.</p>
</body>
</html>';
```

The important part here is that the HTML version is a complete HTML page, like one you would view in your Web browser.

**4.** Create the `Mail_Mime` object.

```
$mime = new Mail_Mime();
```

**5.** Set the email body.

```
$mime->setTXTBody($text);
$mime->setHTMLBody($html);
```

These two methods establish the body of the email, one in plain text and the other in HTML.

**6.** Set the headers.

```
$mime->setFrom('me@address.com');
$mime->setSubject('Testing HTML
→ Email');
```

You should obviously change the *from* value to something meaningful. If using an SMTP server, you'll likely need to use that server's corresponding address.

**7.** Retrieve the formatted code.

```
$body = $mime->get();
$headers = $mime->headers();
```

These two functions retrieve the generated result of using the `Mail_Mime` class.

**8.** Invoke the `Mail` class's `factory()` method.

```
$mail =& Mail::factory('mail');
```

I'm glossing over this piece of syntax, which isn't that important so long as you follow it exactly. For the `factory()` function's argument, use *mail*, *sendmail*, or *smtp*. For details on the SMTP option, see the sidebar "Using SMTP with Mail."

**9.** Send the email.

```
$mail->send('you@address.com',
→ $headers, $body);
```

Change the *to* address here to your email address.

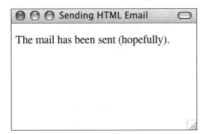

Figure 12.22 The resulting Web page is nothing to be excited about; the real magic occurs behind the scenes.

Figure 12.23 The simple, but functionally valid, HTML email.

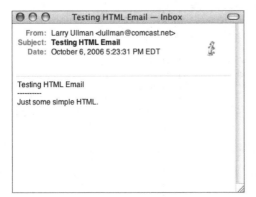

Figure 12.24 The version of the message seen by mail clients that do not allow HTML email.

**10.** Delete the objects and complete the page.

```
unset($mime, $mail);
echo '<p>The mail has been sent
→ (hopefully).</p>';
?>
</body>
</html>
```

The echo() statement is used here just so that something shows in the Web browser.

**11.** Save the file as mail_html.php, place it in your Web directory, and test in your Web browser (**Figure 12.22**).

**12.** Check your email to see the result (**Figure 12.23**).

**13.** If possible, view the plain text alternative version of the email (**Figure 12.24**).

Most mail clients have some way for you to view the plain text alternative. Check your menus, help files, or documentation for suggestions.

# Sending HTML with images

One of the reasons the resulting email in the preceding example is so plain (Figure 12.23) is that it lacks any images, a rudimentary element in Web pages. There are two ways you can incorporate images in your HTML emails. The first is easy and foolproof: just use the img tag, with an absolute URI for the image.

```
<p>Some HTML</p>
<img src="http://www.yoursite.com/path/
→ to/image.ext" />
```

Using this method, when the email is received, the mail client will attempt to download that image from that URI. But this method can also be frowned upon because it's used by very bad people to track when spam reaches an address (the request for the image sends a signal to that server indicating that the address was good).

An alternative is to use the Mail_Mime addHTMLImage() method. Start by putting the img tag in the HTML, but just use the image's exact name as the source:

```
$html = '...<img src="image.ext" />...';
```

Then, add the image using the class:

```
$mime->addHTMLImage('/path/to/
→ image.ext);
```

Then add the HTML to the email:

```
$mime->setHTMLBody($html);
```

## To send email with images:

1. Open mail_html.php (Script 12.6) in your text editor or IDE, if it is not already open.

2. If you want, change the page title (line 6, **Script 12.7**).

   ```
   <title>Sending HTML Email with an
   → Image</title>
   ```

*continues on page 478*

**Script 12.7** An image is built into the HTML email sent by this script.

```
1    <!DOCTYPE html PUBLIC "-//W3C//DTD XHTML 1.0 Transitional//EN"
2         "http://www.w3.org/TR/xhtml1/DTD/xhtml1-transitional.dtd">
3    <html xmlns="http://www.w3.org/1999/xhtml" xml:lang="en" lang="en">
4    <head>
5        <meta http-equiv="content-type" content="text/html; charset=iso-8859-1" />
6        <title>Sending HTML Email with an Image</title>
7    </head>
8    <body>
9    <?php # Script 12.7 - mail_image.php
10
11   /*  This page sends an HTML email.
12    *  This page requires the PEAR Mail and Mail_Mime packages.
13    *  The email now contains an image.
14    */
15
16   // Include the class definitions:
17   require_once ('Mail.php');
18   require_once ('Mail/mime.php');
19
20   // Define the data to use in the email body:
21   $text = 'Testing HTML Email with an Image
22   ----------
23   Just some simple HTML.
```

**Script 12.7** *continued*

```
24    You are not going to see the logo.';
25
26    $html = '<!DOCTYPE html PUBLIC "-//W3C//DTD XHTML 1.0 Transitional//EN"
27           "http://www.w3.org/TR/xhtml1/DTD/xhtml1-transitional.dtd">
28    <html xmlns="http://www.w3.org/1999/xhtml" xml:lang="en" lang="en">
29    <head>
30        <meta http-equiv="content-type" content="text/html; charset=iso-8859-1" />
31        <title>Testing HTML Email with an Image</title>
32    </head>
33    <body>
34    <h1>Testing HTML Email with an Image</h1>
35    <hr />
36    <p>Just some <em>simple</em> HTML.</p>
37    <img src="logo2.png" alt="my logo" />
38    <p>That is what my logo would look like randomly placed in an email.</p>
39    </body>
40    </html>';
41
42    // Create the Mail_Mime object:
43    $mime = new Mail_Mime();
44
45    // Add the image:
46    $mime->addHTMLImage('logo2.png');
47
48    // Set the email body:
49    $mime->setTXTBody($text);
50    $mime->setHTMLBody($html);
51
52    // Set the headers:
53    $mime->setFrom('me@address.com');
54    $mime->setSubject('Testing HTML Email with an Image');
55
56    // Get the formatted code:
57    $body = $mime->get();
58    $headers = $mime->headers();
59
60    // Invoke the Mail class' factory() method:
61    $mail =& Mail::factory('mail');
62
63    // Send the email.
64    $mail->send('you@address.com', $headers, $body);
65
66    // Delete the objects:
67    unset($mime, $mail);
68
69    // Print a message, if you want.
70    echo '<p>The mail has been sent (hopefully).</p>';
71    ?>
72    </body>
73    </html>
```

3. If you want, update the plain text version of the email.

```
$text = 'Testing HTML Email with an
→ Image
----------

Just some simple HTML.
You are not going to see the logo.';
```

4. Change the definition of the HMTL version of the email body so that it includes an image.

```
$html = '<!DOCTYPE html PUBLIC "-
→ //W3C//DTD XHTML 1.0
→ Transitional//EN"
"http://www.w3.org/TR/xhtml1/DTD/
→ xhtml1-transitional.dtd">
<html
xmlns="http://www.w3.org/1999/xhtml"
→ xml:lang="en" lang="en">
<head>
    <meta http-equiv="content-type"
→ content="text/html; charset=
→ iso-8859-1" />
    <title>Testing HTML Email with
→ an Image</title>
</head>
<body>
<h1>Testing HTML Email with an
→ Image</h1>
<hr />
<p>Just some
→ <em>simple</em> HTML.</p>
<img src="logo2.png" alt="my logo" />
<p>That is what my logo would look
→ like randomly placed in an
→ email.</p>
</body>
</html>';
```

The important addition here is the
→ line

```
<img src="logo2.png" alt="my logo" />
```

I've also made minor modifications to the title and other text.

## Sending Email with Attachments

How to send emails with attachments is another common question PHP programmers have. Thanks to `Mail_Mime`, it's surprisingly simple. Whether you're creating plain text or HTML emails, just use the `addAttachment()` method:

```
$mime->addAttachment($file_name,
→ $file_type);
```

The first argument used is the full name and path to the file on the server. This might be `../path/to/mydoc.doc` or `C:\data\spreadsheet.xls`. The second argument is the file's type, like `application/pdf`.

With this one line of code, assuming that it can find the file on the server, you can quickly send attachments with your emails.

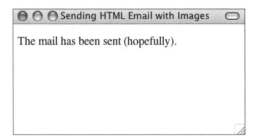

**Figure 12.25** Not much new happening here, but check your email (Figure 12.26)!

**Figure 12.26** The received email now includes an image (built into the message, not fetched from a server).

**Figure 12.27** The plain text alternative of the message shows the image as an attachment (in my mail client).

**5.** After creating the object, add the image.

`$mime->addHTMLImage('logo2.png');`

Because the `src` of the image in the HTML is `logo2.png`, the name of the file here must match that exactly. This code assumes that the file `logo2.png` is in the same directory as this script. To include an image located elsewhere, use an absolute or relative path:

`$mime->addHTMLImage('/path/to/` → `logo2.png');`

Whatever the location of the file on the server, the `src` in the HTML should remain just `logo2.png`.

**6.** If you want, update the email's subject.

`$mime->setSubject('Testing HTML Email` → `with an Image');`

**7.** Save the file as `mail_image.php`, place it in your Web directory, and test in your Web browser (**Figure 12.25**).

**8.** Check your email to see the result (**Figure 12.26**).

**9.** If possible, view the plain text alternative version of the email (**Figure 12.27**).

# AJAX

Of all the buzzwords to enter the computer lexicon in the past couple of years, Ajax may be the "buzziest." Ajax, which stands for *Asynchronous JavaScript and XML* (or not, depending upon whom you ask), changes the client/server relationship so that server interactions can take place without any apparent action on the part of the client. In truth, Ajax is just a label given to functionality that's been present for years, but sometimes a good label helps, and when a powerhouse like Google uses Ajax (for Gmail, Google Suggest, and more), people pay attention.

In this chapter I provide an introduction to the Ajax concept, with PHP and MySQL as its back end. As Ajax is still comparatively new, there are new ideas and debates for each aspect of the technology, but in two different examples I can demonstrate the entire soup-to-nuts of what Ajax is about and, in the process, provide real-world code. Because the heart of Ajax really is JavaScript and the Document Object Model (DOM), the PHP in this chapter will be basic. As sophisticated JavaScript may be new territory for you, the chapter concludes with a discussion of debugging techniques, as resolving Ajax problems requires special approaches.

# Introduction to Ajax

Before getting into the code, you should understand what, exactly, Ajax is and how it differs from what you currently do with PHP. As you know, PHP is primarily a Web-based technology (although it can be used from the command line—see Chapter 11, "PHP's Command-Line Interface"). This means that PHP does its thing whenever a server request is made. A user goes to a Web page or submits a form; the request is made of the server; PHP handles that request and returns the result. Each execution of some PHP code requires an active request and a redrawing of the Web browser (**Figure 13.1**). For the end user, this means they see their browser leave the current page, access the new one, download the new page's content, and display the content, repeating as necessary.

The secret to Ajax is that it can make the server request happen behind the scenes while still changing what the user sees as if they actively made the server request. JavaScript is really the key technology here.

With an Ajax transaction, JavaScript, which does its thing within a Web browser, makes the request of the server and then handles that request. The Web page can then be updated without ever seeming to leave the current page (**Figure 13.2**). In action, this might mean:

1. The end user goes to a Web page.

2. The user types something in a box, clicks a button, or drags something with their cursor.

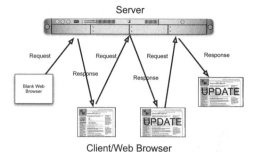

**Figure 13.1** The typical client/server model, where each data transfer is apparent to the end user.

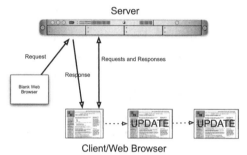

**Figure 13.2** The Ajax model, where the client/server data transfer can happen unbeknownst to the end user.

3. Whatever the user does in Step 2 triggers JavaScript to request something from the server.

4. The server handles that request (using PHP in this chapter), returning some data.

5. JavaScript receives that data and uses it to update the Web page, without reloading it.

Looking at all the technologies involved, you start with (X)HTML, which is the foundation of all Web pages. Then there's JavaScript, which runs in the Web browser, asks for and receives data from the server, and manipulates the HTML by referring to the Document Object Model (DOM, an object-based representation of the elements of a Web page). And finally, on the server, you have our friend PHP. The last technology commonly involved is XML (Extensible Markup Language), which *can be* used in the data transfer. I say "can be," because you don't have to use XML. In fact, this chapter has two examples—one simple, one complex—without any XML.

### ✔ Tip

- Jesse James Garrett coined the term Ajax in February 2005. He has since claimed that Ajax is not an acronym. It just, you know, seems like an acronym.

## What Is Asynchronous?

One of the key components of Ajax is its *asynchronous* behavior. This term, which literally means *not synchronous*, refers to a type of communication where one side (say, the client) does not have to wait for the other side (the server) before doing something else.

In an asynchronous transaction, the user can do something that makes the JavaScript request data from the server. While the JavaScript is awaiting that data, which it'll then display in the Web browser, the user is free to do other things, including other things that involve JavaScript. So the asynchronicity makes the experience more seamless.

On the other hand, you can perform *synchronous* transactions, if you are in a situation where the user should wait until the data is in.

INTRODUCTION TO AJAX

# A Simple Example

One of my personal favorite best uses of Ajax starts with a commonplace Web presence: a registration form (**Figure 13.3**). When using PHP to validate a registration form, there are many steps you'd take, from checking that all the required fields are filled out to validating the values in certain fields (e.g., a valid email address, a valid date of birth). If the registration process requires a username for logging in, PHP would also check the database to see if that username is available. With a traditional model, this check couldn't take place until the form was submitted. With Ajax, this check can take place prior to form submission (**Figure 13.4**), saving the user from having to go back, think up a new username, and resubmit the form, repeating as necessary.

In developing this Ajax example, I'll work the application backward, which I think makes it easiest to understand the whole process (it also leaves the newer information toward the end). For the server-side stuff, it's really basic PHP and MySQL. I won't develop it fully, but you shouldn't have a problem fleshing it out when it comes time for you to implement this in a real site.

**Figure 13.3** The basic registration form.

**Figure 13.4** The availability of the requested username will be indicated prior to submitting the form to the server.

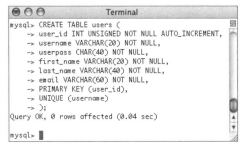

**Figure 13.5** I'll be creating the table in the test database, using the mysql client.

```
mysql> CREATE TABLE users (
    -> user_id INT UNSIGNED NOT NULL AUTO_INCREMENT,
    -> username VARCHAR(20) NOT NULL,
    -> userpass CHAR(40) NOT NULL,
    -> first_name VARCHAR(20) NOT NULL,
    -> last_name VARCHAR(40) NOT NULL,
    -> email VARCHAR(60) NOT NULL,
    -> PRIMARY KEY (user_id),
    -> UNIQUE (username)
    -> );
Query OK, 0 rows affected (0.04 sec)

mysql>
```

**Figure 13.6** Creating the table.

# Creating the database

This example will involve user registration. This might be part of a forum, e-commerce site, or whatever. At the very minimum, a users table is necessary, with fields for the user ID, username, password, first name, last name, and email address. For demonstration purposes, some sample data needs to be entered as well.

## To create and populate the database:

1. Access your MySQL database using the mysql client.

   You can also use phpMyAdmin or whatever other interface you prefer.

2. Select the test database (**Figure 13.5**).

   USE test;

   Since this is just an example, I'll create the table within the test database.

3. Create the users table (**Figure 13.6**).

   CREATE TABLE users (

   user_id INT UNSIGNED NOT NULL

   → AUTO_INCREMENT,

   username VARCHAR(20) NOT NULL,

   userpass CHAR(40) NOT NULL,

   first_name VARCHAR(20) NOT NULL,

   last_name VARCHAR(40) NOT NULL,

   email VARCHAR(60) NOT NULL,

   PRIMARY KEY (user_id),

   UNIQUE (username)

   );

   The table contains just six fields; you'll likely want to expand it for your real-world needs. The user_id is the primary key, and the username field must be unique for each row. I set the userpass field as a CHAR(40), as I'll encrypt passwords using SHA(), which returns a string 40 characters long. The table also has slots for the user's name and email address.

A SIMPLE EXAMPLE

**4.** Populate the users table (**Figure 13.7**).

```
INSERT INTO users (username,
→ userpass, first_name, last_name,
→ email) VALUES
('sherif', SHA('deadwood1'), 'Seth',
→ 'Bullock', 'seth@address.com'),
('Al', SHA('deadwood2'), 'Al',
→ 'Swearengen', 'al@thegem.org'),
('Garret', SHA('deadwood3'), 'Alma',
→ 'Garret', 'agarret@address.net'),
('starman', SHA('deadwood4'), 'Sol',
→ 'Star', 'solstar@bank.com');
```

I'm just throwing in a few random records. You can use your own, type this query exactly as it is, or download the SQL commands from the book's corresponding Web site.

**5.** Confirm the contents of the users table (**Figure 13.8**).

```
SELECT * FROM users;
```

I'm going to focus on debugging quite a bit in this chapter because there are many technologies being used and you are probably less familiar with some of them. The first debugging technique is to know—for certain—what data you have in the server.

### ✔ Tip

■ You don't have to use MySQL for this example; you could use PostgreSQL, Oracle, SQLite, a text file, or even a simple array.

**Figure 13.7** Populating the table.

**Figure 13.8** Make sure you know what's in your database before proceeding! Doing so will make debugging that much easier.

## Programming the PHP

In discussing this example, I state that the Ajax aspect of the application will be to check that a username is available prior to submitting the form to the server. This PHP script, which is the server side of the Ajax process, just needs to check the availability of a provided username.

The script will be written so that it accepts a username in the URL; the script is invoked using:

```
http://hostname/checkusername.php?
→ username=XXXX
```

The PHP script then runs a query on the database to see if this username—*XXXX*—has already been registered. Finally the script should return a message indicating the availability of that username. This should all be quite easy for even a beginning PHP programmer.

One little quirk with this page: It will not use any HTML (gasp!). As this page won't be intended to be viewed directly in a Web browser, HTML is unnecessary.

## To create the PHP script:

**1.** Create a new PHP script in your text editor or IDE (**Script 13.1**).

```
<?php # Script 13.1 -
→ checkusername.php
```

**Script 13.1** This simple PHP script takes a submitted username (passed in the URL) and sees if it is already recorded in the database. Simple text messages are displayed, indicating the status.

```
 ⊖ ⊖ ⊖                                    📄 Script
1    <?php # Script 13.1 - checkusername.php
2
3    /*  This page checks a database to see if
4     *  $_GET['username'] has already been registered.
5     *  The page will be called by JavaScript.
6     *  The page returns a simple text message.
7     *  No HTML is required by this script!
8     */
9
10   // Validate that the page received $_GET['username']:
11   if (isset($_GET['username'])) {
12
13       // Connect to the database:
14       $dbc = @mysqli_connect ('localhost', 'username', 'password', 'test') OR die ('The
     availability of this username will be confirmed upon form submission.');
15
16       // Define the query:
17       $q = sprintf("SELECT user_id FROM users WHERE username='%s'", mysqli_real_escape_string($dbc,
     trim($_GET['username'])));
18
19       // Execute the query:
20       $r = mysqli_query($dbc, $q);
21
22       // Report upon the results:
23       if (mysqli_num_rows($r) == 1) {
24           echo 'The username is unavailable!';
25       } else {
26           echo 'The username is available!';
27       }
28
29       mysqli_close($dbc);
30
31   } else { // No username supplied!
32
33       echo 'Please enter a username.';
34
35   }
36   ?>
```

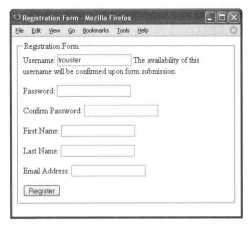

**Figure 13.9** If the PHP script could not connect to the database, then the availability of the username could not be determined. That information could be shown in the registration form.

2. Validate that the page received a username.

```
if (isset($_GET['username'])) {
```

No use in querying the database without a username!

3. Connect to the database.

```
$dbc = @mysqli_connect ('localhost',
→ 'username', 'password', 'test') OR
→ die ('The availability of this
→ username will be confirmed upon
→ form submission.');
```

For sake of simplicity, I'm hard-coding the database connection into this script (as opposed to including a MySQL file for that purpose). Note that I'm using the MySQL Improved extension, available as of PHP 5 and MySQL 4.1. If you're using older versions of either technology, you'll want to switch to the `mysql_*` functions.

You will likely need to change the MySQL access information provided here to values that correspond to a valid username/password/hostname for your server.

If a connection to the database cannot be established, this page returns a generic message. This isn't strictly necessary, but remember that anything returned by this script will be displayed on the HTML form page (**Figure 13.9**).

*continues on next page*

**4.** Define and execute the query.

```
$q = sprintf("SELECT user_id FROM
→ users WHERE username='%s'",
→ mysqli_real_escape_string($dbc,
→ trim($_GET['username'])));
$r = mysqli_query($dbc, $q);
```

The query will be

```
SELECT user_id FROM users WHERE
→ username='XXXX'
```

To create it, I use the `sprintf()` function (see Chapter 1, "Advanced PHP Techniques," if you are not familiar with it). The provided username will be trimmed and run through the `mysqli_real_escape_string()` function for improved security.

**5.** Report upon the results of the query.

```
if (mysqli_num_rows($r) == 1) {
    echo 'The username is
→ unavailable!';
} else {
    echo 'The username is
→ available!';
}
```

This script just prints a string indicating the results of the query. These are the two primary responses, assuming there were no errors.

**6.** Close the database connection and complete the page.

```
    mysqli_close($dbc);
} else {
    echo 'Please enter a username.';
}
?>
```

The `else` clause here applies if no username was supplied when calling the script.

**7.** Save the file as `checkusername.php` and place it in your Web directory.

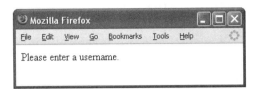

**Figure 13.10** Without providing a username in the URL, this is the result.

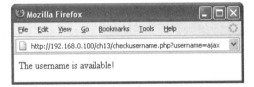

**Figure 13.11** If the provided username has not been registered, the PHP script displays this message (and nothing more).

**Figure 13.12** If the provided username has been taken, this is the result.

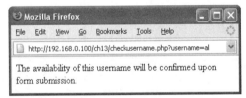

**Figure 13.13** If the PHP script could not connect to the database in order to perform the query, this message is shown.

## Testing the PHP

To fully understand what's happening in the client, it's best to understand what the server side of things is doing. Toward that end, you should quickly confirm what checkusername.php does in different situations. To do so, run it directly in your Web browser, offering different usernames in the URL.

You should know by now how to test a PHP script, of course. The important point here is that debugging an Ajax application begins by confirming what the server is sending back to the client.

### To test the PHP script:

1. Load checkusername.php in your Web browser (**Figure 13.10**).

2. Rerun the script, providing an available username in the URL (**Figure 13.11**).

   Doing so is just a matter of adding ?username=*XXXX* to the end of the URL.

3. Rerun the script, providing an unavailable username in the URL (**Figure 13.12**).

   Use one of the registered usernames (see Figure 13.8 or your own users table contents). So I might test the script with ?username=al.

4. If you want, check the result if the PHP script couldn't connect to the database (**Figure 13.13**).

   The easiest way to do so is to change the connection parameters so that they are invalid.

**A SIMPLE EXAMPLE**

## Writing the JavaScript, part 1

For many PHP programmers the JavaScript will be the most foreign part of the Ajax process. It's also the most important, so I'll go through the thinking in detail. I'm breaking the JavaScript code into two sections: the creation of the `XMLHttpRequest` object and the use of said object. The first chunk of code will be used by both examples in this chapter (and can pretty much be used by any Ajax application you write). The second chunk of code will be application-specific.

To start, you'll need to create an object through which all the magic happens. For this purpose, there is the `XMLHttpRequest` class. The functionality defined within this class is at the heart of all Ajax capabilities.

If the user's browser supports the `XMLHttpRequest` (which I'll show you how to test for in the next script), you'll want to make an object of this type:

```
var ajax = new XMLHttpRequest();
```

Windows Internet Explorer 5.*x* and 6.*x* do not support `XMLHttpRequest` and instead need to use an `ActiveXObject`:

```
var ajax = new
ActiveXObject("Microsoft.XMLHTTP");
```

And that's really it to creating the object. Even if you've never done any JavaScript programming before, this is easy enough to follow. In this next script, I'll formally implement the two lines of code but wrap it in some conditionals and `try...catch` blocks (see Chapter 8, "Real-World OOP," for a discussion of PHP `try...catch`) to make sure it's done right.

**Script 13.2** This JavaScript file creates an object called ajax of a browser-supported type. This object will be used by the other JavaScript files (Scripts 13.3 and 13.6).

```
1    // Script 13.2 - ajax.js
2
3    /*  This page creates an Ajax request
     object.
4    *  This page is included by other pages
     that
5    *  need to perform an XMLHttpRequest.
6    */
7
8    // Initialize the object:
9    var ajax = false;
10
11   // Create the object...
12
13   // Choose object type based upon what's
     supported:
14   if (window.XMLHttpRequest) {
15
16       // IE 7, Mozilla, Safari, Firefox,
     Opera, most browsers:
17       ajax = new XMLHttpRequest();
18
19   } else if (window.ActiveXObject) { //
     Older IE browsers
20
21       // Create type Msxml2.XMLHTTP, if
     possible:
22       try {
23           ajax = new
     ActiveXObject("Msxml2.XMLHTTP");
24       } catch (e1) { // Create the older
     type instead:
25           try {
26               ajax = new
     ActiveXObject("Microsoft.XMLHTTP");
27           } catch (e2) { }
28       }
29
30   }
31
32   // Send an alert if the object wasn't
     created.
33   if (!ajax) {
34       alert ('Some page functionality is
     unavailable.');
35   }
36
```

## To write some of the JavaScript:

**1.** Create a new JavaScript script in your text editor or IDE (**Script 13.2**).

```
// Script 13.2 - ajax.js
```

**2.** Initialize a variable.

```
var ajax = false;
```

In JavaScript you should declare variables using the keyword var. Here I declare the variable (called *ajax*, but it could be called anything) and initially set its value to *false*.

**3.** Create the XMLHttpRequest object, if supported.

```
if (window.XMLHttpRequest) {
    ajax = new XMLHttpRequest();
```

If the browser supports the XMLHttpRequest object type, a new object of that type will be created. This will be the case for most browsers, including Internet Explorer 7 (but not earlier versions), Firefox, Mozilla, Safari, and Opera.

**4.** Check if ActiveXObject is supported.

```
} else if (window.ActiveXObject) {
```

If the browser does not support XMLHttpRequest, then an object of type ActiveXObject should be created. This only applies to Internet Explorer versions prior to 7.

**5.** Try to create the ActiveXObject object.

```
try {
    ajax = new
→ ActiveXObject("Msxml2.XMLHTTP");
} catch (e1) {
    try {
        ajax = new
→ ActiveXObject("Microsoft.XMLHTTP");
    } catch (e2) { }
}
```

*continues on next page*

Microsoft has developed several different flavors of `ActiveXObject XMLHTTP`. Ideally, you'd like to use the most current one. Since there's no way of testing what versions are supported by the current browser, two `try...catch` blocks will attempt to make the object. If an object of type `Msxml2.XMLHTTP` cannot be created, then an attempt is made to make one of type `Microsoft.XMLHTTP`.

Nothing is done with any caught exceptions, as a more general error handling later in the script will suffice.

**6.** Complete the main conditional.

```
}
```

This closes the `else if` clause begun in Step 4.

**7.** Send an alert if the object wasn't created.

```
if (!ajax) {
    alert ('Some page functionality
→ is unavailable.');
}
```

If `ajax` is false, meaning that none of the attempts to declare it as an object succeeded, then the entire Ajax application won't work. In such a case, a simple message is displayed to the end user (**Figure 13.14**), although you don't have to do that.

**8.** Save the file as `ajax.js` and place it in your Web directory.

This file should be put in the same directory as `checkusername.php`.

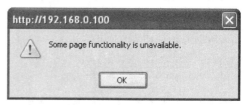

**Figure 13.14** If the user's browser supports JavaScript but none of the attempts to make the `XMLHttpRequest` object succeeds, this alert is displayed.

## ✔ Tips

■ If you have an Ajax application that performs multiple Ajax transactions in the same Web browser, you'll want to modify the code in `ajax.js` so that a JavaScript function returns an `XMLHttpRequest` object. Then you would call this function, assigning the returned value to a new variable for each separate Ajax transaction. This may make more sense to you once you've completed the first Ajax example.

■ People are often (understandably) confused about this point, but JavaScript is unrelated to the programming language Java. JavaScript is an implementation of a scripting language called ECMAScript.

# Writing the JavaScript, part 2

The first sequence of JavaScript instructions creates the `ajax.js` file. The code in that file creates an `XMLHttpRequest` object, tailored for the Web browser in use. Once you've established the object, you can begin using it, starting by opening a connection. Provide to the `open()` method the type of request to make—GET, POST, or PUT—and the URL to use:

```
ajax.open('get', 'scriptname.php');
```

The object is called `ajax`, defined in the `ajax.js` file. It opens a connection to `scriptname.php` on the server, to which it will make a GET request.

With this first example (checking a username's availability), you'll need to modify that `open()` code to pass the username along to the script. You already know how to do this:

```
ajax.open('get', 'checkusername.php?
→ username=XXXX');
```

Adding ?username=*XXXX* to the URL achieves the desired result. If you look back at how the `checkusername.php` script is used (Figures 13.11 and 13.12), this will make more sense.

The next step is to name the JavaScript user-defined function to be called when the PHP script returns its results. The `onreadystate-change` property takes this value. This property is one of five important `XMLHttpRequest` object properties listed in **Table 13.1**. Assign to this property the name of the function, without any parentheses:

```
ajax.onreadystatechange =
→ call_this_function;
```

So the JavaScript will send the request to the server, the server will send back a reply, and, at that time, the `call_this_function()` function will be called. This function, defined in a little bit, will take the returned data and update the Web page accordingly.

The last step in this sequence is to send the request. For GET requests, you should provide the value `null` as its only argument:

```
ajax.send(null);
```

That wraps up the "making the request" JavaScript; next is the handling of the returned results (what the server-side PHP script sends back). The first thing you'll want to do is confirm that the request was successful. To do so, check that the `readyState` is equal to 4 (see **Table 13.2** for the list of `readyState` values).

```
if (ajax.readyState == 4) {
    // Handle the returned data.
```

*continues on next page*

**Table 13.1** You'll rely upon these XMLHttpRequest properties in your JavaScript code.

| XMLHttpRequest Properties | |
|---|---|
| PROPERTY | CONTAINS THE… |
| onreadystatechange | Name of the function to be called when the readyState property changes. |
| readyState | Current state of the request (see Table 13.2). |
| responseText | Returned data as a string. |
| responseXML | Returned data as XML. |
| status | HTTP status code returned. |

**Table 13.2** The five readyState values, of which the last one is the most important for knowing when to handle the returned data.

| XMLHttpRequest readyState Values | |
|---|---|
| VALUE | MEANING |
| 0 | uninitialized |
| 1 | loading |
| 2 | loaded |
| 3 | interactive |
| 4 | complete |

The `readyState` just indicates the status of the request process: at first it's uninitialized, then the server page is loading, then it's completely loaded; next up is some interaction and eventually the request is completed. Often these states will change very quickly.

Along with the `readyState` value, you can also check the `status` property to know if it's safe to process the returned data.

```
if ( (ajax.readyState == 4) &&
(ajax.status == 200) ) {
```

The `status` corresponds to the possible HTTP status codes, with which you might already be familiar. **Table 13.3** has a small sampling of them.

Having created the `XMLHttpRequest` object, having performed the transaction, and having confirmed the server results, the final step is to use the returned data to alter the Web browser content. The easiest way to access that data is by referring to the `responseText` property. This attribute stores the results of the server request (i.e., the PHP page), which, in this case, is one of the string messages (*The username is unavailable!*, *The username is available!*, etc.).

In this example, the JavaScript will take this message and place it in the HTML. To do that, the JavaScript uses the DOM (Document Object Model, see the accompanying sidebar "The Document Object Model") to identify where on the page the text should go. Then the `innerHTML` property is assigned a value:

```
document.getElementById('location_name')
→ .innerHTML = 'Some message';
```

**Table 13.3** Every requested server page returns an HTTP status code. For Ajax purposes, 200 is the code to watch for.

| Common HTTP Status Codes | |
|---|---|
| CODE | MEANING |
| 200 | OK |
| 204 | No content |
| 400 | Bad request |
| 401 | Unauthorized |
| 403 | Forbidden |
| 404 | Not found |
| 408 | Timeout |
| 500 | Internal server error |

## The Document Object Model

The Document Object Model is a representation of an HTML page (also XML data) in a tree form. For example, the base of an HTML tree is the entire page, found within HTML tags. From that base there are two main branches: the HEAD and the BODY. Within each of these there are going to be many other branches, like the TITLE in the HEAD or a P in the BODY.

The DOM provides an object-oriented way to reference each branch and leaf on this tree. For example, `document.form.username` refers to the `username` input in a form.

Rather than navigating the entire tree, you can quickly address a specific element by using `document.getElementById('id_name')`. Thus `document.form.username` and `document.getElementById('username')` are the same thing (provided that the form has an input with an ID of *username*).

This is just a basic introduction to the DOM. You can either trust me and go with the examples as is, or search the Web for more information on this concept.

## To complete the JavaScript:

**1.** Create a new JavaScript script in your text editor or IDE (**Script 13.3**).

```
// Script 13.3 - checkusername.js
```

*continues on next page*

**Script 13.3** The second JavaScript file defines two functions specific to the Ajax application being developed. One function makes the request, and the second handles it.

```
1    // Script 13.3 - checkusername.js
2
3    /*  This page does all the magic for applying
4     *  Ajax principles to a registration form.
5     *  The users's chosen username is sent to a PHP
6     *  script which will confirm its availability.
7     */
8
9    // Function that starts the Ajax process:
10   function check_username(username) {
11
12       // Confirm that the object is usable:
13       if (ajax) {
14
15           // Call the PHP script.
16           // Use the GET method.
17           // Pass the username in the URL.
18           ajax.open('get', 'checkusername.php?username=' + encodeURIComponent(username));
19
20           // Function that handles the response:
21           ajax.onreadystatechange = handle_check;
22
23           // Send the request:
24           ajax.send(null);
25
26       } else { // Can't use Ajax!
27           document.getElementById('username_label').innerHTML = 'The availability of this username
     will be confirmed upon form submission.';
28       }
29
30   } // End of check_username() function.
31
32   // Function that handles the response from the PHP script:
33   function handle_check() {
34
35       // If everything's OK:
36       if ( (ajax.readyState == 4) && (ajax.status == 200) ) {
37
38           // Assign the returned value to a document element:
39           document.getElementById('username_label').innerHTML = ajax.responseText;
40
41       }
42
43   } // End of handle_check() function.
```

**2.** Begin defining the main function.

```
function check_username(username) {
```

This is the function that will be called when something happens in the Web browser. It takes one argument: the username. This will be passed to the PHP script.

**3.** Check that the request object has a value.

```
if (ajax) {
```

A conditional checks if `ajax` has a value. This is an important check because the `ajax.js` code may not have been able to make a valid request object.

As for variable scope, you can reference `ajax` in this function because in JavaScript, variables declared outside of any function are automatically available within them. This differs from PHP.

**4.** Open the connection.

```
ajax.open('get',
→ 'checkusername.php?username=' +
→ encodeURIComponent(username));
```

This code is similar to what I show in the introduction to these steps. In JavaScript, you cannot place variables within quotation marks, so the username must be concatenated (using the plus sign) to the URL. For safety's sake, I'm using the `encodeURIComponent()` function, which makes any submitted value safe to pass in the URL (for example, it'll turn spaces into URL-safe pluses).

**5.** Declare what function handles the response.

```
ajax.onreadystatechange =
→ handle_check;
```

This line states that when the `readyState` value of the object changes, the `handle_check()` function should be called.

**6.** Send the request.

```
ajax.send(null);
```

**7.** Complete the `if (ajax)` conditional.

```
} else {
    document.getElementById
→ ('username_label').innerHTML =
→ 'The availability of this username
→ will be confirmed upon form
→ submission.';
}
```

The easiest way to change the HTML page using JavaScript (and without reloading the browser) is to refer to an element's `innerHTML` value. In the page's HTML, there will be a SPAN tag with a name of *username_label*. This line of code says that that element's "innerHTML"—the stuff between the tags—should be set to *The availability of....*

**8.** Complete the `check_username()` function.

```
}
```

**9.** Begin defining the function for handling the request result.

```
function handle_check() {
    if ( (ajax.readyState == 4) &&
→ (ajax.status == 200) ) {
```

Because the `handle_check()` function will be called every time the `readyState` changes, it should check to make sure that the request is complete before doing its thing. This conditional checks two things: that the `readyState` is completed (4) and that the server returned an OK status (200).

**10.** Complete the `handle_check()` function.

```
        document.getElementById
→ ('username_label').innerHTML =
→ ajax.responseText;
        }
} // End of handle_check() function.
```

Like the code in Step 7, the HTML will be changed using the `innerHTML` attribute. Here, after a successful request, that attribute is assigned the value of `ajax.responseText`. That property stores, as a string, whatever was returned by the server.

**11.** Save the file as `checkusername.js` and place it in your Web directory.

This file should be put into the same directory as `checkusername.php` and `ajax.js`.

## ✔ Tips

■ Some Ajax examples you might come across will use `escape()` instead of `encodeURIComponent()` for safeguarding data passed to the server. The `escape()` method only works on ASCII characters, leaving out-of-range characters unencoded. Conversely, `encodeURIComponent()` works on all UTF-8 characters, making it safer.

■ One modification you could make is to separate the `handle_check()` conditional so that the `readyState` and `status` properties are validated separately:

```
if (ajax.readyState == 4) {
    if (ajax.status == 200) {
            document.getElementById
→ ('username_label').innerHTML =
→ ajax.responseText;
    } else {

document.getElementById('username_
→ label').innerHTML = 'The
→ availability of this username will
→ be confirmed upon form
→ submission.';
    }
}
```

The main benefit would be that you could take separate steps if the process completes (`readyState ==4`) but the status was something other than OK (200).

■ One of the constant Ajax debates is whether or not one should use the `innerHTML` property. It has been deprecated by the W3C (World Wide Web Consortium, which governs Web standards), meaning that it could disappear in future standards. But browsers don't really live and die by standards, and using `innerHTML` is so popular, that I doubt your Ajax code will be rendered useless in the near future. The alternative is to use something called *nodes*, which can be tedious, and are not universally supported.

# Creating the HTML

By this point in time in the Ajax application's development, all of the challenging coding has been completed. Besides actually making the HTML page with the registration form, two things still need to be accomplished:

◆ An event defined that starts the Ajax process

◆ A place created in the HTML where the resulting message will be placed

For the first item, some JavaScript event must call the check_username() function. **Table 13.4** lists some common events. For this form, I'll attach an onchange() event to the username form input.

For the second item, some understanding of the Document Object Model (see the sidebar "The Document Object Model" earlier in the chapter) is required. For this example, where one string is returned by the server, you can make an empty SPAN to be filled by the JavaScript.

**A SIMPLE EXAMPLE**

**Table 13.4** A handful of the available JavaScript events. The word "element" can refer to a form field, an image, a button, even a link. The word "focus" means that the cursor is placed within that form element (as one common example).

| Common JavaScript Events | |
|---|---|
| EVENT | OCCURS WHEN... |
| onfocus | An element gains focus. |
| onblur | An element loses focus. |
| onchange | A form element's value or state changes. |
| onreset | The form is reset. |
| onsubmit | The form is submitted. |
| onclick | A mouse is clicked on an element. |
| onload | The HTML page has completely loaded. |

## To create the HTML form:

1. Create a new HTML page in your text editor or IDE (**Script 13.4**).

```
<!DOCTYPE html PUBLIC "-//W3C//DTD
→ XHTML 1.0 Transitional//EN"
"http://www.w3.org/TR/xhtml1/DTD/
→ xhtml1-transitional.dtd">
<html
xmlns="http://www.w3.org/1999/xhtml">
<head>
```

```
<title>Registration Form</title>
<script src="ajax.js"
type="text/javascript"
→ language="javascript"></script>
<script src="checkusername.js"
→ type="text/javascript"
→ language="javascript"></script>
</head>
<body>
<!-- Script 13.4 - register.html
```

*continues on next page*

**Script 13.4** The HTML page that includes the two JavaScript files, makes the form, and ties the form into the JavaScript.

```
1    <!DOCTYPE html PUBLIC "-//W3C//DTD XHTML 1.0 Transitional//EN"
2          "http://www.w3.org/TR/xhtml1/DTD/xhtml1-transitional.dtd">
3    <html xmlns="http://www.w3.org/1999/xhtml">
4    <head>
5        <title>Registration Form</title>
6        <script src="ajax.js" type="text/javascript" language="javascript"></script>
7        <script src="checkusername.js" type="text/javascript" language="javascript"></script>
8    </head>
9    <body>
10   <!-- Script 13.4 - register.html
11   /*  This page has the HTML registration form.
12    *  The JavaScript code is included in the HEAD.
13    */
14   -->
15   <form action="register.php" method="post">
16   <fieldset>
17   <legend>Registration Form</legend>
18
19   <p>Username: <input name="username" type="text" size="20" maxlength="20"
     onchange="check_username(this.form.username.value)" /> <span id="username_label"></span></p>
20
21   <p>Password: <input name="pass1" type="password" /></p>
22
23   <p>Confirm Password: <input name="pass2" type="password" /></p>
24
25   <p>First Name: <input name="first_name" type="text" size="20" maxlength="20" /></p>
26
27   <p>Last Name: <input name="last_name" type="text" size="20" maxlength="20" /></p>
28
29   <p>Email Address: <input name="email" type="text" size="20" maxlength="60" /></p>
30
31   <input name="submit" type="submit" value="Register" />
32
33   </form>
34   </fieldset>
35   </body>
36   </html>
```

In the first part of this page, the most important consideration is the inclusion of both JavaScript files: `ajax.js` and `checkusername.js`.

**2.** Begin the HTML form.

```
<form action="register.php"
→ method="post">
<fieldset>
<legend>Registration Form</legend>
```

To clarify one possible point of confusion, the `action` value here is `register.php`. This is a separate script from `checkuser-name.php`. That file is used for Ajax purposes and only confirms the availability of a username. The purpose of `regis-ter.php` is to handle the entire form. That would likely also involve confirming the username's availability, but it would validate the entire form as well, and then actually record the new registrant in the database.

I have not, in this chapter, created `register.php`, but it should be pretty easy to put together.

**3.** Create the username input.

```
<p>Username: <input name="username"
→ type="text" size="20"
→ maxlength="20"
→ onchange="check_username(this.form.
→ username.value)" /> <span
→ id="username_label"></span></p>
```

For the HTML page, this line ties into all the JavaScript functionality. First, the input is called *username* and a JavaScript event is attached to it. That event says that when the value of this input changes, the `check_username()` function should be called, passing that function the username input's value. This gets the Ajax ball rolling.

**Figure 13.15** The registration form when the user first arrives.

After the input, a SPAN is added, with an id (not a name) of *username_label*. This is part of the DOM, and the JavaScript function that handles the server result will dynamically assign text to this SPAN. When the form is first loaded, this area after the username is blank (**Figure 13.15**).

**4.** Complete the HTML form.

```
<p>Password: <input name="pass1"
→ type="password" /></p>
<p>Confirm Password: <input
→ name="pass2" type="password" /></p>
<p>First Name: <input
→ name="first_name" type="text"
→ size="20" maxlength="20" /></p>
<p>Last Name: <input name="last_name"
→ type="text" size="20"
→ maxlength="20" /></p>
<p>Email Address: <input name="email"
→ type="text" size="20"
→ maxlength="60" /></p>
<input name="submit" type="submit"
→ value="Register" />
</form>
```

**5.** Complete the HTML page.

```
</fieldset>
</body>
</html>
```

**6.** Save the file as register.html and place it in your Web directory.

All four files—checkusername.php, ajax.js, checkusername.js, and register.html—should be in the same directory.

## Testing the application

That's it! You've now created an entire Ajax application from scratch. You have created four files:

- ◆ checkusername.php
- ◆ ajax.js
- ◆ checkusername.js
- ◆ register.html

These should all be in the same folder in your Web directory. Now, to test the application...but first: If yours does not work as it should (as it does in the following figures), you'll need to use some good old-fashioned debugging work to solve the problem. I discuss how to debug Ajax applications at the end of this chapter.

A SIMPLE EXAMPLE

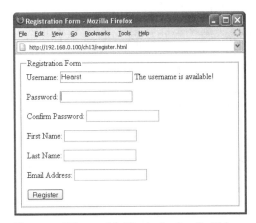

**Figure 13.16** The result (without reloading the Web page) if a username is available.

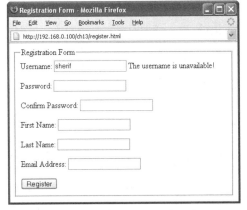

**Figure 13.17** The result (without reloading the Web page) if a username is unavailable.

## To test the Ajax application:

1. Load `register.html` in a Web browser.

   How you load `register.html` is very important. You absolutely must access it through a URL! This might mean `http://localhost/register.html` or `http://www.example.com/register.html`. If you just open the HTML file without going through a URL, then the request for the PHP script will not be made to the server and it won't work.

2. Type an available username in the first text box, and then press Tab (**Figure 13.16**).

   Nothing will happen until you press Tab or click in one of the other text inputs. At that point, the JavaScript will see that the value of the username has changed, triggering the event, and calling the `check_username()` function.

3. Change the username value to an unavailable one (**Figure 13.17**).

   You don't have to reload the page or do anything special; just delete what you typed in Step 2, type something new, and press Tab.

## ✔ Tip

- If you submit the form, you'll get a page not found error, because the form is sent to a `register.php` script, which has not been created. When you want to implement this application in a live Web site, write your own `register.php` that validates and handles the form as you otherwise would.

# Full-Fledged Ajax

This chapter begins with a "simple" demonstration of Ajax, which turns out to be not all that simple. The overall premise was that the server returns a string that is put into the HTML page. Accomplishing this requires one PHP script, two JavaScript files, and an HTML document. But what if you want to return a lot of data to the client? You can take heart in knowing that doing so won't require that much more work.

In this next, "full-fledged" example, the user will enter their U.S. zip code in a form field (**Figure 13.18**) and click the submit button. Using Ajax, the browser will then be updated to show a list of stores in order of how close they are (in miles) to the supplied zip code (**Figure 13.19**). Much of the technology involved will be the same as it was in the "simple" example. The main difference is that a new idea is required for conveying between the server and the client not only the data but also what that data is. In particular, the server will send back to the JavaScript several pieces of information—a name, an address, a city, a state, and so on—for several stores. The receiving page must be able to differentiate between each piece of data.

The old-school and common way of doing just that is to use XML. But XML can be a bit of a pain to work with, and there is an easier answer: JSON (JavaScript Object Notation). JSON is a "lightweight data-interchange format" (see www.json.org) that JavaScript can intuitively work with. So in this next example, the biggest changes will involve creating and using JSON instead of working with a plain string.

**Figure 13.18** The simple form as the user sees it upon first loading the page.

**Figure 13.19** The Ajax-generated result (without reloading the page) after the user clicks the submit button.

**Figure 13.20** One sample MySQL result using the query from the PHP script.

[{"name":"Fishmonger's Heaven","address":"Pier 9","city":"MORRISONVILLE","state":"WI","zip":"53571","phone":"(123) 000-7890","distance":"132"},{"name":"Kiosk","address":"St. Charles Towncenter 3890 Crain Highway","city":"WELLSVILLE","state":"MO","zip":"63384","phone":"(123) 888-4444","distance":"277"},{"name":"Ray's Shop","address":"49 Main Street","city":"FAIRDEALING","state":"MO","zip":"63939","phone":"(123) 456-7890","distance":"394"},{"name":"Megastore","address":"34 Suburban View","city":"MUSELLA","state":"GA","zip":"31066","phone":"(555) 456-7890","distance":"656"},{"name":"Hoo New","address":"576b Little River Turnpike","city":"WOODSTOWN","state":"NJ","zip":"08098","phone":"(123) 456-0000","distance":"662"}]

**Figure 13.21** A JSON representation of the query results in Figure 13.20.

## Creating the Database

The database in this example will be the zips database, exactly the same as it was created in Chapter 3. The database contains two tables: stores, which lists a bunch of stores, and zip_codes, which contains the latitude and longitude values for every U.S. zip code.

If you have not yet created this database on your server, get thee to Chapter 3 and follow the steps therein.

Note that this database also contains one stored function, called return_distance(). This function performs the math that calculates the distance between two latitudes and longitudes. Stored functions, and the creation of this one in particular, are also covered in Chapter 3. If you are not using at least version 5 of MySQL (or a database application that supports stored procedures), you'll need to see Chapter 3 for alternatives because the query used in this example's PHP script will not work for you.

## Programming the PHP

The database for this example does not need to be created as it was created in Chapter 3, "Advanced Database Concepts." See the sidebar for details or if you have not yet created the database. As for the PHP script used by this Ajax example, it'll differ from checkusername.php in three ways:

◆ The MySQL query will return a table of data (**Figure 13.20**).

◆ The PHP script needs to return this array of data, or an indication that no data is being returned.

◆ If an array of data is returned, it should be in JSON format.

In the preceding example, it really didn't matter what, if anything, MySQL returned because the PHP script was going to return (i.e., print) a string message no matter what. Here, there'll be a distinction between returning an array of data or nothing.

As for returning the data in the JSON format, that format isn't too hard to understand (go to www.json.org for specifics of the syntax) or to create for yourself in PHP. **Figure 13.21** shows the data in Figure 13.20 in JSON format. That being said, the success of the JavaScript using the JSON data relies upon this format being exactly correct. To better guarantee that end, I recommend using the PECL json package (see http://pecl.php.net/package/json). If you can't or don't want to install a PECL package for this example, then there are several JSON scripts written in PHP available online. Just download and use one of them.

## To create the PHP script:

1. Create a new PHP script in your text editor or IDE (**Script 13.5**).

   ```php
   <?php # Script 13.5 - stores_json.php
   ```

   *continues on page 510*

**Script 13.5** This PHP script accepts a U.S. zip code in the URL and uses it to fetch a list of stores from the database. The list is then returned in JSON format.

```php
1    <?php # Script 13.5 - stores_json.php
2
3    /*  This page queries a database, returning
4     *  a list of 10 stores and how far away
5     *  they are from the submitted zip code.
6     *  The page will be called by JavaScript.
7     *  No HTML is required by this script!
8     */
9
10   $zip = FALSE; // Flag variable.
11
12   // Validate that the page received $_GET['zip']:
13   if ( isset($_GET['zip']) &&
14        ( (strlen($_GET['zip']) == 5) || (strlen($_GET['zip']) == 10) )
15        ) {
16
17       // Chop off the last four digits, if necessary.
18       if (strlen($_GET['zip']) == 10) {
19           $zip = substr($_GET['zip'], 0, 5);
20       } else {
21           $zip = $_GET['zip'];
22       }
23
24       // Make sure it's numeric:
25       if (is_numeric($zip)) {
26
27           // Connect to the database:
28           $dbc = @mysqli_connect ('localhost', 'username', 'password', 'zips') OR die ('null');
29
30           // Get the origination latitude and longitude:
31           $q = "SELECT latitude, longitude FROM zip_codes WHERE zip_code='$zip'";
32           $r = mysqli_query($dbc, $q);
33
34           // Retrieve the results:
35           if (mysqli_num_rows($r) == 1) {
36
37               list($lat, $long) = mysqli_fetch_array($r, MYSQLI_NUM);
38
39           } else { // Invalid zip.
```

*(script continues on next page)*

**Script 13.5** *continued*

```
 |  ⊜ ⊜ ⊜                                      📄 Script
40              $zip = FALSE;
41              mysqli_close($dbc);
42          }
43
44      } else { // Invalid zip.
45          $zip = FALSE;
46      }
47
48  }
49
50  if ($zip) { // Get the stores and distances.
51
52      // Big, important query:
53      $q = "SELECT name, CONCAT_WS('<br />', address1, address2), city, state, s.zip_code, phone,
    round(return_distance($lat, $long, latitude, longitude)) AS dist FROM stores AS s LEFT JOIN
    zip_codes AS z USING (zip_code) ORDER BY dist ASC LIMIT 5";
54      $r = mysqli_query($dbc, $q);
55
56      if (mysqli_num_rows($r) > 0) {
57
58          // Initialize an array:
59          $json = array();
60
61          // Put each store into the array:
62          while (list($name, $address, $city, $state, $zip, $phone, $distance) =
    mysqli_fetch_array($r, MYSQLI_NUM)) {
63
64              $json[] = array('name' => $name,
65              'address' => $address,
66              'city' => ucfirst(strtolower($city)),
67              'state' => $state,
68              'zip' => $zip,
69              'phone' => $phone,
70              'distance' => $distance);
71
72          }
73
74          // Send the JSON data:
75          echo json_encode($json) . "\n";
76
77      } else { // No records returned.
78          echo 'null';
79      }
80
81      mysqli_close($dbc);
82
83  } else { // Invalid zip.
84      echo 'null';
85  }
86  ?>
```

**2.** Validate that the page received a zip code.

```
$zip = FALSE;
if ( isset($_GET['zip']) &&
    ( (strlen($_GET['zip']) == 5) ||
→ (strlen($_GET['zip']) == 10) )
    ) {
```

To start, I assume that no valid zip code has been received. Then I use a conditional that checks if a zip code was passed to this script in the URL and, if so, if it's either exactly five or ten characters in length. A U.S. zip code will be either 12345 or 12345-6789, so this script should accept both lengths.

**3.** Trim off the last four digits of the zip code, if necessary.

```
if (strlen($_GET['zip']) == 10) {
    $zip = substr($_GET['zip'],
→ 0, 5);
} else {
    $zip = $_GET['zip'];
}
```

This conditional results in having a zip code, now stored in `$zip`, that's exactly five characters long. The zip codes in the database never use the -6789 extensions, so that can be chopped off.

**4.** Confirm that the zip code is numeric.

```
if (is_numeric($zip)) {
```

This is the last validation routine for the zip code. By this point in the script, the zip code must be exactly five characters long. All that is left to do is confirm that it is numeric (because a submitted zip code of *pizza* would match every check thus far).

**5.** Connect to the database.

```
$dbc = @mysqli_connect ('localhost',
→ 'username', 'password', 'zips') OR
→ die ('null');
```

As with the other PHP script, I'm hard-coding the database connection instead of including an external file. Unlike the last example, though, if a database connection couldn't be made, I don't want to return a message, just a null value (which, in truth, is a string with a value of *null*, not a real null). You'll see how this is used in the following JavaScript.

**6.** Define and execute the query.

```
$q = "SELECT latitude, longitude FROM
→ zip_codes WHERE zip_code='$zip'";
$r = mysqli_query($dbc, $q);
```

This first query—the script contains two—both validates the zip code (that it's an actual U.S. zip code) and retrieves that zip code's latitude and longitude. That information will be necessary for calculating distances between the given zip code and each store.

**7.** Retrieve the results of the query.

```
if (mysqli_num_rows($r) == 1) {
    list($lat, $long) =
→ mysqli_fetch_array($r, MYSQLI_NUM);
} else {
    $zip = FALSE;
    mysqli_close($dbc);
}
```

If one row was returned, the zip code is valid. Otherwise, the `$zip` variable should be set as `false`, because it's invalid.

**8.** Complete the conditionals begun in Steps 4 and 2.

```
        } else {
                $zip = FALSE;
        }
}
```

If the first five characters of the provided zip code are not numeric, the flag variable is set as `false`.

**9.** If the zip code is valid, perform the main query.

```
if ($zip) {
        $q = "SELECT name,
→ CONCAT_WS('<br />', address1,
→ address2), city, state,
→ s.zip_code, phone,
→ round(return_distance($lat, $long,
→ latitude, longitude)) AS dist FROM
→ stores AS s LEFT JOIN zip_codes
→ AS z USING (zip_code) ORDER BY
→ dist ASC LIMIT 5";
        $r = mysqli_query($dbc, $q);
```

Getting to this main query is really the point of the whole script. As you can see in Figure 13.20, this query returns a store's name, full address, phone number, and distance from the given zip code. It calculates that distance using the `return_distance()` stored procedure. For more discussion of this query, see Chapter 3.

**10.** Fetch the data from the query.

```
if (mysqli_num_rows($r) > 0) {
        $json = array();
        while (list($name, $address,
→ $city, $state, $zip, $phone,
→ $distance) =
→ mysqli_fetch_array($r,
→ MYSQLI_NUM)) {
```

If at least one row was returned, it should be fetched. Before using a loop that does that, an array is initialized. This array will store the JSON data.

**11.** Add each record to the `$json` array.

```
$json[] = array('name' => $name,
'address' => $address,
'city' =>
→ ucfirst(strtolower($city)),
'state' => $state,
'zip' => $zip,
'phone' => $phone,
'distance' => $distance);
```

The `while` loop builds up a multidimensional array, where the main array has one array for each store. The subarrays contain each store's data, indexed by data type (name, address, …). Because the zip code database I used in Chapter 3 has each city's name in all capital letters (again, see Figure 13.20), I make the name all lowercase, then capitalize the first letter, prior to storing this information in the array.

**12.** Complete the `while` loop and print the data.

```
}
echo json_encode($json) . "\n";
```

If you've installed the json PECL package, this is all you need to do to have the script return properly formatted JSON data (Figure 13.21).

*continues on next page*

**13.** Complete the page.

```
    } else {
            echo 'null';
    }
    mysqli_close($dbc);
} else {
    echo 'null';
}
?>
```

If no records were returned by the query, then *null* is printed. The same applies if no valid zip code was provided.

**14.** Save the file as stores_json.php, place it in your Web directory, and test in your Web browser (**Figures 13.22**, **13.23**, and **13.24**).

Remember that you'll need to test this by appending ?zip=*XXXXX* or ?zip=*XXXXX-XXXX* to the URL.

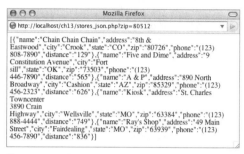

**Figure 13.22** The result if a valid zip code was supplied.

**Figure 13.23** The result if no or an invalid zip code was supplied.

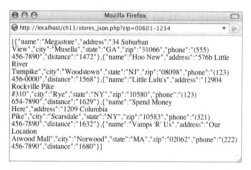

**Figure 13.24** The result using another valid zip code.

## Writing the JavaScript

Once you've written the server side of things (the PHP script), you can move to the JavaScript. The `ajax.js` file will still be used by this application to create the `XMLHttpRequest` object. But another JavaScript file will be required that makes the server request and handles the returned data. In this example, the first part of that equation will be simple, very much like the `checkuser-name.js` `check_username()` function. The second part of the equation—handling the returned data and displaying it in the Web page—will require new code, as the returned data is in the JSON format.

For starters, the returned data will still be accessed through the `responseText` attribute. But that value will be a string (as shown in Figure 13.24), not easily usable. To turn it into a more accessible format, you'll run it through the `eval()` function. You could do something like

```
var data = eval('(' + ajax.responseText
→ + ')');
```

The extra parentheses are necessary in order for this to work—just trust me on this one. After running the JSON data through `eval()`, you can refer to individual elements using the `data[x].attribute` syntax. The overall variable—`data`—is an array, meaning a specific element is at `data[0]`, `data[1]`, and so on. Each array element is an object, whose attributes are at `.attribute`. You'll see this better in the following script.

### Performing Synchronous Transactions

This chapter's examples perform asynchronous transactions. You might, however, want to perform synchronous ones. You'd do so in situations where you don't want the user to be doing anything else while the JavaScript is waiting for the server response.

To do this, set the `open()` method's third argument to `false`:

```
ajax.open('get', 'scriptname.php',
→ false);
```

If not provided, this third argument has a default value of `true`, which is to say that performing asynchronous transactions is the default behavior.

## To write the JavaScript:

1. Create a new JavaScript script in your text editor or IDE (**Script 13.6**).

   ```
   // Script 13.6 - stores.js
   ```

*continues on page 516*

**Script 13.6** In this JavaScript page, data is received in the JSON format, which is then accessed using object notation.

```
1    // Script 13.6 - stores.js
2
3    /*  This page does all the magic for applying
4     *  Ajax principles to a store retrieval form.
5     *  The users's zip code is sent to a PHP
6     *  script which will return data in JSON format.
7     */
8
9    // Function that starts the Ajax process:
10   function get_stores(zip) {
11
12       if (ajax) {
13
14           // Call the PHP script.
15           // Use the GET method.
16           // Pass the zip code in the URL.
17           ajax.open('get', 'stores_json.php?zip=' + encodeURIComponent(zip));
18
19           // Function that handles the response:
20           ajax.onreadystatechange = handle_stores;
21
22           // Send the request:
23           ajax.send(null);
24
25           return false;
26
27       } else { // Can't use Ajax!
28           return true;
29       }
30
31   } // End of get_stores() function.
32
```

*(script continues on next page)*

**Script 13.6** *continued*

```
33    // Function that handles the response from the PHP script:
34    function handle_stores() {
35
36        // If everything's OK:
37        if ( (ajax.readyState == 4) && (ajax.status == 200) ) {
38
39            // Check the length of the response:
40            if (ajax.responseText.length > 10) {
41
42                // Send the response, in object form,
43                // to the show_stores() function:
44                show_stores(eval('(' + ajax.responseText + ')'));
45
46            } else {
47                document.getElementById('list').innerHTML = '<p>No stores matched your search.</p>';
48            }
49
50        }
51
52    } // End of handle_stores() function.
53
54    // Function that shows the list of stores:
55    function show_stores(stores) {
56
57        // Initialize a string:
58        var message = '';
59
60        // Get each store:
61        for (var i = 0 ; i < stores.length ; i++) {
62
63            // Add to the string:
64            message += '<h2>' + stores[i].name + '</h2>'
65            + '<p>' + stores[i].address + '<br />'
66            + stores[i].city + ', ' + stores[i].state + ' '
67            + stores[i].zip + '<br />'
68            + stores[i].phone + '<br />(approximately '
69            + stores[i].distance + ' miles)</p>';
70
71        }
72
73        // Place the string in the page:
74        document.getElementById('list').innerHTML = message;
75
76    } // End of show_stores() function.
```

**2.** Begin defining the main function.

```
function get_stores(zip) {
    if (ajax) {
```

This is the function that will be called when something happens in the Web browser. It takes one argument: the zip code. This will be passed to the PHP script. Prior to that, though, a conditional confirms that ajax has a value.

**3.** Create the request.

```
ajax.open('get',
→ 'stores_json.php?zip=' +
→ encodeURIComponent(zip));
ajax.onreadystatechange =
→ handle_stores;
ajax.send(null);
```

All of this code is much like that in checkusername.js, although a different URL and variable are used.

**4.** Complete the get_stores() function.

```
            return false;
    } else {
            return true;
    }
} // End of get_stores() function.
```

Unlike check_username() this function will return a Boolean value. I'm doing this because of the way that the function will be called in the HTML page. Specifically, it'll be called when the user clicks the submit button. That code is:

```
onclick="return
→ get_stores(this.form.zip.value)"
```

Because of the return in that statement, whether or not the form is submitted depends upon what value is returned by the get_stores() function. If an ajax request could be made, then false is returned, stopping the form from being submitted to the server (because the data is already accessible). If an ajax request could not be made, true is returned and

**Figure 13.25** If the PHP script does not return any data, this message is displayed in the HTML page.

the form will be sent to the server. This is desired because if an `ajax` request could not be made, the user should still be able to get the information somehow.

5. Begin defining the function for handling the request result.

```
function handle_stores() {
     if ( (ajax.readyState == 4) &&
→ (ajax.status == 200) ) {
```

This code is the same as it was in `checkusername.js`.

6. Handle the returned data.

```
if (ajax.responseText.length > 10) {
     show_stores(eval('(' +
→ ajax.responseText + ')'));
} else {
document.getElementById('list').
→ innerHTML = '<p>No stores matched
→ your search.</p>';
}
```

The PHP script will return either the data in JSON format (if the query worked) or the word *null* (if the query doesn't return any results, if an invalid zip code is used, or if the database connection cannot be made). As a simple test to see if the stores were returned, check if the length of the response is greater than 10 (or some other small number, allowing for both *null* and some extra spaces). So if just *null* is returned, the length will be less than 10 and the form will show that no match was made (**Figure 13.25**). If any JSON data was returned, then the length will be greater than 10 and the `show_stores()` function is called. This function is sent one argument: the `eval()` version of the `responseText`. The end result will be that `show_stores()` receives an array of JSON objects containing all the store data.

*continues on next page*

**7.** Complete the `handle_stores()` function.

```
    }
} // End of handle_stores() function.
```

**8.** Begin defining the `show_stores()` function.

```
function show_stores(stores) {
    var message = '';
```

As I mention in Step 6, this function receives one argument: a bunch of JSON data, assigned to the variable `stores`. Then a string is initialized. This function will take all the JSON data and concatenate it to the `message` variable, which will then be assigned to the HTML.

**9.** Loop through the JSON data.

```
for (var i = 0 ; i < stores.length ;
→ i++) {
    message += '<h2>' +
→ stores[i].name + '</h2>'
    + '<p>' +  stores[i].address +
→ '<br />'
    + stores[i].city + ', ' +
→ stores[i].state + ' '
    + stores[i].zip + '<br />'
    + stores[i].phone + '<br
→ />(approximately '
    + stores[i].distance + '
→ miles)</p>';
}
```

## Ajax Frameworks

If you'd rather not mess with all this hand-coding of JavaScript, there are tons of freely available Ajax frameworks floating about the Internet. Just a couple of examples are Rico (www.openrico.org), Dojo (www.dojotoolkit.org), script.aculo.us (http://script.aculo.us), XAJAX (www.xajaxproject.org), and SAJAX (www.modernmethod.com/sajax). What you can do with these frameworks is quite impressive!

The main downside to these is that they often use Ruby (or Ruby on Rails) or some other technology for the back end. This means that while the client side of things can be a snap to put together, you'll need to put more effort into figuring out how to tie the client to the server (your PHP code). But doing so isn't impossible, particularly with decent documentation and many Web searches, and may be well worth your time.

It would also be worth your while to consider the PEAR HTML_AJAX package (Arpad Ray, one its developers, was kind enough to help out on this chapter). It's a PHP-specific option, of course, so it may be much easier to integrate into your Web sites.

**The page at http://localhost says:**

<h2>Fishmonger's Heaven</h2><p>Pier 9<br />Morrisonville, WI 53571<br />(123) 000-7890<br />(approximately 132 miles)</p>

OK

**Figure 13.26** The HTML of a single returned store record (I use a JavaScript alert to display it—see the debugging section at the end of the chapter).

A simple for loop can access every stores element. The variable is an array of objects, each object representing one of the records returned by the MySQL database. In the loop, you can refer to stores.length to see how many items are in the array (like count($stores) in PHP). For each element in the array, the loop refers to stores[i].

Then, all you need to do is refer to the attributes of that object (the object being stores[i]). These attributes correspond to the array indexes set in the PHP script: *name*, *address*, *city*, *state*, *zip*, *phone*, and *distance*. Each of these values is concatenated to the message variable, along with some HTML. **Figure 13.26** shows an individually formatted record.

**10.** Complete the show_stores() function.

        document.getElementById('list').
    → innerHTML = message;

    } // End of show_stores() function.

All that's left to do is assign the compiled message variable to the proper HTML element's innerHTML.

**11.** Save the file as stores.js and place it in your Web directory.

This file should be put into the same directory as stores_json.php and ajax.js.

## ✔ Tip

■ Using the JavaScript eval() function can be unsafe if the source of the evaluated code cannot be trusted. In such cases, a JSON parser could be used instead:

    show_stores(ajax.responseText.
    → parseJSON());

## Creating the HTML

The last step for this second example is to make the HTML page. Like register.html, this file must:

◆ Include the required JavaScript.

◆ Define an event that triggers the Ajax process.

◆ Have a place in the HTML page for the result to go.

As I mention in the steps for stores.js, the event will be the clicking of the submit button. As for the last item, a DIV with an id of *list* (matching that in the JavaScript) will be defined.

### To create the HTML form:

1. Create a new HTML page in your text editor or IDE (**Script 13.7**).

```
<!DOCTYPE html PUBLIC "-//W3C//DTD
→ XHTML 1.0 Transitional//EN"
"http://www.w3.org/TR/xhtml1/DTD/
→ xhtml1-transitional.dtd">
<html xmlns="http://www.w3.org/1999/
→ xhtml">
<head>
    <title>Find Stores</title>
    <script src="ajax.js"
→ type="text/javascript"
→ language="javascript"></script>
    <script src="stores.js"
→ type="text/javascript"
→ language="javascript"></script>
</head>
<body>
<!-- Script 13.7 - stores.html
```

Make sure that you include ajax.js and stores.js.

**Script 13.7** This HTML page includes the two required JavaScript files and shows an HTML form.

```
1   <!DOCTYPE html PUBLIC "-//W3C//DTD XHTML
    1.0 Transitional//EN"
2        "http://www.w3.org/
    TR/xhtml1/DTD/xhtml1-transitional.dtd">
3   <html xmlns="http://www.w3.org/1999/
    xhtml">
4   <head>
5       <title>Find Stores</title>
6       <script src="ajax.js"
    type="text/javascript"
    language="javascript"></script>
7       <script src="stores.js"
    type="text/javascript"
    language="javascript"></script>
8   </head>
9   <body>
10  <!-- Script 13.7 - stores.html
11  /*  This page has a simple HTML form.
12   *  The JavaScript code is included in
    the HEAD.
13   */
14  -->
15  <form action="find_stores.php"
    method="post">
16
17  <p>Your Zip Code: <input name="zip"
    type="text" size="10" maxlength="10" />
    <input name="submit" type="submit"
    value="Find a Store" onclick="return
    get_stores(this.form.zip.value)" /></p>
18
19  </form>
20
21  <div id="list"></div>
22
23  </body>
24  </html>
```

**Figure 13.27** The HTML page upon first loading it.

**2.** Make the HTML form.

```
<form action="find_stores.php"
→ method="post">
<p>Your Zip Code: <input name="zip"
→ type="text" size="10"
→ maxlength="10" /> <input
→ name="submit" type="submit"
→ value="Find a Store"
→ onclick="return
→ get_stores(this.form.zip.value)"
→ /></p>
</form>
```

The form contains two elements: the input box for the zip code and the submit button. The JavaScript `onclick()` event is tied to this button.

If the `get_stores()` function returns the value `true`, the form would be submitted to `find_stores.php`. I have not, in this chapter, created `find_stores.php`, but it would do exactly what `stores.php` does, except it would display the data in an HTML page instead of printing it in JSON format.

**3.** Create the `DIV`.

```
<div id="list"></div>
```

After the form, a `DIV` is added, with an id (not a `name`) of *list*. This is part of the DOM that JavaScript will dynamically assign text to. When the form is first loaded, this area after the zip code is blank (**Figure 13.27**).

*continues on next page*

Full-Fledged Ajax

**4.** Complete the HTML page.

```
</body>
</html>
```

**5.** Save the file as `stores.html`, place it in your Web directory, along with `stores.php`, `ajax.js`, and `stores.js`, and test in your Web browser (**Figures 13.28** and **13.29**).

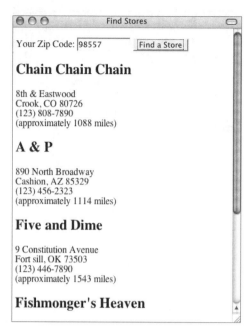

**Figure 13.28** Enter a zip code and click the button to fetch the data.

**Figure 13.29** Enter a different zip code and click the button to fetch the new data.

# Debugging Ajax Applications

Debugging your Ajax applications can be quite challenging because:

◆ There are so many technologies involved (PHP, MySQL, JavaScript, DOM, and HTML).

◆ You may be less familiar with JavaScript and DOM.

◆ Much of what happens goes on behind the scenes.

◆ Because of the JavaScript, you really need to test your applications on multiple browsers and platforms to ensure universal reliability.

In my experience developing Ajax applications from scratch, I've picked up quite a few useful debugging techniques, outlined in the following steps.

## Making POST Requests

I didn't have the need to in this chapter's two examples, but you can perform POST requests with Ajax instead of GET ones. To do so, start by naming that method when invoking the open() function:

```
ajax.open('post', 'scriptname.php');
```

Then you'll need to pass the data when calling the send() method. The data should be a string in the format of

*arg1=value&arg2=value&arg3=value…*

You might accomplish this by doing something like:

```
var post_data = 'first_name=' +
encodeURIComponent(first_name) +
'&last_name=' +
encodeURIComponent(last_name)
+'&city=' + encodeURIComponent(city);
```

Finally:

```
ajax.send(post_data);
```

## To debug Ajax applications:

**1.** Run your applications through a URL!

For the PHP to work, it must be accessed through `http://`. This means that you must load your HTML page through `http://`.

**2.** Test your PHP script separately.

This is something I include as a step for both Ajax examples. Be in the habit of doing this automatically, not just when things go awry.

**3.** Test your database queries separately.

This, and many other unmentioned techniques, are essential to debugging your PHP scripts, should Step 2 indicate a problem. Print out the exact query(ies) PHP is running (**Figure 13.30**) and use another interface, like the `mysql` client or phpMyAdmin, to confirm the results.

**4.** Validate, if appropriate, the data returned by the PHP script.

If the JavaScript function handling the returned data expects to receive XML or JSON, then the returned text *must be in strict XML or JSON format*. To validate that, follow Step 2, and then use a validation tool (search the Web) to confirm that the data conforms to the proper format.

**Figure 13.30** When PHP pages run dynamically generated queries on a database, it's best to know exactly what that query is.

**Figure 13.31** JavaScript alert prompts, while generally annoying, can be valuable debugging tools.

**Figure 13.32** This alert reveals the data, in JSON format, received by the JavaScript from the PHP page.

5. Use JavaScript alerts to indicate what's going on.

Since so much is going on behind the scenes, it's often necessary to shed some light on the processes. Add code like

```
alert('in the check_username()
function');
```

to your JavaScript code (e.g., put that alert as the first line in the `check_username()` function). Then, when you test the application, you'll see what the JavaScript is trying to do (**Figure 13.31**).

6. Use JavaScript alerts to indicate the values of variables.

There are three families of values you'll need to confirm:

◆ Values received by a function:

```
alert(zip);
```

Use this for any JavaScript function, like the one triggered by the HTML event or the one called when the PHP script returns its value.

◆ Values returned by the PHP script:

```
alert(ajax.responseText);
```

Since `responseText` stores the data you'll deal with in the JavaScript, confirming its value is a great debugging technique (**Figure 13.32**).

◆ Values to be assigned to HTML elements:

```
alert(message);
```

You could also have problems in writing new HTML to the Web page. In such cases, you'll need to confirm if the problem is in the message being written (tested using such an alert) or in the writing process itself (i.e., assigning a value to `innerHTML`).

*continues on next page*

**DEBUGGING AJAX APPLICATIONS**

**7.** Make sure you reload your Web browser after making changes.

Failure to do so is a common, and very frustrating, mistake.

**8.** Test with multiple browsers.

With JavaScript and HTML, different browsers can behave differently, so see how your applications behave in multiple browsers. Of the multiple browsers you test on, the first one should be good, like Firefox, and not quirky, like Internet Explorer.

**9.** Watch the method—GET or POST— being used.

Some browsers (I'm looking at you, Internet Explorer) cache GET page requests, so it might look as if the changes you made didn't take effect. Also, it's possible that using POST in your Ajax won't work properly with the PHP script (it's odd, but I've witnessed it myself), so try switching methods to rule that out as a culprit. To allow for any method in your PHP script, use $_REQUEST instead of $_POST or $_GET.

**Figure 13.33** Firefox's JavaScript console.

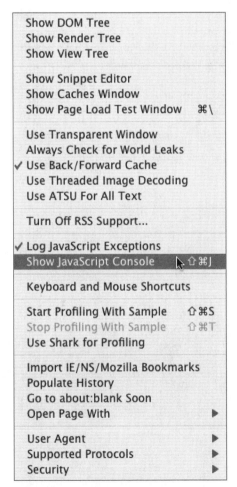

**Figure 13.34** Safari's Debug menu, which needs to be enabled in order to appear.

**10.** Use a JavaScript console.

Good browsers, like Firefox and Safari, can show JavaScript errors in a separate window (**Figure 13.33**), which will save you some grief. To enable this on Firefox, you'll need to opt for installing the Development Tools during installation. On Safari, enable the Debug menu (**Figure 13.34**), where you can access the JavaScript console.

**11.** Use a JavaScript debugger.

Firefox users benefit greatly from the Venkman debugger (www.mozilla.org/projects/venkman/). Internet Explorer users have the Microsoft Script Debugger.

## Know When You Shouldn't Use Ajax

Ajax is, without a doubt, pretty cool, but what's cool isn't always what's best (despite what you thought in high school). As with any technology, employ Ajax because you *should* (when it adds useful features without adding more problems and excluding users), not because you *can* or *know how*.

Since Ajax relies upon JavaScript, one potential problem is that not all users enable JavaScript and it can run differently on different browsers. A well-implemented Ajax example can work seamlessly on any browser, but you really need to be thorough. You can also create a non-Ajax version of a system for those with JavaScript disabled: not difficult, but again, something you do need to think about.

Another problem is that Ajax renders the browser's history feature unusable. For that matter, you can't bookmark Ajax pages the way you can search results (the page itself can be book-marked, but not after some interaction). So by adding functionality, your Ajax application will remove common features. And Ajax requests still require a server connection and the data transfer, so they don't save any resources, just reallocate them.

Finally, I'll point out that there's an argument to be made that IFrames offer similar function-ality to Ajax but without some of its downsides.

# 14

# XML AND PHP

XML, the Extensible Markup Language, is one of the most used technologies for sharing data between computers and applications. XML provides a format for storing not just information but also information about the information (aka *meta-information*). XML, like HTML, is based on Standard Generalized Markup Language, or SGML, which means that you'll see numerous similarities between the two (in fact, XHTML, is a combination of them). Early versions of PHP supported XML, PHP 4 improved upon that support, and PHP 5 took things even further.

This chapter begins with a basic introduction to XML: what it is, the proper XML syntax, and how to make your own XML document. From there, PHP will take over, both for reading and creating XML documents. You'll learn about and use the two primary XML handling methods. The chapter wraps up with a demonstration of creating RSS (Really Simple Syndication) feeds, an increasingly popular feature of Web sites and just one use of XML.

XML AND PHP

# What Is XML?

XML, which is governed by the World Wide Web Consortium (W3C), was created with several goals in mind:

◆ To be a regulated standard, not the proprietary technology of any one company

◆ To act as a highly flexible way to store nearly any type of information

◆ To be easily readable by humans and still usable by computers

◆ To be able to check itself for validity and integrity

While XML itself is not actually a markup language—despite its name—it provides a foundation for you to manufacture your own markup language. A markup language is used to help define or describe pieces of information. For example, the HTML code `<strong>Giant</strong>` indicates that the word *Giant* should be displayed in emphasized text.

With XML you use tags to encapsulate pieces of information in defined chunks. XML tags (or *elements* as they are formally called) are the opposite of HTML tags in that they define what something is but do not reveal how that something should be displayed. Whereas the purpose of HTML is to *present* information, the purpose of XML is to *identify* information.

**WHAT IS XML?**

## XML and...

Because XML is all about providing an independent way to store and transmit data, it's often intertwined with other networking technologies. You'll see other acronyms, like RPC (Remote Procedure Calls), SOAP (which used to be an acronym but technically isn't anymore), WSDL (Web Services Description Language), and REST (Representational State Transfer). All of these help create Web services: where part of the content of one Web site is based upon data requested from another Web site. Google, eBay, PayPal, Amazon, Yahoo!, and others all offer ways to use their data in your applications.

Every book having its limitations, you won't find examples of these here. Sadly, this chapter alone can only offer a mere introduction to XML. But that knowledge—basic XML—is key to implementing Web services in your own site when you're ready.

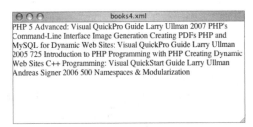

**Figure 14.1** Firefox (here, on Macintosh) automatically parses an XML document to display it in a more meaningful form.

**Figure 14.2** Safari (also for Macintosh) shows XML files as plain text, with the tags treated as unknown HTML (you can still see them in the source of the page).

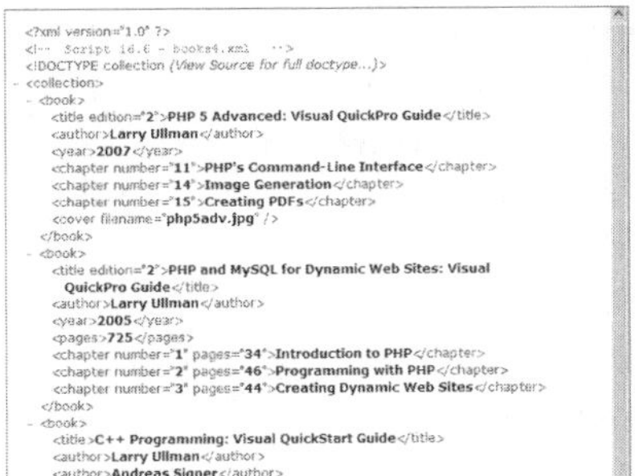

**Figure 14.3** Internet Explorer (on Windows) is also able to render XML data.

The power of XML is that you are not limited to any predetermined set of tags; you can actually use XML to come up with your own. Once you have created your markup language (your own definition of elements), you can begin to store data formatted within the newly defined tags.

XML documents can be created in any text editor or IDE. But they cannot necessarily be read in a Web browser like any old Web page (**Figures 14.1**, **14.2**, and **14.3**). You can use PHP to turn XML data into a browser-readable format, as you'll see by chapter's end.

# XML Syntax

Before doing anything with XML, you must understand how XML documents are structured. An XML document contains two parts:

◆ The prolog or XML declaration

◆ The data

The XML prolog is the first line of every XML file and should be in the form

`<?xml version="1.0"?>`

It indicates the XML version and, sometimes, the text encoding or similar attributes. There are actually two versions of XML—1.0 and 1.1—but the differences aren't important here and using version 1.0 is fine.

The main part of the XML document is the content itself. This section, like an HTML page, begins and ends with a root element. Each XML document can have only one root.

Within that root element will be more nested elements. Each element contains a start tag, the element data, and an end tag:

`<tag>data</tag>`

One example might involve products for an e-commerce store (**Script 14.1**). In this example, `store` is the root element.

The XML rules for elements insist upon the following:

◆ XML tags must be balanced in that they open and close (for every `<tag>` there must be a `</tag>`).

◆ Elements can be nested but not intertwined. HTML will let you get away with a construct like `<strong><em>Soul Mining</strong></em>`, but XML will not.

**Script 14.1** An XML document representing two products in a virtual store.

```
1    <?xml version="1.0"?>
2    <!-- Script 14.1 - store.xml -->
3    <!DOCTYPE store SYSTEM "store.dtd">
4    <store>
5      <product>
6        <name>T-Shirt</name>
7        <size>XL</size>
8        <color>White</color>
9        <price>12.00</price>
10     </product>
11     <product>
12       <name>Sweater</name>
13       <size>M</size>
14       <color>Blue</color>
15       <price>25.50</price>
16       <picture filename="sweater.png" />
17     </product>
18   </store>
```

As for the tag names, they are case-sensitive. You can use letters, numbers, and some other characters, but tag names cannot contain spaces or begin with the letters *xml*. They can only begin with either a letter or the underscore.

Before getting into an example, two last pieces of information. First, it is safe to use white space outside of elements but not within the tags or between them (XML is generally sensitive to white space, unlike PHP or HTML). Second, you can place comments within an XML file—for your own use, not for any technical purposes—by using the same syntax as HTML:

```
<!-- This is my comment. -->
```

To start down the XML path, you'll hand-code an XML document: a partial listing of the books I've written (with apologies for the self-centeredness of the example).

## To write XML:

**1.** Begin a new XML document in your text editor or IDE (**Script 14.2**).

```
<?xml version="1.0"?>
<!-- Script 14.1 - books1.xml -->
```

**2.** Open with the root element.

```
<collection>
```

For a file to be proper XML, it must use a root element. All of the content of the page will be stored between the opening and closing tags of this element. You can make up the name of this element, as is the case with all of your elements.

**3.** Add a book to the file.

```
<book>
<title>PHP 5 Advanced: Visual
→ QuickPro Guide</title>
<author>Larry Ullman</author>
<year>2007</year>
</book>
```

This book is represented by one element, book, with three nested elements: title, author, and year.

**4.** Add another book.

```
<book>
<title>PHP and MySQL for Dynamic Web
→ Sites: Visual QuickPro
→ Guide</title>
<author>Larry Ullman</author>
<year>2005</year>
<pages>725</pages>
</book>
```

This book has a fourth nested element: pages. It is perfectly acceptable, even common, for similar elements to have different subelements.

**Script 14.2** This is a basic XML document containing information about three books.

```
1    <?xml version="1.0"?>
2    <!-- Script 14.2 - books1.xml -->
3    <collection>
4      <book>
5        <title>PHP 5 Advanced: Visual QuickPro
         Guide</title>
6        <author>Larry Ullman</author>
7        <year>2007</year>
8      </book>
9      <book>
10       <title>PHP and MySQL for Dynamic Web
         Sites: Visual QuickPro Guide</title>
11       <author>Larry Ullman</author>
12       <year>2005</year>
13       <pages>725</pages>
14     </book>
15     <book>
16       <title>C++ Programming: Visual QuickStart
         Guide</title>
17       <author>Larry Ullman</author>
18       <author>Andreas Signer</author>
19       <year>2006</year>
20       <pages>500</pages>
21     </book>
22   </collection>
```

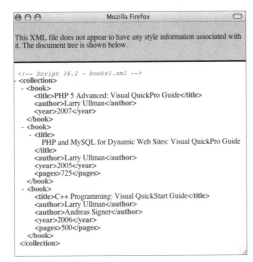

**Figure 14.4** How Firefox displays the `books1.xml` file.

**5.** Add a third and final book.

```
<book>
<title>C++ Programming: Visual
→ QuickStart Guide</title>
<author>Larry Ullman</author>
<author>Andreas Signer</author>
<year>2006</year>
<pages>500</pages>
</book>
```

This record is different from the other two in that it has two authors. Each piece of author data (the name) is placed within its own **author** element (rather than putting both names within one element).

**6.** Complete the XML document.

```
</collection>
```

This closes the root element.

**7.** Save this file as `books1.xml`.

If you want, view it in a Web browser (**Figure 14.4**).

# Attributes, Empty Elements, and Entities

The preceding section of the chapter and the books1.xml file demonstrate the basic syntax of an XML document. There are three more concepts to cover before learning how to handle XML with PHP.

An element, as already described, has both tags and data. This is like HTML:

```
<p>some text here</p>
```

Also like HTML, XML elements can have attributes:

```
<tag attribute_name="value">data</tag>
<p class="highlight">some text here</p>
```

XML elements can have an unlimited number of attributes, the only restriction being that each attribute must have a value. You could not do:

```
<tag attribute_name>data</tag>
```

You can use either single or double quotes for quoting your attribute values, but you must use quotes and you should be consistent about which type you use.

Attributes are often used with empty elements. An empty element is one that doesn't encapsulate any data. As an HTML example, `<br />` is an empty element. Just as XHTML requires the space and the slash at the end of an empty element, so does XML:

```
<tag attribute_name="value" />
```

For example, you might have this:

```
<picture image_name="me.jpg" />
```

The last little idea to throw out here is the *entity*. Some characters cannot be used in XML data, as they cause conflicts. Instead, a character combination is used, starting with the ampersand (&) and ending with the semicolon (;). **Table 14.1** lists five of the predeclared XML entities.

**Table 14.1** Use these five entities in your data whenever one of these special characters is required.

## XML Entities

| ENTITY | MEANING |
| --- | --- |
| &amp; | & |
| &lt; | < |
| &gt; | > |
| &apos; | ' |
| &quot; | " |

## To use attributes, empty elements, and entities:

1. Open books1.xml in your text editor or IDE, if it is not already open.

2. Add edition numbers to the first two books (**Script 14.3**).

   ```
   <title edition="2">PHP 5 Advanced:
   → Visual QuickPro Guide</title>

   <title edition="2">PHP and MySQL for
   → Dynamic Web Sites: Visual QuickPro
   → Guide</title>
   ```

To indicate that these two titles are second editions, an attribute is added to their title elements, with values of 2. The third book, which is in its first edition, won't have this attribute, although you could add it with a value of 1.

*continues on next page*

**Script 14.3** Attributes, empty elements, and entities have been added to the XML document to better describe the data.

```
1    <?xml version="1.0"?>
2    <!-- Script 14.3 - books2.xml -->
3    <collection>
4      <book>
5        <title edition="2">PHP 5 Advanced: Visual QuickPro Guide</title>
6        <author>Larry Ullman</author>
7        <year>2007</year>
8        <chapter number="11">PHP&apos;s Command-Line Interface</chapter>
9        <chapter number="14">Image Generation</chapter>
10       <chapter number="15">Creating PDFs</chapter>
11       <cover filename="php5adv.jpg" />
12     </book>
13     <book>
14       <title edition="2">PHP and MySQL for Dynamic Web Sites: Visual QuickPro Guide</title>
15       <author>Larry Ullman</author>
16       <year>2005</year>
17       <pages>725</pages>
18       <chapter number="1" pages="34">Introduction to PHP</chapter>
19       <chapter number="2" pages="46">Programming with PHP</chapter>
20       <chapter number="3" pages="44">Creating Dynamic Web Sites</chapter>
21     </book>
22     <book>
23       <title>C++ Programming: Visual QuickStart Guide</title>
24       <author>Larry Ullman</author>
25       <author>Andreas Signer</author>
26       <year>2006</year>
27       <pages>500</pages>
28       <chapter number="12">Namespaces &amp; Modularization</chapter>
29     </book>
30   </collection>
```

**3.** Add a couple chapters to the first book.

```
<chapter number="11">PHP&apos;s
→ Command-Line Interface</chapter>
<chapter number="14">Image
→ Generation</chapter>
<chapter number="15">Creating
→ PDFs</chapter>
```

Three chapters are added, each having an attribute of number, with a value of the chapter's number. Chapter 11, whose name is *PHP's Command-Line Interface*, requires the apostrophe entity (&apos;).

**4.** Add a couple chapters to the second book.

```
<chapter number="1"
→ pages="34">Introduction to
→ PHP</chapter>
<chapter number="2"
→ pages="46">Programming with
→ PHP</chapter>
<chapter number="3"
→ pages="44">Creating Dynamic Web
→ Sites</chapter>
```

To demonstrate multiple attributes, these chapters contain information about their number and page count. It is not a problem that the XML file contains both elements called pages and attributes with the same name.

**5.** Add a chapter to the third book.

```
<chapter number="12">Namespaces &amp;
→ Modularization</chapter>
```

I'm entering just this one chapter, to demonstrate the ampersand entity.

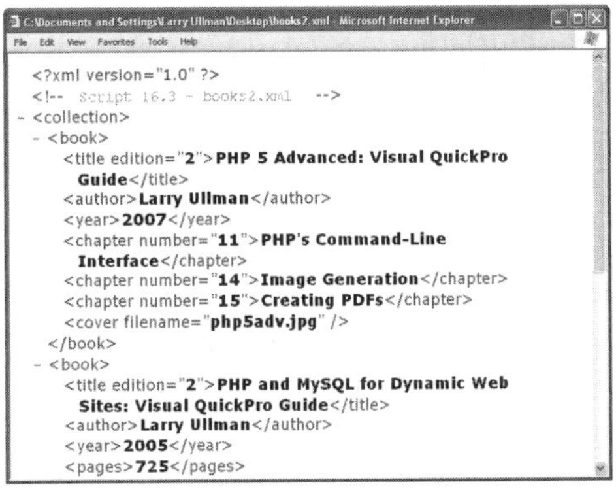

**Figure 14.5** The updated books2.xml in Internet Explorer.

**6.** Add an empty element to the first book.

`<cover filename="php5adv.jpg" />`

The cover element contains no data but does have an attribute, whose value is the name of the cover image file.

**7.** Save this file as books2.xml.

If you want, view it in a Web browser (**Figure 14.5**).

## ✔ Tips

■ Whether you use a nested element or an attribute is often a matter of choice. The first book in books2.xml could also be reflected as (omitting a couple elements for brevity):

```
<book>
<title>PHP 5 Advanced: Visual
→ QuickPro Guide</title>
<edition>2</edition>
<chapter>
<number>11</number>
<name>PHP&apos;s Command-Line
→ Interface</name>
</chapter>
<chapter>
<number>14</number>
<name>Image Generation</name>
</chapter>
<cover>php5adv.jpg</cover>
</book>
```

■ HTML has dozens upon dozens of predeclared entities, including the five listed in Table 14.1.

■ You can also create your own entities in a Document Type Definition file, discussed next in the chapter.

**ATTRIBUTES, EMPTY ELEMENTS, AND ENTITIES**

# Document Type Definitions

XML files primarily contain data, as you've already seen in the first three scripts. That data can also be associated with a *schema*, which is a guide for how the XML document should be formatted. A schema can be put together in many kinds of ways, the DTD, a Document Type Definition, being one of the older, standard methods (included in the definition of XML 1.0). For the simple examples in this chapter, a DTD will suffice. A DTD or any other schema is used to validate an XML document. They are optional, though, as XML data can be used with or without validation.

To associate a DTD with an XML file, a reference line is placed after the prolog but before the data:

```
<?xml version="1.0"?>
<!DOCTYPE name SYSTEM "filename.dtd">
<name>
```

The syntax begins `<!DOCTYPE name`. This is similar to HTML documents that begin with `<!DOCTYPE html`, stating that the root element of the file is the `html` tag. Within the document type declaration, you can define your elements or you can reference an external document that contains these definitions. For the declaration to point to an external file, your document type declaration would be

```
<!DOCTYPE name SYSTEM
→ "/path/to/filename.dtd">
```

where `filename.dtd` is the included file and */path/to* is a Uniform Resource Indicator, or URI, pinpointing where that file is on the server.

Now that the XML file references the DTD, that file must be created. This process is called *document modeling*, because you are creating a paradigm for how your XML data should be organized. A DTD defines every element and attribute in your markup language.

The syntax for defining an element is

```
<!ELEMENT name TYPE>
```

where *name* is the name of the new tag and it will contain content of type *TYPE*.

**Table 14.2** lists the three primary element types and their meanings.

Applying this to the e-commerce example (Script 14.1), some of the elements could be defined like so:

```
<!ELEMENT name (#PCDATA)>
<!ELEMENT size (#PCDATA)>
<!ELEMENT price (#PCDATA)>
<!ELEMENT picture EMPTY>
```

The last element, picture, is of type EMPTY because it has no content (it has an attribute of filename).

The rules just defined seem to cover the XML in Script 14.1, but there are still a couple of missing pieces. First, there's another element used, that of product, which contains all of the other elements. To define it:

```
<!ELEMENT product (name, size, price,
→ picture)>
```

This states that product contains four other elements in the order of name, size, price, and picture. Definitions can be more flexible by using regular expression–like syntax.

```
<!ELEMENT product (name, size*, price,
→ picture?)>
```

This line indicates that product can contain up to four elements. One element, size, can be listed anywhere from zero to multiple times. Another element, picture, is entirely optional, but if present, there can be only one. **Table 14.3** lists the pertinent characters for defining elements.

*continues on next page*

**Table 14.2** These are the three main element types, although an element can also consist of other elements or mixed data.

| Element Types | |
| --- | --- |
| TYPE | ASSOCIATION |
| (#PCDATA) | Generally text (specifically Parsed-Character Data) |
| EMPTY | Nothing |
| ANY | Anything |

**Table 14.3** The four symbols here reflect their regular expression counterparts and are used to more specifically define an element.

| Element Type Symbols | |
| --- | --- |
| SYMBOL | MEANING |
| ? | Optional (zero or one) |
| + | At least one |
| * | Zero or more |
| \| | Or |

You can extend this even further by dictating that an element contain other elements, parsed-character data, or nothing, using the OR character:

```
<!ELEMENT thing (other_element | #PCDATA
→ | EMPTY)>
```

The second problem with the current model for Script 14.1 is that it doesn't reflect the `picture` element's attribute (the `filename`). To allow elements to have attributes, make an attribute list within the DTD. This can be done only after defining the elements (or at least, the attributes of an element must be defined after the element itself has been defined).

```
<!ATTLIST element_name
attribute_name attribute_type
→ attribute_description
>
```

The `attribute_name` field is simply a text string like *color* or *alignment*. The `attribute_type` indicates the format of the attribute. **Table 14.4** lists the possibilities.

Another possibility is for an attribute to be an enumerated list of possible values:

```
<!ATTLIST element_name
attribute_name (value1 | value2)
→ "value1"
>
```

The preceding code says that `element_name` takes an attribute of `attribute_name` with possible values of `value1` or `value2`, the former being the default.

The third parameter for an attribute—the attribute's description—allows you to further define how it will function. Possibilities include `#REQUIRED`, meaning that an element must use that attribute; `#IMPLIED`, which means that the attribute is optional; and `#FIXED`, indicating that the attribute will always have the same value. To round out the definition of the `picture` element for Script 14.1, an attribute should be added:

```
<!ATTLIST picture
filename NMTOKEN #REQUIRED
>
```

Now that you've seen the foundation of defining elements, you can write a Document Type Definition that corresponds to the books XML.

**Table 14.4** There are more options for your attribute type field, but these four cover the basics.

| Element Attribute Types | | |
|---|---|---|
| TYPE | MEANING | EXAMPLE |
| CDATA | Character Data | General text |
| NMTOKEN | Name Token | String (without white space) |
| NMTOKENS | Several Name Tokens | NMTOKENS separated by white spaces (e.g., "Jessica Zoe Sam") |
| ID | Unique Identifier | Text or numerical, but it must be unique for each element |

**DOCUMENT TYPE DEFINITIONS**

## To write a Document Type Definition:

1. Create a new document in your text editor or IDE (**Script 14.4**).

   ```
   <!-- Script 14.4 -->
   ```

2. Define the collection element.

   ```
   <!ELEMENT collection (book+)>
   ```

   The first element to be declared is the root element, collection. It consists only of one or more book elements.

   *continues on next page*

**Script 14.4** The DTD file will establish all the rules by which the book XML pages must abide.

```
1    <!-- Script 14.4 -->
2
3    <!ELEMENT collection (book+)>
4
5    <!ELEMENT book (title, author+, year, pages?, chapter*, cover?)>
6
7    <!ELEMENT title (#PCDATA)>
8    <!ELEMENT author (#PCDATA)>
9    <!ELEMENT year (#PCDATA)>
10   <!ELEMENT pages (#PCDATA)>
11   <!ELEMENT chapter (#PCDATA)>
12   <!ELEMENT cover EMPTY>
13
14   <!ATTLIST title
15   edition NMTOKEN #IMPLIED
16   >
17
18   <!ATTLIST chapter
19   number NMTOKEN #IMPLIED
20   pages NMTOKEN #IMPLIED
21   >
22
23   <!ATTLIST cover
24   filename NMTOKEN #REQUIRED
25   >
```

**3.** Define the book element.

```
<!ELEMENT book (title, author+, year,
→ pages?, chapter*, cover?)>
```

This tag will contain up to six other tags: title, author, and year, which are required; chapter, which is optional and can be listed numerous times; and pages and cover_image, both of which are optional but can occur only once. The author is also flagged as being allowed multiple times.

**4.** Define the title, author, year, pages, and chapter elements.

```
<!ELEMENT title (#PCDATA)>
<!ELEMENT author (#PCDATA)>
<!ELEMENT year (#PCDATA)>
<!ELEMENT pages (#PCDATA)>
<!ELEMENT chapter (#PCDATA)>
```

Each of these elements contains only character data.

**5.** Define the cover element.

```
<!ELEMENT cover EMPTY>
```

This one item is different from the others because the element will always be empty. The information for this element will be stored in the attribute.

**6.** Define the attributes for title and chapter.

```
<!ATTLIST title
edition NMTOKEN #IMPLIED
>
<!ATTLIST chapter
number NMTOKEN #IMPLIED
pages NMTOKEN #IMPLIED
>
```

The title element has one optional attribute, the edition. The chapter element has two attributes—number and pages—both of which are optional.

## Well-Formed and Valid XML

Two ways of describing an XML document are *well formed* and *valid*. A *well-formed* XML document conforms to the XML standard. These are the rules discussed in the "XML Syntax" section of this chapter. A *valid* XML document is both well formed and adheres to the rules laid out in its associated schema or Document Type Definition file.

Most XML data can be used as long as it is well formed, which is why many discussions of XML don't even go into the topics of schema and DTD. But being valid is, for obvious reasons, better.

**7.** Define the attribute for cover.

```
<!ATTLIST cover
filename NMTOKEN #REQUIRED
>
```

The cover element will take one mandatory attribute, the filename of type NMTOKEN, which means it will be a string (e.g., *image.jpg*). Keep in mind that the element itself is not required, as defined in the book tag. So the XML file should either include cover with a filename attribute or not include it at all.

**8.** Save this file as collection.dtd.

Now that the document modeling is done, the DTD needs to be linked to the XML file.

**9.** Open books2.xml (Script 14.3) in your text editor or IDE.

**10.** After the prolog but before the root element, add the doctype declaration (**Script 14.5**).

```
<!DOCTYPE collection SYSTEM
→ "collection.dtd">
```

*continues on next page*

**Script 14.5** The books file now references the corresponding DTD (Script 14.4).

```
1    <?xml version="1.0"?>
2    <!-- Script 14.5 - books3.xml -->
3    <!DOCTYPE collection SYSTEM "collection.dtd">
4    <collection>
5    <book>
6    <title edition="2">PHP 5 Advanced: Visual QuickPro Guide</title>
7    <author>Larry Ullman</author>
8    <year>2007</year>
9    <chapter number="11">PHP&apos;s Command-Line Interface</chapter>
10   <chapter number="14">Image Generation</chapter>
11   <chapter number="15">Creating PDFs</chapter>
12   <cover filename="php5adv.jpg" />
13   </book>
14   <book>
15   <title edition="2">PHP and MySQL for Dynamic Web Sites: Visual QuickPro Guide</title>
16   <author>Larry Ullman</author>
17   <year>2005</year>
18   <pages>725</pages>
19   <chapter number="1" pages="34">Introduction to PHP</chapter>
20   <chapter number="2" pages="46">Programming with PHP</chapter>
21   <chapter number="3" pages="44">Creating Dynamic Web Sites</chapter>
22   </book>
23   <book>
24   <title>C++ Programming: Visual QuickStart Guide</title>
25   <author>Larry Ullman</author>
26   <author>Andreas Signer</author>
27   <year>2006</year>
28   <pages>500</pages>
29   <chapter number="12">Namespaces &amp; Modularization</chapter>
30   </book>
31   </collection>
```

**11.** Save the file with these new changes (I've also changed its name to `books3.xml`). Place this file and `collection.dtd` in your Web directory (in the same folder), and test in your Web browser (**Figure 14.6**).

## ✔ Tips

■ There are other ways of creating a schema, including XML Schema. More sophisticated than a DTD, and having vastly different syntax, XML Schema serves the same purpose but requires a whole new body of knowledge.

■ One of the great things about XML is that you can write your own DTDs or make use of document models created by others, which are freely available online. Developers have already written models for books, recipes, and more.

■ If you get into developing complex XML applications, you may want to learn about namespaces, which is another way to group elements. Check an XML reference for more information.

■ **Script 14.6** shows `books3.xml` (Script 14.5) with the element definitions within the document instead of using an external DTD.

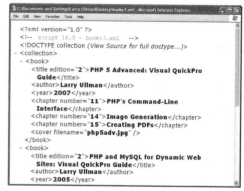

**Figure 14.6** The `books3.xml`, in Internet Explorer, which indicates the added doctype.

**Script 14.6** To define the elements in the XML file, the DTD reference could be replaced.

```
1    <?xml version="1.0"?>
2    <!-- Script 14.6 - books4.xml -->
3    <!DOCTYPE collection [
4
5    <!ELEMENT collection (book+)>
6
7    <!ELEMENT book (title, author+, year, pages?, chapter*, cover?)>
8
9    <!ELEMENT title (#PCDATA)>
10   <!ELEMENT author (#PCDATA)>
11   <!ELEMENT year (#PCDATA)>
12   <!ELEMENT pages (#PCDATA)>
13   <!ELEMENT chapter (#PCDATA)>
14   <!ELEMENT cover EMPTY>
15
16   <!ATTLIST title
17   edition NMTOKEN #IMPLIED
18   >
19
20   <!ATTLIST chapter
21   number NMTOKEN #IMPLIED
22   pages NMTOKEN #IMPLIED
23   >
24
25   <!ATTLIST cover
26   filename NMTOKEN #REQUIRED
27   >
28
29   ]>
30   <collection>
31   <book>
32   <title edition="2">PHP 5 Advanced: Visual QuickPro Guide</title>
33   <author>Larry Ullman</author>
34   <year>2007</year>
35   <chapter number="11">PHP&apos;s Command-Line Interface</chapter>
36   <chapter number="14">Image Generation</chapter>
37   <chapter number="15">Creating PDFs</chapter>
38   <cover filename="php5adv.jpg" />
39   </book>
40   <book>
41   <title edition="2">PHP and MySQL for Dynamic Web Sites: Visual QuickPro Guide</title>
42   <author>Larry Ullman</author>
43   <year>2005</year>
44   <pages>725</pages>
45   <chapter number="1" pages="34">Introduction to PHP</chapter>
46   <chapter number="2" pages="46">Programming with PHP</chapter>
47   <chapter number="3" pages="44">Creating Dynamic Web Sites</chapter>
48   </book>
49   <book>
50   <title>C++ Programming: Visual QuickStart Guide</title>
51   <author>Larry Ullman</author>
52   <author>Andreas Signer</author>
53   <year>2006</year>
54   <pages>500</pages>
55   <chapter number="12">Namespaces &amp; Modularization</chapter>
56   </book>
57   </collection>
```

# Parsing XML

There's more to XML than just composing XML documents and DTD files, although that is the basis of XML. One thing you can do with XML is parse it. Parsing XML is a matter of using an application or library to access XML files and...

- Check if they are well formed

- Check if they are valid

- Access the stored data

A parser, in short, takes XML files and breaks them down into their various pieces. As an example, the code `<artist>Air</artist>` consists of the opening tag (`<artist>`), the content (*Air*), and the closing tag (`</artist>`). While this distinction is obvious to the human eye, the ability of a computer to pull meaning out of a string of characters is the power of XML.

There are two types of XML parsers: event-based and tree-based. The former goes into action when an event occurs. An example of an event would be encountering an opening tag in an XML file. By reading an entire file and doing things at each event, this type of parser—also called a SAX (Simple API for XML)—manages the entire XML document. Expat, to be demonstrated next, is an event-based parser.

The second parser type views an XML file and creates a tree-like representation of the entire thing that can then be manipulated. These are primarily DOM (Document Object Model) systems such as libxml. **Figure 14.7** shows how Script 14.1 would be represented as a DOM tree. SimpleXML, covered later in the chapter, is a DOM parser.

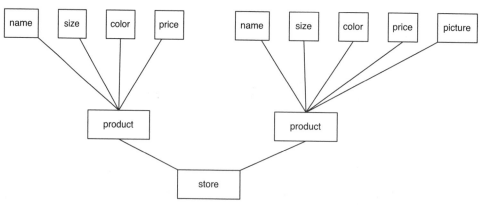

**Figure 14.7** A DOM, or tree, representation of the store XML file (Script 14.1).

## Parsing XML with Expat

Using Expat with PHP is a four-step process:

1. Create a new parser.

2. Identify the functions to use for handling events.

3. Parse the file.

4. Free up the resources used by the parser.

The first step is accomplished using `xml_parse_create()`.

```
$parser = xml_parser_create();
```

The second step is the most important. Because Expat is an event-handler parser, it makes use of callback functions when encountering events. The primary events that occur are reading:

◆ An opening tag

◆ The content between tags

◆ A closing tag

You need to tell PHP what user-defined functions should be called when each of these events occurs. For the opening and closing tags, use the `xml_set_element_handler()` function:

```
xml_set_element_handler ($parser,
→ 'open_element_function',
→ 'close_element_function');
```

For the tag content, use `xml_set_character_data_handler()` to name the callback function:

```
xml_set_character_data_handler ($parser,
→ 'data_function');
```

Now, when the parser encounters the different events, it will automatically send that content to the proper function.

Parsing the file requires the use of the `xml_parse()` function, which takes two arguments (and an optional third).

```
xml_parse ($parser, $data,
→ $stopping_point);
```

This function is first fed the pointer or reference to the parser, and then the information to be parsed. The third argument tells the parser when to stop working.

Finally, you should free up the resources used by the parser by calling

```
xml_parser_free ($parser);
```

One use of PHP and XML is to turn XML documents into HTML so that the information can be displayed in the browser (especially because some of the currently available browsers will not do this automatically). As an example, I'll write a PHP script that uses Expat to make a legible Web page from an XML file.

## To parse XML with PHP:

1. Create a new document in your text editor or IDE, beginning with the standard HTML (**Script 14.7**).

```
<!DOCTYPE html PUBLIC "-//W3C//DTD
→ XHTML 1.0 Transitional//EN"
"http://www.w3.org/TR/xhtml1/DTD/
→ xhtml1-transitional.dtd">
<html xmlns="http://www.w3.org/1999/
→ xhtml" xml:lang="en" lang="en">
<head>
     <meta http-equiv="content-type"
→ content="text/html; charset=iso-
→ 8859-1" />
     <title>XML Expat Parser</title>
     <style type="text/css"
→ title="text/css" media="all">
.tag {
     color: #00F;
}
.content {
     color: #C03;
}
.attribute {
     color: #063;
}
.avalue {
     color: #000;
}
</style>
</head>
<body>
<pre>
<?php # Script 14.7 - expat.php
```

I add the `<pre>` tag here because I'll be using spaces throughout the page to align my code and I want the Web browser to honor them. And yes, that means this isn't valid XHTML, but that's a price I'm willing to pay in this example.

Notice that I've also declared four CSS classes to help with the formatting of the output.

*continues on page 553*

**Script 14.7** This script uses PHP in conjunction with the Expat library to parse XML documents, turning them into an HTML page.

```
1    <!DOCTYPE html PUBLIC "-//W3C//DTD XHTML 1.0 Transitional//EN"
2           "http://www.w3.org/TR/xhtml1/DTD/xhtml1-transitional.dtd">
3    <html xmlns="http://www.w3.org/1999/xhtml" xml:lang="en" lang="en">
4    <head>
5        <meta http-equiv="content-type" content="text/html; charset=iso-8859-1" />
6        <title>XML Expat Parser</title>
7        <style type="text/css" title="text/css" media="all">
8    .tag {
9         color: #00F;
10   }
11   .content {
12        color: #C03;
13   }
14   .attribute {
15        color: #063;
16   }
17   .avalue {
18        color: #000;
19   }
```

*(script continues on next page)*

```
      ┌─────────────────────────────────────────────────────────────┐
      │ ⊖ ⊖ ⊖                        📄 Script                        │
20    </style>
21    </head>
22    <body>
23    <pre>
24    <?php # Script 14.7 - expat.php
25
26    /*  This script will parse an XML file.
27     *  It uses the Expat library, an event-based parser.
28     */
29
30    // Define some constants to represent
31    // the greater-than and less-than symbols.
32    define ('LT', '<span class="tag">&lt;');
33    define ('GT', '&gt;</span>');
34
35    // Function for handling the open tag:
36    function handle_open_element ($p, $element, $attributes) {
37
38        // Make the element lowercase:
39        $element = strtolower($element);
40
41        // Do different things based upon the element:
42        switch ($element) {
43
44            case 'collection':
45                echo LT . $element . GT . "\n";
46                break;
47
48            case 'book': // Indent books two spaces:
49                echo '  ' . LT . $element . GT . "\n";
50                break;
51
52            case 'chapter': // Indent four spaces:
53                echo '    ' . LT . $element;
54
55                // Add each attribute:
56                foreach ($attributes as $key => $value) {
57                    echo ' <span class="attribute">' . strtolower($key) . '="<span class="avalue">' .
      $value . '</span>"</span>';
58                }
59                echo GT;
60                break;
61
62            case 'cover': // Show the image.
63
64                // Get the image info:
65                $image = @getimagesize ($attributes['FILENAME']);
66
67                // Make the image HTML:
68                echo "<img src=\"{$attributes['FILENAME']}\" $image[3] border=\"0\" /><br />\n";
69                break;
70
```

*(script continues on next page)*

**Script 14.7** *continued*

```
71          // Indent everything else four spaces:
72          default:
73              echo '    ' . LT . $element . GT;
74              break;
75
76      } // End of switch.
77
78  } // End of handle_open_element() function.
79
80  // Function for handling the closing tag:
81  function handle_close_element ($p, $element) {
82
83      // Make the element lowercase:
84      $element = strtolower($element);
85
86      // Indent closing book tags 2 spaces,
87      // Do nothing with cover,
88      // Do nothing special with everything else.
89      if ($element == 'book') {
90          echo '  ' . LT . '/' . $element . GT . "\n";
91      } elseif ($element != 'cover') {
92          echo LT . '/' . $element . GT . "\n";
93      }
94
95  } // End of handle_close_element() function.
96
97  // Function for printing the content:
98  function handle_character_data ($p, $cdata) {
99      echo "<span class=\"content\">$cdata</span>";
100 }
101
102 # --------------------
103 # End of the functions.
104 # --------------------
105
106 // Create the parser:
107 $p = xml_parser_create();
108
109 // Set the handling functions:
110 xml_set_element_handler ($p, 'handle_open_element', 'handle_close_element');
111 xml_set_character_data_handler ($p, 'handle_character_data');
112
113 // Read the file:
114 $file = 'books3.xml';
115 $fp = @fopen ($file, 'r') or die ("Could not open a file called '$file'.\n</body>\n</html>\n");
116 while ($data = fread ($fp, filesize($file))) {
117     xml_parse ($p, $data, feof($fp));
118 }
119
120 // Free up the parser:
121 xml_parser_free($p);
122 ?>
123 </pre>
124 </body>
125 </html>
```

2. Define the necessary constants.

```
define ('LT', '<span
→ class="tag">&lt;');
define ('GT', '&gt;</span>');
```

My script will mimic what the built-in Firefox or Internet Explorer parser does with XML files (see Figure 14.6). To this end, I'll frequently be printing out the greater-than and less-than symbols in a blue font. The start of the tags (the less-than symbol) will also start the span with the CSS class association. The close of the tags (the greater-than symbol) will close this same span.

3. Begin the function for handling opening tags.

```
function handle_open_element ($p,
→ $element, $attributes) {
$element = strtolower($element);
```

The function that will be called whenever an opening tag is encountered by the parser will be handle_open_element(). This function will receive from the parser the parser reference, the name of the element, and an associative array of any attributes that element contains. As an example, the chapter element can have both number and pages attributes. Upon encountering that tag, the parser will send this function the values $p (for the parser), chapter (the name of the element), and an array that could be defined like so:

```
$attributes = array ('NUMBER' => 1,
→ 'PAGES' => '34');
```

(One oddity is that every element and attribute name is received in all-uppercase letters, so I use the strtolower() function to turn them back into a lowercase form.)

4. Begin a switch for handling the different elements.

```
switch ($element) {
    case 'collection':
        echo LT . $element . GT
→ . "\n";
        break;
    case 'book':
        echo ' ' . LT .
→ $element . GT . "\n";
        break;
```

Depending on the element received, the function will do different things. For the root element, collection, the element name will be printed as a tag (<collection>), using the HTML entity versions of < and > stored in the constants. For the book elements, the same rules applied, but the tag is indented two spaces.

5. Add a case for chapter elements.

```
case 'chapter':
    echo '   ' . LT . $element;
    foreach ($attributes as $key =>
→ $value) {
        echo ' <span
→ class="attribute">' .
→ strtolower($key) . '="<span
→ class="avalue">' . $value .
→ '</span>"</span>';
    }
    echo GT;
    break;
```

For the chapter element, I'll want to loop through the $attributes array, printing each name/value pair (or key/value pair).

*continues on next page*

**6.** Add a case for cover elements.

```
case 'cover':

        $image = @getimagesize
→ ($attributes['FILENAME']);

        echo "<img
→ src=\"{$attributes['FILENAME']}\"
→ $image[3] border=\"0\" /><br />\n";

        break;
```

If the element is the cover, I'll place the image itself in the page in lieu of referring to the textual name of the element or its attributes.

**7.** Complete the `switch` and the function.

```
        default:

                echo '    ' . LT
→ . $element . GT;

                break;

    }

}
```

The default case will apply to the `title`, the `pages`, the `year`, and the `author`. Each will be indented four spaces.

**8.** Write the function for handling any closing elements.

```
function handle_close_element ($p,
→ $element) {

    $element = strtolower($element);

    if ($element == 'book') {

            echo '  ' . LT . '/' .
→ $element . GT . "\n";

    } elseif ($element != 'cover') {

            echo LT . '/' . $element
→ . GT . "\n";

    }

}
```

This function is more straightforward than its predecessor. All this does is send a formatted version of the tag to the browser, assuming the tag is not the closing cover tag. The book tag is indented two spaces, everything else four.

**9.** Script the final function.

```
function handle_character_data ($p,
→ $cdata) {

        echo "<span class=\"content\">
→ $cdata</span>";

}
```

The `handle_character_data()` function will be used for the information between the opening and closing tags. It will be printed in its own CSS class. Note that the parser does not capitalize this information as it does the element and attribute names.

**10.** Create a new parser and identify the functions to use.

```
$p = xml_parser_create();

xml_set_element_handler ($p,
→ 'handle_open_element',
→ 'handle_close_element');

xml_set_character_data_handler ($p,
→ 'handle_character_data');
```

**11.** Read and parse the XML file.

```
$file = 'books3.xml';

$fp = @fopen ($file, 'r') or die
→ ("Could not open a file called
→ '$file'.\n</body>\n</html>\n");

while ($data = fread ($fp,
→ filesize($file))) {

        xml_parse ($p, $data,
→ feof($fp));

}
```

To parse the file I first try to open it using `fopen()`. Then I loop through the file and send the retrieved data to the parser. The main loop stops once the entire file has been read, and the parser is told to stop once the end of the file has been reached.

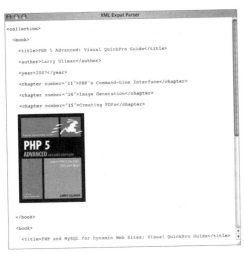

**Figure 14.8** Running books3.xml through the PHP-Expat parser generates this HTML page, viewable in any browser.

**Figure 14.9** The parsed XML document in Firefox.

**12.** Free up the parser and complete the page.

```
xml_parser_free($p);
?>
</pre>
</body>
</html>
```

**13.** Save the file as expat.php, place it in your Web directory, along with books3.xml (Script 14.5), collection.dtd (Script 14.4), and the php5adv.jpg image file (downloadable from the book's Web site, www.dmcinsights.com/phpvqp2/; click Extras).

**14.** Test in your Web browser (**Figures 14.8** and **14.9**).

### ✔ Tips

- Remember when working with XML to always use formal PHP tags (<?php and ?>). The informal PHP tags (<? and ?>) will conflict with XML tags.

- There are many PEAR classes specifically for handling XML data.

- For more on the Expat functions, see www.php.net/xml.

- The method of parsing the XML data and displaying it in a Web site used in this example is more a demonstration than something you would do on a live site. In all likelihood, you would take XML data and either use XSLT (Extensible Stylesheet Language Transformation) or different HTML to display it in a nicer format.

- The Expat library can read an XML document, but it cannot validate one.

# Using SimpleXML

Added in PHP 5 is a great tool for working with XML documents, called SimpleXML. While not as elaborate as other DOM-based parsers, SimpleXML is terrifically easy to use, with several nice built-in features.

To start the process off, use the `simplexml_load_file()` function to load an XML file into an object.

```
$xml = simplexml_load_file
→ ('filename.xml');
```

Alternatively, you could use `simplexml_load_string()` if you had a bunch of XML stored in a string.

From there, there are many ways you could go. To refer to specific elements, you would use the format `$xml->elementname`. If there are multiple items of the same element, you could treat them like arrays:

```
echo $xml->elementname[0];
```

Looking at the DOM in Figure 14.7, there is `$xml->product[0]` and `$xml->product[1]`.

For nested elements, just continue this syntax:

```
echo $xml->product[0]->name;
echo $xml->product[1]->price;
```

Using a `foreach` loop, it's easy to access every element in a tree:

```
foreach ($xml->product as $product) {
    // Do something with:
    // $product->name
    // $product->size
    // etc.
}
```

Attributes are easy to access as well, by referring to them like an array:

```
$xml->elementname['attribute'];
```

Let's parse the `books3.xml` file using SimpleXML this time. Instead of just printing out the tags and the data, we'll create a better-formatted Web page.

## Modifying XML

The SimpleXML library also makes it easy to modify the XML data. The `addChild()` and `addAttribute()` methods let you add new elements and attributes. You can also change the value in an element by using the assignment operator:

```
$xml->product->name = 'Heavy
→ T-Shirt';
```

## To use SimpleXML:

1. Create a new document in your text editor or IDE, beginning with the standard HTML (**Script 14.8**).

```
<!DOCTYPE html PUBLIC "-//W3C//DTD
→ XHTML 1.0 Transitional//EN"
"http://www.w3.org/TR/xhtml1/DTD/
→ xhtml1-transitional.dtd">
<html xmlns="http://www.w3.org/1999/
→ xhtml" xml:lang="en" lang="en">
```

```
<head>
    <meta http-equiv="content-type"
→ content="text/html; charset=iso-
→ 8859-1" />
    <title>SimpleXML Parser</title>
</head>
<body>
<?php # Script 14.8 - simplexml.php
```

*continues on page 559*

**Script 14.8** The SimpleXML library provides an easy, DOM-based way to access all of the data in an XML file.

```
1   <!DOCTYPE html PUBLIC "-//W3C//DTD XHTML 1.0 Transitional//EN"
2       "http://www.w3.org/TR/xhtml1/DTD/xhtml1-transitional.dtd">
3   <html xmlns="http://www.w3.org/1999/xhtml" xml:lang="en" lang="en">
4   <head>
5       <meta http-equiv="content-type" content="text/html; charset=iso-8859-1" />
6       <title>SimpleXML Parser</title>
7   </head>
8   <body>
9   <?php # Script 14.8 - simplexml.php
10
11  /*  This script will parse an XML file.
12   *  It uses the simpleXML library, a DOM parser.
13   */
14
15  // Read the file:
16  $xml = simplexml_load_file('books3.xml');
17
18  // Iterate through each book:
19  foreach ($xml->book as $book) {
20
21      // Print the title:
22      echo "<h2>$book->title";
23
24      // Check for an edition:
25      if (isset($book->title['edition'])) {
26          echo " (Edition {$book->title['edition']})";
27      }
28
29      echo "</h2><p>\n";
30
31      // Print the author(s):
32      foreach ($book->author as $author) {
33
34          echo "Author: $author<br />\n";
```

*(script continues on next page)*

**Script 14.8** *continued*

```
35
36          }
37
38          // Print the other book info:
39          echo "Published: $book->year<br />\n";
40
41          if (isset($book->pages)) {
42              echo "$book->pages Pages<br />\n";
43          }
44
45          // Print each chapter:
46          if (isset($book->chapter)) {
47              echo '<ul>';
48              foreach ($book->chapter as $chapter) {
49
50                  echo '<li>';
51
52                  if (isset($chapter['number'])) {
53                      echo "Chapter {$chapter['number']}: \n";
54                  }
55
56                  echo $chapter;
57
58                  if (isset($chapter['pages'])) {
59                      echo " ({$chapter['pages']} Pages)\n";
60                  }
61
62                  echo '</li>';
63
64              }
65              echo '</ul>';
66          }
67
68          // Handle the cover:
69          if (isset($book->cover)) {
70
71              // Get the image info:
72              $image = @getimagesize ($book->cover['filename']);
73
74              // Make the image HTML:
75              echo "<img src=\"{$book->cover['filename']}\" $image[3] border=\"0\" /><br />\n";
76
77          }
78
79          // Close the book's P tag:
80          echo "</p>\n";
81
82      }
83
84      ?>
85      </body>
86      </html>
```

2. Read the file.

```
$xml = simplexml_load_file
→ ('books3.xml');
```

This one line is all you need to read in the entire XML document.

3. Create a loop that iterates through each book element.

```
foreach ($xml->book as $book) {
```

The XML file contains several **book** elements. With each iteration of this loop, another of the **book** elements will be assigned (as an object) to the **$book** variable. If the XML file is the tree shown in **Figure 14.10**, then **$book** at this point is one of the branches of the tree.

*continues on next page*

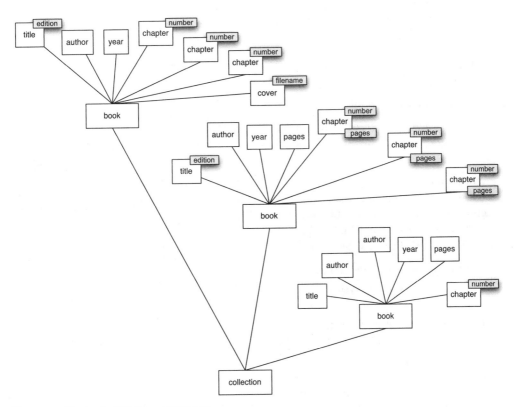

**Figure 14.10** The books XML file as a DOM tree.

**4.** Print the book's title.

```
echo "<h2>$book->title";
```

Referring to a subelement is this easy. For the first iteration of the loop, this is the equivalent of directly referring to `$xml->book[0]->title`.

The title will be printed within H2 tags, which are started here.

**5.** Print the book's edition, if applicable.

```
if (isset($book->title['edition'])) {
    echo " (Edition {$book-
→ >title['edition']})";
}
echo "</h2><p>\n";
```

The `isset()` function can be used to test if an element or attribute exists, as if it were any other variable. If the `edition` attribute exists, it'll be printed in parentheses: (Edition *X*). Then the title's closing H2 tag is printed, followed by a starting P tag (all of a book's information will be printed between one pair of paragraph tags).

**6.** Print the author(s).

```
foreach ($book->author as $author) {
    echo "Author: $author<br />\n";
}
```

Another `foreach` loop can iterate through all the authors. Remember that, by definition in the `collection.dtd` file, each book element has at least one author subelement, but it can also have multiple.

**7.** Print the year and the page count.

```
echo "Published: $book->year
→ <br />\n";
if (isset($book->pages)) {
    echo "$book->pages Pages
→ <br />\n";
}
```

**8.** Begin the process of printing each chapter.

```
if (isset($book->chapter)) {
    echo '<ul>';
    foreach ($book->chapter as
→ $chapter) {
```

A book may or may not have any chapter elements in it, but could have multiple. The `isset()` checks if any exist. If so, the chapters will be printed as an unordered list. Another `foreach` loop will access each chapter.

**9.** Print the chapter information.

```
echo '<li>';
if (isset($chapter['number'])) {
    echo "Chapter
→ {$chapter['number']}: \n";
}
echo $chapter;
if (isset($chapter['pages'])) {
    echo " ({$chapter['pages']}
→ Pages)\n";
}
echo '</li>';
```

The chapter's name will be printed within LI tags. If the chapter has a `number` or `pages` attribute, that information should be printed as well.

**10.** Complete the chapter's `foreach` loop and conditional.

```
    }
    echo '</ul>';
}
```

**11.** Handle the book's cover.

```
if (isset($book->cover)) {
    $image = @getimagesize
→ ($book->cover['filename']);
```

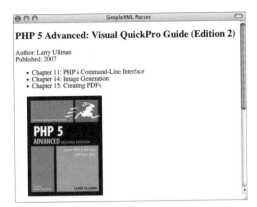

**Figure 14.11** The beginning of the books data, as viewed in Firefox.

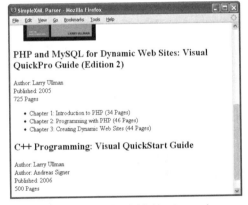

**Figure 14.12** The second and third book records.

```
    echo "<img src=\"{$book-
→ >cover['filename']}\" $image[3]
→ border=\"0\" /><br />\n";
}
```

If a cover element exists, the image's information is gathered from the file on the server and the appropriate HTML img tag is generated.

**12.** Close the P tag for this book and complete the page.

```
        echo "</p>\n";
    }
?>
</body>
</html>
```

**13.** Save the file as simplexml.php, place it in your Web directory, along with books3.xml (Script 14.4), collection.dtd (Script 14.5), and the php5adv.jpg image file (downloadable from the book's Web site, www.dmcinsights.com/phpvqp2/; click Extras).

**14.** Test in your Web browser (**Figures 14.11** and **14.12**).

### ✔ Tips

■ The asXML() method returns the loaded XML data as an XML string.

■ Because PHP treats elements and attributes as objects, you'll need to cast them to strings if you want to use them for comparison or in any standard string functions.

■ SimpleXML also supports XPath, a language used to perform queries (search for data) within XML.

■ The DOM parsers, like SimpleXML, will require more memory on the server than SAX parsers because they load the entire XML data into a variable.

# Creating an RSS Feed

RSS, which stands for Really Simple Syndication (it used to mean Rich Site Summary or RDF Site Summary), is a way for Web sites to provide listings of the site's content. Normally this list contains at least the titles of articles, plus their descriptions (and by "article," think of any type of content that a site might offer). Users access these feeds using an RSS client (many Web browsers support RSS, as well). If they want to read more of an article, there's a link to click, which takes them to the full Web page. RSS is a great convenience and has become popular for good reasons.

RSS feeds are just XML files that have already-established tags. RSS documents begin with the rss root element, with a mandatory attribute called version. You'll want to use the latest version of RSS for that value, which is 2.0 at this writing. So an RSS document starts with:

```
<?xml version="1.0"?>
<rss version="2.0">
```

After that, all RSS files contain a single channel element. Nested within this element are others, like title, description, and link, all of which describe the RSS feed.

```
<channel>
<title>Name of the RSS Feed</title>
<description>Description of the RSS
→ Feed</description>
<link>Link to the Web site</link>
```

Those three elements are required within channel. There are many optional ones, too, like language (e.g., *en-us*), copyright, managingEditor (an email address), webMaster (also an email address), and so on. See the formal specifications at www.rssboard.org/rss-specification for more.

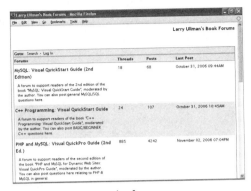

**Figure 14.13** My supporting forums.

The channel also contains multiple item elements, each item being a piece of content (an article). The item elements also have title, description, link, and other nested elements.

```
<item>
<title>Article Title</title>
<description>Article
→ Description</description>
<link>Link to this article</link>
</item>
```

None of the item subelements are required, except that either a title or description must be present. You might also use author (an email address) and pubDate (the article's publication date). This last one is tricky because its value must be in the RFC 822–specified format. If you don't know what that is offhand, it's: *Wed, 01 Nov 2006 16:45:23 GMT*.

That's really all there is to it! Remember: RSS is just formatted XML. If you understand XML, you can create RSS.

For this example, I'll create something that may be somewhat particular but is tremendously useful. As part of my Web site (www.DMCinsights.com), I use the Phorum software (www.phorum.org) to create a support forum for readers (**Figure 14.13**). Each book I've written has its own forum, meaning there are quite a few. To simplify looking through all of these forums, I want to create an RSS feed that displays the latest newly created threads across every forum, using the subject and part of the thread's body as the title and description. If you aren't using Phorum or don't care about this feature, you'll only need to change a wee bit of this code to create the RSS feed you do want.

CREATING AN RSS FEED

## To create an RSS feed:

1. Begin a new document in your text editor or IDE (**Script 14.9**).

   ```
   <?php # Script 14.9 - forum_rss.php
   ```

**Script 14.9** This PHP script uses a MySQL query to generate an RSS feed.

```
 1    <?php # Script 14.9 - forum_rss.php
 2
 3    /*  This script will create an RSS feed.
 4     *  The feed content will be recent Phorum threads.
 5     */
 6
 7    // Send the Content-type header:
 8    header('Content-type: text/xml');
 9
10    // Create the initial RSS code:
11    echo '<?xml version="1.0"?>
12    <rss version="2.0">
13    <channel>
14    <title>Larry Ullman&apos;s Recent Forum Threads</title>
15    <description>The most recent threads started in Larry&apos;s supporting book
      forums.</description>
16    <link>http://www.dmcinsights.com/phorum/</link>
17    ';
18
19    // Connect to the database:
20    $dbc = @mysql_connect ('localhost', 'username', 'password') OR die ("</channel>\n</rss>\n");
21    @mysql_select_db('database') or die ("</channel>\n</rss>\n");
22
23    // Define the query:
24    // Change this query for different sources!
25    $q = 'SELECT message_id, forum_id, subject, LEFT(body, 200), datestamp FROM p5_messages WHERE
      status=2 and parent_id=0 order by datestamp desc LIMIT 50';
26
27    // Retrieve the results:
28    $r = mysql_query($q);
29    while ($row = mysql_fetch_array($r, MYSQL_NUM)) {
30
31        // Print each record as an item:
32        echo '<item>
33    <title>' . htmlentities($row[2]) . '</title>
34    <description>' . htmlentities($row[3]) . '...</description>
35    <link>http://www.dmcinsights.com/phorum/read.php?' . $row[1] . ',' . $row[0] . '</link>
36    <guid>http://www.dmcinsights.com/phorum/read.php?' . $row[1] . ',' . $row[0] . '</guid>
37    <pubDate>' . date('r', $row[4]) . '</pubDate>
38    </item>
39    ';
40
41    } // End of while loop
42
43    // Complete the channel and rss elements:
44    echo '</channel>
45    </rss>
46    ';
47
48    ?>
```

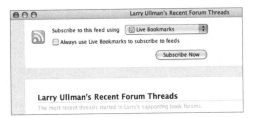

**Figure 14.14** Firefox, which supports RSS, shows the channel element's `title` and `description` values at the top of the page.

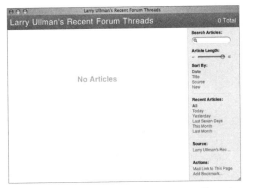

**Figure 14.15** A database connection failure still results in a valid RSS feed, but with no articles (being viewed in Safari on Mac OS X here).

**2.** Send the Content-type header.

`header('Content-type: text/xml');`

This page will have a *.php* extension, because it's a PHP page that must be properly handled by the Web server. But to create an XML page, a header should be sent with the proper *Content-type*.

**3.** Create the initial RSS code.

```
echo '<?xml version="1.0"?>
<rss version="2.0">
<channel>
<title>Larry Ullman&apos;s Recent
→ Forum Threads</title>
<description>The most recent threads
→ started in Larry&apos;s supporting
→ book forums.</description>
<link>http://www.dmcinsights.com/
→ phorum/</link>
';
```

These lines of XML get the ball rolling. To start, there's the XML prolog, required in all XML documents. Next is the `rss` element and the opening `channel` tag. Within the `channel`, three tags are used to help describe this feed (**Figure 14.14**).

**4.** Connect to the database.

```
$dbc = @mysql_connect ('localhost',
→ 'username', 'password') OR die
→ ("</channel>\n</rss>\n");
@mysql_select_db('database') or die
→ ("</channel>\n</rss>\n");
```

If you want to use another database or resource for your feed (like a text file or different database application), you'll need to change this code.

If a database connection couldn't be made, the XML page is completed, resulting in no articles in an RSS reader (**Figure 14.15**).

*continues on next page*

CREATING AN RSS FEED

**5.** Define the query.

```
$q = 'SELECT message_id, forum_id,
→ subject, LEFT(body, 200), datestamp
→ FROM p5_messages WHERE status=2 and
→ parent_id=0 order by datestamp desc
→ LIMIT 50';
```

Understanding this query requires a knowledge of the Phorum software and its database design. I'm selecting the `message_id` and `forum_id` values, which are used in creating the link to a thread. I also select the thread's `subject` and the first 200 characters in its `body`, which will be used as the `title` and `description` values in the feed. The `datetime` will be used for the `pubDate`.

If you don't want to (or can't) follow this example exactly, just change this query to retrieve any data that's represented in your Web site. You could even select something from one of the other databases created in this book.

**6.** Retrieve the results.

```
$r = mysql_query($q);

while ($row = mysql_fetch_array($r,
→ MYSQL_NUM)) {
```

**7.** Print each record as an item.

```
echo '<item>
<title>' . htmlentities($row[2]) .
→ '</title>
<description>' .
→ htmlentities($row[3]) .
→ '...</description>
<link>http://www.dmcinsights.com/
→ phorum/read.php?' . $row[1] . ',' .
→ $row[0] . '</link>
<guid>http://www.dmcinsights.com/
→ phorum/read.php?' . $row[1] . ',' .
→ $row[0] . '</guid>
<pubDate>' . date('r', $row[4]) .
→ '</pubDate>
</item>
';
```

This is the most important part of the whole script, where each item is generated. First, you have the opening item tag. Then, there's the title, which is the subject of the forum thread and becomes the title of the article in the feed. After that is the description, which is what will be printed in the feed describing the article. For that value, I use some of the thread's body. For both the title and the description, the retrieved value is run through the htmlentities() function because XML does not allow many characters that might appear.

Next is the link element, which is a link to the actual "article" online. In this case, it's a link to the thread itself in the forum. After that is an element called a guid, which isn't required but is a good idea. This is a unique identifier for each item. The URL, which will be unique for each item, can be used here as well.

Finally, there's the pubDate, which needs to be in an exact format. Fortunately, PHP's date() function has a shortcut for this: *r*. This makes the formatting a lot easier!

*continues on next page*

CREATING AN RSS FEED

**8.** Complete the `while` loop.

```
} // End of while loop
```

**9.** Complete the `channel` and `rss` elements.

```
echo '</channel>
</rss>
';
```

**10.** Complete the PHP page.

```
?>
```

**11.** Save the file as `forum_rss.php`, place it in your Web directory, and load it in an application that supports RSS feeds (**Figures 14.16** and **14.17**).

### ✔ Tips

- If you want to confirm that you've generated a valid RSS feed, check out `http://feedvalidator.org`.

- Because of some perceived issues with RSS, an offshoot format called Atom was created. Meant to define a better standard for feeds, Atom is an open standard (unlike RSS, which is both closed and frozen from further development). Although Atom is worth considering, many of the largest Web sites still use RSS 2.0 for their feeds.

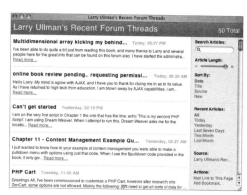

**Figure 14.16** Viewing the RSS feed in Safari.

**Figure 14.17** Viewing the RSS feed in Firefox.

# INDEX

INDEX

INDEX